THE POETRY OF

THE FAERIE QUEENE

THE POETRY OF

THE FAERIE QUEENE

BY PAUL J. ALPERS

PRINCETON UNIVERSITY PRESS

1 9 6 7

In Memory of Rosemond Tuve

Preface

The purpose of this book is to bring *The Faerie Queene* into focus—to enable the ordinary reader and student to trust Spenser's verse, and scholars and critics to agree on what the realities of the poem are and on the ways in which it is profitable to discuss and investigate them. I hope that my aims and arguments will be clear from the text itself, and I want only to say a word here about the organization of the book. Part I is addressed to describing and understanding the surface of *The Faerie Queene;* it concerns both the practical problem of the right relation between the reader and the poem, and more theoretical problems about the nature of the reality constituted by Spenser's verse. Part II concerns the interpretation of *The Faerie Queene;* it uses a variety of historical materials to ask what kinds of meanings are to be found in a number of episodes and, finally, a major canto of the poem. Part III draws on the arguments and conclusions of the first two parts to discuss, in the most general way, the nature of Spenser's poetry. The last two chapters are more illustrative than argumentative. They are intended to show first the kinds of continuities that exist in whole books of *The Faerie Queene,* and second the unique power of Spenser's verse to put us in possession of man's traditional wisdom about himself and of the truths contained in the traditions of European poetry.

Parts of Chapter 1 appeared as an article, "Narrative and Rhetoric in *The Faerie Queene,*" in *Studies in English Literature,* II (1962), pages 27–46.

Quotations from *The Faerie Queene* are from *The Works of Edmund Spenser: A Variorum Edition,* edited by Edwin Greenlaw, et al., Baltimore, 1932–1957, cited in the notes as *Variorum.* For *Orlando Furioso* I have used the text of Santorre Debenedetti and Cesare Segre, Bologna, 1960, and the prose translation of Allan Gilbert, New York, 1954, with the permission of S. F. Vanni, Publishers. For Latin authors I have used the texts and translations of the Loeb Classical Library. All unidentified translations are mine. Biblical passages are from the Great Bible (1540); New Testament passages are quoted from *The New Testament Octapla,* edited by Luther A. Weigle. Quotations from Shakespeare are from *Works,* edited by George Lyman Kittredge, Boston, 1936. Except for expanding contractions, I have not altered any of the texts cited.

I owe a great deal to many people: to Douglas Bush and Harry Levin, who patiently supervised the doctoral dissertation in which I first tried to work out some of my ideas; to Reuben A. Brower, who taught me to frame critical questions and pursue intelligible answers; to my wife Svetlana, and to Stephen Orgel, David Kalstone, Roger Sale, and Jonas A. Barish for their friendship and intellectual companionship as well as for their services to this book; to Josephine Miles and Norman Grabo for giving the manuscript the kind of reading that encourages by its very stringency and intelligence; to my graduate students at Berkeley, who made teaching Spenser a joy and with whom many of the ideas in this book were worked out; finally, for favors great and small, to Herschel Baker, Elizabeth Closs, Martha Craig, Robert M. Durling, Donald Friedman, Christopher Ricks, Thomas P. Roche, Jr., and Ann Stanford. I should also like to thank the American Council of Learned Societies for a grant-in-aid that enabled me to do much of the research for this book, and the Warburg Institute, and particularly E. H. Gombrich, its director, and J. B. Trapp, for their hospitality during my months in London.

My greatest obligation is one that I can now discharge only by an act of commemoration. Rosemond Tuve gave me the support of intelligent understanding at a time when I was most discouraged about my work on Spenser. For most of the years I worked on this book, she was both its most discerning critic and its most appreciative audience. Indeed it was only when her magnificent *Allegorical Imagery* appeared, after I had completed my manuscript, that I realized how similar were the conclusions about Spenser towards which, starting from quite different materials and problems, we had both been working. Miss Tuve's powers and disinterestedness are apparent on even the densest pages of her writings, but one had to know her to realize fully how penetrating and flexible her mind was, and how profoundly she was motivated by love of the literature she studied. By her friendship, as well as by her example, she made you want your writing to be worthy of its subject. I hope this book is, and that in being so it is worthy of her.

P. J. A.
Berkeley, California
March 7, 1966

Contents

PART I

Chapter One

The Rhetorical Mode of
Spenser's Narrative

I

The main problem that faces a reader of *The Faerie Queene* was stated by Joseph Addison, in his "Account of the Greatest English Poets":

> Old *Spenser* next, warm'd with poetick rage,
> In ancient tales amus'd a barb'rous age;
> An age that yet uncultivate and rude,
> Where-e'er the poet's fancy led, pursu'd
> Thro' pathless fields, and unfrequented floods,
> To dens of dragons, and enchanted woods.
> But now the mystick tale, that pleas'd of yore,
> Can charm an understanding age no more;
> The long-spun allegories fulsom grow,
> While the dull moral lyes too plain below.
> We view well-pleas'd at distance all the sights
> Of arms and palfries, battels, fields and fights,
> And damsels in distress, and courteous knights.
> But when we look too near, the shades decay,
> And all the pleasing landscape fades away.[1]

The problem Addison indicates is the relation between the rich and elaborate surface of *The Faerie Queene* and its poetic meaning. For Addison, as for many readers today, "the dull moral" is both too insistent and too simple to allow narrative realities to take on a complex and substantial life of their own. Romantic criticism defended Spenser from such complaints by skimming off the surface and leaving the moral alone. This is the burden of Hazlitt's famous remark that Spenser's allegory is a painted dragon, and Hazlitt esteemed Spenser precisely because he was persuaded to follow "where-e'er the poet's fancy led." Modern commentators have in turn rescued Spenser from the romantics by arguing that the moral of *The Faerie Queene* is as com-

[1] Lines 17–31, in *The Miscellaneous Works of Joseph Addison*, ed. A. C. Guthkelch, London, 1914, 2 vols.

3

plex and interesting as the surface of chivalric events and exotic landscapes. But the tendency of modern studies has been to expound Spenser's ideas, and there has recently been a reaction against the abstractness and aridity of much interpretation of *The Faerie Queene*. Book after book now urges us to return to the surface of the poem and to find its meanings there. Yet we still have no account of *The Faerie Queene* that new readers find persuasive or that scholars and critics find trustworthy. The movement back to the surface of the poem is entirely right in its motives and aims. But we still wander in a dark wood, because we have not made clear to ourselves just what constitutes the surface of *The Faerie Queene,* or in what way it holds our attention and expresses meanings of the complexity and human importance that we expect to find in great poetry.

The main initial impediment to our understanding of *The Faerie Queene* is a false assumption about the relation in it between narrative events and poetic meaning. Consider Ruskin's analysis of Book I— one of the first reactions against the romantic tendency to dismiss or minimize Spenser's allegory:

> [Holiness], in the opening of the book, has Truth (or Una) at its side, but presently enters the Wandering Wood, and encounters the serpent Error; that is to say, Error in her universal form, the first enemy of Reverence and Holiness. . . . Having vanquished this first open and palpable form of Error, as Reverence and Religion must always vanquish it, the Knight encounters Hypocrisy, or Archimagus: Holiness cannot detect Hypocrisy, but believes him, and goes home with him; whereupon, Hypocrisy succeeds in separating Holiness from Truth; and the Knight (Holiness) and Lady (Truth) go forth separately from the house of Archimagus. Now observe; the moment Godly Fear, or Holiness, is separated from Truth, he meets Infidelity, or the Knight Sans Foy. . . .[2]

Ruskin simply translates the narrative materials of Book I into abstract terms. Characters and settings are given consistent symbolic identifications, and the narrative action indicates their conceptual relations. Ruskin makes what is still the fundamental assumption of Spenserian criticism—that the sequence of stanzas in *The Faerie Queene* is equivalent to the narrative materials, or (to use a handier term) the fiction, of the poem. As exemplary or dramatic narrative, Spenser's fiction is taken to be real, according to the conventional sus-

[2] *The Stones of Venice*, Appendix 2: "Theology of Spenser," in John Ruskin, *Works*, ed. E. T. Cook and A. Wedderburn, London, 1903–1912, 11, 251–252.

pension of disbelief we grant to any romance or novel. As allegory, the fiction is understood to be less real than its conceptual translation, but it nevertheless provides both the terms and the syntax of the translation. "What happens" poetically is taken to be identical with, or at least determined by, "what happens" fictionally. Whatever the specific content or meaning, it is expressed by the characters and settings that constitute and the events that take place in the putative reality of the poem.

However, when we read the poem on this assumption, we find numerous inconsistencies, some of which produce major interpretive difficulties. We find inconsistencies, I think, because our criterion of consistency is not valid. In turning narrative materials into stanzas of poetry, Spenser's attention is focused on the reader's mind and feelings and not on what is happening within his fiction. His poetic motive in any given stanza is to elicit a response—to evoke, modify, or complicate feelings and attitudes. His stanzas, then, are modes of address by the poet to the reader. For this reason, I call his use of narrative materials *rhetorical*.

The most striking instance in which this approach resolves a fictional inconsistency is the problem of why the figure of Time is in the Garden of Adonis. According to Spenser's myth, the flowers in the garden are souls or forms that are sent out into the world; having lived and died on earth, they return to the Garden of Adonis to be replanted and reborn. The garden itself is a spontaneously flowering paradise and projects the idea that nature is permanent because its change is orderly. Literally, then, it is simply a mistake to place wicked Time with his scythe in the Garden of Adonis: the realm he rules is the earth below, and he represents a principle of sudden and final death that is presumably resolved by the orderly cycles of the garden.[3]

[3] The problem is not that Spenser places a figure named Time in the garden, but that he depicts Time as a destroyer, an agent of death, not of change. As Brents Stirling long ago pointed out, Spenser never represents the Garden of Adonis as changeless: "The Philosophy of Spenser's 'Garden of Adonis,'" PMLA, 49 (1934), 501–538. But the words that describe Time's actions—"mow," "flings," "wither," "fowly mard," and "beates downe"—all suggest final destruction; there is a sharp contrast with the terms of preceding stanzas, all of which suggest a process—"chaungefull" (stanza 33, which ends, "so like a wheele around they runne from old to new") and "decayes" and "fade," which appear jointly in both stanzas 37 and 38. Stirling maintains that "there is nothing inconsistent in Time mowing down the 'flowring herbes and goodly things'" (p. 526), but his argument depends on identifying change and death. The depiction of Time will not support, as the rest of the canto will, the formula used of Adonis, "eterne in mutabilitie" (3.6.47).

Robert Ellrodt (*Neoplatonism in the Poetry of Spenser*, Geneva, 1960, pp.

Yet poetically Time's presence is perfectly valid. The potency of the image of a natural paradise depends on our understanding the idea of change that it corrects and resolves. In order to make us aware of earthly mutability, Spenser is willing to neglect both his fable and its philosophic coherence. He sets these aside in order to introduce concepts, and their attendant feelings, that are relevant to our understanding of the Garden of Adonis. In the stanza preceding the description of Time, Spenser explains the continuity of matter. "The substance is not chaunged," he says, but forms are:

> For formes are variable and decay,
> By course of kind, and by occasion;
> And that faire flowre of beautie fades away,
> As doth the lilly fresh before the sunny ray.
>
> (3.6.38)

Spenser returns to the flowers of the garden by means of an image developed in the course of direct address to the reader. In the next four stanzas, he lays out the double suggestion of the image of the lily—on the one hand the inevitability of decay, and on the other the sense of benignity and naturalness given by "sunny ray."

The first of these stanzas is the presentation of earthly time:

> Great enimy to it, and to all the rest,
> That in the *Gardin* of *Adonis* springs,
> Is wicked *Time,* who with his scyth addrest,
> Does mow the flowring herbes and goodly things,
> And all their glory to the ground downe flings,
> Where they doe wither, and are fowly mard:

77–84) and William Nelson (*The Poetry of Edmund Spenser*, New York, 1963, pp. 210–215) have shown that the Garden of Adonis is not a realm of Platonic forms, but a storehouse of what Plotinus and, following him, Augustine called *rationes seminales* (cf. *FQ* 3.6.30). "According to Augustine," Ellrodt says, "God created all things, present and future, simultaneously. All living beings not fully developed in the first act of creation—whether plants, beasts or the bodies of men—were preformed in the *rationes seminales,* or invisible germs, not to be mistaken for the eternal 'ideas,' which were not created, but pre-existed in the divine mind or Word from all eternity" (p. 77). Such "seeds" have a temporal aspect inherent in them—they are created in time and they grow in time—but again this explains no more than the presence of change in the garden. Nelson, p. 213, simply identifies the description of Time's mowing with change. Ellrodt recognizes the distinction between change and death, and he rightly says that the flowers of stanza 39 "cannot be the pre-existent seeds but the actual beings they produced." But he then goes on to argue that these distinctions "could not but be blurred in the poetic myth" (p. 81).

6

> He flyes about, and with his flaggy wings
> Beates downe both leaues and buds without regard,
> Ne euer pittie may relent his malice hard.

>   (3.6.39)

Time is more the activated abstraction of a sonnet than a fictional personage. The striking details of the stanza impress us primarily as emphatic diction, and not as the attributes of an emblematic character. "Wicked," "mow," "to the ground downe flings," "wither," "fowly mard," "beates downe," "malice hard"—this series runs through the stanza and is juxtaposed with the language of delicate pastoral— "flowring herbes," "glory," "leaues and buds." Spenser is multiplying statements about the action of earthly time. Even where there is a sense of fictional action, it is in the service of direct address to the reader. Time's wings, which ordinarily represent swiftness of flight, are here instruments of destruction, and the effect of this change in narrative materials is to give continuity and emphasis to the poet's statements.

The stanza that follows is also conceived as an address to the reader:

> Yet pittie often did the gods relent,
> To see so faire things mard, and spoyled quight:
> And their great mother *Venus* did lament
> The losse of her deare brood, her deare delight;
> Her hart was pierst with pittie at the sight,
> When walking through the Gardin, them she saw,
> Yet no'te she find redresse for such despight.
> For all that liues, is subiect to that law:
> All things decay in time, and to their end do draw.

>   (3.6.40)

The first line directly echoes the last line of the stanza on Time and produces an important shift of tone. "Ne euer pittie may relent his malice hard" has a note of finality and rigor. "Yet pittie often did the gods relent" conveys tender solicitude for Time's victims. Venus' mourning is produced, so to speak, by our responding to Spenser's statements and to the verbal linking of the two stanzas. By the same token, Spenser can elicit from Venus' fictional tenderness a tone of direct address that is both delicate and grave. His concluding explanation of the goddess's helplessness is really a summary statement of Time's dominion over nature. It is from this rhetorical point that he

7

presents the garden as a paradise (3.6.41–42). And even here he begins by saying, "But were it not, that *Time* their troubler is." In a strict philosophical sense, this concession is absurd, but poetically it places the vision of "continuall spring, and haruest . . . both meeting at one time" in a wider context of human feeling about time.

The poetic coherence of *The Faerie Queene* is usually described in terms of fictional consistency; but it is rather to be found in the coherence of the reader's feelings and attitudes. One of the puzzles of the poem is the ending of Book I, when the Red Cross Knight leaves Una. Spenser does not explicitly address the reader, but we can solve the interpretive dilemma only by recognizing that the mode of his narration is rhetorical:

> Yet swimming in that sea of blisfull ioy,
> He nought forgot, how he whilome had sworne,
> In case he could that monstrous beast destroy,
> Vnto his Farie Queene backe to returne:
> The which he shortly did, and *Vna* left to mourne.
>
> (1.12.41)

If the knight's separation from Una does not mean separation from Truth, as it did earlier in the book, then what does it mean? The question is perplexing if we assume that a continuous fiction is the main vehicle of Spenser's meaning. But surely Spenser's intention is clear enough. The holy knight still bears his burden of flesh, and therefore must resume a life of heroic action. Marriage to Una symbolically tells us about the knight's election and his moral condition, but it is not the literal truth about his human experience. As literal experience, the marriage is a "sea of blisfull ioy" and suggests permanent earthly happiness—precisely what is not possible for man since the Fall. Una's mourning, then, suggests the pathos of the fact that the servant of God does not enjoy the eternal bliss of the saints in heaven.

There is a further fictional inconsistency in the departure of the Red Cross Knight. He has already promised the hermit Contemplation that he will forsake arms and take up a "Pilgrims poore estate" (1.10.64), and this vow is directly contradicted by the vow to return to the Fairy Queen. Yet both vows serve the same poetic purpose: each in its context enlarges the reader's understanding of the conflicting imperatives that involve the elected man. The vow to the Fairy Queen, which is not mentioned until the last canto, is introduced simply to be used as a poetic device in the conclusion of Book I. In fictional terms, this conclusion must seem clumsy if not meaningless. But it is entirely true to the reader's sense of Spenser's central concern—human experience seen under the aspect of man's relation to God.

Each stanza in *The Faerie Queene* is conceived as an address to the reader, but we do not feel, as we do in *Paradise Lost,* that a decisive voice speaks to us. Spenser's manner of address is much more self-effacing than Milton's—so much so that C. S. Lewis finds it possible to claim that "outside the proems to the books and cantos he scarcely writes a line that is not for the story's sake."[4] Nevertheless, Spenser's style is not, as Lewis proposes, "to be judged as the style of a story-teller"; it makes sense only as a rhetorical instrument, a means of appealing to the reader's feelings and awarenesses. Without attempting a comprehensive discussion of Spenser's style, I would like to examine a crucial phenomenon in his poetry—the pictorial effects in which his well-known verbal sensuousness seems to be in the service of fictional narration.

It has always been assumed that in his pictorial stanzas, Spenser's purpose is primarily imitative or descriptive: his language is chosen to render a "real" object, which of course can be symbolic or emblematic.[5] But we often find that a striking pictorial effect is not identical with visual description:

> For round about, the wals yclothed were
> With goodly arras of great maiesty,
> Wouen with gold and silke so close and nere,

[4] *English Literature in the Sixteenth Century*, Oxford, 1954, p. 389.

[5] The most extreme statement of this view is Joseph B. Dallett, "Ideas of Sight in *The Faerie Queene*," ELH, 27 (1960), 87–121. Dallett treats Spenser's reader as an "ideal spectator" who exists *within the fiction,* and he argues that "many of the descriptions (including those with optical 'absurdities') are analogous to methods of representation found abundantly in the fine arts" (p. 98). See also W. B. C. Watkins, *Shakespeare and Spenser*, Princeton, 1950, pp. 223–258 ("Spenser's Palace of Art"); Rudolf Gottfried, "The Pictorial Element in Spenser's Poetry," in *That Soueraine Light*, ed. W. R. Mueller and D. C. Allen, Baltimore, 1952, pp. 123–133; Carl Robinson Sonn, "Spenser's Imagery," ELH, 26 (1959), 156–170. Watkins' chapter is an engaging and sensitive essay in the tradition of comparing Spenser to various painters. Gottfried complains that Spenser's "pictures" are very bad paintings, and therefore concludes that the pictorial element in his poetry is insignificant. Sonn argues that Spenser does not attempt to paint pictures, but uses concrete details in formal images that convey abstracts or universals. But he assumes that when Spenser's language is pictorial it renders the sensory experience of objects in the external world. He recognizes that some of Spenser's sensuous imagery offers "no chance of sensuous identification with the object" (p. 166), but he so completely explains these images in terms of abstractions that he is unable to account for their sensuousness, which he describes as "transient," "superficial," or "sublimated" (pp. 167–168).

That the rich metall lurked priuily,
As faining to be hid from enuious eye;
Yet here, and there, and every where vnwares
It shewd it selfe, and shone vnwillingly;
Like a discolourd Snake, whose hidden snares
Through the greene gras his long bright burnisht
          backe declares.   (3.11.28)

Several words and phrases that support a pictorial effect are not at all descriptive—for example, "vnwares," "vnwillingly," and most notably "faining to be hid from enuious eye," where Spenser directly suggests the kind of feeling that Busyrane's tapestries induce. Other phrases that do have a visual reference are persuasive because they are suggestive moral formulas—"close and nere," "lurked priuily," "hidden snares." A great deal of quasi-visual effect is achieved through verse rhythms, particularly in the sixth and ninth lines. Spenser is using all the verbal resources of his poetry; our sense of physical immediacy comes specifically from our experience of words and their poetic disposition, and not from any optical illusion. The last line is the most distinctly pictorial, yet we are hardly meant to see the color green. The effect of the line comes from the rhythmic crowding of words, and we are to hear the alliterated formula, "greene gras." Literally, the "long bright burnisht backe" of the snake is like a fitfully gleaming golden thread. But through alliteration, rhythm, and the concluding "declares" with its strong rhyme, Spenser makes us feel we are dazzled, our field of vision filled—nor do we remember that the snake is "discolourd." The stanza has a pictorial effect because Spenser wants to achieve a certain psychological impact, not because he wants to render real visual experience.[6] He impresses upon us, as if it were a di-

---

[6] The following lines from the *Divine Comedy* genuinely attempt to render real visual experience. Tasso cites them as an example of *evidenza* or *energia*, "that power which makes us seem to see the things that are narrated": Torquato Tasso, *Prose diverse*, ed. Cesare Guasti, Florence, 1875, 1, 257:

Come le pecorelle escon del chiuso
Ad una, a due, a tre, e l'altre stanno
Timidette atterrando l'occhio e 'l muso,
E ciò che fa la prima, e l'altre fanno,
Addossandosi a lei s' ella s' arresta,
Semplici e quete, e lo 'mperchè non sanno.
                    (*Purg.* 3.79–84)

As the sheep come forth from the fold by ones, and twos, and threes, and the others stand timid, holding eye and muzzle to the ground; and what the first does the others also do, huddling themselves to it if it stop, silly and quiet, and wherefore know not.

rect sensation, the sinister moral atmosphere of Busyrane's palace.

The nondescriptive character of Spenser's "pictures" was recognized by Coleridge, in a comment on a line about Dissemblance, in the masque of Cupid: "And her bright browes were deckt with borrowed haire" (3.12.14). "Here, as too often in this great poem, that which is and may be known, but cannot *appear* from the given point of view, is confounded with the visible. It is no longer a mask-figure, but the character, of a Dissembler."[7] The solution to this difficulty is to recognize that Spenser's pictorial stanzas are not mimetic descriptions, but "speaking pictures" in Sidney's sense:

> Whatsoeuer the Philosopher sayth shoulde be doone, hee [the poet] giueth a perfect picture of it in some one, by whom hee presupposeth it was doone. . . . A perfect picture I say, for hee yeeldeth to the powers of the minde an image of that whereof the Philosopher bestoweth but a woordish description: which dooth neyther strike, pierce, nor possesse the sight of the soule so much as that other dooth. . . . No doubt the Philosopher with his learned definition, bee it of vertue, vices, matters of publick policie or priuat gouernment, replenisheth the memory with many infallible grounds of wisdom, which, notwithstanding, lye darke before the imaginatiue and iudging powre, if they bee not illuminated or figured foorth by the speaking picture of Poesie.[8]

We ordinarily understand "speaking picture" to mean "a picture that speaks." But Sidney does not attribute to poetry any formal analogies with painting, nor does he think poetry is vivid because it renders the visual experience of external objects. He is speaking of the psychological effect of poetry. The poem enables the reader's imagination to function properly: he can, as Sidney says elsewhere in this passage, "satisfie his inward conceits with being witnes to it selfe of a true lively knowledge." Poetry immediately implants in the mind images that the completely sound and regenerate man would produce by his ordinary psychological activity.[9] Observe that Sidney does not limit the re-

---

The text is that of C. H. Grandgent, rev. edn., New York, 1933. The translation is by Charles Eliot Norton.

[7] *Coleridge's Miscellaneous Criticism*, ed. T. M. Raysor, Cambridge, Mass., 1936, p. 39.

[8] Sir Philip Sidney, *An Apologie for Poetrie*, in *Elizabethan Critical Essays*, ed. G. Gregory Smith, Oxford, 1904, 1, 164–165.

[9] For an account of Renaissance psychological ideas that are relevant to this passage, see Perry Miller, *The New England Mind: The Seventeenth Century*, Cambridge, Mass., 1939, chapters 9 and 10.

sources of poetry in order to make it pictorial. All that he says assumes the full exploitation of the verbal resources that specifically belong to poetry and have nothing to do with painting. "Speaking picture," then, means speaking that is so vivid, has so much of its own life, that it gives immediacy and clarity to its subject matter.[10] The presentation of Time in the Garden of Adonis is a speaking picture in this sense. In using the traditional phrase as a metaphor for the psychological effect of poetry, Sidney deals with a crucial problem in any didactic theory—to show that the knowledge conveyed by poetry is necessarily dependent on the emotional force and quasi-sensory immediacy of verse.

The relation between Spenser's pictorial language and his rhetorical use of narrative materials becomes very clear in Calidore's vision of the Graces, where pictorial experience is part of the fictional action. Spenser attempts neither a real description nor a dramatization of the hero's visual experience, but rather directly conveys the vision and its significance to the reader. Hence at the climax of the passage, the observing hero and what he sees vanish into a heroic simile. The vision begins when Calidore comes to an open green on the top of Mount Acidale:

> There he did see, that pleased much his sight,
> That euen he him selfe his eyes enuyde,
> An hundred naked maidens lilly white,
> All raunged in a ring, and dauncing in delight.
>
> (6.10.11)

Spenser does not paint a picture or portray Calidore as first seeing, then responding. Descriptive elements are absorbed into a rendering of Calidore's response, which is completely identified with our experience in reading the passage. Thus two clauses that render quality of response intervene between the verb "see" and its object "naked maidens"; feeling and rhythm are dammed up so that the release will imitate Calidore's surprise and delight. This rhythmic effect and the shift of tone it produces in the next to last line account for the extraordi-

---

[10] Compare Daniel, *Musophilus*, lines 177–182:

> When as perhaps the words thou scornest now
> May liue, the speaking picture of the mind,
> The extract of the soule that laboured how
> To leaue the image of her selfe behind,
> Wherein posteritie that loue to know
> The iust proportion of our spirits may find.

Poems and A Defence of Ryme, ed. A. C. Sprague, Cambridge, Mass., 1930.

nary impression the word "naked" makes on most readers. From the remarks of critics, we would gather that the vision of the Graces is the healthy analogue of the long erotic description of Acrasia's damsels (2.12.63–68).[11] Not at all—this single line is almost all we see of the dancing maidens. There are, after all, a hundred of them, and we are not meant to see a naked human body any more than Wordsworth meant to describe, or meant us to see, the leaves and petals of the ten thousand daffodils that danced in the breeze. Pictorial description renders real visual experience, while Spenser's diction uses visual suggestions to make us experience the words themselves.

The next stanza decisively shows the difference between pictorial description and the rhetorical use of pictorial diction:

> All they without were raunged in a ring,
> And daunced round; but in the midst of them
> Three other Ladies did both daunce and sing,
> The whilest the rest them round about did hemme,
> And like a girlond did in compasse stemme:
> And in the middest of those same three, was placed
> Another Damzell, as a precious gemme,
> Amidst a ring most richly well enchaced,
> That with her goodly presence all the rest much graced.
>
> (6.10.12)

Clearly there is no pictorial equivalence between the two images in this stanza: if the lady is in the center of a ring of dancing maidens, she cannot be described as the jewel set into a ring for the finger. But it would be absurd to complain that Spenser is visually confusing, for he has no desire to be visually convincing. He uses sensory impressions to give a quasi-physical presence to images and words that express value.

The rationale of Spenser's verbal sensuousness is exceptionally clear in the profound and breathtaking stanza that concludes the vision. Although it is a heroic simile, it is not announced by the usual "like" or "as": the modification of the poet's voice does not suggest that he is turning from the narration of action (which scarcely exists at this point) in order to state an analogy. Spenser begins with "Looke," and his simile continues and intensifies our experience of the preceding stanza:

[11] See, for example, C. S. Lewis, *The Allegory of Love*, Oxford, 1936, p. 331, and Northrop Frye, *Fables of Identity*, New York, 1963, p. 86.

Looke how the Crowne, which *Ariadne* wore
Vpon her yuory forehead that same day,
That *Theseus* her vnto his bridale bore,
When the bold *Centaures* made that bloudy fray
With the fierce *Lapithes,* which did them dismay;
Being now placed in the firmament,
Through the bright heauen doth her beams display,
And is vnto the starres an ornament,
Which round about her moue in order excellent.

(6.10.13)

What Spenser makes us "see" is not a fixed image, an emblem in the usual sense, but a transformation of turbulence and fury into order and beauty. Our experience is specifically an experience of words and is modulated and developed in the very act of reading. The process is quite explicit in this stanza, for the crux of the simile has no iconographic or fictional reason for being there. The Centaurs and the Lapiths are not at all necessary to Ariadne's crown—they belong to another myth—nor does their bloody fray correspond to any part of the Graces' dance. Yet once there, the bloody fray is both relevant and necessary—as the syntax of the sentence makes us recognize.[12]

There is a temporal dimension in our reading of any poem, and in a narrative poem it is conventionally identified with a sequence of fictional events. But in *The Faerie Queene,* as our last example shows, time is the dimension of verbal events—the lines and stanzas that evoke and modify the reader's responses. An episode in *The Faerie Queene,* then, is best described as a developing psychological experience within the reader, rather than as an action to be observed by him. By heeding this distinction, we can solve one of the most perplexing interpretive problems in the poem: why is Amoret tortured by Busyrane? As W. B. C. Watkins remarks, her "captivity and torture by Busyrane seem sadism unrelated to her character or desert, since as Belphoebe's twin, she is clearly designed to represent a second kind of chastity closer to Spenser's heart—married faithfulness."[13] The puzzle arises because the meaning of the episode is taken to be a simple translation of the story into abstract terms. Thus, "Britomart rescues Amoret from Busyrane" means "Chastity rescues Amoret from Lust." We are then led to search for what Watkins calls an "indefinable . . .

---

[12] See below, pp. 102–106, for a discussion of the relation of Spenser's pictorialism to sixteenth-century critical ideas.

[13] *Shakespeare and Spenser,* p. 206.

fault"[14] in Amoret that is symbolized by her torture. If we take Amoret not as a dramatic individual but as an embodied concept, we are in the same dilemma, because we must find a concept that is in need of rescue from Lust.

There seems to me no way of juggling fictional terms to produce a plausible interpretation of the episode, much less one that adequately suggests its vastness and intensity. In this episode a series of speaking pictures that creates our psychological experience as it unfolds has a clear priority over the narration of an action. Britomart disappears the moment she enters Busyrane's castle, and Spenser presents directly to the reader the series of mythological tapestries (3.11.28–46). More important, we feel no break between this long set piece and the end of canto 11, in which Britomart reappears and fictional action nominally begins. There is complete continuity from one part to the other, because the end of the canto develops and expands the poetic experience begun in the presentation of the tapestries. The image of Cupid's darts is carried over to the description of his statue (3.11.48), and it is in the context established by the tapestries that we feel the menacing brilliance of that description. Taken by itself, Spenser's parenthetical "Ah man beware, how thou those darts behold" is merely a pious exclamation; in the context of his continual admiration of the persuasive liveliness of the tapestries, it records the intensification of our involvement as we move further into Busyrane's palace. When we proceed into the next room, the living walls of gold and the spoils of mighty conquerors (3.11.51–52) again intensify images of the tapestries.

The role of fictional action in this canto is to support the reader's psychological experience of images and their transformations. Spenser makes this explicit by reintroducing Britomart in the middle of the reader's exploration of the first room:

> And vnderneath his feet was written thus,
> *Vnto the Victor of the Gods this bee*:
> And all the people in that ample hous
> Did to that image bow their humble knee,
> And oft committed fowle Idolatree.
> That wondrous sight faire *Britomart* amazed,
> Ne seeing could her wonder satisfie,
> But euer more and more vpon it gazed,
> The whiles the passing brightnes her fraile
>   sences dazed. (3.11.49)

[14] *Ibid.*, p. 66

Britomart's daze is not something to be observed; it intensifies the reader's reaction to the dazzling effect of the palace. Britomart's actions in this episode never have the fictional independence that would place the reader in the role of an observer of an action. Rather they are poetic devices that develop the reader's responses and that frequently merge with a direct rendering of them. Britomart's vigil in canto 12 is absorbed into Cupid's masque, an emblematic procession of the psychological impulses that are engendered by and that characterize erotic feeling. Action in these cantos consistently turns into images that speak directly to the reader.

The nominal action at the beginning of canto 12 is Britomart's lying in wait to observe her enemy and Amoret, the object of her quest. But in fact Britomart is no more present as the masque marches by than she was when the tapestries were presented. It is the reader who first sees Amoret, and Amoret is primarily identified with her torture, the image Spenser wishes to impress upon us:

> Her brest all naked, as net iuory,
> Without adorne of gold or siluer bright,
> Wherewith the Craftesman wonts it beautify,
> Of her dew honour was despoyled quight,
> And a wide wound therein (O ruefull sight)
> Entrenched deepe with knife accursed keene,
> Yet freshly bleeding forth her fainting spright,
> (The worke of cruell hand) was to be seene,
> That dyde in sanguine red her skin all snowy cleene.
>
> (3.12.20)

Spenser begins by developing the suggestion of artificiality in the commonplace comparison of skin to ivory. He praises Amoret's beauty in terms that recall the sinister glamor of the palace, and thus suggests the puzzling presence of a beautiful woman in Busyrane's masque. When he presents Amoret's torture, Spenser directly identifies our psychological experience with the process of reading. Subordinate clauses and exclamations intervene between the major grammatical elements, "a wide wound" and "was to be seene"; each is a separate unit that presents a single aspect of a multiple response to Amoret's wound. The strikingly simple last line emerges from a context of deliberate confusions with which Spenser draws us in more closely.

Once what we may call the emblematic presence of the wound is achieved, Spenser continues to involve the reader:

At that wide orifice her trembling hart
Was drawne forth, and in siluer basin layd,
Quite through transfixed with a deadly dart,
And in her bloud yet steeming fresh embayd:
And those two villeins, which her steps vpstayd,
When her weake feete could scarcely her sustaine,
And fading vitall powers gan to fade,
Her forward still with torture did constraine,
And euermore encreased her consuming paine.

(3.12.21)

After fully presenting the emblem, Spenser does the reverse of allowing us to observe it as complete and amenable to decisive understanding. In the final lines, he makes us participate in Amoret's pain; we have a sense not only of the fact that she is tortured, but also of her endurance of torment. This stanza is the last we see of her for the moment, and we are left at a peak of tension. By thus heightening the sense of mystery that characterizes the verse throughout this episode, Spenser makes it explicit that Britomart's quest is not an action we observe, but is identified with our experience of reading. When Britomart finally enters Busyrane's inner chamber, all the figures of the masque disappear, and we see only Amoret, bound and still tortured (3.12.30–31). The object of our quest is the image of the pure heart transfixed by the cruel dart of desire, and Britomart's "rescue" of Amoret is a resolution of this image:

The cruell steele, which thrild her dying hart,
Fell softly forth, as of his owne accord,
And the wyde wound, which lately did dispart
Her bleeding brest, and riuen bowels gor'd,
Was closed vp, as it had not bene bor'd,
And euery part to safety full sound,
As she were neuer hurt, was soone restor'd.

(3.12.38)

The meaning of these lines lies in the profoundly erotic sense of relaxation, wonder, and wholeness after the terrors of the palace have reached their height in the preceding stanzas (3.12.36–37). By bringing the reader into intimate contact with his verse, Spenser creates feelings and awarenesses that cannot be stated by a conceptual translation of fictional action.

17

Amoret's torture is a conventional image that has occurred throughout Book III. It now emerges as the culminating expression of the major issue of the book—the compatibility of sexual desire and spiritual value in human love. The meanings the image carries are most succinctly indicated by Spenser's exclamation at the sight of Busyrane tormenting Amoret: "Ah who can loue the worker of her smart?" (3.12.31). "Worker of smart" is an epithet for the object of desire,[15] and Spenser's sententious outcry asks, "Who can be a human lover?" Human love must involve the flesh and hence must involve desire and pain. Spenser's conception of chastity as marriage rather than virginity demands that he keep this point firmly in view, and Amoret's torture is the most drastic and comprehensive statement of it. Her torment presents something characteristic of all human love and not the unique suffering of an individual. The healing of her heart, then, expresses the resolution of problems with which the whole book is concerned, and in which Britomart—rocked by the storms of love and wounded by Malecasta and Busyrane (3.1.65, 12.33; cf. 4.6)—is fully implicated. Amoret's torture and release are a direct rendering of awarenesses that have developed in the reader throughout the book, and particularly in those passages of the final episode that have very little to do with fictional action—Busyrane's tapestries and the masque of Cupid.

In all the climactic episodes of *The Faerie Queene,* Spenser brings us into extraordinarily close, almost physical contact with his verse, in order that our psychological experience be identified as closely as possible with the direct experience of language in the activity of reading. The immediacy of the reader's psychological experience is the sign of all these episodes—the human wretchedness of the Cave of Despair, the menacing glitter of Busyrane's palace, the oppressiveness of Mammon's cave, the seductive *otium* of the Bower of Bliss. Amoret's torture is a crucial problem because it is confusing on a very simple level where Spenser's meaning is usually clear. In this episode, Spenser was able to find and express vast significance in a story that has no clear allegorical translation. In most episodes, of course, allegorical significance is plain enough in its general outlines, because symbolic encounters, emblematic figures, and the like were simply raw narrative material to Spenser. But confusion sets in the moment we try to elabo-

---

[15] Calidore's beloved, Pastorella, is called "his wounds worker" (6.10.31), and cf. *Hymne in Honour of Love*, lines 31–32:

> And ye faire Nimphs, which oftentimes haue loued
> The cruell worker of your kindly smarts.

rate the significance of the allegory by treating details of language as if they were fictional details.[16]

II

The idea that *The Faerie Queene* is a coherent fiction implies and is based on the broader idea that the narrative poem is a "world." In its simplest forms, this analogy is obvious, and we appeal to it quite casually. But when the various senses in which we call a narrative poem a world are brought together, they make a comprehensive and powerful nexus of ideas. The narrative poem is and has been thought to be a world because its constituent elements (characters, actions, and settings) imitate or are analogous to those of the real world; because it is a self-contained, coherent, and intelligible structure; and because the poet is like God.[17] Without insisting that these three ideas must necessarily occur together, we can observe that they frequently and naturally do. They do, for example, in the following passage from Tasso's *Discorsi del Poema Eroico,* which can serve as our basic statement of the analogy:

> As in this wonderful realm of God, which is called the world, one sees the sky scattered or highlighted with such a variety of stars, and the air and the sea full of birds and fish, and so many animals, both fierce and gentle, inhabiting the earth, in which we are accustomed to wonder at brooks and fountains and lakes and fields and meadows and woods and mountains; . . . for all that, the world is single which holds in its lap so many and so diverse things, its form and essence are single, the knot is single with which its parts are

---

[16] The phrase "continued allegory, or dark conceit" in the Letter to Raleigh refers to the symbolic nature of Spenser's materials, but it does not guarantee or even imply that a fiction with a continuous double significance is the main vehicle of poetic meaning in *The Faerie Queene.* Spenser would have found exactly this notion of allegory in Tasso's preface to *Gerusalemme Liberata,* which he certainly knew but from which he borrows nothing in his own prefatory letter. Spenser's formula "dark conceit" is based on the rhetoricians' definition of allegory as the local device of continued metaphor ("dark" is the stock epithet for the figure in rhetorical handbooks). Furthermore, in his remarks on *Gerusalemme Liberata,* Spenser does not follow the allegorical interpretation of the heroes that Tasso develops by rationalizing the fiction of his poem. The only possible conclusion is that Tasso's division of a heroic poem into the imitation of actions and the allegory hidden beneath this surface (*Prose,* 1, 301) meant very little to Spenser.

[17] For a penetrating history of the idea of "the poem as heterocosm," see M. H. Abrams, *The Mirror and the Lamp,* New York, 1953, pp. 272–285.

19

brought together and bound in discordant concord; and, with nothing lacking in it, yet there is nothing there which does not serve for either necessity or ornament: so by the same token I judge that an excellent poet (who is called divine for no other reason than that making himself like the supreme maker in his workings [*al supremo artefice nelle sue operazioni assomigliandosi*], he comes to participate in his divinity) can make a poem in which, as in a little world, here we read of armies drawn up, here of battles on land and sea, here of sieges of cities, . . . there deeds of cruelty, of boldness, of courtesy, of magnanimity, there the events of love, now happy now unhappy, now joyous now pitiful: but that nonetheless the poem is single that contains so much variety of material, its form and its soul are single; and that all these things are composed in such a way that one thing looks to another, one thing corresponds to another, one thing depends on another either necessarily or plausibly, so that if one single part is taken away or has its place changed, the whole is destroyed.[18]

When Tasso says that a poem is a world because it is single, the single soul or form he refers to is what he calls the fable—the comprehensive and controlling action that is assumed to exist (or felt to be missing) in each book of *The Faerie Queene*.[19] But there is no reason to think that Spenser shared Tasso's concept of the heroic fable. Tasso says that the *Aeneid* has an ideal action for an epic: "The most noble action, beyond all the others, is the coming of Aeneas into Italy, because the argument is grand and illustrious in itself; but most grand and most illustrious since it looks to the Roman Empire, to which it gave rise."[20] English critics of the sixteenth century do not speak of Aeneas's travels and their destiny; the "argument" of the *Aeneid* is always stated in terms of the moral qualities of its hero. Thus Sidney calls Aeneas "a vertuous man in all fortunes" and describes the *Aeneid* as a series of moral exempla:

> Only let *Aeneas* be worne in the tablet of your memory; how he gouerneth himselfe in the ruine of his Country; in the preseruing his old Father, and carrying away his religious ceremonies; . . . how in storms, howe in sports, howe in warre, howe in peace, how a fugitiue, how victorious, how besiedged, how besiedging, howe to

[18] *Prose*, 1, 154–155.
[19] See *Prose*, 1, 126, 135–136, 142.
[20] *Ibid.*, 1, 121.

strangers, howe to allyes, how to enemies, howe to his owne; lastly, how in his inward selfe, and how in his outward gouernment.[21]

Similarly Spenser, in the Letter to Raleigh, classifies epic poems by the type of virtue, ethical or political, that their heroes exemplify.

The *Apologie for Poetrie* provides considerable support for our view of *The Faerie Queene* as a continual address to the reader rather than as a fictional world. Sidney justifies the poet's use of fiction, but he does not describe or analyze poetic fictions. For example, he does not raise what is, for Tasso, a central question—whether the narrative of a heroic poem should be historically true. Sidney's criterion of truth is not the nature of the fiction in itself, but its didactic efficacy. He consistently describes poetry as a moral influence operating on the reader's mind. Hence his golden world is entirely different from the world of the poem that Tasso describes: "Nature neuer set forth the earth in so rich tapistry as diuers Poets haue done, neither with plesant riuers, fruitful trees, sweet smelling flowers, nor whatsoeuer els may make the too much loued earth more louely. Her world is brasen, the Poets only deliuer a golden."[22] What interests Sidney is not the structure or the constituent elements of this world (compare the abundance of detail in Tasso's passage), but its effect on a human "inhabitant." His metaphor renders the attractiveness of poetry; hence he clinches his statement with the fine wistfulness of "nor whatsoeuer els may make the too much loued earth more louely." Sidney then goes on to say that Nature never produced such excellent men as the heroes of epic poetry:

> Neither let this be iestingly conceiued, because the works of the one be essentiall, the other, in imitation or fiction; for any vnder-standing knoweth the skil of the Artificer standeth in that *Idea* or fore-conceite of the work, and not in the work it selfe. And that the Poet hath that *Idea* is manifest, by deliuering them forth in such excellencie as hee hath imagined them. Which deliuering forth also is not wholie imaginatiue, as we are wont to say by them that build Castles in the ayre: but so farre substantially it worketh, not onely to make a *Cyrus,* which had been but a particuler excellencie, as Nature might haue done, but to bestow a *Cyrus* vpon the worlde, to make many *Cyrus's,* if they wil learne aright why and how that Maker made him.[23]

---

[21] *An Apologie for Poetrie,* in *Elizabethan Critical Essays,* 1, 166, 179–180.
[22] *Ibid.,* 1, 156.   [23] *Ibid.,* 1, 157.

For Tasso, the poet resembles "il supremo artefice nelle sue operazioni" because he creates his own little world, the poem. For Sidney, the poet "substantially worketh" by creating virtuous men.

In the two passages in *The Faerie Queene* in which Spenser refers to his poem as a world, his use of the analogy resembles Sidney's rather than Tasso's. The simpler passage is the beginning of Book VI:

> The waies, through which my weary steps I guyde,
> In this delightfull land of Faery,
> Are so exceeding spacious and wyde,
> And sprinckled with such sweet variety,
> Of all that pleasant is to eare or eye,
> That I nigh rauisht with rare thoughts delight,
> My tedious trauell doe forget thereby;
> And when I gin to feele decay of might,
> It strength to me supplies, and chears my dulled
>   spright.   (6.Proem.1)

For Spenser, as for Sidney, the interest of the metaphorical landscape lies in what it suggests of human response to poetry. Spenser hardly pretends to describe "this delightfull land of Faery"; the crucial words in the first five lines almost all refer to feelings induced by this land. Not only vocabulary but also syntax indicates the orientation of Spenser's metaphor: the "that" clause that completes the first sentence takes us completely inside the poet's mind. Hence in the following stanzas, poetic landscape becomes Parnassus and "the sacred noursery / Of vertue" which Spenser asks the Muse to reveal to him (6.Proem. 3). The opening lines of this proem are so often quoted as if they were meant to be a direct characterization of the poem, that it is worth emphasizing how different they are from, say, Dante's at the beginning of *Purgatorio:*

> Per correr migliori acque alza le vele
> Omai la navicella del mio ingegno,
> Che lascia dietro a sè mar sì crudele.

To run over better waters the little vessel of my genius now hoists her sails, as she leaves behind her a sea so cruel. (*Purgatory* 1.1–3)

The metaphor of the "better waters" and the "cruel sea" exactly corresponds to the fact that hell is a place with certain characteristics and purgatory is another place with certain other characteristics. But Spenser, who has just completed the harshest book in the poem, is not pointing to parts of the poem that can be thought of as external to him. He is characterizing his own mental experience as a poet—quite wonderfully, I think, with its mixture of delight and tedium—and he is about to ask the Muses for inspiration. The important affinities of the passage are with the internal landscape of Milton's

> Yet not the more
> Cease I to wander where the Muses haunt
> Clear Spring, or shady Grove, or Sunny Hill,
> Smit with the love of sacred Song; but chief
> Thee *Sion* and the flow'ry Brooks beneath
> That wash thy hallow'd feet, and warbling flow,
> Nightly I visit.[24]

In his most important comparison of his poem to a world, Spenser answers the charge that his poem "Of some th' aboundance of an idle braine / Will iudged be, and painted forgery," because "none, that breatheth liuing aire, does know, / Where is that happy land of Faery" (2.Proem.1):

> But let that man with better sence aduize,
> That of the world least part to vs is red:
> And dayly how through hardy enterprize,
> Many great Regions are discouered,
> Which to late age were neuer mentioned.
> Who euer heard of th'Indian *Peru?*
> Or who in venturous vessell measured
> The *Amazons* huge riuer now found trew?
> Or fruitfullest *Virginia* who did euer vew?
>
> Yet all these were, when no man did them know;
> Yet haue from wisest ages hidden beene:
> And later times things more vnknowne shall show.
> Why then should witlesse man so much misweene
> That nothing is, but that which he hath seene?
> What if within the Moones faire shining spheare?
> What if in euery other starre vnseene
> Of other worldes he happily should heare?
> He wonder would much more: yet such to some appeare.
>
> (2.Proem.2–3)

24 John Milton, *Paradise Lost*, 3.26–32, ed. Merritt Y. Hughes, New York, 1962.

23

Compare the opening stanzas of canto 7 of *Orlando Furioso,* a passage which Spenser surely had in mind:

> Chi va lontan da la sua patria, vede
> cose, da quel che già credea, lontane;
> che narrandole poi, non se gli crede,
> e stimato bugiardo ne rimane:
> che 'l sciocco vulgo non gli vuol dar fede,
> se non le vede e tocca chiare e piane.
> Per questo io so che l'inesperïenza
> farà al mio canto dar poca credenza.
>
> Poca o molta ch'io ci abbia, non bisogna
> ch'io ponga mente al vulgo sciocco e ignaro.
> A voi so ben che non parrà menzogna,
> che 'l lume del discorso avete chiaro;
> et a voi soli ogni mio intento agogna
> che 'l frutto sia di mie fatiche caro.
> Io vi lasciai che 'l ponte e la riviera
> vider, che 'n guardia avea Erifilla altiera.

He who goes far from his native land sees things far different from what until then he believed, and afterward when he tells of them, he is not believed and is thought a liar, for the foolish multitude will not put faith in him if it does not openly and plainly see and touch them. From this I know that inexperience will make my song gain little belief.

Whether I get little or much of it, I do not need to care about the foolish and ignorant throng. I am certain it will not appear false to you who have the clear light of reason; and every purpose of mine struggles to make dear to you alone the fruit of my labors. I left you when they saw the bridge and the stream the proud Erifilla had in charge. (*OF* 7.1–2)

Ariosto's comparison of his poem to a strange land and himself to a returned traveler is completely adequate to justifying the fanciful, allegorical episodes on Alcina's island. He can treat *l'inesperïenza* as the essential fault of the foolish crowd, and his lively confidence in the clear-witted reader is expressed by his setting us right back in the place where he left us: the final lines, by their very utterance, affirm that Alcina's island exists.[25] Spenser, on the other hand, is concerned

[25] In Harington's translation of this passage, the fit reader is represented as one who is "discreete and wise," and his credence is a matter of moral under-

less with the existence of a strange place than with the presence and quality of a belief. His metaphor is that of an explorer, who thinks what he might see, rather than a returned traveler, who knows what he has seen. Hence instead of Ariosto's down-to-earth assertions, his stanzas consist of questions. These are not merely "rhetorical"—questions in form but assertions in fact. The questions do suggest affirmations, but at the same time they express a sense of wonder, which becomes explicit at the end:

> What if within the Moones faire shining spheare?
> What if in euery other starre vnseene
> Of other worldes he happily should heare?
> He wonder would much more: yet such to some appeare.

There is a beautiful poise here between a very firm sense that something can be so, and a capacity for limitless marveling at what might turn out to be so. We note that the role Spenser adopts is not that of an explorer, but of an observer of explorers. The final "yet such to some appeare" is so firm and decisive precisely because Spenser does not claim to be one of those "some." He has made the affirmation hold true even when the fact exceeds what we can conceive. The kind of affirmation Spenser makes is very different from, say, Tasso's insistence that his fable be historically true, which is the high and serious version of Ariosto's claims to veracity. Spenser is not involved in such claims about events or places external to him. He is encouraging the reader to trust in his feelings of being moved, excited, interested, morally enlightened as he reads the poem. What is so wonderful about Spenser's stanzas is that they enact the affirmation implicit in Sidney's, "The poet . . . nothing affirmes and therefore neuer lyeth."

Almost any problem or topic we consider in *The Faerie Queene* in-

---

standing. Hence in a marginal note he identifies the *sciocco vulgo* of stanza 1 as "those that cannot understand the allegorie," and for Ariosto's lines about *l'inesperïenza*, he substitutes:

> Therefore to them, my tale may seeme a fable,
> Whose wits to vnderstand it are not able.

The second stanza concludes not by returning us to the scene of the narrative action, but by appealing to the reader's self-understanding:

> For some there are, may fortune in this booke,
> As in a glasse their acts and haps to looke.

John Harington, *Orlando Furioso in English Heroical Verse*, London, 1591, 7.1–2. These changes have been noticed by Hallett Smith, *Elizabethan Poetry*, Cambridge, Mass., 1952, pp. 317–318.

volves asking whether the poem is a world.[26] For example, Time's presence in the Garden of Adonis, which is usually considered a problem in the coherence of Spenser's thought, can equally well be stated as a problem of the identity of a place. Time's ravages in *a* garden are entirely relevant to that canto; the apparent inconsistency lies in Time's laying waste that particular garden. Hence we find one critic trying to solve the dilemma by saying, "The poet does not simply continue his description of the garden: here he creates a new and different space, substituting a second garden for the first. Momentarily, however, there is confusion: it is as if Time had not left the stage when the scene was changed."[27] The most direct and explicit way to test whether Spenser thought of his poem as a world is to examine his use of divine intervention in the ordinary course of events. Clearly a Christian poet who thinks of his poem as a world must decide whether it is one in which providential intervention occurs. We need not expect or require that *The Faerie Queene* be a poem like *Gerusalemme Liberata,* in which God directs all the major action. The question is whether the instances of providential intervention in *The Faerie Queene* reveal any pattern within a putative world or justify our thinking of Providence as an agent in the poem.

There are four clear instances of providential intervention in *The Faerie Queene,* one of which—the angel's succouring of Guyon—is a special case, since it involves a celestial being. The other three are the satyrs' rescue of Una from Sansloy (1.6.5–8), Belphoebe's discovery of the wounded Timias (3.5.27), and Proteus' rescue of Florimell from the lecherous old fisherman (3.8.27–30). In each of these cases the person rescued gets into more trouble. Proteus turns out to be as lustful as the fisherman and imprisons Florimell at the bottom of the sea. Belphoebe cures Timias' physical wounds, but inflicts a deadlier wound of love. Though the satyrs provide a pastoral retreat for Una, it is only a temporary respite; as soon as she returns to the world of men to seek her knight, she is deceived again by Archimago. If we really trusted these events to establish a pattern, the first thing we would notice is a taste for irony on the part of Spenser's Providence. Or we might say that the contradiction between a claim like "Prouidence heauenly passeth liuing thought, / And doth for wretched mens reliefe make way" (3.5.27) and the ensuing events is not to be at-

---

[26] See below, pp. 203 and 249, for its relevance to problems of iconography and interpretation of character.

[27] Harry Berger, Jr., "Spenser's Gardens of Adonis: Force and Form in the Renaissance Imagination," UTQ, 30 (1960–1961), 140.

tributed to God Himself, but is a confusion in the mind of Spenser, the little god of the poem. But these problems arise only if we treat Spenser's assertions of providential intervention as literal claims about a world. What we find, in fact, is that these passages have a clear rhetorical purpose: at particular points in the poem, Spenser uses them to direct and extend the reader's emotional responses and awareness of issues.

The most imposing of these passages is the satyrs' rescue of Una from Sansloy's assault:

> So when he saw his flatt'ring arts to fayle,
> And subtile engines bet from batteree,
> With greedy force he gan the fort assayle,
> Whereof he weend possessed soone to bee,
> And win rich spoile of ransackt chastetee.
> Ah heauens, that do this hideous act behold,
> And heauenly virgin thus outraged see,
> How can ye vengeance iust so long withhold,
> And hurle not flashing flames vpon that Paynim bold?
>
> (1.6.5)

The idea of providential intervention enters the passage as an intensified reaction to a stock situation, the maiden in distress. The poet's role here is not that of the god who can call on supernatural forces to intervene, but that of the human being who shares Una's distress. Of course this role could be adopted ironically: to pretend to feel amazement at the heavens' indifference could be a way of indicating an assurance that heaven will act in the desired way. If this were indeed the case, the extravagance of Spenser's question would be melodramatic and vulgar. In fact that extravagance is turned to wonderful account in the next stanza:

> The pitteous maiden carefull comfortlesse,
> Does throw out thrilling shriekes, and shrieking cryes,
> The last vaine helpe of womens great distresse,
> And with loud plaints importuneth the skyes,
> That molten starres do drop like weeping eyes;
> And *Phoebus* flying so most shamefull sight,
> His blushing face in foggy cloud implyes,
> And hides for shame. What wit of mortall wight
> Can now deuise to quit a thrall from such a plight?
>
> (1.6.6)

27

We see that Spenser is far from claiming that the heavens will behave in the way he has desired. The result of Una's cries is a very pointed bit of poetic artifice. Where we expected that the translation of our feelings into action would take the form of a rescue, it in fact takes the form of an emphatic pathetic fallacy. The poetic realization of our feelings is thus, in an entertaining way, completely problematic. The concluding question leaves us with only the resources of our mortal wits, and with a sense of puzzlement very different from the simple outrage expressed at the end of the preceding stanza.

As usual, Spenser is not imitating an action, but evoking and manipulating our responses. It is in the context of understanding created by these two stanzas that we read about the providential rescue of Una:

> Eternall prouidence exceeding thought,
> Where none appeares can make her selfe a way:
> A wondrous way it for this Lady wrought,
> From Lyons clawes to pluck the griped pray.
> Her shrill outcryes and shriekes so loud did bray,
> That all the woodes and forestes did resownd;
> A troupe of *Faunes* and *Satyres* far away
> Within the wood were dauncing in a rownd,
> Whiles old *Syluanus* slept in shady arber sownd.
>
> (1.6.7)

Taken by itself, this stanza might seem to treat Providence as a dramatic agent in the poem. But as an answer to the question with which the preceding stanza ends, the resonant opening lines of this stanza become part of Spenser's exploitation of our expectations and desires. This playing with the reader has its classic form in the passage he is imitating here:

> Chi narrerà l'angoscie, i pianti, i gridi,
> l'alta querela che nel ciel penètra?
> Maraviglia ho che non s'apriro i lidi,
> quando fu posta in su la fredda pietra,
> dove in catena, priva di sussidi,
> morte aspettava abominosa e tetra.
> Io nol dirò; che sì il dolor mi muove,
> che mi sforza voltar le rime altrove.

Who will relate the anxieties, the tears, the shrieks, the high lamentation that pierces into the sky? I wonder that the shores did not open when she was put on the cold rock, where in chains, without aid, she awaited horrible black death. I shall not tell it, for sorrow so moves me that it compels me to turn my rimes elsewhere.[28]

The reader has to wait two cantos to find out how Angelica is rescued. Spenser plays with the reader's expectations not by so direct a joke, but by turning the awe suggested by the opening lines of the stanza into the charm of the pastoral scene at the end. The rescue itself, in the next stanza, is a rather comic event. The satyrs rush to see what the disturbance is, and Sansloy, never having seen such a "rude, misshapen, monstrous rablement," takes to his horse and flees (1.6.8). What is wonderful about the rescue is its disarming simplicity. The satyrs, true pastoral figures in William Empson's sense,[29] are both better than and inferior to man. Their frank response to Una's beauty is genuinely innocent in its tenderness and awe; Spenser can even call them "incontinent" in their haste, whereas in human terms the word would suggest Sansloy's lust.[30] At the same time, their innocence turns out to be simply ignorance in respect to Una and what she represents (1.6.19).

Providential intervention in this episode is a product of our involvement, both emotional and mental, in Una's helplessness, and is not an assertion about the causation of events within a putative world. By the same token, the meaning of the episode is not the mere assertion, "Providence protects Truth." The feeling that Una is special, that Providence does care for her, gives us reassurance, just as the satyrs' affectionate awe does. On the other hand, we are aware that just as the satyrs' worship is not adequate, neither is a rescue that has been called providential precisely because it is not made by a human knight. The pastoralism of the satyrs brings out the pathos of the Red Cross Knight's defection from Una, for to adore so lovely a being seems the easiest and most natural act for a creature. At the same time, the pastoral mode reinforces the irony of Una's rescue—that she will not be truly secure until she is reunited with her human knight, she will be helpless so long as he is. Una is able to leave the satyrs only with the help of the "noble warlike knight" Satyrane (1.6.20). He immedi-

[28] *Orlando Furioso*, 8.66. This outburst occurs when Angelica is exposed to the Orc. The narrative action of Spenser's episode is derived from another episode in *Orlando Furioso*, Odorico's assault on the chaste Isabella (*OF* 13.26–29).

[29] See *Some Versions of Pastoral*, London, 1935, p. 15 *et passim*.

[30] For this play on words, see 2.9.1 and *As You Like It*, 5.2.43.

ately leads her into another of Archimago's deceptions (1.6.34–48), but it is in the context of man's fallen world that Una must find her peace—a point emphasized by the fact that the reader is as much fooled by Archimago here as are Una and Satyrane. One objects to saying that "Providence protects Truth" is the meaning of this episode, because so simply confident a claim does not adequately represent all that Spenser makes us understand. It could do so only if our role as observers were decisively that of beings (angels, perhaps) who could view the action from the standpoint of Providence. This is precisely the effect Spenser would produce if, in the role of little god, he made us feel that Providence were an agent that could be counted on to act in a certain way within the world of the poem.

We have already observed that if Spenser literally holds Providence responsible for the protection of Florimell, he has a good deal to account for when Proteus puts her in prison. But no such claims or problems arise. As in the rescue of Una, Spenser uses the heavens' intercession for Florimell to develop the reader's response to a stock situation:

> The silly virgin stroue him to withstand,
> All that she might, and him in vaine reuild:
> She struggled strongly both with foot and hand,
> To saue her honor from that villaine vild,
> And cride to heauen, from humane helpe exild.
> O ye braue knights, that boast this Ladies loue,
> Where be ye now, when she is nigh defild
> Of filthy wretch? well may shee you reproue
> Of falshood or of slouth, when most it may behoue.

> (3.8.27)

From the end of this stanza, one would think that Spenser was about to introduce providential care as a rebuke to human indifference. But instead we are given two versions of an appropriate reaction to Florimell's distress—one human, one divine:

> But if that thou, Sir *Satyran*, didst weete,
> Or thou, Sir *Peridure*, her sorie state,
> How soone would yee assemble many a fleete,
> To fetch from sea, that ye at land lost late;
> Towres, Cities, Kingdomes ye would ruinate,
> In your auengement and dispiteous rage,
> Ne ought your burning fury mote abate;

30

But if Sir *Calidore* could it presage,
No liuing creature could his cruelty asswage.

But sith that none of all her knights is nye,
See how the heauens of voluntary grace,
And soueraine fauour towards chastity,
Doe succour send to her distressed cace:
So much high God doth innocence embrace.

(3.8.28–29)

Spenser provides two ways of seeing a rescue that are appropriate to Book III. First he suggests the tyrannical force of love, which good knights as well as bad feel in Book III. With the shift from phrases like "burning fury" to "voluntary grace" and "innocence," he then suggests the natural harmony of the universe—most notably seen in the Garden of Adonis—which gives a sanction to human love and shows its painfulness to be ultimately benign. Both these views of love support the presentation of the rescue and its consequences. Florimell's shrieks are heard by Proteus, the "Shepheard of the seas" while he wanders "along the fomy waues driuing his finny droue" (3.8.29–30). The rescue comes from the sea in its friendliest aspect—a pastoral realm populated by mythological figures. This image of the sea, far from being a proof of providential protection, is one of several ways in which Spenser examines the pastoral vision of love in its relation to actual human feeling. It has already been prominent in canto 4, where the inherent irony of treating the sea under the aspect of humanized nature is brought out by the contrast between Britomart's storms of love and Cymoent's delicate seclusion.[31] At the beginning of this episode, nature sympathizes with Florimell's plight:

For th'aire was milde, and cleared was the skie,
And all his windes *Dan Aeolus* did keepe,
From stirring vp their stormy enmitie,
As pittying to see her waile and weepe.

(3.8.21)

But the condition of this calm is made clear in the next line: "But all the while the fisher did securely sleepe." The pastoral image of the sea

[31] See 3.4.7–10, 13, 22–23, 31–34, 42–43. The description of Proteus' chariot being drawn by fish resembles the description of Cymoent's chariot (3.4.33). And Proteus, like Cymoent, has an underground bower (3.8.37). The way in which Spenser tests the pastoral vision of love as a rendering of actual human experience is discussed in chapter 11.

31

is not a fixed reality in Spenser's little world, but a poetic image that is constantly subject to modifications. Its "reality" lies in the reader's grasp of what it suggests: it is thus amenable to the irony of Proteus' lustful wooing, while the literal claim of a providential rescue is not.[32]

Belphoebe's rescue of Timias is a slighter example than the two we have examined, but here too we find the idea of providential intervention entering as an extension of our responses and desires. When Timias has been wounded and lies "wallowd all in his own gore," Spenser exclaims, "Now God thee keepe, thou gentlest Squire aliue" (3.5.26), and then says, in the next stanza:

> Prouidence heauenly passeth liuing thought,
> And doth for wretched mens reliefe make way;
> For loe great grace or fortune thither brought
> Comfort to him, that comfortlesse now lay.
>
> (3.5.27)

These lines make our feelings anticipate Timias' exclamation when he awakens and sees Belphoebe:

> Mercy deare Lord (said he) what grace is this,
> That thou hast shewed to me sinfull wight,
> To send thine Angell from her bowre of blis,
> To comfort me in my distressed plight?
>
> (3.5.35)

The irony of the episode—that in curing Timias' physical wounds, Belphoebe inflicts a deadlier wound of love (see 3.5.41–43)—is also

---

[32] This is not to say that Spenser does not want us to see Florimell's chastity as a divinely sanctioned virtue. A dozen stanzas later, he praises her in terms that strongly recall the way he speaks of the heavens' voluntary grace:

> Eternall thraldome was to her more liefe,
> Then losse of chastitie, or chaunge of loue:
> Die had she rather in tormenting griefe,
> Then any should of falsenesse her reproue,
> Or loosenesse, that she lightly did remoue.
> Most vertuous virgin, glory be thy meed,
> And crowne of heauenly praise with Saints aboue,
> Where most sweet hymmes of this thy famous deed
> Are still emongst them song, that far my rymes exceed.
> (3.8.42)

These lines do not justify the heavens' earlier intervention, but rather prove that Spenser is concerned with our responses to Florimell and our attitude towards love, and not with claims about a putative world. The two passages are equivalent praises of chastity, whereas they conflict as statements about providential direction of human events. One says that Providence does succor innocence; the other says that suffering on earth will be rewarded in Heaven.

an irony against these lines. But clearly it is directed against a human mode of praising beauty and not against Providence as the cause of events in a world.

It is rather striking to realize that all three of these episodes are imitations of Ariosto,[33] and that Spenser is consistently interested in Ariosto's way of addressing his reader. We have already observed (above, n. 28) that he imports into the narrative outline provided by Odorico's assault on Isabella the potent rhetoric and explicit joking of Ariosto's bewailing Angelica's distress. Spenser imitates this stanza once again when he bids farewell to Florimell in prison (3.8.43), and his praise of Florimell's chastity (3.8.42–43) is taken from Ariosto's praise of Isabella's chastity (*OF* 29.26–27). The address to Florimell's knights, which produces the heavens' "voluntary grace," is an imitation of a stanza in which Ariosto energetically laments the absence of Angelica's knights (*OF* 8.68). In Belphoebe's rescue of Timias, the reminder that the reader has already met Belphoebe imitates a common Ariostan device that occurs in the episode Spenser is imitating here, the idyll of Angelica and Medoro (*OF* 19.17; cf. 3.5.27). Spenser concludes this episode by praising Belphoebe's chastity (3.5. 51–55). The image of the rose with which he begins is borrowed from Ariosto's address to Angelica's knights when she gives herself to Medoro (*OF* 19.31–33), and the rhetorical mode itself, the address to the female readers of the poem, is one Spenser seems to have considered specifically Ariostan.[34] Ariosto, of all poets, most dazzlingly manages his poem as a little world, but Spenser's central interest in these passages is in the way Ariosto speaks in his own voice and extends or manipulates the reader's reactions. Insofar as he is interested in Ariosto's management of his poem, he seems to see it as an exploitation of the reader's expectations.

The only other important example of providential intervention in *The Faerie Queene,* the angel's descent to succor Guyon, produces no consequences that would make us question the intentions of Providence. But it is nonetheless clear that the purpose of this episode is to evoke certain awarenesses and attitudes in the reader. In the second of the two introductory stanzas, Spenser says:

[33] For a full account of the relation of these episodes to *Orlando Furioso,* see chapter 6.

[34] Most of these addresses occur in Book III, in which Spenser is consciously emulating Ariosto, and the other two major ones, 3.1.49 and 3.9.1–2, both imitate *OF* 22.1–3. Other passages in which Ariosto addresses his female readers are *OF* 10.5–9, 28.1–2, 29.2–3, 30.1–3, 37.7–24, and 38.1–6.

> How oft do they, their siluer bowers leaue,
> To come to succour vs, that succour want?
> How oft do they with golden pineons, cleaue
> The flitting skyes, like flying Pursuiuant,
> Against foule feends to aide vs millitant?

(2.8.2)

The force of these questions lies in qualities of voice, diction, and imagery, rather than in any sense the poem gives us of literal evidence to support the implied claims. In fact it is wonderfully bold of Spenser to ask these questions immediately after Guyon has defied a "foule feend" alone and unaided. Similarly, the angel says to the Palmer that he will not forget Guyon, but will "euermore him succour, and defend / Against his foe and mine" (2.8.8). But we do not expect the angel to aid Guyon in the Bower of Bliss; indeed, any hint of angelic super-vision would destroy the significance of his conquest there.[35] Spenser is not introducing the angel as an agent in the world of the poem; he is making a point. The purpose of the fictional event is exactly the same as that of the opening address to the reader:

> O th'exceeding grace
> Of highest God, that loues his creatures so,
> And all his workes with mercy doth embrace,
> That blessed Angels, he sends to and fro,
> To serue to wicked man, to serue his wicked foe.

(2.8.1)

It has long been recognized that Spenser is not calling Guyon a wicked person. He is changing our perspective, giving us a different way to see Guyon: for all his moral heroism, he is still a man, and is therefore dependent on God's grace. The portrayal of the angel extends what is suggested by the opening stanza, and in particular gives us a sense of God's love that is appropriate at this point in the poem. Spenser is no

---

[35] Compare *Gerusalemme Liberata*, 7.78ff. Raimondo, going out to meet the pagan Argante, prays that God help him, a "weak old man," as he did David, a "weak youth" against Goliath (7.78). God selects an angel, who is identified as the guardian angel who has watched over Raimondo since he was a babe (7.80); this angel protects Raimondo from all Argante's blows (7.87, 92), and when Oradino, prompted by Satan, treacherously wounds him with an arrow, the angel ensures that the wound is slight (7.102). Tasso does not, indeed, explain why God permitted Satan to prevent Raimondo's victory, but we may assume that it is the same explanation as that given a dozen stanzas later for the Christians' failure to achieve what seems an imminent victory: "it was not the day that God had written in his eternal decrees" (7.114).

longer concerned, as he was in Book I, with man's radical dependence on grace. Through his portrait of the angel (2.8.5–6), in which pagan imagery and decorative loveliness dominate, he now suggests the accessibility of the grace that sustains the virtuous man.

It seems to me unnecessary to discuss all the minor examples of providential intervention in *The Faerie Queene*.[36] But one incident is particularly instructive and confirms the conclusions we have reached. In his battle with the dragon, the Red Cross Knight is saved, on the first day, by falling into the Well of Life and on the second day by falling under the Tree of Life. Spenser introduces the first of these accidents (as we may call them) by saying, "It fortuned (as faire it then befell)" (1.11.29), and the second by saying, "It chaunst (eternall God that chaunce did guide)" (1.11.45). Surely it would be absurd to say that the first fall is really an accident and that God is responsible only for the second. The parenthetical "eternall God that chaunce did guide" is meant to intensify our feeling and knowledge that the knight's victory is inevitable; it is not an assertion that God has begun to direct events at this point. It is just this kind of definitive assertion that Spenser is unwilling to make in his poem. Whatever his attitude might have been towards divine direction of real human affairs, his attitude in *The Faerie Queene* is best expressed by Arthur's reply when Una asks him what has brought him to Fairyland:

> Full hard it is (quoth he) to read aright
> The course of heauenly cause, or vnderstand
> The secret meaning of th'eternall might,
> That rules mens wayes, and rules the thoughts of
>   liuing wight.
>
> For whither he through fatall deepe foresight
> Me hither sent, for cause to me vnghest,
> Or that fresh bleeding wound, which day and night
> Whilome doth rancle in my riuen brest,
> With forced fury following his behest,
> Me hither brought by wayes yet neuer found,
> You to haue helpt I hold my selfe yet blest.
>
>   (1.9.6–7)

[36] For example, 1.7.12, 1.10.9, 3.3.24, 3.7.27, 4.7.23, 4.11.1, 5.9.42, 6.4.10. I call these minor examples, because the apparent claim of providential direction is briefer or less explicit than in the passages I have discussed.

Chapter Two

Narrative Materials and
Stanzas of Poetry

I

"Literally . . . a poem's narrative is its rhythm or movement of words,"
Northrop Frye has remarked. But "when we think of a poem's narra-
tive as a description of events, we no longer think of the narrative as
literally embracing every word and letter. We think rather of a se-
quence of gross events, of the obvious and externally striking elements
in the word-order."[1] In Frye's terms, the argument of the last chapter
is that we have forsaken the literal narration of *The Faerie Queene,*
the continuous flow of words, for a kind of narration that is really not
there. But if Spenser's narration is not a descriptive fiction, if *The
Faerie Queene* is not a world, of what does its surface consist? The
"gross events" of *The Faerie Queene* are verbal phenomena—lines
and stanzas of poetry. Their constituent elements are verbal formulas,
not observed details in a putative world. Spenser's stanzas are frankly
arrangements of words, and do not purport to imitate or create a real-
ity external to the speaker. What is striking, of course, is that Spen-
ser's words are prompted by and derive from narrative materials. We
have so far equated "narrative materials" and "fiction," but we should
now recognize the difference between them. Tasso, speaking of the
poet's materials, observes: "Before this has been subjected to the
artifice of epic, it is called matter. After it has been disposed and
treated by the poet, and clothed with eloquence, it forms the fable,
which is no longer matter, but the form and soul of the poem."[2] Pre-
cisely what interests us in *The Faerie Queene* is the fact that Spenser
transforms his narrative materials not into parts of a fiction, but into
stanzas of poetry, arrangements of words.

Consider the following stanza (the first line refers to the Red Cross
Knight's harsh penitential discipline):

> In which his torment often was so great,
> That like a Lyon he would cry and rore,
> And rend his flesh, and his owne synewes eat.

[1] *Anatomy of Criticism,* Princeton, 1957, pp. 78–79.
[2] Torquato Tasso, *Prose diverse,* ed. Cesare Guasti, Florence, 1875, 1, 126.

His owne deare *Vna* hearing euermore
His ruefull shriekes and gronings, often tore
Her guiltlesse garments, and her golden heare,
For pitty of his paine and anguish sore;
Yet all with patience wisely she did beare;
For well she wist, his crime could else be neuer cleare.

(1.10.28)

This is an interesting example, because if the stanza really does purport to imitate actions, we are asked to believe that Una's tearing her clothing and hair exemplifies wise patience. But if this is not the case, what do we mean by saying that the narrative materials are transformed simply into a stanza, an arrangement of words? We mean, first of all, that individual lines of verse work independently, even when they are based on the same narrative event. This is especially evident in the use made of the knight's suffering in the second half of the stanza. His shrieks and groanings in line 5 are assimilated to Una's suffering—through the intervening fourth line, through the adjective "ruefull" and through the rhyme-word "tore," which suggests a suffering on Una's part that matches the knight's. By the time we reach line 7, the "paine and anguish sore" seem as much hers as his, and the next line shows how much Spenser counts on our responding in this way. The independence of the line as a unit is most artfully exploited in lines 5 and 6. Despite the enjambment, "tore" is kept quite separate from its objects in the next line, both because it is a rhyme-word and because alliteration and formulaic balance assert the independence of "Her guiltlesse garments, and her golden heare." The effect of this is to draw our attention from "tore her guiltlesse garments" as a representation of action, and to leave us satisfied with it as a conventional formula expressing sorrow and anguish. The effect is decisively established by the fact that we do not make a full stop after "golden heare," but continue on to the next line, which completes the b-rhymes. The movement of lines 4–7 does not allow us to isolate the action of tearing, but carries it directly over into the feeling it expresses.

Spenser's managing of the four middle lines indicates a second aspect of the way in which he transforms narrative materials into an arrangement of words. Although each line is an individual unit, we group the lines into distinct subdivisions of the stanza—in this case, lines 1–3, 4–7, and 8–9. The lines are organized not by the narrative events that give rise to them (and that, in another poem, they would be imitating), but by the groupings imposed by various verbal means.

37

(The rhyme scheme of the stanza, as further illustrations will make clear, does not in itself impose any specific groupings; it simply provides a formal structure that can be used in support of these groupings, as the b-rhyme is used in this stanza.) These groupings are extremely important in Spenser's stanzas, and attention to them is almost always rewarded. In this stanza, for example, each of the middle four lines in some way expresses cherishing love. At the same time as Una's sufferings are assimilated to the knight's "paine and anguish," the tenderness associated with her distinctively modifies the quality of feeling in the stanza and hence its significance. The wise patience with which the stanza ends is felt to be not heroic resistance, but an expression of loving understanding and solicitude.

The next stanza shows that Spenser's special transformation of narrative materials is what makes his poetry allegorical:

> Whom thus recouer'd by wise Patience,
> And trew *Repentance* they to *Vna* brought:
> Who ioyous of his cured conscience,
> Him dearely kist, and fairely eke besought
> Himselfe to chearish, and consuming thought
> To put away out of his carefull brest.

> (1.10.29)

From Una's patience, we move to Patience, the spiritual physician who has supervised the discipline imposed on the knight. But we notice a curious typographical trick in this stanza: Patience, unlike Repentance, is not italicized (as it is in 1.10.23), and hence is not treated as a proper name. What Spenser wishes, surely, is that we avoid recognizing "Patience" as the name of a personification, an agent external to the knight, until we have fully absorbed the word as the name of a moral virtue. In this way we are made to feel that the knight has recovered through his own patience, just as his repentance has been his own. We now see how important it is that Una's sorrowing is assimilated to the knight's spiritual anguish in the preceding stanza. Her experience, which in narrative terms is simply a reaction to the knight's suffering, becomes through the poetry a part of it. It is this that enables Spenser to play his trick with "Patience" and to turn Una's joyous affection into the injunction to the knight "Himselfe to chearish."

Examining even one of Spenser's stanzas gives us a sense of the resources he had at his command. Without accumulating further exam-

38

ples, we can appreciate the long aside in which William Empson gives what is much the most perceptive account we have of the stanza of *The Faerie Queene:*

> Spenser concentrates the reader's attention on to the movement of his stanza: by the use of archaic words and constructions, so that one is at a safe distance from the exercise of an immediate judgment, by the steady untroubled flow of similar lines, by making no rapid change of sense or feeling, by sustained alliteration, parallel adjectives, and full statement of the accessories of a thought, and by the dreamy repetition of the great stanza perpetually pausing at its close. *Ababbcbcc* is a unit which may be broken up into a variety of metrical forms, and the ways in which it is successively broken up are fitted into enormous patterns. The first quatrain usually gratifies the ear directly and without surprise, and the stanzas may then be classified by the grammatical connections of the crucial fifth line, which must give a soft bump to the dying fall of the first quatrain, keep it in the air, and prevent it from falling apart from the rest of the stanza.
>
> It may complete the sense of the quatrain, for instance, with a couplet, and the stanza will then begin with a larger, more narrative unit, *ababb,* and wander garrulously down a perspective to the alexandrine. Or it may add to the quatrain as by an afterthought, as if with a childish earnestness it made sure of its point without regard to the metre, and one is relieved to find that the metre recovers itself after all. For more energetic or serious statements it will start a new quatrain at the fifth line, with a new sentence; there are then two smaller and tighter, repeatedly didactic, or logically opposed, historically or advancing, units, whose common rhyme serves to insist upon their contrast, which are summed up and reconciled in the final solemnity of the alexandrine. In times of excitement the fifth line will be connected both ways, so as to ignore the two quatrains, and, by flowing straight on down the stanza with an insistence on its unity, show the accumulated energy of some enormous climax; and again, by being connected with neither, it will make the stanza into an unstressed conversational device without overtones of rhythm, picking up stray threads of the story with almost the relief of prose. It would be interesting to take one of the vast famous passages of the work and show how these devices are fitted together into larger units of rhythm, but having said that every use of the stanza includes all these uses in the reader's apprehension of it I may have

39

said enough to show the sort of methods Spenser had under his control; why it was not necessary for him to concentrate on the lightning flashes of ambiguity.[3]

Empson does more than describe the variety of Spenser's stanza. He grasps the fact that individual uses of it are not discrete and separate from each other, but are, for the poet, exploitations of a complex set of possibilities; from the reader's standpoint, this means that "every use of the stanza includes all these uses in [his] apprehension of it." Thus when we say that the stanza we have examined has three major groupings—lines 1–3, 4–7, and 8–9—we do not mean that this is one fixed subtype of the Spenserian stanza that has been imposed from outside on the formulas and devices of the stanza. We are speaking of a set of choices that the stanza makes as it progresses—for example, the choice between a stop after "golden heare" and the direct continuing of the verse into "For pitty of his paine and anguish sore." Empson rightly says that the most important and frequent of such choices occur in and around the fifth line, but they can occur anywhere in the stanza. Groupings in Spenser's stanzas are almost always quite definite, because the independence of each line is not threatened by the combinations into which it enters (by contrast think of Milton's blank verse, in which the possibilities seem infinite, not just numerous). Hence it is often convenient to think and speak about one of Spenser's stanzas as if it were a static object. This is not really misleading, so long as we remember that Spenser's stanza is not a predetermined mold or set of such molds, but an experience of language that is temporal and not spatial. Our sense of a stanza's organization depends on active perceptions as we follow the movement of the verse, and our descriptions and interpretations of individual stanzas must always recognize this fact.

II

We begin with a trick of narration that shows how decisively Spenser's verse constitutes a verbal, not a fictional, reality, and at the same time shows us one of the most important ways in which Spenser manages his stanza. The following passage describes Venus' and Diana's discovery, while they are searching for Cupid, of Chrysogone and her newborn twins, Belphoebe and Amoret:

> So long they sought, till they arriued were
> In that same shadie couert, whereas lay

[3] *Seven Types of Ambiguity*, 3rd edn., London, 1953, pp. 33–34.

Faire *Crysogone* in slombry traunce whilere:
Who in her sleepe (a wondrous thing to say)
Vnwares had borne two babes, as faire as springing day.

Vnwares she them conceiu'd, vnwares she bore:
She bore withouten paine, that she conceiued
Withouten pleasure: ne her need implore
Lucinaes aide: which when they both perceiued,
They were through wonder nigh of sense bereaued,
And gazing each on other, nought bespake:
At last they both agreed, her seeming grieued
Out of her heauy swowne not to awake,
But from her louing side the tender babes to take.

(3.6.26–27)

The trick lies in the use to which Spenser puts "which when they both perceiued" in the second stanza. In narrative terms, "which" can only refer to Chrysogone lying unconscious with the babies next to her. But our grammatical instincts tell us that it refers to what immediately precedes it, and this is the effect Spenser intends, even though the preceding lines convey things of which Venus and Diana are not aware. The goddesses' wonder, which in narrative terms derives from the surprised discovery of babes in the woods, is transmuted into an intensification of the reader's sense of wonder at the miraculous birth. What the goddesses have perceived, in effect, is the preceding lines of verse.

Phrases based on the formula "which X perceived" would seem to be involved in rendering fictional events. In *The Faerie Queene*, however, they are in the service not of a fiction, but of the verbal events of individual stanzas—a characteristic purpose being to divide the stanza into two major groups of verse. At the height of Arthur's battle with Orgoglio, the device appears in two consecutive stanzas:

And in his [Arthur's] fall his shield, that
    couered was,
Did loose his vele by chaunce, and open flew:
The light whereof, that heauens light did pas,
Such blazing brightnesse through the aier threw,
That eye mote not the same endure to vew.
Which when the Gyaunt spyde with staring eye,
He downe let fall his arme, and soft withdrew
His weapon huge, that heaued was on hye
For to haue slaine the man, that on the ground did lye.

And eke the fruitfull-headed beast, amaz'd
At flashing beames of that sunshiny shield,
Became starke blind, and all his senses daz'd,
That downe he tumbled on the durtie field,
And seem'd himselfe as conquered to yield.
Whom when his maistresse proud perceiu'd to fall,
Whiles yet his feeble feet for faintnesse reeld,
Vnto the Gyant loudly she gan call,
O helpe *Orgoglio,* helpe, or else we perish all.

(1.8.19–20)

In each stanza the first five lines render the physical impact of Arthur's shield, its dazzling and stunning effect. The last four lines render a particular sense of helpless enfeeblement in creatures who were formerly powerful and threatening. In neither stanza is the formula "which X perceived" strikingly at variance with the narrative action; yet we find that each stanza exemplifies Spenser's characteristic handling of narrative materials. In the first stanza we feel that "which" refers to the whole of the two preceding lines, and not simply to the "blazing brightnesse" which is its literal reference. The difference between the two ways of reading becomes clear when we reach "He downe let fall his arme, and soft withdrew," which derives its force much more from the line "That eye mote not the same endure to vew" than from a purely physical rendering of bright light (note the echoing of this line in "with staring eye" in the next). In the second stanza, the beast has decisively "tumbled on the durtie field" before we see him reeling for faintness. If rendered action were Spenser's concern, the stanza would be impossible or at best clumsy. But "Whiles yet his feeble feet for faintnesse reeld" is a poetic stroke that is essential to the significance and organization of the stanza. Without it, "perceiu'd to fall" would unequivocally mean "perceived to have fallen," and Duessa's cry would be simply the result of the beast's downfall. Instead it is made part of the process of being overwhelmed. The last four lines of this stanza extend and complicate the sense of defeat in the first five, in which the victim's helplessness is entirely a matter of being physically stunned. With Duessa's cry human consciousness enters into the experience of being overcome by the shield, and the sense of being enfeebled and diminished, far from being a mere sign of victory over an external enemy, emerges as part of the psychological experience of illuminating grace.[4]

[4] Other interesting uses of "which X perceived" and similar formulas are

Needless to say, Spenser does not always divide a stanza into more or less equal halves. We can best understand the possibilities of his stanza by going through one of the more varied sequences:

There the most daintie Paradise on ground,
It selfe doth offer to his sober eye,
In which all pleasures plenteously abound,
And none does others happinesse enuye:
The painted flowres, the trees vpshooting hye,
The dales for shade, the hilles for breathing space,
The trembling groues, the Christall running by;
And that, which all faire workes doth most aggrace,
The art, which all that wrought, appeared in no place.

(2.12.58)

We are particularly aware that the groupings in this stanza (lines 1–4, 5–7, and 8–9) are not a static form imposed from without, but result from choices made as the stanza progresses. The voice makes a marked shift when the formal regularities of the list begin at line 5, and because we are conscious of sustaining a set movement in lines 5–7 we are equally conscious that the list is not continued to the end of the stanza (as it is in 2.12.23 and 36). If it were, our sense of this "daintie Paradise" would be rather monotonous and limited, for our pleasure would lie in passively recording the details of an ideal landscape. But the last two lines draw our attention to the quality of mind that has created these details, and our pleasure becomes an active savoring of a particular kind of refined accomplishment. The final lines exploit our consciousness of the artifice of the list, and they utilize (as a continuation of the list would not have) the sense we had in lines 5–7 that listing is an action of the mind.

The next stanza directly sets out to create and characterize a mental activity and the quality of the pleasure it gives:

One would haue thought, (so cunningly, the rude,
And scorned parts were mingled with the fine,)

1.1.22, 1.5.2, 1.10.56, 2.4.16, 3.4.18. In most cases, of course, these formulas involve no fictional anomalies, but 3.1.40 amusingly has the knights beholding what they hear. 3.4.52 is interestingly atypical: our double perspective on Arthur (see below, p. 396) is developed by quite dramatic means, but much depends on the fact that the grammatical reference of "Which when the Prince beheld" is ambiguous. These formulas most frequently appear in the first lines of stanzas. The most interesting example is 3.9.23, where the knights "behold" not Britomart in the fiction, but Minerva in the simile.

That nature had for wantonesse ensude
Art, and that Art at nature did repine;
So striuing each th'other to vndermine,
Each did the others worke more beautifie;
So diff'ring both in willes, agreed in fine:
So all agreed through sweete diuersitie,
This Gardin to adorne with all varietie.

(2.12.59)

This is verse that does exactly what it describes. The words "cunningly" and "mingled" are supported by the parenthetical comment and the enjambment in the first two lines; "nature" literally ensues "Art" into the next line; inverted word order supports the meaning of line 5, as normal word order supports that of line 6; the phrase "agreed in fine" concludes both a line and a sequence of rhymes. The stanza builds up to the phrase "sweete diuersitie," which is supported not only by the content of the lines and couplets—in each of which antagonists are harmonized—but also by the very conduct of the stanza. This is the first stanza we have seen in which there are no clear blocks of verse. Each line seems quite separate, with its own distinct movement and force. The first four lines are a syntactic unit, but they are broken into separate pieces by the parenthetical aside in lines 1 and 2, and the management of the enjambment in lines 3 and 4. Because of the separateness of the first seven lines, the last two strike us, much more than they usually do, as a concluding couplet. There is indeed a sweet diversity of lines here, and they serve to adorn the stanza, like the garden, "with all varietie."

In the next stanza, by contrast, there is a good deal of homogeneity:

And in the midst of all, a fountaine stood,
Of richest substaunce, that on earth might bee,
So pure and shiny, that the siluer flood
Through euery channell running one might see;
Most goodly it with curious imageree
Was ouer-wrought, and shapes of naked boyes,
Of which some seemd with liuely iollitee,
To fly about, playing their wanton toyes,
Whilest others did them selues embay in liquid ioyes.

(2.12.60)

The stanza could be divided after line 4, but the difference between the two halves is less distinctly felt than in other instances. The mode

44

of diction and the nature of our experience do not notably change from one half to the next. "Most goodly," beginning line 5, repeats the kind of rhetorical gesture found in "Of richest substaunce" and "So pure and shiny." Even the vivid "curious imageree" serves as much to intensify the preceding lines as to introduce a new kind of experience. Probably the most important choice made within the stanza is not to develop the suggestions of "curious" and "ouer-wrought." Instead the last three lines treat the "naked boyes" as if they were real, not carved, and the diction is free of the self-indulgent qualities that we find elsewhere in the Bower of Bliss. Instead of turning the attractiveness of the fountain into a sense of sterile or corrupting artifice, this stanza associates the images on the fountain with something equally important in expressing the moral condition of the Bower of Bliss—"liquid ioyes."

The sense of artifice and of "liquid ioyes" are both developed in the next stanza:

> And ouer all, of purest gold was spred,
> A trayle of yuie in his natiue hew:
> For the rich mettall was so coloured,
> That wight, who did not well auis'd it vew,
> Would surely deeme it to be yuie trew:
> Low his lasciuious armes adown did creepe,
> That themselues dipping in the siluer dew,
> Their fleecy flowres they tenderly did steepe,
> Which drops of Christall seemd for wantones to weepe.
>
> (2.12.61)

This stanza concerns a *trompe-l'oeil,* but we search in vain for any visual deception. All the physical terms in the first three lines describe the "rich mettall": a "trayle" is "a trailing ornament (carved, molded, or embroidered) in the form of a wreath or spray of leaves or tendrils" (*OED*), and the only color we see is "purest gold." Our deception is rendered not by any sensory experience, but by "natiue hew" and "so coloured." These more general terms produce the direct address in which Spenser, keeping his voice poised between wondering and warning, makes it explicit that any deception that occurs is impossible without our active assent and enjoyment. Spenser uses the division of the stanza wonderfully when he returns us to the ivy in line 6. The relatively flat verbs of the middle lines, "vew" and "deeme," become the vivid activities of the last four lines, and these personifying verbs are the main source of the feeling of self-indulgence with

45

which the stanza ends. At the same time, line 6 suddenly returns us to sensuous experience, and thus releases the sense of luxuriance that comes from the richness and felicity of the verse.

The variations among these four stanzas should make it clear that general statements about Spenser's stanza or the devices he uses cannot provide an adequate account of individual stanzas. For example, in the stanza last discussed, the line "For the rich mettall was so coloured" can be associated, for its diction and the way it addresses the reader, with either the two lines that precede or the two lines that follow it. We cannot define all the possibilities of Spenser's stanza by considering it as a unit, because its variety and flexibility come not from a property of the stanza itself, but from a property of the individual line—the independence that is uncompromised by any combinations into which it enters. In Spenser's verse, even syntactic connections, as we shall see in the next chapter, do not override the independence of the line. Because of the rhyme scheme, certain groupings will predominate in Spenser's stanza. But the rhyme scheme is very permissive (largely because of the number and distribution of b-rhymes), and in any given instance it will not rule out a particular combination of lines. Hence we must add to our view of the stanza as a single unit our awareness of it as nine independent lines that can enter into all possible combinations and groupings. We must ask, then, how narrative materials become not stanzas, but lines of poetry.

III

Spenser's treatment of the line as an independent unit can be seen in every stanza of *The Faerie Queene*. The special aspect of this phenomenon with which we are now concerned is illustrated by the following stanza:

> So was that chamber clad in goodly wize,
> And round about it many beds were dight,
> As whilome was the antique worldes guize,
> Some for vntimely ease, some for delight,
> As pleased them to vse, that vse it might:
> And all was full of Damzels, and of Squires,
> Dauncing and reueling both day and night,
> And swimming deepe in sensuall desires,
> And *Cupid* still emongst them kindled lustfull fires.
>
> (3.1.39)

The activities cited in the last three lines are of very different sorts. Malecasta's courtiers are not swimming in the sense that they are dancing and reveling; not only is "swimming" metaphoric, it is not even clear whether it suggests an action or a quality of feeling. To complicate matters, the last line is not exactly like either of the other two. Clearly it does not describe something that is actually going on in Malecasta's chamber, but given that the line is metaphoric, its mythical action is more graphically rendered than is the swimming of the preceding line. Our question is how these three lines, based on such different materials (respectively, narrative action, metaphor, and myth), are made compatible with each other, so that we can read them as a coherent listing of the various things that go on in Malecasta's castle.

Part of the explanation is certainly the nature of the stanza. When one has read seven consecutive lines, each one lucid and independent by virtue of end-stopping, rhyme, and formulaic character, then one is entirely ready to accept another such line, especially when it is syntactically parallel to the preceding one. However, the main reason that one is not jolted by "swimming" is that dancing and reveling are not rendered as specific dramatic actions; they are part of a single formula that indicates the general character of the activity at Malecasta's castle—"Dauncing and reueling both day and night." Similarly, we do not read "swimming" as a separate word indicating an action to be compared with dancing and reveling, but as part of the formula, "swimming deepe in sensuall desires." The two lines are compatible because Spenser turns the narrative action of the one and the metaphor of the other into the same kind of line of poetry—a formula, such as a satirist might use, that suggests the nature of courtiers' activities.

In the final line, stanza form again helps to make the line compatible with what precedes it. We are not surprised that the alexandrine is an especially vivid line, set off from the rest of the stanza—an effect achieved here through grammar (the line contains the only active main verb in the second half of the stanza) and heightened pictorialism. But alexandrine or not, this line would jar if it really rendered a specific action, performed by a specific character. Even while he exploits the sense of activity in "kindled," Spenser accommodates this line to the formulaic, moralistic character of the two preceding lines. For one thing, the word less suggests a specific action than it would if the line read, say, "And *Cupid* still lit lustfull fires emongst them all." As it is, the phrase "still emongst them" does not necessarily go

47

with the action, but clings just as much to Cupid, the courtiers' tute-
lary deity. Even more important, the phrase "kindled lustfull fires,"
like "swimming deepe in sensuall desires," is a commonplace. We do
not have to imagine these phrases as literal actions in order to feel
their force or understand their significance. This fact enables Spenser
to make physical and moral terms homogeneous. We can see this in
the patterns of alliteration and verbal suggestion in the last two lines.
In "kindled lustfull fires," Spenser clearly does not mean literal flames
but fires that symbolize lust; still, if we take the phrase literally, fires
that are lustful are those that burn eagerly, and this is an important
characterizing quality of lust. In most poetry, apprehending so full a
meaning requires a conscious recognition of its various elements. In
Spenser the mind holds the phrase without analyzing it, and as if vari-
ous meanings were resonances of the single verbal formula. Clearly
this effect would be impossible if the meanings in question did not
overlap in the way they do in this phrase. In using commonplace for-
mulas, Spenser is able to count on an immediacy and obviousness
that, far from robbing them of poetic effectiveness, is essential to the
particular fusion of lucidity and suggestiveness that he achieves.

The stanza in which Una tears her hair in grief over the Red Cross
Knight's torment is another instance of Spenser's willingness to take a
stock formula as a stock formula, and not primarily as the rendering
of an action. He can go very far in counting on us to assume this dis-
tinction:

> In this great passion of vnwonted lust,
> Or wonted feare of doing ought amis,
> He started vp, as seeming to mistrust
> Some secret ill, or hidden foe of his:
> Lo there before his face his Lady is,
> Vnder blake stole hyding her bayted hooke,
> And as halfe blushing offred him to kis,
> With gentle blandishment and louely looke,
> Most like that virgin true, which for her knight
>   him took.   (1.1.49)

We are not, of course, to see a baited hook under the stole of Archi-
mago's apparition: "bayted hooke" is a common metaphor for a dan-
gerous allurement, and the false Una is felt to be concealing not an
object, but a purpose. The line is especially bold because Spenser
means it to have pictorial impact—"Lo there before his face his Lady
is"—without its rendering a real picture. But the source of its impact

48

—the voice that enters the stanza with "Lo"—explains why we do not confuse rhetorical and descriptive intentions here. Precisely because the line is produced by a distinct and vivid voice, we realize that this is a verbal formula being used by a speaker.

In these first two examples, the metaphoric action would be impossible or absurd as narrative action. But even when a metaphor is related to or based on the narrative action, we must still regard it as belonging to a verbal reality—characteristically, a conventional formula —and not to a fictional action or world. Here is the Red Cross Knight after he has left Una and is traveling from Archimago's house (the second "he" in line 1 is Archimago, who has just disguised himself as the Red Cross Knight):

> But he the knight, whose semblaunt he did beare,
> The true *Saint George* was wandred far away,
> Still flying from his thoughts and gealous feare;
> Will was his guide, and griefe led him astray.
>
> (1.2.12)

It would be possible to consider "wandred far away" as the literal action and the last line as one of its possible metaphoric developments. But "Still flying from his thoughts and gealous feare" cannot be accommodated to either side in this dichotomy of literal and metaphoric. Though clearly metaphoric, it is not a development of the literal action: "flying" has a sense of urgency that is not conveyed in "wandred far away," and we take it as a direct rendering of the knight's psychological condition (cf. 3.12.12). The presence of this line has an important effect on the next: it draws our attention to "will" and "griefe" as active psychological agents. The line then renders actions of the mind, like "flying from fear," and suggests the knight's experience of being out of control, run by his feelings. The effect is to give "led him astray" its full life as a general moral formula, instead of tying it to the narrative action of "wandred far away."

All Spenser's materials, metaphors as well as narrative actions, become formulaic lines of poetry. When the action is itself metaphoric, Spenser still produces his characteristic kind of poetic narration, and not what we usually think of as allegorical narrative. Consider the Red Cross Knight's spiritual cure at the hands of Patience:

> Who [Patience] comming to that soule-diseased knight,
> Could hardly him intreat, to tell his griefe:
> Which knowne, and all that noyd his heauie spright
> Well searcht, eftsoones he gan apply reliefe

49

Of salues and med'cines, which had passing priefe,
And thereto added words of wondrous might:
By which to ease he him recured briefe,
And much asswag'd the passion of his plight,
That he his paine endur'd, as seeming now more light.

(1.10.24)

We might expect Spenser to narrate the healing of the knight as a co-
herent physical action, but lines 5 and 6 seem to exemplify the in-
discriminate mixing of concrete and abstract that we associate with
allegory in its decay. Modern readers are perhaps quick to be dis-
pleased in this matter, but in these lines there are perfectly rational
grounds for our objections. If "med'cines" is a metaphor for "words,"
then line 6 is simply a label, and one wonders why Spenser would
bother with pretending that this spiritual healing is a physical cure. On
the other hand, if "words" are really as different as "thereto added"
suggests, one wonders what the "salues and med'cines" of Patience
might be, and one still feels that it is jarring to have a line that requires
translation of a metaphor followed by one that does not. But the final
lines justify what Spenser has done. The double meaning of "passion"
(physical pain and vehement feeling) would have been felt if he had
kept to the merely physical description of healing. But the full reso-
nance of "much asswag'd the passion of his plight"—our uncertainty
whether the knight's pain itself or the emotional disorder it provoked
has been reduced—would be impossible without our being able to
think of physical healing and moral advice as separate experiences.
The puzzle which here, perhaps, is only an overtone becomes the cen-
ter of meaning in the alexandrine: we cannot tell whether the knight's
pain has become more endurable, or whether he has become better
able to endure pain. Clearly we are to take in both meanings, the point
being that in a disease of the soul, to endure the pain is in fact to re-
duce it. The human truth of this truism is brought home to us because
Spenser, by presenting human endurance as a reality separate from
the metaphoric description of healing, has enforced the full meaning
of "as seeming now more light." We usually associate such fullness of
meaning in allegory with scrupulous attention to the fiction, because
we think of the poet as finding significances inherent in a metaphoric
action. But instead of dramatizing the comparison of patience to a
physician,[5] Spenser develops individual lines from each side of the

[5] Compare Shakespeare, Sonnet 147:

> My Reason, the physician to my Love,
> Angry that his prescriptions are not kept,

metaphoric equation. We apprehend each physical detail or moral formula not as part of a single dramatic reality, but as one of the many ways in which a common metaphor manifests its significance.

The materials of moral metaphor are handled in the same way in the next stanza:

> But yet the cause and root of all his ill,
> Inward corruption, and infected sin,
> Not purg'd nor heald, behind remained still,
> And festring sore did rankle yet within,
> Close creeping twixt the marrow and the skin.
> Which to extirpe, he laid him priuily
> Downe in a darkesome lowly place farre in,
> Whereas he meant his corrosiues to apply,
> And with streight diet tame his stubborne malady.
>
> (1.10.25)

This stanza intensifies our sense of the virulence of sin and the misery it causes. We also have a stronger sense of man's helplessness: whereas "he his paine endur'd" suggested some moral strength in the knight, this stanza makes us feel only that something must be done to him. One's first impression is of a description of physical disease, but this is in fact to be found only in lines 4 and 5. All the other details, vivid as they are, are as much moral as physical terms. "Inward corruption, and infected sin" are both commonplaces of the sort that we accept literally, without needing to translate their metaphors.[6] "Corrosiues" are caustic medicines, but the metaphoric intent brought out by "his" (specifying that these are the remedies of Patience) is supported by the fact that the word is a common moral metaphor (*OED* 3). Most important, we cannot tell whether the last line describes a genuine medical cure or the metaphoric taming of the flesh by asceticism. Because of the independence of his lines, Spenser is able to give a direct physical description of disease and its pain in lines 4 and 5, without therefore making us treat the terms in the rest of the stanza as first and foremost medical. His freedom from committing himself to a literal description of disease appears in the phrase "Which to ex-

---

> Hath left me, and I desperate now approve
> Desire is death, which physic did except.

[6] "Corruption," as a glance at OED will confirm, has both physical and moral meanings firmly established in 1590. OED cites this passage as the second to use "infected" in a moral sense (the first is dated 1570), but the obsolete participial adjective "infect" has a long listing of moral uses.

tirpe," which begins a new block of verse, and which returns us to terms in which moral meanings are as present as physical ones. "Extirpe" literally means "root out," and would thus apply very well to the medical treatment of the knight. But as an English word it primarily suggests a moral action, as it does when Lucio, in *Measure for Measure,* says: "Yes, in good sooth, the vice is of a great kindred— it is well allied; but it is impossible to extirp it quite, friar, till eating and drinking be put down" (3.2.110). Spenser fully exploits the physical meaning of "extirpe." But the poetic process is that of endowing a word with its full meaning, not of finding moral significance in a kind of physical action.[7] Similarly the stanza as a whole does not describe a physical disease, but renders the phrase "soule-diseased" (stanza 24) in terms that are especially vivid because of their physical suggestions.

The overlapping of meanings continues in the next stanza:

> In ashes and sackcloth he did array
> His daintie corse, proud humors to abate,
> And dieted with fasting euery day,
> The swelling of his wounds to mitigate,
> And made him pray both earely and eke late:
> And euer as superfluous flesh did rot
> *Amendment* readie still at hand did wayt,
> To pluck it out with pincers firie whot,
> That soone in him was left no one corrupted iot.

> (1.10.26)

Again we cannot determine whether the ascetic regimen is medical or moral, for "proud humors" has both physiological and moral mean-

---

[7] The word "extirpe" presents fairly complicated problems, and I would like to give a fuller explanation of my reading. OED lists three meanings for "extirp" and "extirpate," which is interchangeable with it (what follows combines what is given under the two words): (1) the literal meaning, "to root up (plants)"; (2) "To root out, exterminate (a family, sect, or nation)"; (3) "To root out, eradicate (an immaterial thing, e.g. heresy, vice, etc.)." The second meaning is not relevant here. Under the first, OED cites a special meaning in surgery, "To root out, remove (anything spoken of as having roots)" and cites this passage. But except for the first citation, a surgery handbook of 1541, the word does not appear as a surgical term until 1767. On the other hand, there are abundant uses of the word in the third sense; it appears to be felt as a vigorous term and is used with a great deal of feeling for its literal meaning. I think this is the way Spenser uses it here. At the very least we can claim that he does not intend the word to be strictly physical, and that its force is not dependent on the metaphor of physical healing.

ings. But in lines 4 and 5 the two kinds of meaning are decisively separated, and Spenser uses the separation as a transition to a new kind of action—another familiar form of allegory, in which personifications are the dramatic agents. Simply reading the stanza tells us what has happened: the physical and moral elements that were fused at the beginning are separated and then recombined. The effect is to make it impossible to regard the action described in the last four lines as a direct continuation of the curing of the disease as it is described earlier. Looking back over the three stanzas, we find there is hardly any fictional continuity between the "salues and med'cines," the "streight diet," and the actions of Amendment. Our sense of progressing intensity in the ordeal of being purged comes specifically from the way Spenser increases our feeling of the strength of the knight's spiritual disease and the severity with which it must be treated. If we were regarding the fiction, we would say that Spenser had introduced (rather clumsily) a new "literal level" in this stanza. But precisely because this passage is based on traditional forms of allegory, it makes clear that the "literal level" of *The Faerie Queene* is not a narrative action, but whatever verbal combination of physical and moral elements the verse we are reading presents to us.

The physical immediacy of the lines about Amendment suggests that Spenser's poetic narration will at last take the form of a coherent action. But Spenser is no more tied to a fictional mode in this allegory of personifications than he was in using the materials of metaphoric action:

> And bitter *Penance* with an yron whip,
> Was wont him once to disple euery day:
> And sharpe *Remorse* his hart did pricke and nip,
> That drops of bloud thence like a well did play;
> And sad *Repentance* vsed to embay,
> His bodie in salt water smarting sore,
> The filthy blots of sinne to wash away.
> So in short space they did to health restore
> The man that would not liue, but earst lay at
> > deathes dore. (1.10.27)

Penance performs a literal action—something done to the knight by way of discipline—while "sharpe *Remorse* his hart did pricke and nip" directly renders an internal experience. Penance has a great deal of dramatic presence as a personification, while "Remorse" affects us primarily as an abstract noun. Spenser makes the two kinds of action compatible by means with which we are now familiar—turning his materials, in line 3, into a common verbal formula that is immediately acceptable to us as a reality in itself. He thus enables us to feel—what is essential to the stanza and the whole passage—that both imposed discipline and internal experience are part of a single process—a feeling he encourages by beginning the first, third, and fifth lines with the same basic formula. The two aspects of the knight's restoration are brought together in the action of Repentance. Although it could not possibly be considered a direct rendering of internal experience, Spenser evokes the knight's suffering, so that line 7 suggests the experience of being cleansed as much as it expresses the purpose of the personification, Repentance.[8] In the final line, our double sense of the knight's recovery—that it is a genuine change in him, yet it had to be imposed from without—is wonderfully rendered by the phrase, "The man that would not liue." It seems to mean both "the man who refused to live (and hence would have died without external aid)" and, especially when we feel the force of "earst," "the man whose refusal to live is a thing of the past."

If the passage ended here, our sense of the knight's recovery would be dominated by the discipline he has undergone. But in the next stanza, as we have seen, Una's suffering and endurance are assimilated to the knight's, and our sense of spiritual amendment is made to center on internal experience. In the last stanza of the passage, the personifications become the knight's own spiritual strengths, and not only "Patience" but also "trew *Repentance*" is felt to be an abstract noun rather than a personification. The trick of making us apprehend the names of personifications directly as abstract nouns (and *vice versa*) is frequent in *The Faerie Queene* and can be thrilling in its effects.[9] We can take it as a final example of the way in which fictional materials are transmuted into verbal formulas.

I V

Narrative materials are not the same as a poetic fiction, but are literally materials—capable of being turned into more than one kind of

---

[8] We have especially good reason to be conscious of the independence of individual lines here, because the effect of these three lines is due to Spenser's changing "His blamefull body in salt water sore," in 1590, to "His bodie in salt water smarting sore," in 1596. Note that it is as important that he removed "blamefull"—which could be said only from the point of view of the discipliner—as that he added "smarting."

[9] See 1.1.18, 1.4.35, 2.4.44 (discussed below, p. 231), 3.10.55 (discussed below, p. 219), 3.12.12 (line 7), 7.6.6.

poetic narration. Nothing illustrates this more strikingly than a comparison of the story of Phedon (*FQ* 2.4.17–36) with its source in *Orlando Furioso,* the story of Ariodante and Ginevra (4.51–6.16). The most familiar form of the story is the main plot of *Much Ado about Nothing.* In Ariosto's version, it begins when Rinaldo lands in Scotland and is told about the impending death of Ginevra, the daughter of the king. She has been accused of being unchaste, and according to an ancient law she will be killed unless her accuser is challenged and defeated in battle within a month of the accusation. Rinaldo immediately sets out for the Scottish court, and on his journey he rescues a lady from two villains who are about to murder her. The lady turns out to be Dalinda, Ginevra's lady-in-waiting, and as they travel she tells Rinaldo the story of her mistress. Ginevra was loved by the Italian knight Ariodante and loved him in return; since he was a favorite of the king, there seemed no impediment to their marriage. But the jealous Polinesso, the Duke of Albany, tells Ariodante that he is Ginevra's lover, and that a few nights hence Ariodante can see her let him into her bedchamber. Polinesso is in fact the lover of Dalinda, who loves him so much that she does not question his request that she dress for this night in her mistress' clothes. Their meeting place is a bedchamber of Ginevra's which they use because it overlooks an uninhabited area of the city; no one can see a man climbing up to the balcony of this room. Polinesso tells Ariodante to hide in a ruined dwelling directly opposite the balcony. Ariodante agrees, but fearful that Polinesso may be planning simply to ambush him, he brings along his brother, Lurcanio. If Polinesso's story is true, Ariodante does not want Lurcanio to see Ginevra's shame, so he tells him to stay at a distance and only to come if he hears Ariodante call. But driven both by concern and by natural curiosity, Lurcanio comes much closer and is thus able, first to see Polinesso (whom he does not recognize) climb the rope let down to him by Dalinda dressed as Ginevra, and, second, to stop Ariodante from killing himself on the spot. Ariodante promises to calm himself, but leaves the court secretly the next morning. Nothing is heard of him for eight days until a traveler stops at the court to tell that he has seen Ariodante throw himself from a cliff into the sea. Lurcanio is so enraged at Ginevra for causing his brother's death that he accuses her, despite his knowledge that the king and the people will turn their favor towards him into hatred. No one is willing to challenge Lurcanio, partly because he is so powerful a warrior, partly because he is an honorable man, and it is assumed that he would not swear to anything that was not true. The king, meanwhile, proposes to conduct his own investigation and to begin with his daughter's chambermaids. Dalinda, fearful that she and Polinesso will be undone, appeals to Polinesso for help. He promises to have her taken in safety to one of his castles, but he secretly plans to have her escorts kill her, and she is at the point of death when Rinaldo hears her screams and rescues her.

Perhaps the intricacy of this summary will indicate the degree to which Ariosto devotes his attention to external dramatic action. This becomes clear when we consider how important seeing is in the episode. The central deception, of course, is visual, and Ariodante's cryptic message to Ginevra is that "the whole cause of his harsh and sad fate was that he had seen too much" (5.60, cf. 58). But more important is the fact that seeing is regarded as the essential means of human knowledge. Ariodante insists on seeing before he believes (5.41). He tells the traveler to make his fate "manifesto" to Ginevra, and the traveler provides a visual description of Ariodante's leap from the cliff (5.57,59). Words like *manifestar, rivelar,* and *mostrar* occur throughout the episode, and reach their climax in the trial by battle, the point of which is to render a moral decision in full public view. Thus Rinaldo, saying "Now we shall see the outcome" (5.86), offers to prove the truth of his story by fighting Polinesso, and the king and the people watching the battle "all hope that God will make plain that unjustly she was called unchaste" (5.87). In a context in which seeing is believing, Polinesso's trick is poetically and dramatically of a piece with the rest of the episode, and not bizarrely magnified in importance, like the "ocular proof" of the handkerchief in *Othello.* Even mental experiences that do not involve visual experience are spoken of as if they did. Dalinda says that she was so blind with love that she could not see the "thousand sure signs" that Polinesso did not love her (5.11), and that Polinesso's proposal to dress her as Ginevra "was only too plain a fraud" (5.26). Dalinda's fine scorn for Polinesso and herself characteristically finds expression in exclamations beginning "Vedi," "See," and that word, with its mocking tone and its reminder that everything really is obvious, contains much of the ironic force of the episode. Here is Dalinda's comment on Polinesso's revealing, a few days after he becomes her lover, that he is a suitor for Ginevra's hand:

> Vedi s'in me venuto era arrogante,
> s'imperio nel mio cor s'aveva assunto;
> che mi scoperse, e non ebbe rossore
> chiedermi aiuto in questo nuovo amore.

See if he had become arrogant toward me, if he had taken to himself empire over my heart, for to me he revealed this new love and did not blush to ask my aid. (5.12)

Dalinda begins with anger at Polinesso, but in the second line, which describes a natural phenomenon of love, she is mocking herself. Similarly at the end of her narration, her indignation turns into a sense that the joke was on her:

> Hai sentito, signor, con quanti effetti
> de l'amor mio fei Polinesso certo;
> e s'era debitor per tai rispetti
> d'avermi cara o no, tu 'l vedi aperto.
> Or senti il guidardon che io ricevetti,
> vedi la gran mercé del mio gran merto;
> vedi se deve, per amare assai,
> donna sperar d'essere amata mai.

You have heard, Sir, with how many deeds I made Polinesso sure of my love, and you see plainly whether by such causes he was bound to hold me dear or not. Now hear of the recompense I received; see the great reward for my great merit; see whether, because she loves much, a woman can hope to be loved always. (5.72)

And the last line of her narration is, "Ve' come Amor ben chi lui segue, tratta!"—"See how Love treats even those who follow him" (5.74).

The ironic force of Dalinda's "Vedi" depends on our feeling that what she asks us to see is perfectly clear and obvious. And it is precisely the clarity of dramatic events that produces the particular wit and sadness of the episode. The complexities of love are expressed not by any single action or character, but by the way in which the characters' various desires, purposes, and actions—each of them lucid and easy to account for—become entangled with each other. The feelings and awarenesses aroused by this comic spectacle can be seen most economically by comparing Rinaldo's first reaction to Ginevra's plight with the speech he makes on intervening in the trial by battle, when he knows the whole story. When he first hears of Ginevra, Rinaldo expresses outrage at the law that condemns her to death:

> Sia maladetto chi tal legge pose,
> e maladetto chi la può patire!

Debitamente muore una crudele,
non chi dà vita al suo amator fedele.

Sia vero o falso che Ginevra tolto
s'abbia il suo amante, io non riguardo a questo:
d'averlo fatto la loderei molto,
quando non fosse stato manifesto.

May he be cursed who established such a law, and cursed he who can endure it! A cruel woman fitly dies, but not she who gives life to her faithful lover.

Whether it is true or false that Ginevra has taken her lover to her, I pay no attention to that; I would praise her highly for having done it, if it had not been known. (4.63–64)

He goes on for three more stanzas in this vein; Harington justly remarks that he sounds like all the young gentlemen "that make so light of their sweet sinne of lecherie."[10] When Rinaldo intervenes in the trial by battle, his notions of the way in which a knight can champion truth and right have changed:

Rinaldo disse al re:—Magno signore,
non lasciar la battaglia più seguire;
perché di questi dua qualunche more,
sappi ch'a torto tu 'l lasci morire.
L'un crede aver ragione, et è in errore,
e dice il falso, e non sa di mentire;
ma quel medesmo error che 'l suo germano
a morir trasse, a lui pon l'arme in mano.

L'altro non sa se s'abbia dritto o torto;
ma sol per gentilezza e per bontade
in pericol si è posto d'esser morto,
per non lasciar morir tanta beltade.
Io la salute all'innocenzia porto;
porto il contrario a chi usa falsitade.
Ma, per Dio, questa pugna prima parti,
poi mi dà audienza a quel ch'io vo' narrarti.

Rinaldo said to the King: "Mighty lord, do not let the contest go further, because whichever one of these two dies, be assured that wrongfully you let him die. One believes he is right but is in er-

---

[10] John Harington, *Orlando Furioso in English Heroical Verse*, London, 1591, p. 29.

ror, and he speaks falsely and does not know that he is lying; yet the same error that dragged his brother to death puts weapons in his hands.

"The other does not know whether he is right or wrong, but has put himself in peril of death only through his courtesy and goodness, in order not to let so much beauty die. I bring safety to innocence; I bring the opposite to him who uses treachery. But in God's name, first break off this contest; then give me a hearing for what I wish to relate to you." (5.83–84)

Rinaldo does not, of course, say this ironically, but the speech gives a profoundly ironic perspective on human action, because it suggests the complete helplessness of human motives and actions. It is not simply that the formulas for Lurcanio's error are comprehensible only to those (Rinaldo and the reader) who know the whole intricate story. It is also that the verbal complications do not render a confusion in Lurcanio's mind. Quite the reverse, Lurcanio is perfectly clear about what he feels and the stand he takes—he knows, after all, what he has seen. So the verbal complications attach themselves entirely to our sense of the episode and make us feel that the dramatic actors in it, precisely because they act on such clear impulses and for such clear purposes, are hopelessly unaware of and lost in the human entanglements of the situation. Rinaldo speaks of the disguised knight in exactly this way, as if he were a sort of youthful Quixote. Yet he describes precisely those motives that impelled him to set out to defend Ginevra. But now that the whole story is known, bringing safety to the innocent is not a matter of an ordinary knight's dramatic action. It specifically depends on a *deus ex machina,* and the king appropriately "raised his hands to God, who had so well provided him with such aid as that one [Rinaldo] was" (5.91).

The nature of Spenser's use of these materials can be seen in the first two stanzas of Phedon's narration:

> It was a faithlesse Squire, that was the sourse
> Of all my sorrow, and of these sad teares,
> With whom from tender dug of commune nourse,
> Attonce I was vpbrought, and eft when yeares
> More rype vs reason lent to chose our Peares,
> Our selues in league of vowed loue we knit:
> In which we long time without gealous feares,
> Or faultie thoughts continewd, as was fit;
> And for my part I vow, dissembled not a whit.

59

It was my fortune commune to that age,
To loue a Ladie faire of great degree,
The which was borne of noble parentage,
And set in highest seat of dignitee,
Yet seemd no lesse to loue, then loued to bee:
Long I her seru'd, and found her faithfull still,
Ne euer thing could cause vs disagree:
Loue that two harts makes one, makes eke one will:
Each stroue to please, and others pleasure to fulfill.

(2.4.18–19)

Where Ariosto gives us dramatic characters, each separate from the others, pursuing his own desires, and caught up in his own schemes and thoughts, Spenser produces images and formulas that express complete unity. Instead of showing the behavior of two people to each other, he describes feelings or purposes they share. In these stanzas it is quite literally true that "Loue that two harts makes one, makes eke one will."

Our sense of dealing with a single mind, rather than with three different characters, is brought out in the next stanza, which draws the third leg of the triangle:

My friend, hight *Philemon,* I did partake,
Of all my loue and all my priuitie;
Who greatly ioyous seemed for my sake,
And gratious to that Ladie, as to mee,
Ne euer wight, that mote so welcome bee,
As he to her, withouten blot or blame,
Ne euer thing, that she could thinke or see,
But vnto him she would impart the same:
O wretched man, that would abuse so gentle Dame.

(2.4.20)

Naming a character ordinarily gives him a separate identity, but Philemon means simply "my friend," and he is very much the sharer "of all my loue and all my priuitie." The stanza describes dramatic behavior, but it seems like that of a lover to his lady. The final exclamation is one that would be made about a lover, and it has hardly any connection with the narrative action. It is Phedon who is abused by Philemon, who can be said to abuse Claribella only in the sense that he speaks injuriously of her. Even if this meaning of the word were available to Spenser,[11] we do not limit ourselves to it as we read the line.

[11] OED (sense 7) cites *Othello* 5.1.123 as the first use in this sense.

The resonance of "abuse" comes from its participation in a formulaic exclamation, and not from the way it corresponds to dramatic action.

Even when Philemon deceives Phedon, dramatic personages and events are drawn together into the phenomena of a single mind. At first Philemon says only that he has heard that Claribella

> Had both distaind her honorable blood,
> And eke the faith, which she to me did bynd;
> And therfore wisht me stay, till I more truth
>   should fynd.   (2.4.22)

The brevity of Philemon's revelation is in key with his recommendation of caution. But the next stanza produces a sudden increase in emotional intensity by means of an initial formula that takes us directly into the feelings of the jealous lover:

> The gnawing anguish and sharpe gelosy,
> Which his sad speech infixed in my brest,
> Ranckled so sore, and festred inwardly,
> That my engreeued mind could find no rest,
> Till that the truth thereof I did outwrest,
> And him besought by that same sacred band
> Betwixt vs both, to counsell me the best.
> He then with solemne oath and plighted hand
> Assur'd, ere long the truth to let me vnderstand.
>   (2.4.23)

This stanza and a half provides a brief outline of one of the important movements in *Othello*—the friend's casual insinuation produces passionate suffering on the part of the hero, who then binds his friend to him in a pact of heroic resolve. The effect of this movement in Spenser's stanzas can best be seen by following the word "truth." When Philemon "wisht me stay, till I more truth should fynd," the word referred to knowledge of external facts. By the middle of this stanza the truth seems to be something that will be produced from the efforts of Phedon's own mind. Hence Philemon's final assurance "the truth to let me vnderstand" is not simply the office of an external agent. As in *Othello,* the friend's role is produced by the energies of the hero's own mind, and the false friend becomes inextricably part of him. We are not surprised, then, at the way Spenser renders Philemon's fulfilling his promise:

Ere long with like againe he boorded mee,
Saying, he now had boulted all the floure,
And that it was a groome of base degree,
Which of my loue was partner Paramoure:
Who vsed in a darkesome inner bowre
Her oft to meet: which better to approue,
He promised to bring me at that howre,
When I should see, that would me nearer moue,
And driue me to withdraw my blind abused loue.

(2.4.24)

This is the very opposite of Polinesso's offer to Ariodante of ocular proof. What Phedon will see is "that would me nearer moue." The physical details that support this phrase do not constitute a dramatic depiction of Claribella's misbehavior, but appear as a series of formulas, each of which suggests a disturbing quality of feeling. From the coarse heartiness of "boulted all the floure," we go to the social lowness of the groom, then to the suggestion of courtly sexuality in "partner Paramoure," and finally to the "darkesome inner bowre" at the center of the stanza. In the final phrase we are not conscious of what Phedon has been blind to or what he has been abused by. "Blind abused loue" has an absolute force and directly suggests the power and confusion of Phedon's feelings.

The difference between Ariosto's and Spenser's poetic realizations of this story is evident, as one would expect, in their handling of the hero's deception by the maid disguised as her mistress. Ariosto gives a full description of Dalinda in Ginevra's clothes and a clear explanation of why Ariodante and Lurcanio would have been fooled by her appearance (5.47–49). By contrast, here is Spenser's rendering of the scene:

Eftsoones he came vnto th'appointed place,
And with him brought *Pryene,* rich arayd,
In *Claribellaes* clothes. Her proper face
I not descerned in that darkesome shade,
But weend it was my loue, with whom he playd.
Ah God, what horrour and tormenting griefe
My hart, my hands, mine eyes, and all assayd?
Me liefer were ten thousand deathes priefe,
Then wound of gealous worme, and shame of such
    repriefe.
(2.4.28)

"But weend it was my loue, with whom he playd" seems a product not of visual deception, but of the jealous lover's imagination. The preceding line and a half render the viewer's attempt to see, rather than the sight imposed on him, and the psychological energy that explodes in the second half of the stanza comes from the formulas that have been developed over the past several stanzas—"rich arayd," which draws on the erotic glamor of Philemon's speech to Pryene (2.4.25–26), and "that darkesome shade."

Whereas in Ariosto's episode we are observers of a comedy and feel closest to Rinaldo and to Dalinda as she looks back over what happened, in Spenser we are made to feel the change in Phedon from trust and love to the torments of jealousy. But in what sense, then, is Spenser not simply dramatizing the experiences of the jealous lover; why do we say that he turns Ariosto's materials into lines and stanzas of poetry? When we look at the verse of the episode, we do not feel, as we do with Dalinda's self-mockery, that it expresses Phedon's dramatic presence as either hero or narrator. Richness of meaning is no more based on the fictional complexity of Phedon's feelings than it was based on narrative realities in "O wretched man, that would abuse so gentle Dame." Rather, poetic significance is constantly a function of the meanings inherent in formulaic lines of verse. The distinction we are making is apparent in the stanza preceding the one just quoted:

> The whiles to me the treachour did remoue
> His craftie engin, and as he had sayd,
> Me leading, in a secret corner layd,
> The sad spectatour of my Tragedie;
> Where left, he went, and his owne false part playd,
> Disguised like that groome of base degree,
> Whom he had feignd th'abuser of my loue to bee.
>
> (2.4.27)

"The sad spectatour of my Tragedie" could serve as the motto of the whole episode. The paradox of one person being both spectator and actor (for "my Tragedie" means "the tragedy of which I am the hero") awakens our recognition of the way in which Spenser, throughout the episode, has turned the external events that victimize Phedon into the active projections of his own mind. Especially after the inwardness of "in a secret corner layd," we see the "tragedy" as part of a complex psychological phenomenon—the mind feeling that it is about to do something dreadful and being helpless to stop itself. But

Phedon himself—if indeed we feel his presence as the dramatized narrator—is not aware of the meanings that make this so resonant a line. To him "my Tragedie" refers to an external event, and can only mean "the (staged) action that was catastrophic to me."

In the three concluding lines, on the other hand, fictional reference is exceptionally clear. The result is that the meaning of each line is impoverished, even though each contains a formula that Spenser has been at pains to establish and develop earlier in the episode. As we have already seen, "abuse" is a crucial word in two earlier alexandrines; "his owne false part" should draw support from several earlier phrases ("It was a faithlesse Squire," stanza 18; "my falser friend," stanza 21; "This gracelesse man for furtherance of his guile," stanza 25), and we have already seen how effective "groome of base degree" (stanza 24) is as a poetic formula. But "his owne false part playd" so unequivocally indicates an action here, especially when we see that it is part of a theatrical metaphor, and "*that* groome of base degree" so directly points to a specific person, that we are unable to see in them anything but a fiction. What we miss is the way in which such formulas usually convey qualities of feeling—compare, earlier in the stanza, the way "treachour" and "His craftie engin" support "in a secret corner layd." In the final line, "th'abuser of my loue" so clearly refers to the groom that other meanings do not come into play, and there is none of the resonance that we would have expected the phrase to have at this point.

Dramatic clarity robs Spenser's formulaic lines of the kind of potency that we find in the final, and most brilliant, passage of the episode. Phedon, "chawing vengeance all the way," slays Claribella, but his vengeance turns to grief when Pryene confesses:

> Which when I heard, with horrible affright
> And hellish fury all enragd, I sought
> Vpon my selfe that vengeable despight
> To punish: yet it better first I thought,
> To wreake my wrath on him, that first it wrought.
> To *Philemon, false faytour Philemon*
> I cast to pay, that I so dearely bought;
> Of deadly drugs I gaue him drinke anon,
> And washt away his guilt with guiltie potion.

(2.4.30)

The first four lines are perfectly straightforward, and the run-on lines suggest genuine narrative movement. But "to wreake my wrath on him, that first it wrought" is emphatically formulaic and sets the pattern for the rest of the stanza. Phedon means it simply as a circumlocution for Philemon, but in the most literal sense the person who first wrought wrath is the wrathful person himself. The line thus turns Phedon's proposed act of suicide into a moral formula, and with its tautology supported by alliteration, it brings out something important in the nature of wrath—its self-proliferation. The ideas of justice in the last four lines produce formulas that invert the earlier formulas of friendship, and that indicate, as much as they did, that Philemon and his crime are inseparable from Phedon's mind. The reciprocity of "I cast to pay, that I so dearly bought" is not like that of "an eye for an eye," because there is nothing external or measurable to exchange. Spenser's formula, with its unclear fictional references, expresses not the settling of a finite account, but the continual toll taken by a criminal passion—a point explicitly made by the rhetorical and moral reciprocity of the last line.

The matching of "guilt" with "guiltie potion" not only makes an analytic moral point. It also renders a quality of experience that is fully expressed in the next stanza:

> Thus heaping crime on crime, and griefe on griefe,
> To losse of loue adioyning losse of frend,
> I meant to purge both with a third mischiefe,
> And in my woes beginner it to end:
> That was *Pryene;* she did first offend,
> She last should smart: with which cruell intent,
> When I at her my murdrous blade did bend,
> She fled away with ghastly dreriment,
> And I pursewing my fell purpose, after went.

> (2.4.31)

The first two lines—like "guilt with guiltie potion"—heap words on words and render a sense of accumulating anguish. The climax and resolution of these griefs does not, however, take the form of the fiction that seems to be indicated by lines 3 and 4. "In my woes beginner it to end" does not, as the reader thinks it must, refer to Phedon's suicide. It is of course quite implausible as a fictional reference to Pryene, made by Phedon in the role of dramatized narrator. The plausibility and poetic truth of the line lie in the way its meanings recoil on Phedon in the second half of the stanza. He cannot bring his woes to an end, but they do indeed end where they began—in himself. The outgoing energy that is expressed by "That was *Pryene,*"

65

"cruell intent," and "my murdrous blåde did bend" finds no object and manifests itself not in an action, but in the anguished feeling that has become the whole story of this episode. Phedon is literally pursuing not another character, but "my fell purpose." In the next stanza, the internal psychological action becomes an event in the poem:

> Feare gaue her wings, and rage enforst my flight;
> Through woods and plaines so long I did her chace,
> Till this mad man, whom your victorious might
> Hath now fast bound, me met in middle space,
> As I her, so he me pursewd apace,
> And shortly ouertooke: I breathing yre,
> Sore chauffed at my stay in such a cace,
> And with my heat kindled his cruell fyre;
> Which kindled once, his mother did more rage inspyre.
>
> (2.4.32)

Before Furor arrives, Phedon's feelings are described with personifications, and one might expect Furor's intervention simply to act out "rage enforst my flight." But the energies that are registered in almost every line manifest themselves most drastically not in the actions of Furor, but in Phedon's anger itself. Just at the point that Phedon is possessed by a passion, Spenser makes it explicit that this is a human reality, not simply a convention of allegorical narrative. "Breathing yre" could not be an event in an allegorical fiction; it is a locution that directly renders wrathful feeling. It is Phedon who gives life to his captors—"And with my heat kindled his cruell fyre"—and in the next stanza his story ends, not with the personifications of Furor and Occasion, but with the passions of grief and fury:

> Betwixt them both, they haue me doen to dye,
> Through wounds, and strokes, and stubborne handeling,
> That death were better, then such agony,
> As griefe and furie vnto me did bring;
> Of which in me yet stickes the mortall sting,
> That during life will neuer be appeasd.
> When he thus ended had his sorrowing,
> Said *Guyon,* Squire, sore haue ye beene diseasd;
> But all your hurts may soone through temperance
>   be easd. (2.4.33)

The "mortall sting" that sticks in Phedon has been made to seem so relentless and ineradicable, that one is rather surprised at the offer of relief held out by Guyon. The question is whether any human act can ease the kind of anguish Phedon has undergone. This seems to be a moment when Spenser allows simple moral categories to take over the complex realities rendered in his verse. But there is nothing in the Palmer's first words to suggest that he fails to understand the psychological reality that has been presented:

> Then gan the Palmer thus, Most wretched man,
> That to affections does the bridle lend;
> In their beginning they are weake and wan,
> But soone through suff'rance grow to fearefull end;
> Whiles they are weake betimes with them contend:
> For when they once to perfect strength do grow,
> Strong warres they make, and cruell battry bend
> Gainst fort of Reason, it to ouerthrow:
> Wrath, gelosie, griefe, loue this Squire haue layd
>   thus low.   (2.4.34)

"To affections does the bridle lend" may be a commonplace image, but it perfectly brings out both sides of Phedon's tragedy—that he let himself be carried away, there was some fault of will, and yet the affections have an independent energy of their own. The word "suff'rance" embraces the same double idea of moral permission and helplessness. The Palmer's moralizing is genuinely impressive, because it is based on his recognition of the power of the internal forces with which man must deal. Though we are told to deal with passions while they are weak, our "contending" with them is made to seem inherently like heroic struggle. The Palmer does not appeal to the "fort of Reason" until it emerges from the verse as the proper object, so to speak, of the affections' "strong warres" and "cruell battry."

When we stop and think about it, it is surprising that the Palmer speaks only of psychological struggles and says not a word about the murders Phedon committed. But in fact we have to stop and step back from the verse to realize this, because the transformation of actual crimes into psychological disasters has occurred some stanzas before. In Ariosto, the death of Ginevra would have made the episode an irredeemable tragedy. But when Phedon says, "Of which in me yet stickes the mortall sting, / That during life will neuer be appeasd," he refers to the passions of grief and fury, and not to what he has done. One could hardly hope for anything more thoroughgoing by way of transforming narrative materials. The effect in the poetry is that Spenser can give a more severe and fearful rendering of the passions than

Ariosto does, and at the same time can hold out the possibility of averting disaster by an act of temperance. This occurs in the next stanza of the Palmer's speech:

> Wrath, gealosie, griefe, loue do thus expell:
> Wrath is a fire, and gealosie a weede,
> Griefe is a flood, and loue a monster fell;
> The fire of sparkes, the weede of little seede,
> The flood of drops, the Monster filth did breede:
> But sparks, seed, drops, and filth do thus delay;
> The sparks soone quench, the springing seed outweed,
> The drops dry vp, and filth wipe cleane away:
> So shall wrath, gealosie, griefe, loue dye and decay.
>
> (2.4.35)

After the first line, one perhaps expects an instruction to perform some external or psychological action—for example, "Whiles they are weake betimes with them contend." Instead this stanza takes the basic idea of catching the passions when they are weak, and by putting it into a special schematic form, directly creates a psychological action. The basic device of the stanza is simply the continual transferring of attention to new sets of terms. The four terms listed in line 1 are metaphorically equated with four new terms, which then become the realities with which the stanza is concerned. They in turn generate four new terms and the process is repeated. As we follow this process, the passions and their awesome metaphoric equivalents turn into their small beginnings; hence in lines 7 and 8, temperance becomes an easy and even natural process, and the imperative "expell" in the first line turns into the declarative "dye and decay" in the last. Only then does Guyon, in the last stanza of the episode, give real instructions to Phedon:

> Vnlucky Squire (said *Guyon*) sith thou hast
> Falne into mischiefe through intemperaunce,
> Henceforth take heede of that thou now hast past,
> And guide thy wayes with warie gouernaunce,
> Least worse betide thee by some later chaunce.
> But read how art thou nam'd, and of what kin.
> *Phedon* I hight (quoth he) and do aduaunce
> Mine auncestry from famous *Coradin,*
> Who first to rayse our house to honour did begin.
>
> (2.4.36)

By being purged of the passions that so dreadfully transformed him, Phedon becomes a man again, and the sign of his restored humanity is his being named for the first time. It is a wonderful gesture with which to conclude the episode. But considering our interests in this chapter, what should most arouse our wonder is the way the easing of Phedon's hurts was accomplished. Nothing, of course, has happened to him dramatically. It is the reader's mind which, simply by following the devices of the next to last stanza, enacts the process of being purged of passion. The climax of the episode is not an action at all, but a rhetorical scheme, a formal arrangement of words—precisely a stanza of poetry, and nothing else.

Chapter Three

Spenser's Poetic Language

I

In the last chapter we considered the lines and stanzas of Spenser's verse in relation to the narrative materials that give rise to them. In this chapter we shall examine Spenser's verse as language, the product of a speaker; we shall consider it in its relation to the narrator and not to what is narrated. Spenser's poetic language has been out of favor in this century for the very reasons that caused it to be esteemed in the last. The modern reader dislikes Spenser's verse because it answers to an admiring description like Hazlitt's:

> A poetical language rich and varied and magnificent beyond all former, and almost all later example. His versification is, at once, the most smooth and the most sounding in the language. It is a labyrinth of sweet sounds, "in many a winding bout of linked sweetness long drawn out"—that would cloy by their very sweetness, but that the ear is constantly relieved and enchanted by their continued variety of modulation—dwelling on the pauses of the action, or flowing on in a fuller tide of harmony with the movement of the sentiment. It has not the bold dramatic transitions of Shakspeare's blank verse, nor the high-raised tone of Milton's; but it is the perfection of melting harmony, dissolving the soul in pleasure, or holding it captive in the chains of suspense. Spenser was the poet of our waking dreams; and he has invented not only a language, but a music of his own for them. The undulations are infinite, like those of the waves of the sea: but the effect is still the same, lulling the senses into a deep oblivion of the jarring noises of the world, from which we have no wish to be ever recalled.[1]

This view of Spenser's style was accepted for more than a century, but at best it is only a half truth. It is not surprising that C. S. Lewis began his rehabilitation of Spenser by drawing attention to "a poetry far more nervous and masculine—a drier flavour and a wine with more body—than the modern reader has been taught to anticipate."[2] In his

[1] *Lectures on the English Poets*, in William Hazlitt, *Works*, ed. P. P. Howe, London, 1930–1934, 5, 44.
[2] *The Allegory of Love*, Oxford, 1936, pp. 319–320.

later writings he continued to emphasize this aspect of Spenser's style. He speaks of a "Spenser not Golden, not sugared at all (in his manner) but thoroughly good, pressing his tale. . . . It is as direct as good medieval verse: not to be lingered over, carrying us equably forward. Much of the *Faerie Queene* is like that; a 'poetry of statement.' The typical Spenserian line tells you what somebody did or wore or where he went."[3] It should be clear by now that Spenser's style is not an instrument for telling a story. But when Lewis speaks of it in this way, he is obviously thinking of some of the characteristics that we observed in the last chapter—the lucidity of diction, the clarity and independence of the line as a unit, the even and steady pace of the verse.

Lewis was reacting against a nineteenth-century version of Spenser, but his views had been anticipated by both Coleridge and Yeats. Coleridge associated Spenser with Chaucer and Herbert as a practitioner of a plain style "in which every thing was expressed just as one would wish to talk, and yet all dignified, attractive and interesting; and all at the same time perfectly correct as to the measure of the syllables and the rhyme."[4] Yeats, despite his emphasis on Spenser's sensuousness and idyllicism, firmly distinguishes his verse from that of the romantic Spenserians. He quotes a Spenserian stanza from Shelley's narrative poem, *Laon and Cythna,* and says:

> It is now busy with a meteor and now with throbbing blood that is fire, and with a mist that is a swoon and a sleep that is life. It is bound together by the vaguest suggestion, while Spenser's verse is always rushing on to some preordained thought. . . . Poetry [in the nineteenth century] has become more spiritual, for the soul is of all things the most delicately organised, but it has lost in weight and measure and in its power of telling long stories and of dealing with great and complicated events. . . . Spenser's contemporaries, writing lyrics or plays full of lyrical moments, write a verse more delicately organised than his and crowd more meaning into a phrase than he, but they could not have kept one's attention through so long a poem.[5]

It is not surprising that Lewis' account of Spenser's style has impressive antecedents in romantic criticism. The man who describes *The*

---

[3] *English Literature in the Sixteenth Century*, Oxford, 1954, pp. 390–391.
[4] Samuel Taylor Coleridge, *Biographia Literaria*, ed. George Watson, London: Everyman's Library, 1956, p. 223.
[5] William Butler Yeats, *Essays and Introductions*, New York, 1961, pp. 379–381.

Faerie Queene as "a sublime instance of the universal process" and says that Spenser's wisdom is the kind that "exists most often in inarticulate people"[6] is surely to be seen as the last great romantic Spenserian. It is precisely because Lewis belongs to romantic literature that, like Yeats, he can see that Spenser does not.

The two romantic views of Spenser's verse, Hazlitt's and Lewis', though they seem contradictory, are actually quite compatible. To see this, we must consider the problem mentioned at the beginning of this chapter, the relation between speaker and verse. The usual modern view of this relationship has been most influentially stated by F. R. Leavis. *Revaluation* begins by praising the first stanza of Donne's "The Good-Morrow":

> Donne uses in complete dissociation from music a stanza-form that proclaims the union of poetry and music. The dissociation is positive; utterance, movement and intonation are those of the talking voice. And consider the way in which the stress is got on "Did," and the intonation controlled, here:
>
> > I wonder by my troth, what thou, and I
> > Did, till we lov'd?
>
> This is the spirit in which Donne uses the stanza-form—for he does indeed strictly use it: the exigencies of the pattern become means to the inevitable naturalness; they play an essential part in the consummate control of intonation, gesture, movement and larger rhythm.[7]

The praise of Donne is that he has made the formal requirements of the stanza the product of the speaking voice. The reverse condition, in which formal requirements determine the poet's voice, constricts the poet and robs him, as Leavis sees it, of essential resources of the English language. There is a great deal of truth in this position, and it is widely held. One is not at all surprised that in a modern study entitled *The Founding of English Metre,* Sidney has replaced Spenser as the hero:

> The art of poetry achieves the degree of sophistication that allows it to recognize its own limitations; for it is seen that speech is one thing and metre another, although the two must meet. With this recognition, the basic resources of the language can be exploited, not as the order of rhetoric but as the order of speech, and con-

---

[6] *The Allegory of Love,* pp. 358, 359.
[7] *Revaluation,* London, 1936, pp. 11–12.

sciously so. In Sidney's poetry, this recognition leads to wit. . . .
With the ability to control and change the tone of his speech, he
produces the effect of voices speaking, of drama.[8]

We have no trouble finding in Sidney an anticipation of Donne's
achievement:

> This night while sleepe begins with heavy wings
> To hatch mine eyes, and that unbitted thought
> Doth fall to stray, and my chiefe powres are brought
> To leave the scepter of all subject things,
> The first that straight my fancie's error brings
> Unto my mind, is *Stella's* image, wrought
> By *Love's* owne selfe, but with so curious drought,
> That she, me thinks, not onely shines but sings.[9]

Formal devices like enjambment and rhythm are not so expressive as
in Donne, but there can be no doubt that form here is the product of a
speaking voice. The most evident sign of this is Sidney's mastery of
syntax. It is an extraordinary achievement to produce the first four
lines so firmly and still make us recognize that they are syntactically
subordinate to the main clause in lines 5 and 6. We need only observe
the differences of tone and effect in lines 1, 4, 5, and 8 (the a-rhymes)
to recognize how supple and authoritative the voice of the speaker
is here.

Now let us examine a stanza by Spenser. For this comparison we
require a stanza of lyric rather than narrative verse:

> Calme was the day, and through the trembling ayre,
> Sweete breathing *Zephyrus* did softly play
> A gentle spirit, that lightly did delay
> Hot *Titans* beames, which then did glyster fayre:
> When I whom sullein care,
> Through discontent of my long fruitlesse stay
> In Princes Court, and expectation vayne
> Of idle hopes, which still doe fly away,
> Like empty shaddowes, did aflict my brayne,
> Walkt forth to ease my payne
> Along the shoare of siluer streaming *Themmes*,

[8] John Thompson, *The Founding of English Metre*, New York, 1961, p. 140.
[9] *Astrophel and Stella* 38, in *The Poems of Sir Philip Sidney*, ed. W. A. Ringler, Jr., Oxford, 1962.

Whose rutty Bancke, the which his Riuer hemmes,
Was paynted all with variable flowers,
And all the meades adornd with daintie gemmes,
Fit to decke maydens bowres,
And crowne their Paramours,
Against the Brydale day, which is not long:
Sweete *Themmes* runne softly, till I end my Song.

(Prothalamion, 1–18)

W. B. C. Watkins cites this stanza to show Spenser's ability "to handle complex syntax; . . . the shifting rhythms here, the beautiful unfolding of the stanza, are dependent on the arrangement of the sentence."[10] But there is something more seriously wrong with this sentence than the solecism ("When I *whom* sullein care . . . did aflict *my brayne*") that Watkins himself points out. As we read the stanza, it is impossible to grasp the syntax of "did aflict my brayne": one irresistibly takes "shaddowes" instead of "care" to be the subject of the verb. We can read the sentence correctly only by joining "Like empty shaddowes" very forcibly to the preceding line and then, after a decisive pause, giving a firm and independent stress to "did aflict." But it is not simply the comma after "fly away" that discourages us from doing this. A speaking voice does not control and shape the sentence, as it does when Sidney says:

> The first that straight my fancie's error brings
> Unto my mind, is *Stella's* image, wrought
> By *Love's* owne selfe.

In these lines there is a genuine tension between sentence structure and the lines of verse, and the octave maintains its impetus (though the main verb of the sentence has at last appeared) because the claims of both are felt. Because of the syntax, the voice isolates "wrought," and it is thus firmly registered as the rhyme word, even though syntax then impels a strong enjambment with the next line. In Spenser's stanza a speaking voice is never used so actively and decisively. Except for "When I whom sullein care," only two of the many enjambments are necessary—that is, ones in which syntax compels us to continue into the next line. "Delay" (line 3) immediately finds its direct object, and in

> Whose rutty Bancke, the which his Riuer hemmes,
> Was paynted all with variable flowers,

[10] *Shakespeare and Spenser*, Princeton, 1950, pp. 278–279.

the sentence falls into place simply by letting the voice follow the disposition of words into lines of verse. Watkins claims that "the elaborate canzone is sustained by the structure of the sentence,"[11] but surely the reverse is true: the structure of the stanza sustains the sentence. The main effect is one that we observed in the last chapter—single lines being steadily added to one another. Sentence structure does not control our reading even in the periodic structure, "When I whom sullein care, . . . Walkt forth to ease my payne." Our absorption in the lines between "whom" and "brayne" makes it impossible for us to grasp that this is a long subordinate clause and that "I" still lacks a main verb. When Spenser finally produces the main verb, he does not depend on our having kept the structure of the sentence in mind. Instead he uses the redundant "my" to revivify the subject "I," and he brings out the syntactic importance of "Walkt forth to ease my payne" by exploiting a feature of the stanza form—the finality with which the short line repeats the rhyme already sounded in "brayne." And far from expecting us to look back five lines in order to grasp the structure that has been completed, Spenser treats this short line as if it were the beginning of a new sentence, which then unfolds line by line from the main verb phrase.

Hazlitt's description of Spenser's verse comes about not through any special romantic demands he makes of poetry, but simply from assuming the normal relationship between verse form and speaking voice. If we assume that verse movement and coherence are determined by the choices and energies of a human speaker, then Spenser's verse, in which the voice *follows* formal line and stanza structures, will appear to be the product of a peculiarly passive sensibility. Thus G. Wilson Knight, in an essay that is very sympathetic to Spenser, complains that "instead of building up and cohering, the poem is . . . always decomposing. . . . [There is] a sensuousness relaxed, an immorality of technique, which just misses conviction, is over-mentalized and all but decadent."[12] Yeats very acutely saw that if a speaker actually wanted to convey the feelings that Hazlitt and Knight find in Spenser's verse, his poetry would be like Shelley's, with "the rhythm . . . varied and troubled, and the lines . . . broken capriciously."[13] By contrast, Yeats says, Spenser's lines are "like bars of gold thrown ringing one upon another." This is a surprising characterization of Spenser's poetry, but what we have seen about Spenser's treatment of

[11] *Ibid.*, p. 277.
[12] *The Burning Oracle*, London, 1939, p. 14.
[13] *Essays and Introductions*, p. 379.

the individual line should show us that Yeats is right. But when Yeats tells us that the music of *The Faerie Queene* is "like that of the old story-tellers, [with] their energetic pleasure, their rhythmical wills,"[14] and when Lewis says that Spenser's style is the style of a story-teller, "pressing his tale," they are attributing the effects of Spenser's verse to the energies and the will of a dramatically present human speaker. And the moment we make this assumption, we will find ourselves characterizing Spenser's verse as Hazlitt did.

The purpose of this chapter is to analyze Spenser's use of language so that we can trust ourselves to read his verse as it asks to be read. The central problem confronting us appears, in the mouth of a hostile critic, as a familiar complaint about the Spenserian stanza: "The extraordinary skill and variety with which it is handled, always within the limits of its essential monotony, have no doubt contributed greatly to its reputation; but that monotony itself is the sign of a tendency to divorce rhythm from sense, to reduce verse to a flow of harmonious sound which, however skilful, is more like a decadence than the promise of a fresh beginning."[15] Once again, this is very close to Hazlitt's sense of Spenser's verse: Hazlitt simply turns the charge of monotony into a virtue ("the undulations are infinite, like those of the waves of the sea"). There is an essential difficulty here, and it is best indicated by Empson: "The size, the possible variety, and the fixity of this unit [the Spenserian stanza] give something of the blankness that comes from fixing your eyes on a bright spot; you have to yield yourself to it very completely to take in the variety of its movement, and, at the same time, there is no need to concentrate the elements of the situation into a judgment as if for action."[16] Empson is trying to characterize the way in which a passive acceptance of line and stanza form is compatible, in reading Spenser's verse, with a great deal of alertness and attention.

It is perhaps impossible to give a completely abstract or theoretical statement of Spenser's assumptions about language or of the capacity of the human mind to adapt itself to a specialized idiom based on these assumptions. But we can examine a specific phenomenon—the relation between sentence structure and lines of verse—which is a major poetic resource for Spenser, and at the same time results from and reveals his idiosyncratic attitude towards language. To see this will at

---

[14] *Ibid.*, p. 380.
[15] Derek Traversi, "Spenser's *Faerie Queene*," in *The Age of Chaucer*, ed. Boris Ford, London, 1954, p. 221.
[16] William Empson, *Seven Types of Ambiguity*, 3rd edn., London, 1953, p. 34.

least make us feel easy about, even if it does not fully explain, the fact that we can have a full, active contact with Spenser's verse and be appropriately alert to it, without thereby enacting the role of a dramatized human speaker who exploits all the resources of the language. We can then go on to consider the nature of Spenser's verbal formulas as language, rather than as transformations of narrative materials.

II

The question we are asking of the verse of *The Faerie Queene* is: what is the relation between stanza and sentence, or between lines and parts of a sentence? The stanza from the *Prothalamion* suggested that in Spenser's verse the formal requirements of line and stanza carry the sentence, whose structure has little or no independent force. We shall find that this phenomenon is characteristic of the verse of *The Faerie Queene,* and it well explains the "dream-like" or "musical" qualities that readers through the centuries have found in the poem. But it is not so easy as one thinks to say specifically what we mean when we say that sentence structure has little independent force in Spenser's verse. We at first think of the contrast between what Coleridge called the "fluent projection" of Spenser's verse, as opposed to "the deeper and more inwoven harmonies of Shakspeare and Milton."[17]

> There, as in glistring glory she did sit,
> She held a great gold chaine ylincked well,
> Whose vpper end to highest heauen was knit,
> And lower part did reach to lowest Hell;
> And all that preace did round about her swell,
> To catchen hold of that long chaine, thereby
> To clime aloft, and others to excell:
> That was *Ambition*, rash desire to sty,
> And euery lincke thereof a step of dignity.
>
> (2.7.46)

> High on a Throne of Royal State, which far
> Outshone the wealth of *Ormus* and of *Ind,*
> Or where the gorgeous East with richest hand
> Show'rs on her Kings *Barbaric* Pearl and Gold,
> Satan exalted sat, by merit rais'd
> To that bad eminence; and from despair
> Thus high uplifted beyond hope, aspires

[17] *Miscellaneous Criticism*, ed. T. M. Raysor, Cambridge, Mass., 1936, p. 33.

Beyond thus high, insatiate to pursue
Vain War with Heav'n, and by success untaught
His proud imaginations thus display'd.[18]

In Spenser's stanza, each line is a self-contained component of the sentence. It is significant that the one enjambment (after "thereby") produces a line in which the two halves are syntactically parallel, and which thus maintains the correspondence between line and sentence component. The contrast with Milton's postponed verbs and continual enjambments is obvious and is immediately felt when one reads the passages aloud. Yet when we try to use these points of comparison as criteria for analyzing Spenser's verse, we find that they are not so decisive as we had hoped. If simply the use of enjambment is to be a criterion, there are many more enjambments in *The Faerie Queene* than we expect. Similarly the correspondence between verse line and sentence component is too frequent in other Elizabethan narrative poems to be considered a distinguishing characteristic of Spenser's verse.

There is an obvious difficulty in using *Paradise Lost* as a gauge for *The Faerie Queene*. Milton so conspicuously complicates sentence structure that he does not help us determine whether Spenser's verse corresponds to or deviates in its own way from a norm for narrative verse. Similarly lyric poetry cannot provide the basis for a systematic examination of the verse of a heroic poem, even though considering Donne and Sidney is a useful starting point for dealing with Spenser. The relevant comparisons will be between *The Faerie Queene* and other Elizabethan narrative poems, and of these I have chosen Marlowe's *Hero and Leander* and Drayton's *The Barons Warres*. The first seems to me the one Elizabethan narrative as masterful in its mode as Spenser's, and the second is a heroic poem by a disciple of Spenser. If Spenser's verse is really as specialized as it seems, we ought to be able to discriminate it from these poems.

The most useful way to examine sentence structure in these poems is not to distinguish lines and sentences on the basis of inherent structural features, but to pay attention to what happens in the act of reading them.[19] Take the following lines from *The Barons Warres:*

[18] John Milton, *Paradise Lost* 2.1–10, ed. Merritt Y. Hughes, New York, 1962.
[19] It is surprising to find that no mechanical test is adequate or genuinely revealing when we compare the relation between verse form and sentence structure in these poems. By mechanical test I mean one based on some characteristic of language or verse form that exists independently of these particular poems—for example, the use of a particular grammatical construction or of

Whilst EDWARD takes but what they [his advisers]
    onely give,
Whose Nonage crav'd their carefullest Protection,
Who knew to rule, and he but learn'd to live,
From their Experience taking his Direction.

                                                 (6.11)[20]

This passage is very similar to Spenser's verse in the way individual
lines are managed and the way in which sentence components are dis-
tributed among lines of verse. What distinguishes it from Spenser is
the mental activity required of us when we recognize that "Whose" in
line 2 refers to the young king, while "Who" in line 3 refers to his ad-
visers. Simply to understand the lines requires a distinct conscious-
ness of the sentence structure; this demand is particularly striking be-
cause we must resist the suggestion that "Whose" and "Who" refer to
the same person because they appear in the same position in succes-
sive lines of verse.

"Consciousness of sentence structure" may seem an elusive crite-
rion, but we can show with some exactness that Drayton and Marlowe
require it, while Spenser does not. Here is another stanza from *The
Barons Warres:*

    But never doth it surfet with Excesse,
    Each Dish so savorie, season'd with Delight,
    Nor nothing can the Gluttonie suppresse,
    But still it longs, so liquorish is the sight,
    Nor having all, is in desire the lesse,
    Till it so much be tempted, past the Might,

---

inversions or of enjambments. For example, I could find no significant dif-
ference between Spenser's and Marlowe's use of infinitives, or between the
syntax of the enjambments in Book I, canto 1 of *The Faerie Queene* and
sestiad 2 of *Hero and Leander.* Some mechanical tests produce revealing symp-
toms, but not explanations. A canto of *The Barons Warres* has more postponed
main verbs than a canto of *The Faerie Queene*, but if this difference is important
it must reflect a more basic difference between characteristics that are equally
present in stanzas that do not contain periodic sentences. Similarly, there are
rarely two or more consecutive enjambments in *The Faerie Queene*, whereas
there are several stretches of consecutively enjambed verse in *Hero and Leander.*
But *Hero and Leander* also contains long stretches of verse with few or no
enjambments. Obviously we must describe a characteristic of all the verse in
Hero and Leander that makes Marlowe able or liable, as Spenser is not, to
produce a series of enjambments.

[20] All quotations from Drayton are from Michael Drayton, *Works*, ed. J.
William Hebel, Oxford, 1931–1941, 5 vols.

That the full stomacke more then well suffic'd,
Vomits, what late it vilely gourmandiz'd.

(6.23)

We have to recognize that line 2 is an absolute construction, not the subject or object of an ensuing verb, and in line 4 we must recognize that neither "longs" nor "so liquorish" has an ensuing complementary construction. The rejected alternatives are not remote possibilities, but arise perfectly naturally. We again find ourselves resisting some of the suggestions of the verse, and the conflict between verse form and sentence structure accounts for our feeling that our progress through the stanza is rather bumpy. (Drayton increases this effect when, having persuaded us that no line carries over into what follows, he goes against our expectation that the sentence will end at line 5 and pushes it through to the end of the stanza.) The going is bumpy even when we are dealing with parallel constructions, because Drayton makes us work out the grammatical construction of almost every line:

By which, the King with a selected Crue,
Of such as he with his Intent acquainted,
Which he affected to the Action knew,
And in revenge of EDWARD had not fainted,
That to their utmost would the Cause pursue,
And with those Treasons that had not been tainted;
Adventured, the Labyrinth t'assay,
To rowse the Beast, which kept them all at bay.

(6.49)

The effort with which we make our way through the first six lines is capped in the seventh, where we are forced to go back to line 1 to find the subject of "Adventured." A comparison of *The Barons Warres* (1603) with its first version, *Mortimeriados* (1596), shows that Drayton intended us to work consciously at sentence structure.[21] No doubt he meant the effect of difficulty to be a heightening or dignifying of his verse. But it becomes a real vice in *The Barons Warres,* because it so often involves a struggle against verse form: the stanzas more often strike us as fragmented than coherent. Indeed these stanzas from Drayton may suggest to us that the lucidity and ease with which a sentence unfolds in Spenser's stanza is a sign of mastery of language, not of an inability to exploit its resources.

[21] Compare *Mortimeriados*, 2437–2443, with the stanza just quoted; all Drayton's changes increase the effort required of the reader.

Our consciousness of sentence structure can be most clearly observed when there are structural ambiguities or at least genuine possibilities of misconstruing sentence structure. The following lines render Hero's confusion after she has unwittingly allowed herself to invite Leander to her tower:

> And like a planet, mooving severall waies,
> At one selfe instant, she poore soule assaies,
> Loving, not to love at all, and everie part
> Strove to resist the motions of her hart.[22]

"At one selfe instant" can modify either "mooving" or "assaies"; each syntactic choice produces a distinct intonation of the phrase and movement of the line in which it occurs. For two reasons, the phrase is best taken with "mooving." This construction more precisely renders the phenomenon which makes planetary motion an apt simile for Hero's confusion. Second, this choice involves an enjambment and divides the second line; it thus requires a more active use of the speaking voice to keep alive both sentence structure and verse form, and Marlowe continues to exploit this active speaking voice in the interjected "poore soule" and in controlling the rhythm of the hypermetrical third line. Even if this argument is disputed and the other sentence structure preferred, it is clear that the way we speak and mentally grasp these lines depends on which of the two sentence structures we choose.

The next example is not genuinely ambiguous, but it is thoroughly confusing until the right sentence structure is discerned:

> Home when he came, he seem'd not to be there,
> But like exiled aire thrust from his sphere,
> Set in a forren place, and straight from thence,
> Alcides like, by mightie violence,
> He would have chac'd away the swelling maine,
> That him from her unjustly did detaine.
>
> (*Hero and Leander*, 2.117–122)

The first couplet does not make a complete sentence, and having recognized this, we must avoid treating "Set in a forren place" as parallel to "thrust from his sphere." The voice must register the fact that the second line depends on "Set in a forren place" and that that phrase, in its turn, modifies "he." The lines are rather hard to get into focus and might be thought faulty in the way Drayton's stanzas were. But

[22] Christopher Marlowe, *Hero and Leander*, 1.361–364, in *Elizabethan Minor Epics*, ed. Elizabeth Story Donno, London, 1963.

the very active sentence structuring here demanded of us is turned to poetic use: the concentrated effort we give to these lines supports the sense of heroic expenditure of strength in those that follow. Our attention to sentence structure is exploited in a very different way in the opening description of Hero:

> She ware no gloves, for neither sunne nor wind
> Would burne or parch her hands, but to her mind,
> Or warme or coole them, for they tooke delite
> To play upon those hands, they were so white.
>
> (*Hero and Leander*, 1.27–30)

I think it natural to mistake the first couplet for a complete sentence, but even without making this error, we see how forcible is the enjambment from "to her mind" to "Or warme or coole them." The attention secured by this enjambment makes us particularly heed the meaning of "warme or coole" (as opposed to "burne or parch"), and our sense of discriminating attention to language encourages us to participate in the elements' delighting solicitude for Hero.

The consciousness of sentence structure that Marlowe expects is simply the normal attention to language that makes us, in actual speaking and listening, choose one of the possible interpretations of such ambiguous sentences as "The man was killed by the machine" or "They were entertaining women." But in *The Faerie Queene* we are not intended to make a choice when sentence structure is ambiguous. The following lines describe Amoret's appearance in the masque of Cupid:

> After all these there marcht a most faire Dame,
> Led of two grysie villeins, th'one *Despight,*
> The other cleped *Cruelty* by name:
> She dolefull Lady, like a dreary Spright,
> Cald by strong charmes out of eternall night,
> Had deathes owne image figurd in her face,
> Full of sad signes, fearefull to liuing sight.
>
> (3.12.19)

"Cald by strong charmes" can modify either "Lady" or "Spright," and the important point is that there is no need to make a decision either way. Indeed it is essential to the poetry that we somehow have it both ways. Amoret, the prisoner of a diabolical sorcerer, has literally been "Cald by strong charmes out of eternall night," and it is because we feel the line applies to her that the next two lines are so immediate and awesome. Yet the force of the line would be diminished if it modified "Lady" alone. The double syntax makes us feel not simply that Amoret has been "Cald by strong charmes," but that she is "a dreary Spright," and we now see that this phrase has two meanings, both of which are allowed to come into play by the ambiguous structure of the sentence.[23]

Our next example presents a more complicated use of a structural ambiguity:

> And that new creature borne without her dew,
> Full of the makers guile, with vsage sly
> He taught to imitate that Lady trew,
> Whose semblance she did carrie vnder feigned hew.
>
> (1.1.46)

We cannot, and again we need not, decide whether "with vsage sly" modifies "taught" or "imitate." The double grammar makes the allegorical point that the false Una is the creature of Archimago: what characterizes the one characterizes the other. There is a further point of interest here. In line 2, we entertain for a moment the possibility that "with vsage sly" is syntactically parallel to the preceding two phrases (it seems a close echo of "without her dew") and thus modifies "creature." In Marlowe's verse this possibility would be rejected, and our perception of the sentence structure would produce a vigorous enjambment from line 2 to line 3. But the enjambment does not occur here. We continue to entertain the apparent syntax of "with vsage sly," because it makes little difference to the meaning of the passage: it simply makes line 2, rather than line 3, bring out the identity of the false Una and her creator. Note that we do not *choose* the wrong syntax. Rather this is a case of extreme permissiveness; we seem not to have to make the decisions about sentence structure that we ordinarily make.

Before going on to other instances of ambiguous sentence structure in *The Faerie Queene,* I would like to discuss the phenomenon that makes examples like the last one possible. Consider the following stanza:

> Her scattred brood, soone as their Parent deare
> They saw so rudely falling to the ground,
> Groning full deadly, all with troublous feare,
> Gathred themselues about her body round,

[23] For a slighter example of the same structural ambiguity, see 1.1.38.2–3.

Weening their wonted entrance to haue found
At her wide mouth: but being there withstood
They flocked all about her bleeding wound,
And sucked vp their dying mothers blood,
Making her death their life, and eke her hurt
        their good.   (1.1.25)

"Groning full deadly" can modify either "Parent deare" (and thus parallel "falling to the ground") or "all" (and thus parallel "Weening . . . "). In this case we cannot have it both ways. The first of these choices creates an enjambment from line 2 to line 3, a strong caesura in line 3, and another enjambment from line 3 to line 4. The second choice makes line 3 an independent unit, because sentence structure now corresponds to the lines of verse: the subordinate clause ends at the end of line 2, and line 3 gives the subject of the main clause.[24] But on what basis do we make our choice here? There is really no difference in meaning. As the final lines make explicit, with their play on "death" and "dying," we can equally well think of the parent dragon emitting a death groan or of the children giving a deathlike groan at her death. But we must make a choice, and I think we choose the second alternative simply because it is easier: it more readily makes sentence structure compatible with the allocation of words to different lines of verse. The basis of our choice here is a rule that Spenser's verse almost never makes us violate: follow the path of least resistance. This rule, we may note, succinctly states the reason that modern critics dislike Spenser and romantic critics loved him.

We are brought back to the phenomenon that we saw was so important in the last chapter—the independence of the line as a unit in Spenser's verse. We now see that we do not treat the line as a unit at the expense of sentence structure; rather Spenser's ways with sentence structure encourage us to treat the line as a unit. Let us consider a more complex example than the last:

By them the Sprite doth passe in quietly,
And vnto *Morpheus* comes, whom drowned deepe
In drowsie fit he findes: of nothing he takes keepe.

                    (1.1.40)

---

[24] Actually "with troublous feare" is a sentence modifier—it can be construed with either subject or predicate. There is thus still an enjambment from line 3 to line 4, but it is not so strongly felt as it is when we choose the first of the alternative structures.

On first reading, the enjambment between the last two lines seems strong. We assume that "drowned deepe in drowsie fit" is a single, inseparable constituent and thus that a structural necessity forces us to continue from one line to the next. But the two halves of the phrase are quite independent of each other. Spenser could just as well have written "whom in drowsie fit he findes" or "whom drowned deepe he findes" (the preceding stanza tells us that Morpheus' dwelling is where *"Tethys* his wet bed / Doth euer wash, and *Cynthia* still doth steepe / In siluer deaw his euer-drouping hed"). Hence it would be perfectly possible to rewrite these lines, "whom drowned deepe / He findes in drowsie fit." As the lines stand, the immediate echo of "drowned" in "drowsie" makes us feel that this is a single phrase, and the resulting effect of a strong enjambment is poetically important. When we go from the tentative possibility that "drowned deepe" is literal to find "in drowsie fit," we are made to see both the point of a fable—telling us about the steeping of Morpheus' head is a way of telling us about sleep—and the force of a metaphoric locution, "to be drowned in sleep." But the point to observe here is that our sense of a strong enjambment comes not from a genuine structural necessity in the phrase, but from the order of words in the last line. It is, as it were, an enjambment after the fact. Even in this instance our principle of taking the path of least resistance is confirmed. We read these lines correctly by assuming that sentence structure has the easiest relation to the disposition of words into lines, and by thus expecting only a subject and a main verb after "whom drowned deepe."

Structural ambiguity is a genuine poetic resource for Spenser, not just a freakish by-product of his loose sentence structures. The following lines render the invigoration of the Red Cross Knight by Una's call, "Add faith vnto your force":

> That when he heard, in great perplexitie,
> His gall did grate for griefe and high disdaine,
> And knitting all his force got one hand free,
> Wherewith he grypt her gorge with so great paine,
> That soone to loose her wicked bands did her constraine.

> (1.1.19)

We cannot tell whether "so great paine" refers to the knight's painful efforts or to the pain he causes the dragon. This ambiguity is immediately succeeded by another. "That" in the last line is either a relative pronoun or correlative to "so"—in which case the last line is a result clause and we silently supply "he." If we interpret the pain as the dragon's, we are likely to make "That" a relative pronoun; if the pain is the knight's, then "That" will be treated as a conjunction introducing a result clause. But these alternatives are not mutually exclusive. It is possible to make either meaning of "paine" go with either use of "That," and this overlap, or blur, helps us hold in our minds both ways of construing the sentence. Thus, it might be argued that the effect works by our recognizing the ambiguity in "paine" and simply treating "That" as a relative pronoun, which of course retains the ambiguous reference. (This cannot be the only correct reading, because "so . . . that" imposes itself too strongly to be ruled out.) The sentence is exceptionally permissive, and it is able to be so because we are used to treating each line as a unit—an expectation which none of the preceding lines in the stanza violates. We fully take in the next to last line before going on to the last, which in its turn satisfies any or all of our grammatical expectations. We can put this another way by saying that the independence of lines means their separation from each other, and that Spenser's verse keeps us from inspecting the connection between the lines in a way that would make us treat structural possibilities as alternative choices.

An ambiguity like this is a poetic resource for Spenser, because it brings to life a basic assumption of allegory—in this case, that the struggle depicted occurs within a single mind. A related instance occurs in Arthur's battle with Orgoglio, where syntactic ambiguity brings out a connection between Duessa and her beast that is similar to that between Archimago and the false Una:

> The proud *Duessa* full of wrathfull spight,
> And fierce disdaine, to be affronted so,
> Enforst her purple beast with all her might
> That stop out of the way to ouerthroe,
> Scorning the let of so vnequall foe.
>
> (1.8.13)

"Enforst . . . to ouerthroe" can be construed either as "compelled" (*OED* 10) plus a complementary infinitive or as "strengthened" (*OED* 3) plus a purpose clause. The two meanings overlap (the purpose of her strengthening him is the same action that she is compelling him to do), but it is nevertheless important for us to take in the double syntax. It focuses our attention on line 3 (which is made a complete clause by the meaning "strengthened") before we move on to line 4, and in this way the simple narrative action—the rider compelling her steed—is made an allegorical reality. Duessa, we see, is literally filling the beast with her might: her characteristics are his. We may already have noticed that the description of Duessa in the first two lines closely matches the lines describing the beast in the preceding stanza:

> Her dreadfull beast, who swolne with bloud of late
> Came ramping forth with proud presumpteous gate,
> And threatned all his heads like flaming brands.
>
> (1.8.12)

The identity of Duessa and her beast is brought out in a delightful way in the second half of stanza 13. We are told that Timias would not "To *her* yeeld passage, . . . / But with outrageous strokes did *him* restraine" (my italics).

The passages we have examined, though immensely instructive, are of course exceptional. We would like to know what is the normal usage of which such moments are intensifications. The following passage, in which the satyrs kneel before Una, contains both a normal and an abnormal bit of sentence structure:

> Their frowning forheads with rough hornes yclad,
> And rusticke horror all a side doe lay,
> And gently grenning, shew a semblance glad
> To comfort her, and feare to put away,
> Their backward bent knees teach her humbly to obay.
>
> (1.6.11)

We at first treat "feare to put away" as parallel to "to comfort her," but as we continue reading we see that it must go with the last line. The initial mistake seems inevitable, because it is so naturally produced by the ordinary way of reading the verse, and I think we must regard it as a fault. Spenser's verse, unlike Marlowe's, does not encourage or allow us to make the kind of syntactic decision that is required here. In rereading these lines we must either undergo the jolt of the mistake again, or adopt the unusual tactic of remembering the sentence structure that lies ahead. In the lines just before these, on the other hand, we have a normal example of Spenserian sentence structure. If we read the first two lines with particular attention to sentence structure, we find that Spenser apparently wants us to imagine the satyrs laying aside their foreheads, and the visual absurdity is strengthened by the phrase, "with rough hornes yclad." But this difficulty goes unnoticed in our normal reading of the lines. "Rusticke horror" makes perfect sense as the object of "lay aside" (here in a very common metaphoric sense) and we are not at all prompted to seek out the earlier direct object. The separation of lines partly causes this effect, but even more important is the fact that "rusticke horror" recapitulates the preceding line, so that we are willing to understand it as the complete direct object of the verb. The formula includes both the satyrs' physical appearance and their frowns, which are what they can actually be thought to be laying aside.

We read these lines correctly by taking the path of least resistance, but there is a sense in which this rule applies to any grammatical discourse that is not ambiguous. We assume that a poet's sentences will be grammatical, and we often read without paying particular attention to their structure. At the same time, however, we assume that paying attention to sentence structure will be helpful and interesting, and in *Hero and Leander* it is. But particular attention to sentence structure is almost never helpful in reading *The Faerie Queene*. This is the general rule, whose intensified version is that we do not have to make a choice between alternatives when sentence structure is ambiguous. It seems a disagreeable prospect to have to avoid paying attention to sentence structure. But as we shall see, the requisite minimum of attention is secured not by prohibition, but by a firm and involving use of other aspects of language.

The mental processes by which we recognize that a sentence is grammatical are very complex, but no one, I think, would claim that they are conscious. We assume that any utterance is a grammatical sentence, and our awareness of sentence structure needs to become conscious attention only when this expectation is threatened. A deviant usage makes us ask, "Is this sentence really grammatical?" An ambiguity makes us ask, "How is this sentence grammatical?" Except for explicit problems like these, the reader or listener takes his sentence structure as it comes. We can see the difference between conscious attention and unconscious awareness in the following passage from *Hero and Leander*:

> Yet as she went, full often look'd behind,
> And many poore excuses did she find,
> To linger by the way, and once she stayd,
> And would have turn'd againe, but was afrayd,
> In offring parlie, to be counted light.
> So on she goes, and in her idle flight,
> Her painted fanne of curled plumes let fall,
> Thinking to traine Leander therewithall.
>
> (2.5-12)

88

If we make the natural mistake of treating "was afrayd" (line 4) as the completion of a clause, we must consciously restructure the sentence when we discover the complementary infinitive in the next line. But in the last three lines, sentence structure takes care of itself; the participial phrase in the last line in no way makes us question the fact that or the way in which the sentence is grammatical. However, recognizing that a sentence is grammatical is the minimum condition, not the full act, of understanding. A good reading of these lines possibly requires and is certainly facilitated by a conscious attention to sentence structure. There is a great difference between the last line as it stands and the ostensible equivalent, "She thought to traine Leander therewithall." The latter would be simply a knowing remark, set apart from the action. "Thinking" immediately enters the sentence to modify "she," and thus makes us reinterpret "let fall" as an act of volition the moment after we have seen it as an accident. The wit of the line lies in the precision with which the grammatical turn renders our seeing through Hero's helpless little attempt to fool Leander and herself. At every point in the passage conscious attention to sentence structure makes for better reading. To see that lines 3 and 4 are grammatical, we need only read line by line, as we read *The Faerie Queene*. But the lines come to life dramatically when we heed the force of "and," and connect, as a single action, Hero's stopping and her desire to turn.

In *Hero and Leander* the speaking voice structuring a sentence is played off against the formalities of meter, not as a special effect, but as a normal mode of verse that delights. In Spenser's verse, on the other hand, sentence structure is consistently subordinated to the steady progression of lines and the verbal formulas they carry:

> And all that preace did round about her swell,
> To catchen hold of that long chaine, thereby
> To clime aloft, and others to excell:
> That was *Ambition*, rash desire to sty,
> And euery lincke thereof a step of dignity.
>
> (2.7.46)

"Thereby" arouses certain grammatical expectations which are satisfied in the next line, but we should treat this syntactic link in the loosest way. If we pay conscious attention to it, "clime aloft" can have only its physical meaning in the allegorical narrative, whereas taken by itself, it has the force of both narrative action and moral phrase. But not attending to sentence structure cannot be a simply negative action.

89

If it is natural and a sign of poetic strength, then there must be something to which we *are* paying attention. Here and everywhere in Spenser's verse, we pay attention to individual lines and verbal formulas. Instead of looking between the lines at the syntax of "thereby to clime aloft," we look within them at the progression from a formula that renders physical action ("to catchen hold . . .") to one that combines physical and moral phenomena ("to clime aloft") to the purely moral "others to excell." The verse renders not an action, but an allegorical reality—a permanent condition of the human spirit. The sequence of formulas reaches its peak in the naming of Ambition and its definition as "rash desire to sty [ascend]," which exploits elements of all three preceding formulas. For example, the impetuousness suggested by "rash" is indebted to the purely physical "to catchen hold," rather than to the moral formulas.

It is to some extent misleading to speak of Spenser's specialized sense of language. Loose sentence structure, double syntax, and the like are found in much Elizabethan poetry—most notoriously, perhaps, in Shakespeare's sonnets. As a linguistic phenomenon, Spenser's ways with sentence structure should be regarded as a specialized development of characteristics and potentialities that belong to Elizabethan English and Elizabethan verse. But this does not mean that Spenser's underplaying of sentence structure is any the less radical or decisive. The following stanza strikingly justifies our rule that it is not helpful to pay attention to sentence structure in the verse of *The Faerie Queene:*

> All cleane dismayd to see so vncouth sight,
> And halfe enraged at her shamelesse guise,
> He thought haue slaine her in his fierce despight:
> But hasty heat tempring with sufferance wise,
> He stayde his hand, and gan himselfe aduise
> To proue his sense, and tempt her faigned truth.
> Wringing her hands in wemens pitteous wise,
> Tho can she weepe, to stirre vp gentle ruth,
> Both for her noble bloud, and for her tender youth.
>
> (1.1.50)

In lines 5 and 6, it seems unquestionably desirable to heed sentence structure. If we register the syntactic link between "aduise" and its complementary infinitives, the voice will stress the infinitive verbs more than the nouns, and our reading will bring out the Red Cross Knight's dramatic intent—"To *proue* his sense, and *tempt* her faigned

90

truth." But several factors, all characteristic of Spenser's verse, encourage us to read line 6 as an independent unit, with the stress falling about equally on verbs and nouns. First, the inversion in line 4 thwarts dramatic clarity and thrust. We would be more likely to heed the structural force of the verbs in the next two lines if line 4 read: "But tempring hasty heat with sufferance wise." Second, "gan himselfe aduise" need not have a complement (cf. *OED* 5). Finally line 6, with its doubling of the infinitive phrase, fulfills only one syntactic function, so that it is perfectly easy to take in the structure of the sentence by following the path of least resistance. We read the stanza, then, as a normal piece of Spenserian verse, and the question is whether we pay a real price in losing the dramatic intonation of line 6. I think we do not and that Spenser gives us all that the rejected reading does and more. The stanza is devoted not to dramatizing, but to making us see the forces that arise and clash in a spiritual conflict like this. Our suggested rewriting of line 4 would render a single, definitive act of dealing with the passions. Spenser's word order underplays the act of control and more strongly suggests that "hasty heat" and "sufferance wise" are separate forces in the mind, fixed in opposition to each other. The poetic force of the phrase "tempt her faigned truth" comes not from its registering a dramatic intent, but from the fact that it has one meaning for the Red Cross Knight and another for us. While it is a direct reminder to us that this is the false Una, it also expresses the knight's moral indignation—"I will test the faith which (I now see) she pretended to me." The double meaning makes us vividly aware how self-thwarting and helpless the soul can be in such a conflict. Note that we have no difficulty at all in grasping the Red Cross Knight's meaning of "faigned truth." We are conscious of his mind and feelings throughout the stanza, and the first two lines are predominantly from his point of view. But his meaning of "faigned truth" arises as a meaning of the phrase, quite independently of the sentence in which it occurs.

There are dozens of stanzas in *The Faerie Queene* that might legitimately be thought to challenge what we have said, and we cannot examine even a fraction of them here. The next two examples, two consecutive stanzas from the Cave of Mammon canto, seem to require some attention to sentence structure; what we say about them can serve to represent the kind of argument that would be brought against other apparent exceptions to our rules. The first stanza follows the arrival of Guyon and Mammon at Mammon's abode:

So soone as *Mammon* there arriu'd, the dore
To him did open, and affoorded way;
Him followed eke Sir *Guyon* euermore,
Ne darkenesse him, ne daunger might dismay.
Soone as he entred was, the dore streight way
Did shut, and from behind it forth there lept
An vgly feend, more fowle then dismall day,
The which with monstrous stalke behind him stept,
And euer as he went, dew watch vpon him kept.

(2.7.26)

There are three forcible enjambments in this stanza, and the question is whether a right reading of them involves attention to sentence structure. There is no doubt that Spenser is *using* sentence structure here. Lines 1, 5, and 6 each impels us into the next line by introducing a new sentence constituent in the middle of the line and by leaving it syntactically incomplete. But it requires no attention to sentence structure to apprehend that "dore" and "dore streight way" require verbs, and that "forth there lept" requires a subject. Here as elsewhere, Spenser underplays the connections between lines and draws our attention to the lines of verse themselves. We feel the link between the two verbs in line 2 much more strongly than the link between "the dore" and "did open." Our interest here is not so much in what the door does (it can only open or remain shut) as in the nature of a heroic entrance into an evil realm. Spenser is concerned to contrast the formula of line 2, which suggests a willing yielding, with the sense of hostility and terror in the lines that follow. The disparity we feel between lines 2 and 4 leads us into lines 5 and 6, where the enjambments generate real narrative excitement: "forth there lept" forces us on to discover *what* leaped forth. But line 7 then detaches itself from the sentence, and we pay attention to it alone. The verse does not attempt to show us the action rendered by the whole sentence, but rather moves us, by means of consciously melodramatic excitement, from the general formula, "Ne darkenesse him, ne daunger might dismay" to a more concrete and terrifying version of it, "An vgly feend [cf. "daunger"], more fowle then dismall day [cf. "darkenesse"]." The enjambments in this stanza simply intensify our linear progression from line to line. Compare the following lines from *Hero and Leander:*

Therefore unto him hastily she goes,
And like light Salmacis, her body throes
Upon his bosome, where with yeelding eyes,

92

She offers up her selfe a sacrifice,
To slake his anger, if he were displeas'd.

(2.45–49)

There are no enjambments as forceful as those in Spenser's stanza, but as we proceed from line to line, we must retain our grasp of the whole sentence and the relation of its parts. We would seriously misunderstand the last two lines if we did not remember where Hero has thrown and how she is offering herself. Indeed, the wit of the next line —"O what god would not therewith be appeas'd?"—exploits the disparity between the action depicted by the whole sentence and the more solemn suggestions of the last two lines when taken by themselves.

A different problem of sentence structure confronts us in the next stanza:

Well hoped he, ere long that hardy guest,
If euer couetous hand, or lustfull eye,
Or lips he layd on thing, that likt him best,
Or euer sleepe his eye-strings did vntye,
Should be his pray. And therefore still on hye
He ouer him did hold his cruell clawes,
Threatning with greedy gripe to do him dye
And rend in peeces with his rauenous pawes,
If euer he transgrest the fatall *Stygian* lawes.

(2.7.27)

The first five lines are a periodic sentence, but even with a postponed main verb, Spenser makes it easy for us to avoid paying attention to sentence structure. By making lines 2, 3, and 4 a sequence of parallel clauses, he encourages us to entrust the grammatical working out of the sentence to the unfolding of the stanza. Moreover, far from being an essential conclusion to the sentence, "Should be his pray" at first strikes us as the flattest phrase in it. We can see why this is so by considering that if the words followed line 3, they would do no more than fulfill two expectations. As readers of romance we expect such a fate if the hero fails his test, and as readers of allegory we expect that moral failures will be punished in kind: thus "pray" simply confirms what is suggested by "couetous hand, or lustfull eye." But when we read "Should be his pray" not within the structure of a sentence, but in a sequence of lines, we see the poetic life the words have. Coming after "Or euer sleepe his eye-strings did vntye," "pray" surprises us by reintroducing the force of "couetous" and "lustfull"; we realize that in this trial a natural human need is a weakness as potentially disastrous as a moral fault. Merely to be human is a danger here, and the sense of being threatened is developed in the final lines with formulas that expand "pray." The increasing terror in lines 6–8 comes not simply from the increasing energy of the verbs, but also from the moral progression from "cruell" to "greedy" to "rauenous," which increasingly brings out the potential identity of the fiend with the hero who fails. Hence when the alexandrine returns to the "If euer" with which the stanza began, the conditions of the trial impress us as genuinely awesome. The fiend is no longer dependent on the moral error (presumably avoidable) of a "hardy guest"; he has become identified with "the fatall *Stygian* lawes."

Finally we should note that there are some real exceptions to our rules for reading Spenser's verse. The question we must ask of these passages is whether the attention to sentence structure they require arises naturally in the specific poetic context. When it does not, as in the example (1.6.11) discussed above, the verse is faulty.[25] But in other instances, Spenser secures the right kind of attention:

> Thereat the feend his gnashing teeth did grate,
> And grieu'd, so long to lacke his greedy pray;
> For well he weened, that so glorious bayte
> Would tempt his guest, to take thereof assay:
> Had he so doen, he had him snatcht away,
> More light then Culuer in the Faulcons fist.
> Eternall God thee saue from such decay.
> But whenas *Mammon* saw his purpose mist,
> Him to entrap vnwares another way he wist.
>
> (2.7.34)

Following the path of least resistance does not produce the right tone of voice in lines 5 and 6. The awe with which those lines should be said depends on our heeding the syntactic connection between them: the voice must connect "snatcht away" with the adverbial of manner in the next line. But in this case the verse enables us to produce the right intonation by making us feel the incursion of the narrator's speaking voice in line 5. That Spenser wants this effect is shown by the frank emergence of the narrator's voice in "Eternall God thee saue from such decay." That he secures the effect naturally is shown by the

---

[25] Other stanzas that have faults of this sort are 1.6.10 and 2.5.14.

fact that it exploits a basic feature of the stanza—the special opportunity it provides for a poetic choice at the beginning of line 5.

III

The lines and stanzas of *The Faerie Queene* are not conceived as the utterances of a speaker who has a dramatic identity and presence. This fact is apparent not only in Spenser's ways with syntax, but also in his use of individual words and formulas. Consider the following stanza:

> Thus being entred, they behold around
> A large and spacious plaine, on euery side
> Strowed with pleasauns, whose faire grassy ground
> Mantled with greene, and goodly beautifide
> With all the ornaments of *Floraes* pride,
> Wherewith her mother Art, as halfe in scorne
> Of niggard Nature, like a pompous bride
> Did decke her, and too lauishly adorne,
> When forth from virgin bowre she comes in th'early
>   morne. (2.12.50)

In Marvell's "The Mower against Gardens," a poem similar to this stanza in both subject and point, the speaker has a precise dramatic relation to the world of man and the world of nature:

> Luxurious Man, to bring his Vice in use,
> Did after him the World seduce:
> And from the fields the Flow'rs and Plants allure,
> Where Nature was most plain and pure.[26]

But in Spenser's stanza, we cannot imagine that "goodly beautifide" and "too lauishly adorne" are uttered by the same speaker about the same "ornaments." The purpose of the stanza is not to define a dramatic attitude, but to unfold the meanings of the formula at the center of the stanza, "all the ornaments of *Floraes* pride." As we come to it, this line expresses the natural attractiveness of a pastoral landscape. But the next line turns the apparently casual personification of Flora into a decisive one; at the same time, the conventional metaphor in "ornaments" is taken seriously and is made to render a sense of artificial excess. We might argue that these lines make the true meaning of line 5 apparent, were it not for the alexandrine, which again repre-

[26] Andrew Marvell, *Poems and Letters*, ed. H. M. Margoliouth, 2nd edn., Oxford, 1952, 2 vols.

sents "*Floraes* pride" as natural and wholesome. In "The Mower against Gardens," the speaker's tone is often elusive, but we have a fairly definite sense of his mixture of wonder and scorn, and we rightly assume that precise definition of his tone improves our grasp of the poem. But in reading this stanza, it is positively wrong to try to define the tone with which one says, "With all the ornaments of *Floraes* pride." The line includes meanings that would dictate very different tones of voice in a speaker dramatically conceived.

For Spenser the meanings of locutions and formulas are inherent in them, and are as independent of a putative speaker as they are independent of specific dramatic situations within the poem. This sense of language is most directly manifested when Spenser brings to life and puts us in possession of the full meaning of conventional formulas and phrases:

> And oft inclining downe with kisses light,
> For feare of waking him, his lips bedewd,
> And through his humid eyes did sucke his spright,
> Quite molten into lust and pleasure lewd.
>
> (2.12.73)

"Molten into lust" is brought alive by the literal liquidity of "bedewd" and "humid." (It in turn brings out the dissipation of self that both Acrasia and her lover experience—for the last line, in true Spenserian fashion, can refer to either or both of them.) The sense of a moral metaphor can be drawn out by other means than reference to the physical phenomena that underlie it:

> The one [spirit] vpon his hardy head him plast,
> And made him dreame of loues and lustfull play,
> That nigh his manly hart did melt away,
> Bathed in wanton blis and wicked ioy.
>
> (1.1.47)

Here two stock locutions vivify each other. A fuller and more complex instance shows that this is not a casual device, but a basic poetic resource that truly reflects a habit of mind:

> There *Atin* found *Cymochles* soiourning,
> To serue his Lemans loue: for he by kind,
> Was giuen all to lust and loose liuing,
> When euer his fiers hands he free mote find:
> And now he has pourd out his idle mind

96

> In daintie delices, and lauish ioyes,
> Hauing his warlike weapons cast behind,
> And flowes in pleasures, and vaine pleasing toyes,
> Mingled emongst loose Ladies and lasciuious boyes.
>
> (2.5.28)

The stanza is a beautiful illustration of the way Spenser, as W. B. C. Watkins says, "sets up a kind of vibration of interrelated meanings among various seemingly simple, direct statements."[27] The meaning of "loose liuing" is unfolded in a series of formulas and conventional phrases, so that even in a sequence of which Spenser was obviously conscious—"pourd out his idle mind," "flowes in pleasures," and "Mingled emongst loose Ladies"—we feel that the connected meanings lie in the phrases themselves, and are not produced or joined together by the will or wit of the poet.

Our relation to the language of *The Faerie Queene* is illustrated by so many of the passages analyzed elsewhere that we need not now examine any more stanzas like those that have been quoted. What we should recognize here is that the treatment of poetic language as if meanings were inherent in it pervades the verse of *The Faerie Queene*. It underlies the most intimate verbal details, as well as those passages in which we consciously attend to the full meaning of words. Watkins has a fine discussion of such a detail:

> Sensitivity to sound values is so instinctive in Spenser that some of his effects which we have been taught to explain by such devices as alliteration, assonance, internal rhyme rather seem to develop meaning through sound relationships, just as in the process of creation selection of imagery at the start seems to beget subsequent images and in part control the development of the poem. For example:

> > Sleepe after toyle, port after stormie *seas,*
> > *Ease* after warre, death after life does greatly
> > *please.*
> >
> > (*Faerie Queene,* 1.9.40)

And in *Richard II.,* the Shakespearean play nearest to Spenser as well as to Marlowe, we find not only similar structural balance, but also this special sound relationship, which cannot be satisfactorily explained either by "internal rhyme" or "pun":

[27] *Shakespeare and Spenser,* p. 284.

> But whate'er I be,
> Nor I nor any man that but man is
> With nothing shall be pleased, till he be *eased*
> With being nothing.

(*Richard II*, 5.5.38–41)

Here the rhyme really represents a common element of meaning in the two words. Even here Shakespeare makes Spenser's simple statement (ease does please) sharper and more causal (nothing doth please *till* ease); the intellectual, soon to precipitate metaphysical wit, enters.[28]

The comparison with Shakespeare shows that in *The Faerie Queene* the common element of meaning seems really to be in the words, independent of a dramatically conceived speaker.

The best study of Spenser's sense of language and its manifestation in his verse is unfortunately not in print—Martha Craig's doctoral dissertation, "Language and Concept in the *Faerie Queene*."[29] Miss Craig analyzes the most notorious oddities of Spenser's style—the elaborate sound patterns and the profusion of archaisms, neologisms, and etymologies—in the light of Plato's *Cratylus,* as it was read by Renaissance Platonists. The dialogue proposes an ideally rational language, in which words, even down to individual sounds, are not merely conventional, but correspond to the realities they name. In such a language etymologies are true philosophical propositions, similarities in sound indicate similarities of meaning, and old words or old forms of words are often truer because they have been less corrupted in the course of time. Miss Craig treats the *Cratylus* not as the source of Spenser's style, but as a statement of the rationale of its most idiosyncratic features.[30] She gives, in effect, a philosophic account of both the interest and the prevalence of the kind of detail noticed by Watkins, and she shows these details at work in the texture of Spenser's verse. She is persuasive and illuminating even on alliteration and assonance, the dreariest commonplaces of Spenserian criticism:

> In the moral commentary, the implicit reasoning of the sound-play changes assertion into argument.

---

[28] *Ibid.*, p. 286.

[29] Yale, 1959. See Miss Craig's "The Secret Wit of Spenser's Language," an essay based on her dissertation, in *Elizabethan Poetry: Modern Essays in Criticism*, ed. Paul J. Alpers, New York, 1967, pp. 447–472.

[30] For evidence that Spenser would have known the *Cratylus* as an authoritative treatise on language, see Craig, "The Secret Wit of Spenser's Language," *Elizabethan Poetry*, pp. 449, 468.

For *miserie* craues rather *mercie,* then repriefe.

(3.8.1)

As for loose loues are *vaine,* and *vanish* into nought.

(1.10.62)

No greater shame to *man* then *inhumanitie.*

(6.1.26)

... Despair uses such sound-play for a neatly specious argument:

Or let him die at *ease,* that liueth here *vneath.*

(1.9.38)

Meliboe argues in a rather different vein.

It is the mynd, that maketh good or ill,
That maketh *wretch* or happie, *rich* or poore.

(6.9.30)

... Such alliteration may transform an apparent string of common-places into an infinitely fine-wrought web of implicit definition, comparison, contrast, and inference.

But *antique* age yet in the *infancie*
Of time, did liue then like an *innocent,*
In *simple* truth and blamelesse chastitie,
Ne then of *guile* had made experiment,
But *voide* of *vile* and treacherous intent,
Held *vertue* for it selfe in soueraine awe:
Then *loyall* loue had *royall* regiment,
And each vnto his *lust* did make a *lawe,*
From all forbidden things his *liking* to withdraw.

(4.8.30)

... The reticulation of sound and sense in the stanza seems to be infinite.

So both agree their bodies to engraue;
The great earthes wombe they open to the sky,
And with sad Cypresse seemely it embraue,
Then couering with a clod their closed eye,
They lay therein those corses tenderly.

(2.1.60)

The similarity of "a*gree*" and "en*grave*" recalls the reverent acceptance of death by Guyon and the Palmer (2.1.29). . . . . The pronounced resemblance of "en*grave*" to "*great*" singles out to some degree the element of "grave" or "serious" in "engrave" and the rhyme with "embrave" suggests that burial renders death beautiful and perhaps even prepares them for a more beautiful life. The alliteration of "clod" and "closed eye" suggests the motif of "from dust to dust" . . .: we think of the insensitivity of the earth to the plight of Amavia and Mordant, their own inability to be aware of sympathy, and, too, the fact that ultimately there is no real occasion for sympathy.[31]

In our normal reading of Spenser's verse, we are surely not conscious of most of the patterns of sound that Miss Craig points out. Such microscopic analyses are valuable less for telling us how to read than for revealing a feeling for and use of language that explains, better than Lewis himself did, what Lewis called the "density" of *The Faerie Queene:*

> Spenser's style . . . still has in view an audience who have settled down to hear a long story and do not want to savor each line as a separate work of art. Much of *The Faerie Queene* will therefore seem thin or overobvious if judged by modern standards. The "thickness" or "density" which I have claimed for it do not come from its language. They come from its polyphonic narrative, from its different layers of meaning, and from the high degree in which Spenser's symbols embody not simply his own experience, nor that of his characters at a given moment, but the experience of ages.[32]

Everyone knows what Lewis is talking about when he speaks of Spenser's language in this way. But it is impossible to think that, in a poem so conscious of words and their arrangements, "density" comes solely from narrative and symbolic materials, independent of their manifestation in language. If *The Faerie Queene* is not thin, then its language will not be.

Consider a stanza chosen at random from an episode in which, if anywhere, Spenser is simply telling a story—Paridell's wooing of Hellenore behind Malbecco's back:

> And otherwhiles with amorous delights,
> And pleasing toyes he would her entertaine,
> Now singing sweetly, to surprise her sprights,

[31] "Language and Concept," pp. 103–105, 107–108.
[32] "Edmund Spenser, 1552–99," in C. S. Lewis, *Studies in Medieval and Renaissance Literature*, Cambridge, 1966, p. 143.

Now making layes of loue and louers paine,
Bransles, Ballads, virelayes, and verses vaine;
Oft purposes, oft riddles he deuysd,
And thousands like, which flowed in his braine,
With which he fed her fancie, and entysd
To take to his new loue, and leaue her old despysd.

(3.10.8)

The formulaic character of most of the lines is itself no argument against Lewis' view that "much of the *Faerie Queene* is . . . a 'poetry of statement.' The typical Spenserian line tells you what somebody did or wore or where he went."[33] But suppose we inspect the stanza with an eye to the full meaning of words and phrases and to the connections that arise between them. "Amorous delights" is a broad term, suggesting a number of narrative realities; in the stanza itself it generates both "layes of loue" and "his new loue." When it is followed by "pleasing toyes," the apparent redundancy serves—as Miss Craig shows Spenser's redundancies often do—to make a distinction. We now ask what is the relation between the two phrases, and the next two lines work it out. Basically, line 3 goes with "pleasing toyes" and line 4 with "amorous delights," but the pleasure of line 3 captures Hellenore's spirits, while line 4, partly by the suggestions of alliteration, assimilates "louers paine" to song. The jumble of line 5 is thus well justified, but when we come to line 6, we must deal with another redundancy. A "purpose," insofar as it is a "pleasing toy," is almost synonymous with "riddle." For just this reason, "riddles" enforces the broader meanings of "purposes" and the manipulation of words brings out, as Miss Craig would say, a true proposition: these riddles have a purpose, or, to heed the word order, these purposes appear in forms that puzzle and please. The double attention to the lover's intent and the mistress's responsiveness has been prepared for by "entertaine," which means both "to treat in a (specified) manner" and "to engage the attention, thoughts, or time of (a person)."[34] Similarly

---

[33] *English Literature in the Sixteenth Century*, pp. 390–391.

[34] OED 8 and 9. OED assigns these meanings to separate historical branches of the word (III, "to maintain relations with" and IV, "To hold engaged, provide occupation for"). But the examples given suggest that there must have been some overlapping and mutual influence. OED makes it clear that the word had a good deal of fluidity and was rapidly acquiring meanings during Spenser's lifetime. This fact exactly suits our view of Spenser's use of language. We are not meant to see a distinct double meaning in "entertaine," but the word does contain—as it were, holds in solution—two relevant meanings, both of which are developed by the rest of the stanza. One can see the difficulties such an example

the military meaning of "surprise" gives an overtone of purposefulness to the basic meaning, "to overcome the mind or will,"[35] while the emphatic duplication of sound in "surprise her sprights" makes two complementary suggestions: Hellenore's spirits are ready to be "taken over" and Paridell has in fact done so. Lines 7 and 8 make explicit the distinction between the minds of lover and mistress. At the same time, "flowed in his braine" and "fed her fancie" suggest how similar their temperaments are, and the alliteration confirms the connections between the meanings of these phrases. The firmness of the last line comes not simply from the patterned contrast of "his new loue" and "her old," but from the fact that these phrases have double meanings that have been well established by the whole stanza. "His new loue" means "the new love he offers," but it also suggests "her new love of him." The presence of the second meaning is ensured by "her old," which primarily refers to the love she formerly felt, and secondarily to the "old love" proferred by her aged husband. Verse like this is easily taken in, but it is neither thin nor, in a bad sense, obvious. The virtues of this stanza come from the same sense of and skill with language of which we are directly conscious in Spenser's richest and most resonant passages.

The notion that words have meaning and truth in themselves is a natural one, and we need not go to the *Cratylus* for it—just as we find Spenser's sense of language exemplified by all aspects of his verse, not just by the idiosyncrasies to which Miss Craig gives her attention. But we may still wonder how a reader apprehends lines and stanzas that exist "by themselves." We have defined the reader's passivity by saying that he does not enact the role of a dramatized speaker. But what, then, is his role, and what was Spenser's notion of the relation between the reader and the language of his poem? The answer to these questions lies in the rhetorical concept of *enargeia* and the peculiar development of the term in Elizabethan criticism. Tasso uses the term in its traditional sense:

---

presents to the makers of a historical dictionary. A distinct new meaning has not crystallized out, and yet it is there *in posse*. Thus the modern meaning of "entertain," "amuse," is the first one we think of in reading this line, but OED claims that its first occurrence is not until 1626.

[35] OED 1b. The military metaphor becomes explicit two stanzas later and is developed for a whole stanza (3.10.10). The modern sense of "surprise"—"to affect with the characteristic emotion caused by something unexpected" (OED 5) —would be relevant here, but it seems not to have been current in Elizabethan English.

Since style is an instrument with which the poet imitates those things that he has set himself to imitate, it must have *energia,* which with words so places a thing before the eyes of another that he seems not to hear of it, but to see it. And this power is more necessary in epic than in tragedy, because epic does not have the help of actors and stage. This power rises from a scrupulous diligence to describe a thing in detail.[36]

Tasso praises as a virtue in narrative poetry the oratorical power which, according to Quintilian, "makes us seem not so much to narrate *(dicere)* as to exhibit *(ostendere)* the actual scene, while our emotions will be no less actively stirred than if we were present at the actual occurrence."[37]

In Elizabethan criticism, *enargeia* acquires different meanings and applications. Chapman makes it a characteristic of all poetic language:

> That, *Enargia,* or cleerenes of representation, requird in absolute Poems is not the perspicuous deliuery of a lowe inuention; but high, and harty inuention exprest in most significant, and vnaffected phrase; it serues not a skilfull Painters turne, to draw the figure of a face onely to make knowne who it represents; but hee must lymn, giue luster, shaddow, and heightening; which though ignorants will esteeme spic'd, and too curious, yet such as haue the iudiciall perspectiue, will see it hath, motion, spirit and life. . . .
>
> Obscuritie in affection of words, and indigested concets, is pedanticall and childish; but where it shroudeth it selfe in the hart of his subiect, vtterd with fitnes of figure, and expressiue Epethites; with that darknes wil J still labour to be shaddowed.[38]

Chapman's change in the meaning of *enargeia* comes partly from his turning pictorial rendering from an aim of style to a metaphor for its vividness, and partly from conflating *enargeia* with another rhetorical

[36] *Discorsi dell'Arte Poetica,* in Torquato Tasso, *Prose diverse,* ed. Cesare Guasti, Florence, 1875, 1, 56–57. In the expanded version of these discourses, the *Discorsi del Poema Eroico,* Tasso included onomatopoetic effects under *energia.* But the principle of accurately rendering sensory phenomena remains the same.

[37] *Institutio Oratoria,* tr. H. E. Butler, London: Loeb Classical Library, 1920–1922, 4 vols., 6.2.32. The pictorial and mimetic nature of *enargeia* is especially evident in Quintilian's later discussion, *Inst. Orat.* 8.3.61–71.

[38] Preface to *Ovid's Banquet of Sense,* in *The Poems of George Chapman,* ed. Phyllis Brooks Bartlett, New York, 1941, p. 49.

term, *energeia,* "which derives its name from action and finds its pe-
culiar function in securing that nothing we say is tame (*otiosa*)."[39]
Italian critics of the sixteenth century consistently interpret *energeia*
as the rendering of visual experience, because as theoreticians they
were concerned with the problem of imitation and as practical critics
with narrative poetry.[40] But Chapman, writing in a less strict and co-
herent tradition, turns *enargeia* from a single mimetic technique into
a general attribute of style. Similarly Puttenham uses *enargeia* and
energeia to provide a basic classification of all poetic figures:

> This ornament then is of two sortes, one to satisfie and delight
> th'eare onely by a goodly outward shew set vpon the matter with
> wordes, and speaches smothly and tunably running: another by cer-
> taine intendments or sence of such wordes and speaches inwardly
> working a stirre to the mynde: that first qualitie the Greeks called
> *Enargia,* of this word *argos,* because it geueth a glorious lustre and
> light. This latter they called *Energia* of *ergon,* because it wrought
> with a strong and vertuous operation; and figure breedeth them
> both, some seruing to giue glosse onely to a language, some to geue
> it efficacie by sence, and so by that meanes some of them serue
> th'eare onely, some serue the conceit onely and not th'eare: there
> be of them also that serue both turnes as common seruitours ap-
> pointed for th'one and th'other purpose. . . . Ornament is but the
> good or rather bewtifull habite of language and stile, and figuratiue
> speaches the instrument wherewith we burnish our language fash-
> ioning it to this or that measure and proportion, whence finally re-
> sulteth a long and continuall phrase or maner of writing or speach,
> which we call by the name of *stile.*[41]

[39] Quintilian, *Institutio Oratoria* 8.3.89.

[40] There is a quite full account of the concept of *enargeia* in Italian criticism
in Baxter Hathaway, *The Age of Criticism,* Ithaca, 1961, pp. 9–22, *et passim.*
See also Rosemond Tuve, *Elizabethan and Metaphysical Imagery,* Chicago,
1947, pp. 29–32. Miss Tuve's discussion concerns broad questions of "illumi-
nation" and "clarity" in poetry; she does not attempt to work out, as the
Italian critics discussed by Hathaway do, the specific meanings and implications
of *enargeia* narrowly defined.

[41] *The Arte of English Poesie,* ed. Gladys Doidge Willcock and Alice Walker,
Cambridge, 1936, pp. 142–143. Puttenham's use of the terms *enargeia* and
energeia is, to my knowledge, unexampled. But I would like to warn the reader
that the history of the terms and the relation between them is more complex
than is indicated by my brief sketch, the purpose of which is simply to indicate
the contrast between Italian and English uses of *enargeia* in the sixteenth cen-
tury. The complications in the classical sources (e.g. Aristotle, *Rhetoric* 3.11)
are compounded by the fact that the vernacular words *energia, énergie,* and
energy can be used for either term. Cf. Joachim Du Bellay, *La Deffence et*

Both Puttenham and Chapman are attempting to unite two aspects of poetry that all readers feel and that any critical theory seeks to explain—the feelings of sensory immediacy, on the one hand, and of cognitive clarity, on the other. Their use of the term *enargeia* is important for two reasons. First it assumes that visual experience is a model for our apprehension of poetry—a notion that is so widespread as to seem almost instinctive and that is enshrined in two great catchwords of European criticism, "speaking picture" and "ut pictura poesis." Second, the different meanings of *enargeia* in Italy and England exactly correspond to the difference, in narrative poetry, between the mimetic pictorialism of Dante, Ariosto, and Tasso, and Spenser's rhetorical use of pictorial diction and detail. Neither Puttenham nor Chapman provides a description of Spenser's style, but they do justify our invoking a broad notion of *enargeia* to explain both the immediacy and the passivity with which we apprehend words and formulas in Spenser's verse:

> And she her selfe of beautie soueraigne Queene,
> Faire *Venus* seemde vnto his bed to bring
> Her, whom he waking euermore did weene,
> To be the chastest flowre, that ay did spring
> On earthly braunch, the daughter of a king,
> Now a loose Leman to vile seruice bound:
> And eke the *Graces* seemed all to sing,
> *Hymen iō Hymen*, dauncing all around,
> Whilst freshest *Flora* her with Yuie girlond crownd.
>
> (1.1.48)

Spenser's poetry would be impossible without the assumption that the phrases "of beautie soueraigne Queene," "chastest flowre," "the daughter of a king," "a loose Leman," and "to vile seruice bound" have equivalent reality. The immediacy and obviousness of each of these formulas exemplify *enargeia* in the broad sense. But this stanza makes the notion explicit, in a sense acts it out, by concluding with a vividly pictorial line that fuses together the motifs of eroticism, naturalness, and sovereignty. Spenser's pictorialism has usually been misunderstood, but it would be surprising if so persistently noticed a phe-

---

Illustration de la Langue Françoyse, ed. Henri Chamard, Paris, 1948, p. 35. Furthermore, the use of these words in literary discourse can be influenced by nonliterary meanings. On *enargeia* see Neil Rudenstine, *Sidney's Poetic Development*, Cambridge, Mass., 1967.

nomenon did not reveal an important truth about his poetry. The notion of *enargeia,* together with our accounts of Spenser's sense of syntax and of meaning, explains why Spenser's verse strikes us today as it did Sir Kenelm Digby three centuries ago:

> Spencer in what he sayth hath a way of expression peculiar to himselfe; he bringeth downe the highest and deepest mysteries that are contained in humane learning, to an easie and gentle forme of delivery; which sheweth he is Master of what he treateth of; he can wield it as he pleaseth: And he hath done this so cunningly, that if one heede him not with great attention, rare and wonderful conceptions will unperceived slide by him that readeth his workes, and he will thinke he hath mett with nothing but familiar and easie discourses: But lett one dwell a while upon them, and he shall feele a strange fulness and roundness in all he sayth.[42]

[42] "A Discourse concerning Edmund Spencer," in E. W. Bligh, *Sir Kenelm Digby and His Venetia*, London, 1932, p. 279; quoted by Craig, "The Secret Wit of Spenser's Language," p. 467.

Chapter Four

The Problem of Structure
in *The Faerie Queene*

In recent studies of *The Faerie Queene,* structure has received more attention than any other critical problem. Yet how true or relevant to our reading is the attempt to describe underlying structures in the poem? Hallett Smith remarks that "we must often stand back from the picture and view it from a distance. The details are so lovely, or so curious, that they sometimes absorb our attention at the expense of the larger outline and meaning of the design."[1] But why should we stand back from the poem? Is not Spenser's "larger outline," the schematic organization of *The Faerie Queene,* the aspect of the poem that is easiest to apprehend and that most takes care of itself as we are reading? Is not Spenser's verse most involving, complex, and illuminating precisely when we are paying attention to its details? The search for structure in *The Faerie Queene* has faced us in the wrong direction, and made us regard our own theories and interpretations rather than the poem itself. This chapter presents two main arguments. First, the books of *The Faerie Queene,* much less the poem as a whole, do not have structures in the ordinary sense of the word; we should stop using the word "structure" and instead speak of the *organization* of cantos, books, and the whole poem. Second, the basic large unit in *The Faerie Queene* is the canto, not the book. (Consider that one can read independently and assign to students, say, the House of Holiness or the Cave of Mammon, as opposed to a canto of the *Divine Comedy* or a book of *Paradise Lost,* or an act of a play by Shakespeare.) The rule for reading that I shall try to establish is that we observe and remember the canto we are reading in much more detail than we retain other cantos and books.

An interest in structure in *The Faerie Queene* is at odds, as Smith's remark suggests, with the way one naturally reads it. The canceled Letter to Raleigh may tempt us to hunt for structure, but it is the natural way of reading that is encouraged and confirmed by Spenser's conduct of his poem and the way he speaks of it. Consider Spenser's

[1] *Elizabethan Poetry*, Cambridge, Mass., 1952, p. 335.

metaphors for himself and his endeavor—the explorer (2.Proem), the mariner (1.12.1, 42), the plowman (3.12.47, orig.; 6.9.1), the traveler through Fairyland (6.Proem.1): traveling and being in motion are essential to each of these roles. It is true that each implies a goal to be reached, but Spenser rarely even speaks of the goal, much less depicts it as attained. The last canto of Book I begins, "Behold I see the hauen nigh at hand," but the haven is a port of call, not the home port (1.12.1); the canto concludes with the poet-mariner readying his ship for "the long voyage whereto she is bent" (1.12.42). Or consider the opening of Book VI, canto 12—the last canto of *The Faerie Queene* in the edition of 1596, which was the final version of the poem that Spenser himself prepared for his readers:

> Like as a ship, that through the Ocean wyde
> Directs her course vnto one certaine cost,
> Is met of many a counter winde and tyde,
> With which her winged speed is let and crost,
> And she her selfe in stormie surges tost;
> Yet making many a borde, and many a bay,
> Still winneth way, ne hath her compasse lost:
> Right so it fares with me in this long way,
> Whose course is often stayd, yet neuer is astray.
>
> (6.12.1)

The last canto of *Orlando Furioso* begins with the metaphor of the poet-mariner sighting the home port (46.1). But in Spenser's stanza the goal itself has almost nothing to do with the sense of accomplishment in the metaphoric voyage. The satisfactions suggested by "Still winneth way" and "yet neuer is astray" lie in the felt quality of a present activity, not in the hope of reaching a final destination. Similarly, in the proem to Book II, Spenser uses his metaphor to render a quality of the activity of exploring. The sense of wonder and receptivity through which he asserts the truth of his poem is nourished by the possibility that new discoveries may occur, but it does not depend on assurances that they will. In the proem to Book VI, the delightful variety of Fairyland makes the poet forget his "tedious trauell": "And when I gin to feele decay of might, / It strength to me supplies, and chears my dulled spright" (6.Proem.1).

The Faerie Queene continually moves ahead, never ceasing to produce and examine moral and psychological realities. Even at the ends of the individual books, the poem does not come to a stop. This is immediately evident in the endings of Books I, III, V, and VI. The

Red Cross Knight returns to the Fairy Queen and leaves Una to mourn his absence; Britomart and Amoret emerge from the House of Busyrane to find Scudamour and Glauce gone; Artegall must endure the assaults of Envy, Detraction, and the Blatant Beast as he makes his way back to the court of the Fairy Queen. We may remember the endings of Books II and IV and the original ending of Book III as full stops in the poem, but none of them are. When Scudamour and Amoret embrace, Britomart envies their happiness; but "In vaine she wisht, that fate n'ould let her yet possesse" (3.12.46 orig.). In the next stanza, the last of the canto, the poet speaks of himself as a plowman who takes off the "sweatie yokes" of his team "till a new day" (3.12.47 orig.). Book IV ends happily, but it pointedly renders the incipient stages, and not the completion, of the union of Florimell and Marinell (cf. 4.12.34–35). Even Book II ends with a sense of continuing, rather than concluded action: "Let *Grill* be *Grill,* and haue his hogg'sh mind, / But let vs hence depart, whilest wether serues and wind" (2.12.87).

Spenser maintains the forward movement of his poem by linking the contiguous books. His most familiar means of doing this (it occurs in Books II, III, and VI) is to bring the hero of one book into the first canto of the next in order to send the new hero off on his adventures. The most interesting of the links between two books is that between Books III and IV. Our assessment of the connection between these books strongly influences our interpretation of them, and discussing the problem will bring out more clearly some of the issues we are considering. It has become habitual for critics to explain Amoret's captivity in Book III by what is revealed in Book IV about her wedding and her education in the Temple of Venus. It is assumed that events narrated in Book IV must be explanations of those in Book III simply because they are prior to them in fictional time. Graham Hough's interpretation is typical:

> It is on her wedding-day "before the bride was bedded" (4.1.3) that Amoret was stolen away from Scudamour by Busirane. Busirane has never cherished any designs on Amoret before; in the image-sequence this appears as an uncaused, inconsequential calamity. Thematically it means that *because* of the wedding she was stolen away; it is *because* their consummation is so much desired and is so close that the lady is tortured and her lover frustrated by the perverse cruelty of amour-passion.[2]

[2] *A Preface to "The Faerie Queene,"* London, 1962, p. 136.

But to explain Amoret's torment by the fact that she was abducted at her wedding feast means that for six years Spenser let Book III stand without providing an essential piece of information for understanding its climactic episode. He was even willing to give the lie, as it were, to the episode, by bringing the two lovers together in a rapturously happy ending. Since Spenser does not mention the abduction from the marriage feast in the Letter to Raleigh (Scudamour seems to be at the court of the Fairy Queen when the news of Amoret's captivity arrives), it is altogether likely that he did not have this event in mind when he first published Book III in 1590. Obviously he thought Book III was intelligible by itself.

When Spenser revised the ending of Book III to keep Amoret and Scudamour apart, he gave himself the opportunity not of providing explanations for Book III, but of exploring the new, though related, issues of Book IV. Let us look at the stanza in Book IV that is supposed to tell us so much about Amoret's torture at the hands of Busyrane:

> For that same vile Enchauntour *Busyran,*
> The very selfe same day that she was wedded,
> Amidst the bridale feast, whilest euery man
> Surcharg'd with wine, were heedlesse and ill hedded,
> All bent to mirth before the bride was bedded,
> Brought in that mask of loue which late was showen:
> And there the Ladie ill of friends bestedded,
> By way of sport, as oft in maskes is knowen,
> Conueyed quite away to liuing wight vnknowen.
>
> (4.1.3)

Critics who treat this stanza as an explanation of Amoret's torture speak of erotic fearfulness and distress—terms that are appropriate to the House of Busyrane. But Spenser's emphasis here is on all that is suggested by the phrase "ill of friends bestedded." Amoret's abduction is due to some failure in friendship, the ties that unite all good men and women to each other, and if there is any inadequacy of erotic feeling, it lies in the (presumably male) heedlessness that allows Amoret to be carried away. It is perfectly appropriate for a masque to conclude by incorporating the person honored into itself.[3] Spenser's concern here is that men can accept something sinister "by way of sport" and as a way of paying joyful honor to a lady. Even the

[3] See Stephen Orgel, *The Jonsonian Masque*, Cambridge, Mass., 1965, pp. 6–7.

110

phrase "before the bride was bedded"—the cornerstone of all analyses of Amoret's erotic torments—is misrepresented by its usual interpretation. What it suggests is a kind of cynical bawdy on the part of the men. Any unhealthy dwelling on the imminent loss of Amoret's maidenhead surely is part of their "mirth," and not a function of the virgin's fears, at which the stanza does not even hint. "True is, that true loue hath no powre / To looken backe; his eyes be fixt before," Spenser says (1.3.30), and the same can be said of the reader of *The Faerie Queene*. This stanza has very little to do with Book III. But it is a fine introduction to a book in which Spenser will repeatedly examine the experience and claims of friendship—the common bond between all men—and their relation to qualities of erotic feeling and the claims of erotic love—an exclusive relationship between two people.

II

The word "structure" is used so complexly and variously in modern criticism, not to mention other areas of thought, that we cannot hope to give a full definition of it. But I think we can specify what the concept means when it is applied to *The Faerie Queene,* and we can at least identify notions of structure that mislead critics of the poem. A. C. Hamilton's *The Structure of Allegory in "The Faerie Queene"* invokes a metaphor that tells us a great deal about what "structure" means to a critic:

> We may expect to find in *The Faerie Queene* an Idea or argument which unifies the whole poem, and in terms of which, as Sidney claims, the poet's skill is to be judged: "any vnderstanding knoweth the skil of the Artificer standeth in that *Idea* or fore-conceite of the work, and not in the work it selfe." That a poet should plan his poem before writing was common practice sanctioned at least as far back as Geoffrie de Vinsauf:
>
> > The hand that seeks a proper house to raise
> > Turns to the task with care; the measured line
> > Of th'inmost heart lays out the work to do,
> > The order is prescribed by the inner man,
> > The mind sees all before a stone is laid,
> > Prepares an archetype . . .
> > So in the poet's secret mind the plan
> > Unwitting grows, and only when 'tis grown
> > Comes poetry to deck the frame with words.[4]

---

[4] Oxford, 1961, p. 50.

The important analogy here is between the frame of a building and some organizing reality in a poem. Like the skeleton in a vertebrate's body, the frame of a building is an independent, rigid construction, not identical with what it inhabits, but essential to its existence. When we speak of the structure of *The Faerie Queene,* we have in mind not only that the poem has some overall organization, but also that the concrete expression of this organization is essential to the existence and coherence of the poem. We can observe that the architectural metaphor makes the minimum claim for structure as essential to a poem. The frame of a building is readily separable from what surrounds it, whereas other metaphors, for example the analogy between poem and world, suggest an organic relationship in which the structure becomes inseparably part of the reality of each detail.

Anyone can see that *The Faerie Queene* is organized in various ways and that Spenser disposed his materials in accordance not only with the titular virtues of the books, but also with such intellectual schemes as the Platonic division of passions into irascible and concupiscent (in Book II), and with such traditional poetic contrasts (which we can regard as both formal and thematic) as that between heroic activity and pastoral retreat. But to continue our architectural metaphor, all the planning and organization is comparable only to a scaffolding—essential to the making of a building, but not to its existence, for it disappears when the building is erected. The concept of structure requires that there be an identifiable reality within the poem that gives it its coherence and indeed its being. This claim, which is also an initial assumption, has nothing to do with the plausibility of the specific analysis offered. It is as present in old-fashioned ideas of plot—according to which only Books I and II have real structures—as it is in the notions of mythic structure that are now so much in favor, and it is no less present in more esoteric theories, like the numerological structure proposed by Alastair Fowler.[5]

I think it is impossible to argue in the abstract that the books of *The Faerie Queene* have no structures. The only way to make the general case is to appeal to the common reader's experience with the poem—the intense absorption in details of the moment, the even progression from line to line and stanza to stanza, the difficulty in remembering details of earlier cantos and books. Otherwise one can only attempt to show that specific structural analyses are not convincing —a tedious and ungrateful task, since to show that Fowler distorts his

[5] *Spenser and the Numbers of Time*, London, 1964.

numerological evidence does not in itself disprove Hamilton's argument that Book I is a five-act tragedy. I propose to argue that neither Book I nor Book II has a plot in the Aristotelian sense—what Tasso called a fable—and that Book IV does not have the kind of "structure of imagery" (in Northrop Frye's phrase) that has been claimed for it. The structures I am disputing are important and familiar enough that disproving their existence should sufficiently indicate the truth of a general position that can be proved only by exhaustive, case by case analysis. Throughout this argument I try to show that Spenser depends on the reader to see and make connections that are not made by any phenomena within the poem. Of course everything we see in the poem and learn from it is caused by it, and what the poem is includes the ordering and disposition of its parts. In *The Faerie Queene* sequence and juxtaposition (of stanzas, passages, episodes, cantos) are of particular importance. But the word to use for Spenser's kind of ordering is "organization," not "structure." "Organization" suggests purposefulness on the poet's part, and it sufficiently indicates that the order in which the parts of the poem are presented to us and the emphases they are given are essential to the meaning of the poem. The word only denies the crucial element in the concept of structure—that the ordering and evaluating of the realities the poem presents is done by one or several specifiable phenomena within it.[6]

It is reasonable to think that there is a plot or fable in Books I and II, because in each of them the knight's quest appears to be of genuine importance. Yet one can hardly claim that the informing reality of Book II is the mission to destroy Acrasia. The feeling that she is the enemy of all knights more or less disappears after canto 1; when Guyon sets out for the Bower of Bliss, the enemies of knighthood who most impress us are Mammon and Maleger. By contrast, the source of Guyon's invasion of the Bower of Bliss—the mission of Carlo and Ubaldo to rescue Rinaldo from Armida (*Gerusalemme Liberata*, cantos 14–16)—is an action developed over three cantos and with an essential relation to the main action of the poem. Until Rinaldo, who is Goffredo's chief lieutenant, returns to the Christian army, the siege of Jerusalem cannot succeed; Rinaldo must therefore be brought to his moral senses so that he will leave the enchantress' garden of pleasure and resume his proper role. Guyon's stated aim is to avenge the

[6] For a view similar to the one taken here, see the discussion of the importance of sequence in *The Faerie Queene* in Roger Sale, "Spenser's Undramatic Poetry," in *Elizabethan Poetry: Modern Essays in Criticism*, ed. Paul J. Alpers, New York, 1967, pp. 422–433.

deaths of Mortdant and Amavia (2.1.61), but when he captures Acrasia, he sets free Verdant, who is simply a representative young knight, about whom we have heard nothing before. This makes perfect sense—Acrasia is kept from destroying another budding hero, as she destroyed Mortdant—but Spenser is certainly not executing a plot such as Tasso described in his criticism or created in his epic poem.

When we think of the last six cantos of Book II, we remember not a developing action, but six separate episodes, each with a decided character of its own in both subject matter and manner. It is surely notable that while cantos 9, 10 and 11 all take place at Alma's Castle, we remember them not as one continuous episode, but as three discrete units—the allegorical survey of the body, the British histories, and the battle with Maleger and his crew. The idea that Alma prepares Guyon to defeat Acrasia may have been the scaffolding for these three cantos, but it certainly does not give them a structure. (Compare *Gerusalemme Liberata*, 14.49ff., where the two warriors sent to find Rinaldo are told about Armida and given instructions for resisting her temptations.) The function of each of these cantos, as of those that precede and follow them, is to reveal specific aspects or create new understanding of temperance seen as a heroic virtue.

Even if we leave aside questions of plot or developing action, we cannot see any consecutive, structured development from one of these cantos to the next. This is best seen by examining the change from canto 8 to canto 11. These two cantos have important similarities: in both, Arthur fights enemies of temperance, in both he is hard pressed and needs the help of weaker beings, and in both Spenser uses the psychomachia, or something resembling it, not so much to show the workings of temperance within the soul, as to make a point about the nature and limits of temperance as a psychological and moral strength. The main difference between the episodes is that canto 11, Arthur's battle with Maleger, is more drastic in its expression of human frailty and more decisive in indicating the dependence of human virtue on God's grace—as if the famous stanzas about God's care for wicked man (2.8.1–2) were turned from the introduction to the foundation of an episode. One would assume that cantos 9 and 10 would tell us something important about the difference between these cantos—that we would be able to trace some development through these cantos, or at least say why what we learn in them changes our sense of human strength. Yet although canto 10 pays much attention to the uncertainties and bloodiness of human history, it does not provide anything essential to our understanding of canto 11. The imperfection and mutability of human history does not necessarily imply the frailty of the hero in his individual moral combats. However, both awarenesses are included in a general Christian sense of man's imperfections. The two cantos are parallel developments from this common center of understanding; it is not the case, as we might have expected, that canto 11 begins where canto 10 leaves off. Indeed Spenser explicitly rounds off canto 10 and makes it complete in itself. The bulk of the canto consists of the British histories that Arthur reads, but it concludes with the Elfin history read by Guyon (2.10.70–76). In it we learn of the descendants of Elfe and Fay, who are an unfallen Adam and Eve. There is no question that we are to take this mythical history seriously as an expression of human possibilities: the last in line of descent from the innocent pair is Gloriana, the Fairy Queen. The presence of this concluding passage makes it quite clear that Spenser's interest is in the ostensible subject of the canto—the nature of human history— and not in preparing for later cantos which can be thought to develop or subsume this one. The alternative perspective on human history in this passage makes the canto a self-contained unit in a book that is continually concerned with the relation between man's natural strengths and his natural frailties.

To say it again, absence of structure does not mean absence of organization and poetic purpose. We surely assent to the claim, which begins the last canto of Book II, that the book has been moving ahead to some purpose:

> Now gins this goodly frame of Temperance
> Fairely to rise, and her adorned hed
> To pricke of highest praise forth to aduance,
> Formerly grounded, and fast setteled
> On firme foundation of true bountihed.
>
> (2.12.1)

But to what do these lines refer? Clearly not to a developing action: we hear of "this frame of Temperance," presumably the poem itself, not of an action or a hero. Even in the light of line 3, we do not want to limit the "firme foundation of true bountihed" to what Guyon himself has seen and undergone in the preceding cantos. Moreover, Arthur's battle with Maleger—which, when we think of the narrative scaffolding, may seem to prepare for Guyon's conquest of Acrasia— provides no dramatic justification for "Formerly grounded, and fast setteled." Everyone remembers the fierceness with which the senses

115

assault the castle, the ghastly tenacity that makes Maleger so just an embodiment of original sin, and the fact that Arthur is baffled, hard pressed, and at one point close to defeat. But even after Arthur's victory, Spenser describes him as enfeebled: in the last two stanzas of the canto, he must be helped to his horse by his squire, and Alma puts him to bed to dress his wounds (2.11.48–49). What then makes us assent to the opening lines of canto 12, even though we cannot point to any structure, or "goodly frame," within the poem, that begins "fairely to rise"? We feel that the book is drawing to a fit conclusion simply because we have experienced and considered heroic temperance from, apparently, every possible perspective. Each of the preceding five cantos is a massive exploration of the nominal virtue of Book II—its psychological workings, its strengths and limitations, its obligations and dignity. Canto 12, far from completing anything begun and developed in preceding cantos, is itself a separate unit. It begins *ab ovo,* and the opening passages recapitulate the first half of the book. When the boat has safely passed between the Gulf of Greediness and the Rock of Reproach, the Palmer comments in a familiar manner (2.12.9), but one we have not heard since Guyon was separated from him by Phaedria. Five stanzas later the trio encounters Phaedria. Clearly Spenser means this canto—the longest in *The Faerie Queene*—to be not just the conclusion of the book, but, so to speak, a little book in itself. It is, as all the commentators have noted, a miniature version of the *Odyssey*.

Arguments against the existence of a plot in Book I are very much like those made about Book II. Just as Guyon vows to avenge Mortdant and Amavia, so the Red Cross Knight undertakes to aid Fradubio and Fraelissa, the knight and lady transformed into trees by Duessa. They cannot become human again until they are "bathed in a liuing well" (1.2.43)—precisely "that liuing well" (1.11.31) into which the Red Cross Knight falls at the end of his first day's battle with the dragon. But though it makes perfect sense to say that the Red Cross Knight has found the well that will release Fradubio and Fraelissa from their bondage, there is not a trace of this narrative action in the poem. We do not feel that this is an aesthetic objection to Book I, because Spenser clearly means both the terms of Fradubio's captivity and the Red Cross Knight's revival by the Well of Life to indicate man's dependence on grace. But that is just the point: the connection between the two episodes is made by the reader's seeing that they have the same point and not, even when there is every opportunity for it, by the completion of a narrative action.

It would be plausible to argue that the final cantos of Book I show a developing action as the final cantos of Book II do not. The Red Cross Knight's encounter with Despair prompts Una to take him to the House of Holiness, where he is strengthened for his battle with the dragon. But this plot idea, which unquestionably served Spenser as scaffolding for this canto, does not exist in the poem as a structure. When Una strikes Despair's knife from the hand of the Red Cross Knight, she speaks to him in the terms in which we usually think of his quest:

> Fie, fie, faint harted knight,
> What meanest thou by this reprochfull strife?
> Is this the battell, which thou vauntst to fight
> With that fire-mouthed Dragon, horrible and bright?
>
> (1.9.52)

This appeal to the knight's sense of shame is genuinely heroic, because it assumes that the specific obligation he has undertaken has become central to his moral being and profession of worth. This heroic self-consciousness is made compatible with—indeed, it directly produces—the Christian self-awareness to which Una appeals, in exactly the same vein, in the next stanza:

> Come, come away, fraile, feeble, fleshly wight,
> Ne let vaine words bewitch thy manly hart,
> Ne diuelish thoughts dismay thy constant spright.
> In heauenly mercies hast thou not a part?
> Why shouldst thou then despeire, that chosen art?
>
> (1.9.53)

A heroic sense of Christianity is surely what we expect to be strengthened when Una, seeing "that yet he was vnfit for bloudie fight" (1.10.2), takes the knight to the House of Holiness.

But instead of strengthening the identification of the knight's quest with his Christian experience, the episode in the House of Holiness separates them. The human actions that get their sanction there are the corporal works of mercy; the Red Cross Knight's colloquy with Contemplation makes him first want to abandon all earthly ends and later, when the hermit says he must complete his quest, vow to return as quickly as possible and "walke this way in Pilgrims poore estate" (1.10.64). The hermit's praise of Cleopolis (1.10.59) and his account of the knight's taking arms (1.10.66) introduce important complications into the passage itself, but they do not change the main

tendency of the whole canto or even of the episode with the hermit.[7]
At the end of the canto, when the knight is about to descend from the
mountain,

> This said, adowne he looked to the ground,
> To haue returnd, but dazed were his eyne,
> Through passing brightnesse, which did quite confound
> His feeble sence, and too exceeding shyne.
> So darke are earthly things compard to things diuine.
>
> (1.10.67)

There is unquestionably a feeling of spiritual strength in the gravity of
the last line. But that this strength is not here expressed by heroic
endeavor is made clear by the remarkably low-pitched terms of the
call to action and departure in the last stanza of the canto:

> So came to *Vna,* who him ioyd to see,
> And after litle rest, gan him desire,
> Of her aduenture mindfull for to bee.
> So leaue they take of *Coelia,* and her daughters three.
>
> (1.10.68)

Yet for all the apparent contradictions introduced by canto 10,
Spenser's intention in it seems perfectly clear. The Red Cross Knight
falls into the clutches of Despair because he has a naive confidence in
his own strength, and takes Sir Trevisan's story as a direct challenge
to his own moral resources (1.9.32). The House of Holiness is a
preparation for the slaying of the dragon, because it shows us that
man's strength depends precisely on rejecting the idea that he has
strengths of his own and on recognizing his frailty and dependence
on God. This paradox, a Christian commonplace, underlies our sense
of the knight's strength in his battle with the dragon—particularly at
the crucial moments when he falls into the Well of Life (1.11.28–36)
and under the Tree of Life (1.11.45–52). What interests us here is
that when we come to canto 11, Spenser simply assumes we are in
possession of the paradox. It is not a lesson that the knight himself
learns, and nothing in canto 10—neither the knight's sense of him-
self, nor what anyone tells him, nor the representation of his quest
—expresses it. In praising Cleopolis and then scorning earthly glory
(1.10.59–60), the hermit gives us the elements of the paradox, but
he himself does not attempt to state it. Nor does Spenser try to ex-
press it by his management of the passage as a whole. In canto 11, we

---

[7] For fuller discussion of this episode, see below, pp. 347–349.

feel that dependence on God produces something distinctly like heroic strength, but the conclusion of canto 10 does not at all prepare us for the terms or the spirit in which Una will address the knight before he goes into battle:

> The sparke of noble courage now awake,
> And striue your excellent selfe to excell;
> That shall ye euermore renowmed make,
> Aboue all knights on earth, that batteill vndertake.
>
> (1.11.2)

Canto 10 is as independent a unit as any of the final cantos of Book II, and Spenser is perfectly content to develop it on its own terms. This means, for example, treating the seven corporal works of mercy and the life of contemplation as the most important expressions of a Christian life. When Spenser returns to heroic knighthood as the expression of a Christian life, he is entirely untroubled by possible contradictions—he even feels free to introduce into canto 12 a vow that contradicts the vow made to the hermit—and he assumes that we will make the necessary shifts in terms and attitudes. Just as in every other book of *The Faerie Queene,* he trusts the reader to see the relation and coherence of the points made and the attitudes expressed by the various parts of the poem. His confidence here is justified first by the availability of the paradox that Christian humility is strength, but also by the way this paradox is supported by some loosely held equations. For one thing, we are meant to feel that the knight gains moral strength, and in canto 11 there is a tacit agreement to equate this with martial strength. Moreover, there is a general sense in which any poem that gives us an understanding of man becomes, by our very absorbing it as readers, a source of spiritual strength. It is probably this feeling that enables us to accept the knight's growth in Christian understanding as a recovery of martial prowess, despite the main tendency of what the hermit says.

Books III and IV have traditionally been regarded as without structure, "merely episodic," because manifestly neither has a plot. However recent criticism has treated imagery (or alternatively, "myth") as a structuring reality in these books. But consider what happens when Northrop Frye—whose influence is present in many of these interpretations—attempts to explain the ending of Book IV:

> Painful or not, it is love that makes the world go round, that
> keeps the cycle of nature turning, and it is particularly the love of

Marinell and Florimell, whose names suggest water and vegetation, that seems linked to the natural cycle. Florimell is imprisoned under the sea during a kind of symbolic winter in which a "snowy" Florimell takes her place. Marinell is not cured of his illness until his mother turns from "watry gods" to the sun, and when he sees Florimell he revives

> As withered weed through cruell winters tine,
> That feeles the warmth of sunny beames reflection,
> Liftes vp his head, that did before decline
> And gins to spread his leafe before the faire
> sunshine   (4.12.34)[8]

Here, as elsewhere in his criticism, one feels that this is the poem as Frye would have written it; it is certainly not the poem that Spenser wrote. There is no evidence that Florimell's imprisonment is a symbolic winter. Spenser's interest is in what it conveys about the situation and suffering of a human lover. Hence its major metaphoric development comes at the end of Florimell's love complaint, when she addresses the sea gods:

> But if that life ye vnto me decree,
> Then let mee liue, as louers ought to do,
> And of my lifes deare loue beloued be:
> And if he shall through pride your doome vndo,
> Do you by duresse him compell thereto,
> And in this prison put him here with me:
> One prison fittest is to hold vs two:
> So had I rather to be thrall, then free;
> Such thraldome or such freedome let it surely be.
>
> But O vaine iudgement, and conditions vaine,
> The which the prisoner points vnto the free,
> The whiles I him condemne, and deeme his paine,
> He where he list goes loose, and laughes at me.
> So euer loose, so euer happy be.
> But where so loose or happy that thou art,
> Know *Marinell* that all this is for thee.
> With that she wept and wail'd, as if her hart
> Would quite haue burst through great abundance
> of her smart.   (4.12.10–11)

[8] "The Structure of Imagery in *The Faerie Queene*," in *Fables of Identity*, New York, 1963, p. 83.

It is hearing his name uttered that makes Marinell love Florimell; the forces of external nature have nothing whatever to do with it:

> All which complaint when *Marinell* had heard,
> And vnderstood the cause of all her care
> To come of him, for vsing her so hard,
> His stubborne heart, that neuer felt misfare
> Was toucht with soft remorse and pitty rare.
>
> (4.12.12)

In the next stanza, Spenser describes how Cupid, "Dame *Venus* sonne that tameth stubborne youth," masters Marinell and makes him "tread his steps anew, / And learne to loue, by learning louers paines to rew" (4.12.13). Far from turning the two lovers into a vegetation myth, Spenser resolves their woes in the terms of human love—terms that are pointedly different from those of the marriage of the Thames and the Medway in the preceding canto. It is no accident that Marinell is wandering around Proteus' abode (and thus comes to hear Florimell's lament) because being half mortal, "He might not with immortall food be fed, / Ne with th'eternall Gods to bancket come" (4.12.4).

Nor is the cure of Marinell's love illness the natural allegory that Frye would make it. The only evidence for his interpretation is that Cymoent leaves the "watry gods" and goes to "the shinie heauen" to find Apollo (4.12.25). Apollo, however, is presented not as the sun, but as the "King of Leaches." The two roles could coalesce, and thus justify Frye's account, if Apollo cured Marinell; but in fact all he does is diagnose his affliction as love. Marinell's cure takes place under the auspices not of medicine, but of law. Cymoent, realizing that Marinell will recover only if Florimell is released, goes to Neptune and complains that Proteus has imprisoned her. Cymoent claims that Proteus, in effect, has violated maritime law (4.12.31), and Neptune, agreeing, "streight his warrant made, / Vnder the Sea-gods seale autenticall, / Commaunding *Proteus* straight t'enlarge the mayd" (4.12. 32).

The passage about Neptune is not very involving and even becomes a bit silly when Spenser parades his legal vocabulary. But it has a real point, and one which the life and intelligence of the rest of the canto make us heed. The last two cantos of Book IV examine the sea as a metaphor and indeed medium for human love. At the beginning of canto 11, the sea is cruel and monstrous, and Florimell seems doomed "vnlesse some heauenly powre her free / By miracle" (4.11.1). As we have seen, Florimell's rescue comes not through any supernatural or natural agency, but is the direct result of her express-ing her love anguish at the beginning of canto 12. In between, the marriage of the Thames and the Medway holds out the promise that harmony can emerge from pain and misery, but the achievement of harmony has to be in human terms. Thus while the marriage proces-sion gives Spenser poetic authority to tease the reader with some sympathetic mourning from the rocks that enclose Florimell,[9] the major poetic transformation of the rocks comes when Florimell uses them as a metaphor for Marinell's hard-heartedness (4.12.7), just as she uses her prison as a metaphor for her suffering for love. As in Book III, Spenser takes it to be axiomatic that pastoral nature cannot adequately express human realities,[10] and the point of portraying Neptune as a just sovereign is that it enables Spenser to humanize the sea—make it express order and peace in human love—without in-voking pastoral imagery or the pathetic fallacy.

Cymoent's sending for Apollo is to be explained by the same frame of reference—the contrast of pastoral and human realities. Cymoent belongs entirely to a world of water deities, while Marinell, whose father was a mortal, belongs to the world of human beings. In Book III, the sea world in which Cymoent dwells is decidedly a pastoral realm, in which, in a version of the story of Thetis and Achilles, she attempts to seclude her son. In Book IV Cymoent joins the gods in the celebration of the rivers' marriage, while Marinell does not. The contrast between the enclosed world of the water deities and the fuller range of human experience is brought out by the fact that Tryphon, "the seagods surgeon" (4.11.6), can cure the physical wound Mari-nell received from Britomart, but cannot even diagnose the ill when Marinell languishes for love of Florimell (4.12.22–24). Cymoent seeks out Apollo because the physician of her own world cannot help her, and what the "King of Leaches" contributes is simply some ordinary human understanding:

[9]   So feelingly her case she did complaine,
        That ruth it moued in the rocky stone,
        And made it seeme to feele her grieuous paine,
        And oft to grone with billowes beating from the maine.
                                                        (4.12.5)

I call this teasing the reader, because the last two lines seem to renege the plain assertion of the pathetic fallacy that precedes them. It is not just that Spenser uses the word "seeme." That word gets support from the fact that the waves, not Florimell's complaint, make the rocks groan, so that we feel not that the rocks participate in human feeling, but simply that this is an appropriate setting for the expression of human grief.

[10] See chapter 11.

Apollo came; who soone as he had sought
Through his disease, did by and by out find,
That he did languish of some inward thought,
The which afflicted his engrieued mind;
Which loue he red to be, that leads each liuing kind.

(4.12.25)

It seems to me both a wonder and a warning when a man as intelligent as Frye has to describe Spenser's poem so inaccurately in order to persuade himself or his reader that it is aesthetically coherent.[11] Surely the trouble lies in our notions of what gives *The Faerie Queene* its coherence—that if it is not plot, it must be imagery or myth or something else specifiable within the putative reality of the poem. The only way to explain why Book IV concludes with the marriage of the Thames and the Medway and the bringing together of Florimell and Marinell is to indicate what the reader sees to be the point of these cantos. They bring to a climax Spenser's dominant concern in Book IV—the way in which experiences of strife, pain, and unhappiness in human love and friendship can somehow turn into experiences of harmony and joy. This is the subject of the story of Florimell and Marinell, and canto 11 is full of images that express or resolve various unruly forces.[12] Moreover, the relation between the two cantos expands and confirms our understanding of harmony in love by bringing into Book IV one of the central phenomena of Book III—the relationship between pastoral nature, which gives a natural sanction to human love, and the emotional realities of human love, which cannot be expressed by pastoral nature.

One might say, of course, that the repeated transformations of strife and pain into joy constitute a phenomenon within the putative reality of Book IV. The difficulty with this argument is that the episodes that make up this series are remarkably disparate when we take them on their own terms. Consider Amoret's fearfulness lest Britomart assert her right of sexual possession and its resolution when Britomart is resolving a complex problem of hospitality (4.1.4–16);

[11] And consider the following misrepresentation of Book II, which is equally remarkable for its magnitude and the casualness with which it is made: "The Bower of Bliss is a parody of Eden, and just as the climax of Book I is St. George's three-day battle with the dragon of death, so the narrative climax of Book II is Guyon's three-day endurance in the underworld. It is the climax at least as far as Guyon's heroism is concerned, for it is Arthur who defeats Maleger and it is really the Palmer who catches Acrasia." *Fables of Identity*, p. 79.

[12] See 4.11.3, 4, 12, 13, 14, 16, 19, 20, 23, 30, 32, 35, 36, 37, 38, 42, 44, 52.

the elaborate machinery of the Cambel and Triamond story, with Cambel's tournament, the translation of the brothers' souls, and the resolution by means of a *dea ex machina* (4.3); Artegall's savagery towards Britomart and the simultaneous resolution of it and Scudamour's jealousy when he shears off her helmet (4.6.1–33); the estrangement and reconciliation of Belphoebe and Timias (4.7.35–8.18); Arthur's and Amoret's exposure to slander (4.8.23–36); Arthur's conversion of the wicked Poeana into a decent lady (4.9.12–16); the harmonizing of boldness and deference when Scudamour takes Amoret from the Temple of Venus (4.10.53–58). One could pick out elements common to some of these episodes, but not to all of them, and none of the phenomena—say, slander or jealousy—is so much more important than any of the others that we can attribute to it the aesthetic organization of the book. The only way in which we can understand the relation between the various episodes in the book is to perceive that each concerns some kind of strife or painfulness in human love, out of which harmony emerges, or which breaks down into discord. The coherence of Book IV is based not on terms found within the poem—not even in generalizing stanzas about jealousy (4.6.1) or the three kinds of love (4.9.1–2)—but on the activity of the reader's mind as he responds to and interprets the parts of the poem.

III

We are now to consider a more intimate manifestation of structure in a poem—the development and coherence of verbal detail that are most familiar to us in Shakespeare's use of metaphor. When we trace a metaphor in one of Shakespeare's plays, we assume that each occurrence of it is essential to the sequence and to the play, and we assume that the ideal reader—to the creation of whom every good piece of criticism contributes—remembers each occurrence and retains his full imaginative experience of it. Such fullness and intimacy of knowledge is required not only by Shakespearean drama, but also by works like the *Divine Comedy* and *Paradise Lost,* although their modes are very different from each other and from that of Shakespeare's plays. When we read these works, remembering earlier passages is often essential to understanding the passage at hand. At the very least we assume that whatever we remember enriches and cooperates with the passage we are reading, and that the more we remember, the better. Now this is not the case in *The Faerie Queene.* If the reader remembers every verbal detail in a book of *The Faerie Queene,* he will be overcome with confusion, rather than awed by a sense of complex imaginative unity. We have by now seen more than enough evidence that Spenser demands and rewards alert and detailed reading. But he does not expect our span of attention and retention to last for more than about a canto, or at most two. In reading almost any work of literature we assume that our attention is uniform throughout: the closeness with which we recall preceding passages is expected to be as great as the closeness with which we read the one at hand. But in *The Faerie Queene* we are expected to remember preceding passages in much less detail than we possess the canto we are reading.

Of the recent critics of Spenser, A. C. Hamilton has most fully attempted to read *The Faerie Queene* with the attention to and the assumptions about verbal detail that we associate with modern criticism of Shakespeare. I want to begin with an interpretation of Hamilton's in which, it seems to me, he comes to grief precisely because he attempts to make connections that Spenser does not encourage us to make or seek out in our reading. Hamilton begins with the erotic dream of the false Una that Archimago sends to the Red Cross Knight:

> And eke the *Graces* seemed all to sing,
> *Hymen iō Hymen*, dauncing all around,
> Whilst freshest *Flora* her with Yuie girlond crownd.
>
> (1.1.48)

"Only later," Hamilton says, "do we understand how this false vision parodies Arthur's vision of the Faery Queen . . . ." He continues:

> The vision is the same, only the false Una offers love now and not when just time has expired. For the knight that time expires only after he slays the Dragon. Then Una will appear, as she seems to appear now, crowned with 'a girland greene' (1.12.8) with the graces singing around her as she is brought to his bed. Then the first state of being 'bathed in wanton blis and wicked ioy' will be fulfilled—as the development of the metaphor suggests—when he is seen 'swimming in that sea of blisfull ioy' (1.12.41). He is tempted to seize for himself what ultimately will be given him by God's will, even as Adam was tempted to seize godhead before just time expired.[13]

One wonders, first of all, what justifies Hamilton in invoking the phrase "iust time expired" (1.9.14) as the context of moral judgment

[13] *The Structure of Allegory in "The Faerie Queene,"* Oxford, 1961, p. 63.

for a love vision that occurs nine cantos earlier. In any case, his connecting the two garlands is very misleading. In canto 12, Una is not crowned with a garland "with the graces singing around her as she is brought to [the knight's] bed." She is crowned by maidens dancing in the fields, and the context is as virginal as it could possibly be: Una is compared to Diana beholding her nymphs (1.12.7), and when the maidens crown her, she "did seeme such, as she was, a goodly maiden Queene" (1.12.8). The garland has nothing to do with the "sea of blisfull ioy" in which the knight swims after his marriage. Indeed if Hamilton had not been so intent on making canto 12 the fulfillment of the knight's erotic vision in canto 1, he might very well have argued that the garland image brings out a contrast between Diana and Venus, who, in the knight's dream, appeared to bring the false Una to his bedside (1.1.48).

But why do we not correct Hamilton by saying that recalling the garland of the false dream brings out the contrast between Venus and Diana? In the first place, remembering the earlier passage with this degree of particularity would burden us with some undoubted verbal parallels in which the moral discriminations are anything but clear: compare "Whilst freshest *Flora* her with Yuie girlond crownd" (1.1.48) with "The comely virgins came, with girlands dight, / As fresh as flowres in medow greene do grow" (1.12.6). Or consider that Spenser wants us to feel the overtones of erotic indulgence in "Yet swimming in that sea of blisfull ioy"—this is what gives the knight's departure to the Fairy Queen its force and pathos—and that he would specifically not want the expression tied down to a sinful meaning, as it would tend to be if we directly recalled "Bathed in wanton blis and wicked ioy" (1.1.47).[14] More broadly, Spenser would not want us to take the contrast of Venus and Diana as a decisive point of structure, because Una is not to remain "a goodly maiden Queene," but is to become the Red Cross Knight's wife. Finally the comparison of Una to Diana would gain nothing from our remembering the Venus of the knight's dream. No one needs to be told who Diana is and what she signifies. More important, the force and decisiveness of the comparison to Diana come from its immediate context —the shift to classical myth from the allusion to Christ's entry into

[14] Compare also "That nigh his manly hart did melt away" (1.1.47) with "His heart did seeme to melt in pleasures manifold" (1.12.40). The phrase "swim (or bathe) in bliss" usually suggests some degree of sensuous indulgence. Cf. "Wife of Bath's Tale," *Canterbury Tales* 3.1252–1253; *Orlando Furioso* 7.27; *Paradise Lost* 11.625.

Jerusalem (Matthew 21:8) in the preceding stanza, and the progression from adolescent to adult virginity in the stanza in which the comparison appears.

Even when we are expected to remember an earlier passage, we get into trouble if we remember it in detail. Take Artegall's sight of Radigund's face when he has unlaced her helmet in order to slay her:

> But when as he discouered had her face,
> He saw his senses straunge astonishment,
> A miracle of natures goodly grace,
> In her faire visage voide of ornament,
> But bath'd in bloud and sweat together ment;
> Which in the rudenesse of that euill plight,
> Bewrayd the signes of feature excellent:
> Like as the Moone in foggie winters night,
> Doth seeme to be her selfe, though darkned be her
>   light.   (5.5.12)

This is undoubtedly meant to remind us of Artegall's battle with Britomart in Book IV, canto 6. In both battles, the sight of the beautiful face fills Artegall with awe and robs him of his martial rage. There are parallel details, which we may or may not remember: in both cases, the beautiful face is covered with sweat (cf. 4.6.19), and the image of the moon has at various points been associated with Britomart (e.g. 3.1.43). But what happens when we attempt to exploit the connections between these battles in the manner encouraged by Milton and Shakespeare? Our sense of Radigund's beauty has a great effect on our evaluation of Artegall's succumbing to it, and we are therefore particularly attentive to the lines, "A miracle of natures goodly grace, / In her faire visage voide of ornament." If Artegall's battle with Britomart is actively present in our minds, here are the passages that we will bring to bear on these two lines:

> What yron courage euer could endure,
> To worke such outrage on so faire a creature?
> And in his madnesse thinke with hands impure
> To spoyle so goodly workmanship of nature,
> The maker selfe resembling in her feature?
>
>   (4.6.17)

> And round about the same [her face], her yellow heare
> Hauing through stirring loosd their wonted band,
> Like to a golden border did appeare,

Framed in goldsmithes forge with cunning hand:
Yet goldsmithes cunning could not vnderstand
To frame such subtile wire, so shinie cleare.
For it did glister like the golden sand,
The which *Pactolus* with his waters shere,
Throwes forth vpon the riuage round about him nere.

(4.6.20)

It seems indubitable that Spenser wants us to take the phrase "workmanship of nature" quite literally as a praise of Britomart's beauty. In the context of these stanzas, the description of Radigund as "a miracle of natures goodly grace" certainly takes on a specific intention and force, but one that simply saddles us with difficulties. Either we must say that Radigund is a more wonderful product of nature than Britomart, with her absence of ornament being the sign of her miraculousness, or we must make the ornamental nature of Britomart's beauty a specific point of superiority to Radigund. Spenser is by no means as hostile to artifice as he has been thought to be, but he surely could not have intended this.

In almost any other poem, these passages would mutually illuminate each other. In *The Faerie Queene,* the details of expression are to be referred solely to the immediate poetic context in which they occur. In the description of Radigund, it is clear why Spenser wishes us to feel that her beauty is natural and good. Unless we accept the truth of the aphorism in the next stanza—"No hand so cruell, nor no hart so hard, / But ruth of beautie will it mollifie" (5.5.13)—we will not feel the force of the moral and psychological dilemma into which Artegall gets himself by surrendering. Moreover, we will not properly understand Radigund's cruelty in keeping Artegall in thraldom (5.5.23–57) if we think it is an expression of innate wickedness, rather than the perversion of a woman's natural endowment—for this episode, far from making a purely political point, is Spenser's greatest criticism of the imperious mistress.

In the same way, the rightness and force of the description of Britomart's hair become clear when we see it in the context of her battle with Artegall. Let us return to the phrase about the "goodly workmanship of nature" and see how it is produced in the episode. Artegall has been severely wounded by Britomart, but she in turn tires, and

He through long sufferance growing now more great,
Rose in his strength, and gan her fresh assayle,

> Heaping huge strokes, as thicke as showre of hayle,
> And lashing dreadfully at euery part,
> As if he thought her soule to disentrayle.
> Ah cruell hand, and thrise more cruell hart,
> That workst such wrecke on her, to whom thou dearest art.
>
> (4.6.16)

The poet's outburst in the last two lines is a genuine cry of dismay —not only because it responds so immediately to the cruelty of Artegall (who is disguised as the Salvage Knight), but also because it resembles the formulas found in love poetry, and thus suggests that the rage and cruelty of the battle are somehow inherent in the relationship of love. But as the poet's outcry continues in the next stanza, it gives a quite different perspective on the battle. "What yron courage euer could endure, / To worke such outrage on so faire a creature?" Artegall's cruelty now seems not inherent in the situation, but wrong and even absurd. If he could see as we do, he need only look in front of him to refrain: the narrative basis of the episode, after all, is a comedy of disguises. The phrase "goodly workmanship of nature," in the next lines, perfectly expresses our moral perspective here. It fully indicates how terrible it would be to "spoyle" a woman's beauty, but it does so by appealing to our confidence in nature and human nature, and without pretending that a woman is a special creature (say, a goddess or angel) whom it would be a special offense to harm. Hence when the artificial description of Britomart's hair confirms this phrase, it also confirms our sense of the naturalness with which the lovers' situation ought to resolve itself.

However, the phrase "goodly workmanship of nature" does not sufficiently explain the pointed poetic artifice of that stanza, and we must recognize yet another way in which the artificial is natural here. The description of Britomart's hair is a conventional Petrarchan praise of the mistress' beauty—a fact of which the artificiality of the stanza is meant to remind us—and much of the force of the stanza comes from our feeling that the beloved is now being properly seen and described. Hence when Artegall feels his power bereft by this stanza and worships Britomart as a heavenly creature, Spenser is able to indicate the literal falsity of his imaginings, without denying the validity of his sense of woman's beauty:

> And he himselfe long gazing thereupon,
> At last fell humbly downe vpon his knee,
> And of his wonder made religion,

> Weening some heauenly goddesse he did see,
> Or else vnweeting, what it else might bee.

(4.6.22)

Exactly the same discriminations are made when Scudamour recovers from the blow Britomart dealt him and sees her:

> When as he plaine descride
> That peerelesse paterne of Dame natures pride,
> And heauenly image of perfection,
> He blest himselfe, as one sore terrifide,
> And turning his feare to faint deuotion,
> Did worship her as some celestiall vision.

(4.6.24)

Scudamour's worship corresponds to our sense of the wonder of the whole episode, but we are not limited to the terms of his adoration. He takes "heauenly image" literally, whereas we—with our much less magical sense of the phrase, "That peerelesse paterne of Dame natures pride"—feel the uniting of the lovers and the solution of Scudamour's jealousy to be firmly grounded in human nature.

It is essential that in Artegall's battle with Radigund we remember the basic parallel with his battle against Britomart—that in both he was disarmed by the sight of a beautiful face. But we are not expected to remember the episode in the same detail with which we were expected to read it. Throughout *The Faerie Queene* it is clear that Spenser expects us to be aware of events (of narrative action or poetic usage) that have occurred earlier in the poem. In the opening cantos of Book II, for example, we meet two women, Medina and Belphoebe, whose heroic poise expresses the virtue of temperance. We are surely expected to remember these heroines when Phaedria calms Guyon and Cymochles (2.6.32–36) and when Mammon introduces Guyon to Philotime (2.7.44–50). Similarly we are expected to be aware that in Book III Spenser continually uses the language and *topoi* of pastoral poetry in order to see how adequately they can provide settings for and expressions of love. Or, to take an example more like the connection between Artegall's two battles, it is clear—for example, from the frequent use of the word "grace"—that when Arthur comes to rescue Guyon in Book II, canto 8, we are expected to remember the role he played in Book I. But whereas in any other poem these correspondences would make us seek out detailed remembrances, in *The Faerie Queene* tact and common sense make us draw the line at the broad and, usually, obvious recollections of the sort that we have just indicated.

By "tact" I mean our sense of our relation to the poem, the degree of intensity and closeness with which we should follow it. If we are to speak with any confidence of this sense of tact in reading *The Faerie Queene,* we ought to be able to explain how the most intense and scrupulous attention to the language of an individual canto is compatible with a broad and general remembrance of what has preceded it. We can find the solution of this dilemma, if it is that, by considering two aspects of the examples we have considered. In the first place, Spenser's passages—even when they arouse our memories of earlier passages—are made completely intelligible by their immediate contexts. Second, Spenser's materials tend to be literary commonplaces and are thus assumed to be part of the equipment of our minds. The expectations, ideas, and feelings about Diana or pastoral celebrations or woman's beauty that Spenser exploits are not ones he has specifically developed in his poem, but are those he assumes we have brought to his poem from our reading of other poetry.

The comparison of passages, episodes, cantos, or books in *The Faerie Queene* often helps us become aware of what the poem makes us perceive and understand. But it is quite a different thing to say that an earlier passage or episode is an *essential* preliminary to our reading any other passage or episode. These two uses of comparison are often confused—in most poems it is probably unnecessary to distinguish them—and the most common form of the confusion in *The Faerie Queene* is interpreting Book II in terms of Book I. Hamilton has given us our most thoroughgoing examples of this kind of interpretation, and it is worth looking at some of them to see how little help this apparently natural procedure is. For example, Hamilton says that Guyon's descent into Mammon's cave "clearly parallels the Red Cross Knight's passage through the house of Pride":

> The house of Richesse corresponds to the house of Pride, both being places of glittering wealth to which the knights are led by a broad beaten highway. Philotime sitting in her "glistring glory" with the suitors around her throne is an infernal Lucifera: her "broad beauties beam great brightnes threw" (2.7.45), even as Lucifera's "bright blazing beautie . . . shone as *Titans* ray" (1.4.8). Guyon descends to see the damned chained in hell where Tantalus, Pilate, and "infinite moe [are] tormented in like paine" (2.7.63),

131

even as the Dwarf sees "the endlesse routs of wretched thralles" (1.5.51) in the dungeon below the house of Pride.[15]

The details noticed in the Cave of Mammon are completely intelligible and have their full force taken by themselves: there is surely nothing surprising about treating the dwelling of the god of riches as an analogue of hell. And for what purpose, in Hamilton's view, does Spenser make us attend to these echoes? "Such parallels," we are told, "only point up the difference between the two knights." This difference is that "throughout his adventure Guyon manifests the power of temperance over those affections through which the Red Cross Knight falls into the bondage of sin. . . . The Red Cross Knight chooses at first to remain aloof from the worldlings of the house of Pride, but after his fight with Sansjoy he yields to Lucifera."[16] But Spenser's point is that the Red Cross Knight, simply because he is a man, is willy-nilly implicated in Lucifera's kingdom, even when he is fighting a virtuous battle against Sansjoy.[17] The Red Cross Knight does not succumb to an affection here; his relation to Lucifera is not analogous to Guyon's relation to Mammon, who, as Hamilton points out, explicitly tempts him. It is hard to see how Hamilton's parallels establish any differences here. Such as they are, they are simply those basic differences of perspective on man of which we are sufficiently informed by the titles "Legend of Holiness" and "Legend of Temperance." Hamilton repeatedly talks about "the significant contrast which the parallel provides,"[18] but all that becomes clear is that the parallels he discovers, if they were ever part of the poem, are scaffolding, not structure.

Hamilton's analyses are an inevitable result of a mistaken assumption about the way meanings are established in *The Faerie Queene*. For example, he says that "from the parallel with Book I we understand that Maleger is the state of sin,"[19] whereas even if the parallels were convincing, it would still be the case that Maleger's identity is established solely by the symbolism and events of the canto in which he appears.[20] As a final example, let us return to Amoret's wound. Frye says her torture represents "the anguish of jealous love,"[21]

---

[15] *Structure of Allegory*, p. 97.   [16] *Ibid.*, pp. 96–97.

[17] See below, pp. 340–343.   [18] *Structure of Allegory*, p. 98.

[19] *Ibid.*, p. 103.

[20] Thus all the evidence adduced by A. S. P. Woodhouse, who first proposed this identification of Maleger, comes from 2.11. See "Nature and Grace in *The Faerie Queene*," ELH, 16 (1949), 221.

[21] *Fables of Identity*, p. 83.

presumably because Malbecco "did his hart with bitter thoughts engore" (3.10.45), has a "wounded mind" (3.10.55) and, in his final transformation, experiences a passion that "doth transfixe the soule with deathes eternall dart" (3.10.59). Frye at least goes back only two cantos to pin down the meaning of the image. When the method is really pushed to its extreme, we find a critic invoking earlier images of the eyes shooting darts into the heart and saying, "In the speaking picture of the deadly arrow through her heart one can read something of the history of her enslavement by Busyrane, and know it is her eye that has opened Amoret's heart to attack."[22] Surely Amoret's torture is a perfect instance of a passage for whose meaning we are not required to go outside its immediate context. It is, of course, a conventional image, and though we are aware that it has continually appeared in Book III, Spenser does not expect or depend on anything more than a general awareness that it is of major importance in expressing the issues of the book. Quite the contrary, he reactivates the image in our imaginations by employing it repeatedly in Busyrane's tapestries and Cupid's statue (3.11.30, 36, 44, 45, 46, 48), and he reawakens not the memory of earlier passages, but perceptions and feelings that he assumes to be part of our equipment for reading the poem and understanding ourselves.

I V

The reader may well ask whether the argument presented in this chapter does not risk throwing out the baby with the bath. Naturally I think and hope not, and chapters 10 and 11 are meant to show the kinds of continuities that exist in whole books of *The Faerie Queene*. I hope that the reader will agree that the analyses and interpretations in those chapters are consistent with the rules for reading maintained in this one, and that he will feel that nothing essential to the unity of individual books is lost. As for the unity of the whole poem, surely we must think of it in a more easygoing way than most studies of Spenser encourage us to. When we consider that almost any way of pairing or grouping the books is plausible and suggestive, and that everyone feels that the free-floating Mutability Cantos "obviously" belong with the rest of the poem, it would appear that we must describe the unity of *The Faerie Queene* in terms of habits of mind, both the poet's and the reader's, and not in terms of a fixed structure.

[22] Joseph B. Dallett, "Ideas of Sight in *The Faerie Queene*," ELH, 27 (1960), 107.

The ideas in this chapter are most in harmony with Rosemond Tuve's treatment of allegory as unfolding the many aspects of broad fundamental ideas, and with her view that the unity of romances comes from the continuities of meaning seen in interwoven stories.[23] *Allegorical Imagery* appeared after this book was written, and perhaps when we have absorbed all that Miss Tuve has shown us, my distinction between the terms "organization" and "structure" will not seem so important as it now does to me. But at present "structure" is a misleading term, because the search for it is so intimately tied up with the modern idea that a poem has a special kind of reality or autonomous being, and that its meanings are established solely in the terms it presents—its world, or universe of significance, or whatever. It is this notion that makes critics assume that a poet who views the universe as ordered from top to bottom will try to embody that order in his poem. But clearly this is not necessarily so. It is precisely when a poet trusts that the universe really is ordered and assumes that the source of order is God, not the individual poet, that he can allow his poem to expatiate freely.[24] It is no mistake that Lewis, who has given us some of the best characterizations of Spenser's trusting habit of mind, is also the critic who has most encouraged us to take *The Faerie Queene* as it comes.

[23] *Allegorical Imagery*, Princeton, 1966; see especially pp. 126–128, 132, 362–370, and the treatment in chapter 4 of Jean de Meun's part of the *Roman de la Rose*.

[24] This point has been well treated by Robert M. Durling, *The Figure of the Poet in Renaissance Epic*, Cambridge, Mass., 1965, pp. 233–234.

PART II

Chapter Five

Interpretation and the
Sixteenth-Century Reader

I

This chapter is an introduction to the next three, in which we shall examine a variety of historical materials in order to consider what kinds of meanings are to be found in *The Faerie Queene*. The first two of these chapters concern traditional problems of Spenserian scholarship; the third addresses a difficult problem of interpretation and is to some extent devoted to showing that false uses of history cause inadequate critical analyses. In this chapter we shall first examine an episode that raises the main problems and themes of this section of the book, and that has the additional advantage of providing a strong case against the arguments I shall make. We shall then consider what evidence there is of the way Spenser's contemporaries read *The Faerie Queene*. Modern scholars often refer to "the Elizabethan reader" or "sixteenth-century readers" as if all Spenser's contemporaries had the same attitudes and responses to his poem, or indeed any poem. This of course is not the case, and the evidence supports other ways of reading *The Faerie Queene* than the excessively solemn or esoteric interpretations in support of which "the sixteenth-century reader" is usually invoked.

Critics have shown little, if any, uncertainty about the meaning of the episode we are going to discuss—the Red Cross Knight's disarming by the fountain and his dalliance with Duessa, just before his capture by Orgoglio (1.7.1–7). The explicit or understood interpretation of the episode is well represented in a recent article by Vern Torczon: "That the Red Cross Knight commits the sin of presumption is clear when one analyzes his over-confident attitude. . . . The removal of his armor indicates that Red Cross no longer thinks he has need for the protective qualities of the shield of faith and the helmet of salvation."[1] Torczon then explains the knight's going from Orgoglio's dungeon to the Cave of Despair by saying that presumption and despair "are part of the psychological process of conversion and regen-

[1] "Spenser's Orgoglio and Despaire," *Texas Studies in Literature and Language*, 3 (1961), 126–127.

eration, and are generally paired when they occur in theological trea-
tises or literary works. Theologians . . . warn often of this dual sin
against hope."[2] One might quarrel about the particular sin that is rep-
resented by the knight's disarming. But everyone would agree that it
is the central allegorical event of the episode and that it represents
some sin or moral lapse. And there would be no disagreement about
the character of Torczon's interpretation—his understanding the
knight's disarming in the context of theological and moral writings.

One aspect of the episode, however, remains puzzling. Spenser de-
votes most of his verse to describing the grove and the fountain in
which the knight is resting, and the major cause of his enfeeblement
is his drinking from the fountain. Yet it is not clear, as it is when he
disarms and when he dallies with Duessa, in what sense this event is
a moral cause of his succumbing to Orgoglio. The solution is clear,
once we recognize the problem. Spenser tells us that the nymph of
the fountain "was out of *Dianes* fauour" (1.7.4):

> The cause was this: one day when *Phoebe* fayre
> With all her band was following the chace,
> This Nymph, quite tyr'd with heat of scorching ayre
> Sat down to rest in middest of the race:
> The goddesse wroth gan fowly her disgrace,
> And bad the waters, which from her did flow,
> Be such as she her selfe was then in place.
> Thenceforth her waters waxed dull and slow,
> And all that drunke thereof, did faint and feeble grow.
>
> (1.7.5)

The nymph has behaved very much like the knight. Instead of adding
a third moral cause of the knight's downfall, the story of her fountain
recapitulates the two causes already presented. Her giving up the
race is analogous to the knight's taking off his armor, and his dalliance
with Duessa is an explicit instance of falling out of the favor of the
goddess of chastity. The passage is a good example of an apparent
fictional event that makes sense only when we grasp its rhetorical
purpose—to comment on and increase our understanding of the
events already described. The rhetorical function of the myth of the
fountain has been recognized by S. K. Heninger, Jr., who says that it
"focuses the moral significance of this episode."[3] What specifically
concerns us now is the nature of the moral commentary that the myth

---

[2] *Ibid.*, p. 127.
[3] "The Orgoglio Episode in *The Faerie Queene*," ELH, 26 (1959), 175.

makes. Heninger rightly says that Spenser has adapted the myth of Salmacis and Hermaphroditus. Enervating powers, twice mentioned by Ovid (*Metamorphoses* 4.286, 15.321), were given to Salmacis' fountain in answer to Hermaphroditus' prayer when he found that he had become but half a man (*Metamorphoses* 4.383–388). Heninger comments:

> Spenser has used only so much of Ovid's legend as he needs. He has eliminated Hermaphroditus completely, and attributes the enervating properties of the water solely to the displeasure of Diana when the indolent Salmacis showed indifference to the chase. Ovid has never had more ardent disciples than the Elizabethans, however, and to Spenser's audience this enchanted spring would inevitably recall Salmacis.

> Since myth was a form of history, it also was subject to moral interpretation; and the venerated tradition of moralizing Ovid would bring with Salmacis' story a moralized meaning. As Golding summarized it in the epistle preceding his translation of the *Metamorphoses:*

> > Hermaphrodite and Salmacis declare that idlenesse
> > Is cheefest nurce and cherisher of all volupteousnesse,
> > And that voluptuous lyfe breedes sin: which linking
> >   all toogither
> > Make men too bee effeminate, unweeldy, weake and
> >   lither.

> The interlude beside the fountain shows Red Crosse being both idle and voluptuous, and Spenser focuses the moral significance of this episode by connecting it with the history of Salmacis. The sinfulness of this dalliance with Duessa makes Red Crosse a proper victim for the Giant, the agent of God's wrath, that inevitably follows.[4]

Heninger assumes that Golding's verses represent the way sixteenth-century readers understood poems. And it is undeniable that for many readers in the sixteenth century, as in the twentieth, interpretations of poems take the form of stringent moral judgments. Before going on to make my case about this episode, I would like to add some more historical evidence in support of Heninger's. The source of this episode is a famous passage in *Orlando Furioso,* in which Ruggiero, after traveling three thousand miles on the back of the winged hippo-

---

[4] *Ibid.,* pp. 174–175.

griff, lands on a beautiful island, disarms, and refreshes himself from a fountain in the midst of a beautiful grove of trees (*OF* 6.19–25). This is the beginning of the most openly moral and didactic part of *Orlando Furioso*—the captivity of Ruggiero's senses by the beautiful sorceress Alcina (like Spenser's Acrasia, a version of Circe), the re-awakening of his reason by the good sorceress Melissa, and his eventual journey to Alcina's virtuous sister, Logistilla. The scene at the fountain truly invites the allegorical interpretation to which the whole of *Orlando Furioso* was subjected in the sixteenth century. The following commentary on the episode is of a piece with Heninger's article and, like Golding's interpretation of Salmacis and Hermaphroditus, could justifiably be invoked as an interpretation of the episode that Spenser adapted from it. Ruggiero, the commentator says,

$$\text{Throws away} \begin{cases} \text{the shield, reason} \\ \text{the helmet, the mind} \\ \text{gauntlets, good deeds} \end{cases} \text{and behold, Ruggiero is lost.}$$

Being thus lost, the man immerses himself in a spring and there refreshes himself. Ah, how true it is that a man thirsting for carnal amusements throws away these three things and immerses himself in those. He puts aside the shield when he intends to give himself completely, with heart uncovered and open to the world's service. He puts aside the helmet as if he no longer needs a mind to raise himself to heaven. He puts aside the gloves because he thinks he no longer wants, perspiring, to perform good deeds, but wants only to immerse himself in pleasures.[5]

The detailed translation of the physical surface of Ariosto's narration can be invoked to justify what at first seems a farfetched modern analysis of Spenser's episode:

What we witness in [the Red Cross Knight's] descent is a passage through the elements of fire, air, water, and earth. When he escapes the sun's "boyling heat" (fire) and bathes his forehead "in the breathing wind" (air), he drinks from the stream (water) as he lies poured out on the ground (earth). Then he is defeated by Orgoglio who is a mass of earthly slime (earth and water) "puft up with emptie wind." . . . Of the knight we may say, then, that as he feeds upon the shade, drinks from the stream, and lies poured

[5] Levantio da Guidicciolo, *Antidoto della Gelosia . . . estratto da l'Ariosto*, Brescia, 1565, pp. 198–199.

out upon the ground, he becomes earth and water, that earthly slime which is Orgoglio. God's image being erased in him, though not totally, he is re-created in Satan's image.[6]

This interpretation can serve as an orthodox account of those parts of our episode that are not interpreted by Torczon and Heninger.

When Heninger says that the Red Cross Knight is "a proper victim for the Giant, the agent of God's wrath," he makes explicit what is mistaken and objectionable about the kind of interpretation he, Torczon, and Hamilton present. When a poetic character is made the object of a categorical moral judgment, there is a large presumption that the reader, who stands outside the poem, is immune from the offense judged. If Heninger's quote from Golding represents our moral understanding of this episode, we assume a position of superintending God's wrath, not of being potential victims of it. In moral and theological writings such difficulties are avoided (though clearly self-righteousness is the gravest hazard of these writings) by the way the individual writer assesses and indicates his relation to the evils he describes, or by the assumptions or conventions of different types of discourse—the fact, for example, that theology is analytic and disinterested, or the special privileges granted to the preacher of a sermon. But when the categorical and all-inclusive statements of moral discourse are presented as the meaning of an episode like this, it is almost inevitable that the reader will feel immune from the character's frailties. It is clear that the Red Cross Knight in this episode is guilty of wrong and sinful actions. But the narrative action is not the whole of the poetry, and Spenser's verse makes us understand that the knight's frailties are ours. William Nelson quotes a wonderful passage from Hooker that indicates the spirit in which Spenser makes us read:

Happier a great deal is that man's case, whose soul by inward desolation is humbled, than he whose heart is through abundance of spiritual delight lifted up and exalted above measure. Better it is sometimes to go down into the pit with him, who, beholding darkness, and bewailing the loss of inward joy and consolation, crieth from the bottom of the lowest hell, "My God, my God, why hast thou forsaken me?" than continually to walk arm in arm with angels, to sit as it were in Abraham's bosom, and to have no

[6] A. C. Hamilton, *The Structure of Allegory in "The Faerie Queene,"* Oxford, 1961, p. 76.

141

thought, no cogitation, but "I thank my God it is not with me as it is with other men." No, God will have them that shall walk in light to feel now and then what it is to sit in the shadow of death.[7]

There is no a priori reason that Spenser should not be concerned to enforce a strict moral judgment in this episode, but the interpretations we have quoted seem quite out of touch with what we experience in reading it. Students always find the episode interesting because, although they know that they are called upon to make a judgment against the Red Cross Knight, they feel that the grove and the fountain are genuinely attractive. Surely this naive response is the right one:

> He feedes vpon the cooling shade, and bayes
> His sweatie forehead in the breathing wind,
> Which through the trembling leaues full gently playes
> Wherein the cherefull birds of sundry kind
> Do chaunt sweet musick, to delight his mind.
>
> (1.7.3)

And after the reconciliation with Duessa:

> Vnkindnesse past, they gan of solace treat,
> And bathe in pleasaunce of the ioyous shade,
> Which shielded them against the boyling heat,
> And with greene boughes decking a gloomy glade,
> About the fountaine like a girlond made;
> Whose bubbling waue did euer freshly well,
> Ne euer would through feruent sommer fade.
>
> (1.7.4)

There are indications of self-indulgence in "He feedes vpon the cooling shade" and "bathe in pleasaunce of the ioyous shade." But the shade *is* pleasant and joyous ("cherefull birds"), and the main effect of these stanzas is to make us feel how natural and attractive is the refreshment offered by this grove. Moreover the motive that would impel a man to partake of this "pleasaunce" is not a frailty of appetite, but the oppression of "the boyling heat" (compare "His sweatie forehead" and "feruent sommer"). It is perfectly natural to give oneself to this grove, and simply reading the verse makes it impossible for us

[7] "A Learned and Comfortable Sermon of the Certainty and Perpetuity of Faith in the Elect," in *Of the Laws of Ecclesiastical Polity*, London: Everyman's Library, 1907, 1, 6–7. Quoted in *The Poetry of Edmund Spenser*, New York, 1963, p. 153.

to sit in judgment on the Red Cross Knight. The opening stanza of the canto shows that Spenser intends this effect:

> What man so wise, what earthly wit so ware,
> As to descry the crafty cunning traine,
> By which deceipt doth maske in visour faire,
> And cast her colours dyed deepe in graine,
> To seeme like Truth, whose shape she well can faine,
> And fitting gestures to her purpose frame,
> The guiltlesse man with guile to entertaine?

$$(1.7.1)$$

These lines make it explicit that we are all in the same moral situation. Unlike many parts of the Bower of Bliss, this grove and fountain do not appeal to corrupted appetites; there is nothing suspicious in their attractiveness.[8] But insofar as our susceptibility to them is a sign of sinfulness, it is only in the sense that all men are sinful, not in the sense in which some men can be called sinful and others virtuous.

The reading I have proposed has as much historical validity as Heninger's. Heninger says that "Spenser has used only so much of Ovid's legend as he needs," but this formula does not adequately account for a major difference between Spenser's myth and Ovid's. Salmacis, alone among the water nymphs, is not a follower of Diana; she refuses to hunt and spends all her time in soft and self-regarding ease by the side of her own pool (*Metamorphoses* 4.302–315). Spenser's nymph, on the other hand, is a huntress who sits down because, like the Red Cross Knight, she is "quite tyr'd with heat of scorching ayre." Spenser has altered the myth—and surely this fact is a historical reality—so that the nymph will less readily be the object of confident moral condemnation. If Spenser's nymph resembles any Ovidian character, it is Arethusa, whose pursuit by Alpheus begins when she lies down, weary from hunting (*Metamorphoses* 5.585–591). Golding's translation of this passage shows that for an Elizabethan reader moralism was not the only quality that would be called Ovidian:

> In comming wearie from the chase of Stymphalus, the heate
> Was fervent, and my traveling had made it twice as great.
> I founde a water neyther deepe nor shallow which did glide

---

[8] The word "gloomy" in 1.7.4 may seem to be what Lewis would call a danger signal. But Spenser does not use this word only for evil or unhappy places, as he does at 2.7.3 and 4.7.38. The details of this description are closest to the "gloomy groue" in the Garden of Adonis (3.6.43).

Without all noyse, so calme that scarce the moving might
    be spide.
And throughly to the very ground it was so crispe and
    cleare,
That every little stone therein did plaine aloft appeare.
The horie Sallowes and the Poplars growing on the brim
Unset, upon the shoring bankes did cast a shadow trim.[9]

The character of this setting is very similar to Spenser's and it is
Ovidian not only by virtue of sensuous description, but also because
of its association with rest from the chase. The vale of Gargaphie—
Ovid's description of which is one of the great progenitors of pas-
sages describing the harmony of art and nature—is a place where
Diana comes when, in Golding's words, she "felt hir selfe waxe faint,
of following of hir game."[10] Similarly, the exposé of the pregnant
nymph Callisto occurs when

    fainting through hir brothers flames and hunting in
        the chace,
She [Diana] found a coole and shadie lawnde through midst
        whereof she spide
A shallow brooke with trickling streame on gravell
        bottom glide.[11]

The grove and fountain as a setting for refreshment after toil can
be seen as an Ovidian convention, and the scene in Book III when
Venus discovers Diana and her nymphs (3.6.17) suggests that Spen-
ser regarded it as one. It is purely arbitrary to say that Golding's
moralizations are part of the Elizabethan reader's Ovid, but that such
descriptions and their association with legitimate rest are not. A
knowledge of this descriptive convention is not necessary for our un-
derstanding of the Red Cross Knight's situation, but it confirms our
sense that the grove is genuinely attractive and that the knight's desire
to drink from the fountain is natural.

Spenser's use of Ariosto is no more to be equated with the com-
mentator's moralizations than is his use of Ovid. Spenser's most direct
borrowing (the first five lines of 1.7.3) conflates two passages of
Ovid-like description:

[9] *Ovid's Metamorphoses: The Arthur Golding Translation* (1567), ed. John
Frederick Nims, New York, 1965, 5.725–732.
[10] *Metamorphoses* 3.163; *Golding*, 3.190.
[11] *Metamorphoses* 2.454–456; *Golding*, 2.565–567.

> facean riparo ai fervidi calori
> de' giorni estivi con lor spesse ombrelle;
> e tra quei rami con sicuri voli
> cantando se ne gìano i rosignuoli.

[The trees] gave shelter with their thick canopies against the fervid heat of summer days; and among these boughs in secure flight the nightingales went singing. (*OF* 6.21)

> Et ora alla marina et ora al monte
> volgea la faccia all'aure fresche et alme,
> che l'alte cime con mormorii lieti
> fan tremolar dei faggi e degli abeti.

And sometimes to the sea and sometimes to the mountain he turned his face, to the fresh restorative breezes that, with soft murmurs, are making the high crowns of the firs and beeches tremble. (*OF* 6.24)

One needs only the evidence of one's senses to say that Ariosto meant these descriptions to be attractive and that the normal sixteenth-century reader would have found them so. But it happens that on this point we can call to witness Simon Fornari, who was the most elaborate and unremitting of Ariosto's allegorizers, and also the most intelligent. Of the initial description of the island where Ruggiero lands (*OF* 6.21–22), Fornari says: "Leaving these two stanzas without an allegorical interpretation would not hamper the allegorical discourse. Because since we understand Ruggiero to be a youth who has been brought by unbridled appetite to wanton love, which cannot flourish except in the midst of opulence and among delights, it was necessary that the poet depict some pleasing, luxurious, and delightful place where that could happen, as he does here."[12] But the main point is that Spenser does not need Fornari's warrant to take Ariosto's stanzas at face value. At no point is it right to assume that Fornari's reading represents Spenser's. Take Fornari's comment on the stanza in which Ruggiero drinks from the fountain: "The thirst of lust is insatiable and without end. That is why if Ruggiero—that is, a young lover— having spent much time in love and endured infinite toils and finding

---

[12] *La Spositione . . . sopra l'Orlando Furioso*, 2, Florence, 1550, 22. Nevertheless, Fornari says, all the details of the description can be taken allegorically, and he goes on to interpret each detail as one of the woes or allurements of love. Spenser may well have been interested in the general character of this reading, but the details of his borrowings from Ariosto have no discernible relation to the details of Fornari's interpretation.

himself burning with love's fire all the more, happens to attain the desired delight, he completely spreads and immerses himself in it, and eagerly refreshes his parched and suffering lips."[13] At first this interpretation strikes us as one that Spenser would accept. But neither Ariosto nor Spenser describes his knight as drinking greedily from the fountain; that is Fornari's addition, and it is essential to his moral interpretation. Spenser's episode unquestionably has more moral gravity than Ariosto's, but to understand how Spenser uses *Orlando Furioso,* we must turn to the poem itself:

> Bagna talor ne la chiara onda e fresca
> l'asciutte labra, e con le man diguazza,
> acciò che de le vene il calore esca
> che gli ha acceso il portar de la corazza.
> Né maraviglia è già ch'ella gl'incresca;
> che non è stato un far vedersi in piazza:
> ma senza mai posar, d'arme guernito,
> tre mila miglia ognor correndo era ito.

At times he wets his dry lips in the clear fresh stream and stirs it with his hands, that the heat kindled in him by the wearing of his corselet might leave his veins. No wonder it annoyed him, for this has not been a showing-off in the public square, but without ever stopping, clad in armor, he has been rushing on three thousand miles every hour.

(OF 6.25)[14]

Ariosto's request that the reader sympathize with Ruggiero's discomfort is in a light vein. But when we consider Spenser's generosity to the Red Cross Knight, we must assume that he considered these lines an important part of Ariosto's meaning, and that he regarded them as adaptable to the graver tone of his own episode. Certainly Spenser is much closer to Ariosto here than to Fornari, who says of these lines: "And to the moral understanding, the breastplate, which he was wearing when he ran three thousand miles, is the annoying weight of the mortal body; which is a greater burden to the spirit when it has reached the third age" (i.e. adolescence, the third age of man, when love's urgings are strongest and reason weakest).[15]

The different ways of reading this episode involve not only moral

---

[13] *Ibid.,* 2, 29.

[14] The last line, as Gilbert observes in a note, is "usually taken as meaning *three thousand miles ever moving at full speed.*"

[15] *Spositione,* 2, 29–30.

attitude, but also notions of the reader's relation to the text of the poem and its details. Heninger's and especially Hamilton's interpretations abstract and rearrange details of the verse to fit into some predetermined framework: the specific interpretation may not be predetermined, but its general character is. As opposed to this, I have been urging the reader to trust Spenser's verse, to take in meanings by attentively and receptively following the details of language. It is essential to read the poem this way even when there is a definite and morally clear-cut action, such as the Red Cross Knight's disarming:

> Who [Duessa] when returning from the drery *Night,*
> She fownd not in that perilous house of *Pryde,*
> Where she had left, the noble *Redcrosse* knight,
> Her hoped pray; she would no lenger bide,
> But forth she went, to seeke him far and wide.
> Ere long she fownd, whereas he wearie sate,
> To rest him selfe, foreby a fountaine side,
> Disarmed all of yron-coted Plate,
> And by his side his steed the grassy forage ate.
>
> (1.7.2)

We first notice that Spenser does not describe the knight, as Ariosto does Ruggiero, disarming himself. Where an active form of the verb would represent the disarming as an act of the will, Spenser's use of the passive participle suggests that it is an inevitable concomitant of his weariness. Moreover the knight is "disarmed all of yron-coted Plate." The language here reminds us not that this is "the armour of a Christian man specified by Saint Paul," as Spenser says in the Letter to Raleigh, but that it is heavy, and that the pastoral setting is a welcome opportunity for removing it. The first half of the stanza too serves to complicate moral issues, and not simply by calling the Red Cross Knight "noble." The sharpness with which "Her hoped pray" opposes the suggestions of strength in "the noble *Redcrosse* knight" focuses the sense of spiritual danger already indicated in "drery *Night*" and "that perilous house of *Pryde*." That we are not immune from this danger would seem implicit in a normal reading of the first four lines, and Spenser puts the matter beyond question by a trick in the fifth. "But forth she went, to seeke him far and wide" sounds like the formulas he habitually uses of Una (cf. 1.2.8, 1.3.3, 1.3.21, 1.6.2). This line makes us directly experience Duessa's power "to seeme like Truth, whose shape she well can faine."

We must now define more specifically the kinds of meaning that

Spenser's verse expresses. The most important point on which to be clear is that he is not interested in moral adjudication. No doubt he would say that the Red Cross Knight is guilty of mistaken and sinful actions here, but Spenser's interest is not in determining judgments about actions. If it were, he would not introduce the episode by speaking of "the guiltlesse man" in the opening stanza. For the moment Spenser is perfectly willing to see men as guiltless in order to make us grasp an essential way of understanding his hero's plight—that no human powers can keep him from being the victim of the world's corruption. Again this is not a definitive judgment, but one of several truths about a complex moral situation. Similarly, Spenser's intention in making the grove and the fountain attractive is not to exculpate the Red Cross Knight, but simply to put us in possession of an essential truth.

The genius of Spenser's poetry is that it holds in focus a variety of moral truths, even when they might conflict if they were structured as a moral judgment. Sometimes disparate elements appear in juxtaposed lines (as lines 2–4 of 1.7.2), sometimes different moral perspectives appear in different parts of a stanza (as in 1.7.5,6), and sometimes various perspectives are fused in the characteristic lucidity of a line like "bathe in pleasaunce of the ioyous shade." From the standpoint of moral awareness, the richest lines of the episode are those that introduce its catastrophe:

> Yet goodly court he made still to his Dame,
> Pourd out in loosnesse on the grassy grownd,
> Both carelesse of his health, and of his fame.

> (1.7.7)

If the verse were conveying and enforcing moral judgments, we would have to say "goodly court" in a mocking or sarcastic tone. To do so would imply either that our criteria of judgment were true standards of courtiership (ironic emphasis on "goodly") or that all courtiership was worthless (ironic emphasis on "court"). But neither of these alternatives is possible. The Red Cross Knight gets into trouble partly because he takes Duessa at face value, as a lady to whom he has knightly obligations. This point is fully developed in their first meeting (see 1.2.21–22, 26–27); it is seen in this episode when Duessa greets the knight "with reproch of carelesnesse vnkind" (1.7.3) and in the courtly framework suggested by "Vnkindnesse past, they gan of solace treat" (1.7.4). On the other hand, if we think Spenser means to reject all chivalry, it is impossible to explain why he says

148

the Red Cross Knight was "carelesse . . . of his fame" or calls him "this gentle knight" as he stoops to drink from the fountain (1.7.6). The right way to read "Yet goodly court he made still to his Dame" is the natural way—to take it as descriptively true. Spenser gives us a full moral understanding of the situation by making us aware— really, assuming we see—that this *is* "goodly court." After the drastic enfeeblement described in the preceding stanza, we see how pathetic is the knight's continuing in his normal behavior. And just because we take "goodly court" at face value, the sense of pathos extends to the code the knight espouses. Chivalry simply facilitates Duessa's machinations, and we find ourselves asking again, "What man so wise, what earthly wit so ware?"

The next two lines contain explicit moral judgments, but we impoverish them if we take their function to be the direct expression of moral judgment. Again we must take the lines at face value. This expression suggests ignoring recondite or complex meanings for "obvious" or "commonsense" ones. But in Spenser's verse, where lucidity is the hallmark and meanings lie on the surface, to take something at face value means to see all its potential meanings. Because of the earlier descriptions of the fountain and the knight's enfeeblement, "pourd out in loosnesse" has a physical as well as a moral validity.[16] The knight's harmony with the setting is ironic in this phrase, but in the next half of the line it is seen from a different perspective. "On the grassy grownd" reminds us of the pastoral setting—the context in which one does pay goodly court to one's lady, and in which being "pourd out in loosnesse" can even suggest an attractive sense of release.[17] The pastoral context is again exploited in the next line. The

[16] In Spenser's two other uses of "pourd out" for sinful self-indulgence, the moral term is supported, as it is here, by the physical circumstances. See 2.2.36 and 3.1.48, 51.

[17] Compare the scene in which Turpine comes upon Arthur sleeping:

Thence passing forth, not farre away he found,
Whereas the Prince himselfe lay all alone,
Loosely displayd vpon the grassie ground,
Possessed of sweete sleepe, that luld him soft in swound.

Wearie of trauell in his former fight,
He there in shade himselfe had layd to rest,
Hauing his armes and warlike things vndight,
Fearelesse of foes that mote his peace molest.

(6.7.18–19)

And the scene in *Virgil's Gnat* in which the shepherd lies down to sleep in an elaborately described grove:

Of trecherie or traines nought tooke he keep,
But looslie on the grassie greene dispredd,

149

description of the grove and the fountain give the word "carelesse"—or rather, keep alive within it—suggestions of ease, *otium,* because they have made us experience the attractiveness of being free from care.[18] The line makes us fully aware of what the Red Cross Knight has done to himself, but it does so as a matter of moral understanding, not of moral judging. Hence Orgoglio's approach in the next lines is not a punishment that we supervise; rather, the humanity that we share with the Red Cross Knight makes us participate in the experience of terror:

> Till at the last he heard a dreadfull sownd,
> Which through the wood loud bellowing, did rebownd,
> That all the earth for terrour seemd to shake,
> And trees did tremble. (1.7.7)

The moral question we have implicitly been dealing with is man's ability to resist Duessa and Orgoglio, and we have been praising Spenser for keeping both sides of the question in focus. But we have not sufficiently noticed the way in which he does remind us of man's strengths—the capacities and obligations of the hero. We must take at face value the description of the knight's transformation: "Eftsoones his manly forces gan to faile, / And mightie strong was turnd to feeble fraile" (1.7.6). The Red Cross Knight is "noble" and a "gentle knight"; the nymph whose case parallels his wrongly "Sat downe to rest in middest of the race." Later in the canto the knight's downfall is described as the destruction of a noble heroism:

> The wofull Dwarfe, which saw his maisters fall,
> Whiles he had keeping of his grasing steed,

> His dearest life did trust to careles sleep.
> (241–243)

Note that Spenser's two other uses of "pour out" in a sinful sense occur in banquet scenes, while on the other hand, the phrase has a quite innocent meaning in *Epithalamion,* 355–356:

> And tymely sleep, when it is tyme to sleepe,
> May poure his limbs forth on your pleasant playne.

Presumably these passages are related to Virgil's describing the farmer on holidays as *fusus per herbam, Georgics* 2.527.

[18] To judge from OED, the meaning, narrowly construed, of "carelesse" here is the neutral, descriptive "unconcerned, not troubling oneself" (sense 2), and not the morally condemnatory "not taking due care, negligent" (sense 3). The former is much more frequent in the sixteenth and seventeenth centuries, and it alone is described as taking a complementary construction introduced by *of* or *about.*

And valiant knight become a caytiue thrall,
When all was past, tooke vp his forlorne weed,
His mightie armour, missing most at need;
His siluer shield, now idle maisterlesse.

(1.7.19)

The important point to note is that there is no way of bringing these reminders of human heroism and the opposing sense of human frailty into a single structure of moral judgment. The moral awareness that makes us see the loss involved when a knight is "carelesse of his health, and of his fame" are not the same as those engaged two lines earlier, where the pathos of "goodly court" depends on our sense of the inadequacy of knightly behavior.

Spenser is able to keep moral perspectives, and what are potentially whole structures of judgment, lying side by side, clearly apprehended and held in poise. As a psychological matter, this achievement depends on his having, and his assuming in the reader, a sense of the truth of many traditional ways of understanding man and representing his lot. As a rhetorical matter, we have to do with an ability to enforce the full meaning of apparently ordinary locutions and at the same time to keep these meanings from canceling out each other. Fully grasping and describing this phenomenon is a task which I attempt to do in chapter 9. For the moment we can simply observe that the rest of this canto confirms the fact that Spenser gives life to alternative moral perspectives in this episode. We are not surprised after the Red Cross Knight's downfall to see Orgoglio associated with the most arrogant displays of human pride (cf. 1.7.13, 16, 18). But we are perhaps not so confident that the canto will conclude by introducing a knight who restores our sense—as he restores Una's—of man's strengths. Arthur is a brave and courteous knight, and he behaves to Una like one, and not like a magical creature. Spenser was quite conscious of turning potential ills into potential goods in his portrait of Arthur. The description of his helmet (1.7.31) is a close imitation of the description of the helmet of the wicked Sultan in *Gerusalemme Liberata* (9.25). And as we shall see in the next chapter, Spenser treats Arthur's shield not simply as a magical object that gives him superhuman powers, but as the occasion for exploring some of the problems of human capacity that we have been considering. After Arthur appears, there are two notable transformations of details from the episode of the Red Cross Knight at the fountain. When Arthur meets Una, "with louely court he gan her entertaine"

151

(1.7.38)—a line that shows how right we were to take "goodly court" at its face value. Even more extraordinary is the famous simile that describes the "bunch of haires" on top of Arthur's helmet:

> Like to an Almond tree ymounted hye
> On top of greene *Selinis* all alone,
> With blossomes braue bedecked daintily;
> Whose tender locks do tremble euery one
> At euery little breath, that vnder heauen is blowne.
>
> (1.7.32)

The last lines are very close to the earlier description of "the breathing wind, / Which through the trembling leaues full gently playes." The reprise of these lines is so remarkable because it brings out an element of human strength—capacities of gladness, confidence, and response to sensuous beauty—in our enjoyment of verses which, the first time they appeared, served primarily to enforce our sense of human frailty.

II

In the next three chapters we shall frequently consider what Spenser expects of his reader by way of mental equipment and moral attitude, and such inquiries are often hag-ridden by the image of "the sixteenth-century reader." The usual view of that hypothetical creature can be seen in an article by Graham Hough, "First Commentary on *The Faerie Queene.*"[19] Hough summarizes the annotations made in 1597 by a man named John Dixon in a copy of the 1590 quarto of the first three books of *The Faerie Queene.* Three types of note predominate —biblical allusions, historical information and allegory, and moral commentary. An example of the latter is the comment on 2.12.32– 33—stanzas that, according to the argument I have made, the reader ought to find attractive: "womanish alluringe baites, and perswasions, wherby fonde intemperat men, are ofte over-come, to the hurte both of soull and bodye." Hough summarizes these notes in the following way:

> Their great interest is that we can see in them for the first time how *The Faerie Queene* impressed itself on a literate but not particularly literary reader in its own day. Dixon reads the poem largely as a celebration of religious and national history, while the romantic element is given very perfunctory attention or none at all.

[19] *Times Literary Supplement,* April 9, 1964, p. 294.

It is also noteworthy that he is as a rule extremely sure-footed in interpreting the allegory while he makes muddles about the surface narrative. Again and again he dives right through the story to the moral purpose underneath. It may be that in this he was not untypical of the readers of Spenser's day.

Hough's closing speculation is sufficiently tentative, but it is nevertheless characteristic of the modern reader's tendency to exaggerate the solemnity of the Elizabethan reader. Hough would not have made such a remark about the two annotators, mentioned in Alastair Fowler's survey of early copies of *The Faerie Queene,* who assiduously mark similes and nothing else. Fowler remarks that "this fondness for Spenser's similes is a feature common to many of the annotators."[20]

[20] "Oxford and London Marginalia to *The Faerie Queene*," N & Q, n.s. 8 (1961), 417. Fowler, who is the most avid iconographer of all Spenser's critics, concludes this brief article by saying, "Perhaps the most important inference to be drawn from these early marginalia is a very general one: that a detailed, emblematic interpretation of Spenser is historically completely justified" (p. 419). But the evidence he presents does not in any way warrant this conclusion. Fowler examined twenty-three early copies of *The Faerie Queene* in the British Museum and the Bodleian Library. Of these only two give him any evidence at all for an emblematic interpretation. One of these has Latin marginalia only to canto 1 of Book I; they consist of about two dozen words, and are what every schoolboy knows—that Una (1.1.4) is *veritas,* indeed *veritas sinceritas,* and that (on 1.1.15) *error unus multorum parens.* The other copy would provide real evidence if it answered to Fowler's description: "Minute, sometimes apparently trivial, details are noted: not only that Atin carries two darts, but even that 'Gyon striketh off Pyrrhocles horshead' (at 2.5.4). In the Medina episode, it rightly matters to him that the stern Huddibras should be entertained by the elder, and not the younger, sister (note to 2.2.16). In Canto 8, almost every physical circumstance of Arthur's battle with Pyrochles and Cymochles is noted" (p. 418). Fowler goes on, but it will be enough to answer these points. I examined this copy of *The Faerie Queene* at the Bodleian (call number F.2.62 Linc, 1590 edn.), and it seems to me that Fowler is simply making the annotations fit his own preconceptions about the poem. The annotator, Sir T. Postumus Hoby, says that "Gyon stryketh of Pyrrhocles horshead" simply by way of summarizing the action of the stanza. These notes occur throughout Guyon's fight with Pyrochles, so that we find next to 2.5.2, "Perrhocles chargeth Gyon," next to 2.5.5, "Pyrrhocles his speach to Gyon," next to 2.5.6, "Pyrrhocles and Gyon encounter on foote," and so forth. Similarly Huddibras' being entertained by the elder sister does not matter to Hoby at all. He is engaged in his usual activity—surely not a strange one to a reader of *The Faerie Queene*—of straightening out the names and numbers of all the players. Thus we find the following notes: at 2.2.13, "Gyon with the Palmer and babe doth come unto a castell wher dwelt three systers, the eldest was named Elyssa; the yongest Peryssa; the seconde Medyna" (here as elsewhere Hoby looks ahead to get the names of the characters); at 2.2.14, "Medyna doth enterteyne Gyon"; at 2.2.17, "Huddybras entertayned by Elyssa the eldest syster"; at 2.2.18, "Sansloy entertayned by Peryssa the yongest syster"; at 2.2.20,

153

Surely they are as typical of Spenser's audience as John Dixon? We need only be reminded of Peele's imitation of a particularly glamorous description of the sun rising,[21] or of Marlowe's imitation of the description of Arthur's helmet,[22] to recognize that "the sixteenth-century reader" would have assented to the praise of Spenser in *The Return from Parnassus:*

> A sweeter Swan then euer song in Poe,
> A shriller Nightingale then euer blest
> The prouder groues of selfe admiring Rome.
> Blith was each vally, and each sheapeard proud,
> While he did chaunt his rurall minstralsye.
> Attentiue was full many a dainty eare,
> Nay, hearers hong vpon his melting tong,
> While sweetly of his Faiery Queene he song,
> While to the waters fall he tun'd her fame,
> And in each barke engrau'd Elizaes name.[23]

The last six lines are a pastiche of Spenserian phrases, and one of the passages the author is remembering is one that John Dixon would have reviled: "Eftsoones they heard a most melodious sound, / Of all that mote delight a daintie eare" (2.12.70). In the sixteenth century, as in the twentieth, some readers of *The Faerie Queene* especially prize the verse when it is sensuous and decorative, while others, in Hough's phrase, dive through the surface of the poem to the presumed moral purpose underneath.

In Spenser's original audience we can discern a split very much like that between the romantic tradition of Spenser criticism and the twentieth-century scholarship that reacted against it. In the present state of critical opinion, attention needs to be drawn to those Elizabethan readers who enjoyed the surface of Spenser's verse. But it is important to recognize that their readings of Spenser are not necessarily more adequate than that of John Dixon. We shall now look at two imitations of *The Faerie Queene* which conclusively show a responsiveness to the surface of the poem, but which also show ways in which this kind of reading can be genuinely superficial. The first is a stanza from Phineas Fletcher's *Piscatory Eclogues:*

"Huddybrass and Sansloy fyght." Similarly his detailed notes to 2.8 are for the purpose of keeping clear a very confusing battle.

[21] *David and Bethsabe,* 7.58–66; cf. *FQ* 1.5.2.

[22] *2 Tamburlane* 4.3.116–124; cf. *FQ* 1.7.32.

[23] Part 2, lines 210–219, in *The Three Parnassus Plays,* ed. J. B. Leishman, London, 1949.

First her I saw, when tir'd with hunting toyl,
In shady grove spent with the weary chace,
Her naked breast lay open to the spoil;
The crystal humour trickling down apace,
Like ropes of pearl, her neck and breast enlace:
The aire (my rivall aire) did coolly glide
Through every part: such when my Love I spi'd,
So soon I saw my Love, so soon I lov'd, and di'd.[24]

This description of the shepherd's mistress, about whom there are no moral ambiguities, is based on Spenser's description of Acrasia:

Her snowy brest was bare to readie spoyle
Of hungry eies, which n'ote therewith be fild,
And yet through languour of her late sweet toyle,
Few drops, more cleare then Nectar, forth distild,
That like pure Orient perles adowne it trild.

(2.12.78)

Into his imitation of this description, Fletcher has woven a line from the description of the damsels bathing in the fountain: "their yellow heare / Christalline humour dropped downe apace" (2.12.65). Fletcher's stanza shows us an Elizabethan reader feeling—as any reader must—the attractiveness of Acrasia and the bathing damsels. Yet Fletcher's verse is self-indulgent and trivial, because it tries to exploit the erotic appeal of Spenser's descriptions without assessing the nature of the reader's involvement in them. Spenser's stanza is not only more morally intelligent than Fletcher's, it also has more erotic and sensuous attractiveness—a striking indication that these two aspects of his depiction of the Bower of Bliss cannot be separated. When Fletcher says, "Her naked breast lay open to the spoil," one can scarcely tell what he means: the article "the" makes "spoil" unintelligible, because it has no antecedent reference. Spenser's "Her snowy brest was bare to readie spoyle" is not only intelligible, but genuinely alluring. This effect is largely due to a grammatical trick. "Her snowy brest was bare," which is rather simple in its sensuousness, is grammatically complete and by itself would be purely descriptive. As the sentence continues, "to readie spoyle" brings out our erotic involvement in Acrasia's nakedness. That this kind of involvement is not, in

[24] Eclogue 7, stanza 10, in *Poetical Works*, ed. Frederick S. Boas, Cambridge, 1908–1909, 2 vols., 2, 215. This imitation of Spenser was noticed by Bain T. Stewart, "A Note on Spenser and Phineas Fletcher," PQ, 26 (1947), 86–87.

Spenser's verse, incompatible with moral clarity is shown as the sentence continues—again without any grammatical necessity—into the next line. "Of hungry eies" reveals that the imaginings to which "readie spoyle" would justifiably give rise if it ended the sentence are equivalent to a corruption of sexual appetite which C. S. Lewis aptly called skeptophilia.[25]

Our second example loses something of the passage it imitates, but it is not morally obtuse, as Fletcher's is. This is a sonnet by Thomas Watson, from the sequence *The Tears of Fancy* (1593):

> Each tree did boast the wished spring times pride
> When solitarie in the vale of loue:
> I hid my selfe so from the world to hide,
> The vncouth passions which my hart did proue.
> No tree whose branches did not brauelie spring,
> No branch whereon a fine bird did not sit:
> No bird but did her shrill notes sweetelie sing,
> No song but did containe a lovelie dit.
> Trees, branches, birds, and songs were framed faire,
> Fit to allure fraile minde to careles ease:
> But carefull was my thought: yet in despaire,
> I dwelt for brittle hope me cannot please.
> For when I view my loves faire eies reflecting,
> I entertaine despaire, vaine hope reiecting.

Lines 5–10 are a direct transcription of the description of Phaedria's island:

> No tree, whose braunches did not brauely spring;
> No braunch, whereon a fine bird did not sit:
> No bird, but did her shrill notes sweetly sing;
> No song but did containe a louely dit:
> Trees, braunches, birds, and songs were framed fit,
> For to allure fraile mind to carelesse ease.

> (2.6.13)

I have heard an eminent Spenserian try to dismiss the attractiveness of these lines by saying that Spenser had made them excessively artificial in order to reflect Phaedria's nature. But Elizabethan poets and readers loved artificiality, and Watson's lifting of this passage shows us that a man who is likely to have been a good reader considered it an unambiguous rendering of a pastoral landscape.

[25] *The Allegory of Love*, Oxford, 1936, p. 332.

Perhaps it is more accurate to say that Watson saw that the stanza could be used in an unambiguous way. The moral complications in Spenser's lines come not from the character of the description, but from the one detail Watson changed. He says "framed faire, / Fit to allure fraile minde" instead of "framed fit, / For to allure fraile mind." This slight change, which is of course due to the rhyme scheme, makes an immense difference in meaning. Watson's landscape is unambiguously "faire"; one understands why it is "fit to allure *a* mind to careless ease," but not why that mind is called "fraile." In Spenser's stanza, "fit" seems at first to be a quasi-adverbial form (*OED* 7) that renders unqualified praise. When we see in the next line that it is an adjective with a complement, we acknowledge the allurement of our frail minds, precisely because we have assented to the attractiveness of the landscape. It is impossible not to accept the apparent syntax of "fit" at the end of line 5: indeed it may well be the true syntax, since line 6 can be construed as a purpose clause that is complementary to "framed." Only by experiencing the pleasures of the landscape, do we understand—in the sense that word has in *The Faerie Queene*—the moral perils revealed as the stanza continues: "Carelesse the man soone woxe, and his weake wit / Was ouercome of thing, that did him please." And lest we think that the stanza is devoted to exposing the truth behind a lovely exterior, consider the last line—"So pleased, did his wrathfull purpose faire appease." Here we see the effect of the island as benign and morally desirable: the line is compatible with, but its meaning is not exhausted by, the narrative fact that Pyrochles' weak wit has been overcome. The stanza is a fine instance of Spenser's willingness and ability to let different moral perspectives lie side by side—not simply for the fun of it, but because, as the rest of the canto makes clear, the desire for pastoral ease is inherently problematic.

In reading *The Faerie Queene,* one apprehends the depths only by staying on the surface. The poem is genuinely hard to keep in focus, so that to tell the reader to trust Spenser's verse, though that is the right advice, does not solve all his difficulties in dealing with it. One problem, however, is quite easily resolved. It is natural, given both the nature of Spenser's verse and the nature of narrative poetry, that we equate trusting the surface of *The Faerie Queene* with sensuous experience. In all the Elizabethan examples we have mentioned, Spenser's readers and imitators have in mind passages of sensuous description, either in the narrative or in similes. As opposed to this, we think of the moralizing reader as diving beneath the surface to an underlying truth. But this opposition is entirely false. Abstract statements and analyses, moral terms and attitudes, are as much a part of the surface of *The Faerie Queene* as descriptions and other evocations of sensuous experience. The next three chapters will show, in various ways, that recognizing this simple fact does a great deal to resolve some of the false dilemmas of Spenserian criticism. To conclude this chapter, I would like to examine a case in which we can see an Elizabethan reader responding to both the sensuous and the moral language which *The Faerie Queene* presented to him.

This reader is Robert Allott, who in 1600 published a dictionary of quotations entitled *England's Parnassus*. Three-fourths of the collection consists of moral statements gathered under headings like "Danger," "Honor," or "Women"; the rest of the book consists of "poeticall comparisons" and descriptions. Allott was a wretched copyist and made many blunders in attribution, and it is only fair to say that the modern editor of *England's Parnassus* has a low opinion of him.[26] However, none of our argument about Spenser's verse depends on the evidence in *England's Parnassus,* and the reader can take what follows for whatever he thinks it is worth.

Most of Allott's quotations from Spenser are the ones we would expect to find in any collection of moral and descriptive gems from *The Faerie Queene*. The aspect of his collection that is worth our considering is the variety of passages that he sometimes brings together under the same heading. Under "Descriptions of Beauty and Personage" he quotes the long catalogue description of Belphoebe (2.3.22–31, no. 2013),[27] the portrait of Charissa suckling her babes (1.10.30, no. 2026), the description of Acrasia that Fletcher imitated (2.12.77–78, no. 2034), the immensely erotic description of Serena on the cannibals' altar (6.8.42, no. 2035), and the description of Una's face shining like the sun (1.3.4, no. 2050). Allott's selections of moral statements often give a good sense of the play of moral understanding in *The Faerie Queene*. Thus under "War" he quotes the words of both Medina and Phaedria when they pacify Guyon and his foes (2.2.30.6–9, no. 1683; 2.6.35.7–9, no. 1686). Under "Life" he quotes arguments from both the Red Cross Knight and Despair (1.9.41.2–5, no. 936; 1.9.43.1–2, no. 937); and the

---

[26] Charles Crawford, in whose edition, Oxford, 1913, almost all the quotations are identified. My own examination of *England's Parnassus* would have been impossible without Crawford's index and notes.

[27] The number following the book-canto-stanza-line numbers is the number of the quotation in Crawford's edition.

other two quotations under this heading evaluate life in quite different ways—Spenser's contemplation of the feebleness of man's state when Arthur is endangered by Maleger (2.11.30.1–5, no. 942) and Britomart's words of encouragement to Scudamour: "Life is not lost, (said she) for which is bought / Endlesse renowm, that more then death is to be sought" (3.11.19, no. 945). Under "Fate" he quotes two "wrong" opinions that are corrected within the poem (3.3.25.4–5, no. 449; 5.4.27.8–9, no. 452), and thus bears witness to Spenser's willingness to entertain moral attitudes, even if they are then placed or judged. (The correction of one of these opinions, 3.3.25.6–9, though it occurs within the same stanza, is given as a separate quotation, no. 454.) Finally, for sheer variety, we have the following items under "Death": Despair's argument about the inevitability of death (1.9.42, no. 288); lines on dying well from the portrayal of the fifth of Mercy's almoners, who "had charge sicke persons to attend" (1.10.41.6–9, no. 297); part of Cymochles' defiant reply when the Palmer asks him not to abuse Guyon's corpse (2.8.14.7–8, no. 303); Guyon's argument that Mortdant and Amavia should be given burial (2.1.59, no. 304); part of Cymoent's lament over Marinell (3.4.38.5–9, no. 307); and finally Amoret's expression of misery when she has been captured by Lust (4.7.11.7–9, no. 309). All these facts about *England's Parnassus* may have no significance. But if they have any, it is that one Elizabethan reader found a liveliness of moral interest in *The Faerie Queene* and that he took Spenser's verse at face value.

Chapter Six

Spenser's Use of Ariosto

I

The idea that Spenser used an allegorized *Orlando Furioso* has not been a major cause of our misreading *The Faerie Queene,* but it has been considered a major piece of historical evidence in support of our misreadings. Students of Spenser commonly draw attention to the fact that *Orlando Furioso* was considered a highly moral poem, and that of the scores of editions that appeared in the sixteenth century, most were supplied with allegorical interpretations. Graham Hough, for example, has recently said:

> It is impossible to say how much of this exegesis Spenser used, but that he did use it, and turn it to good purpose, is quite clear from internal evidence. . . . Some writers have suggested that it was a sort of British or puritan obtuseness in Spenser that made him read the irresponsible Ariosto as allegory. This is mere ignorance. Spenser read Ariosto in the manner of the Italians of his time. So, it would appear, did others. Harington, who cannot be suspected of undue rigour, who is quite capable of producing a slyly tolerant defence of the poem, also regards it as allegorical, on more than one level.[1]

But it is no defense of Spenser (though it may be of England) to say that Italian editors of Ariosto were also obtuse, and one's feeling that the allegorization of Ariosto was a fairly mindless process is not lessened by examining the commentaries that Spenser presumably approved. We ought to say at once that the issue is not that an essentially frivolous and cynical poem has been burdened with solemn meanings that are entirely inappropriate to it. *Orlando Furioso* not only contains genuine allegories; it is also full of heroic behavior, episodes exemplifying the most exquisite sense of honor and loyalty, pathos that, while often grand, is never exaggerated, and a range of comedy that rivals Chaucer's for variety, clarity of vision, and humanity. One's objection to the commentaries is precisely to their

---

[1] *A Preface to "The Faerie Queene,"* London, 1962, p. 119. For the view that Spenser's English seriousness prevented him from seeing Ariosto's irony, cf. Hallett Smith, *Elizabethan Poetry,* Cambridge, Mass., 1952, p. 322.

moral inadequacy. Take this "allegory" of the tale of Ariodante and Ginevra:

> Polinesso tries to bring dissension into the love of Ginevra and her Italian lover; to make us understand that human happiness always has discord and envy as its rivals.
>
> The Italian knight who, driven to despair because of too much trust, wants to kill himself, is an example to us that he who believes too readily ends up in extreme perils.
>
> By Ginevra, who is defended from the false accusation, the innocent are assured that they may confidently hope to be provided by God with defenders in their hour of need.
>
> The example of Polinesso, punished for his bad deeds, demonstrates that he who acts badly, if he prospers for a while, fares badly in the end.[2]

Prose that ticks off these platitudinous morals is incapable of expressing the moral insight and intelligence of the episode it interprets. If such prose really represents "the way Spenser read Ariosto," then there is indeed an essential obtuseness in the way Spenser used *Orlando Furioso* and, one would say, an essential obtuseness in *The Faerie Queene*.

The solution to the difficulty is simply to examine the way in which Spenser actually used Ariosto. It is unthinkable that a mind that is adequately expressed by Toscanella's allegory could have turned the tale of Ariodante and Ginevra into the tale of Phedon, in which the moral sensibility is certainly more severe, but is no less complex and searching than Ariosto's. In the course of this chapter we shall examine most of Spenser's major borrowings from Ariosto. In each case we shall find that the use to which Spenser puts *Orlando Furioso* can only be explained by attributing to him a full and intelligent response to the poem itself. If we assume, on the other hand, that the allegories of the commentators were the spectacles through which he saw the poem, his use of it is inexplicable. To say this is not at all to deny the possibility—which is very strong in some cases—that Spenser got suggestions for his own poem from the commentators on Ariosto's. It simply denies that the prose of the allegories adequately represents the kind of meaning Spenser found in *Orlando Furioso* or the kind of meaning he would think himself to be expressing in *The Faerie Queene*.

[2] Oratio Toscanella, *Bellezze del Furioso,* Venice, 1574, allegory to canto 5.

But first, what is the place of the commentators' allegories in six-teenth-century editions of Ariosto? For there is no reason to think that Spenser's contemporaries, any more than he himself, mindlessly accepted the commentators' prose as an equivalent to Ariosto's poem. Far from controlling the text, they are part of an elaborate editorial apparatus, which (unlike the apparatuses in Renaissance editions of the classics) is distinctly subsidiary to the text, and in which moral commentary is not the only, and often not the predom-inating, feature. One of the most popular sixteenth-century editions of *Orlando Furioso* contains a life of Ariosto and a table of all the characters (along with their major appearances in the poem) as part of the prefatory matter; a full-page wood engraving, an "argument" in ottava rima, and an allegory at the beginning of each canto; annota-tions at the end of each canto in which the editor explains mythologi-cal references, difficult words, and allusions to geography, history, and natural phenomena, and in which he comments on the rhetorical and narrative decorum of various passages; and at the end of the volume about 150 pages with the following items—a discussion of the verbal changes Ariosto made in the poem after the first edition of 1516; annotations that were too lengthy to include with those that follow each canto; verbal changes and improvements that the editor claims Ariosto intended to make in the poem; a gathering of passages that Ariosto imitated from other, mainly Latin, authors; an account of all the fables mentioned in the poem; a consideration of some ap-parent contradictions in the poem; a glossary of all the words that might be obscure "to those who do not know Latin or Italian litera-ture"; and finally an index of the first lines of all the stanzas in the poem.[3]

How does this material reflect the needs and interests of the reader? Much of it provides information and assistance of the sort found to-day in school editions, while the rest seems to indicate a greater inter-est in niceties of verbal and narrative detail than in moral instruction. We would make a similar judgment even without the various items

---

[3] This is an account of the edition published by Vincenzo Valgrisi in Venice, 1556. In the second edition, of 1558, the account of the fables was expanded and to it was added an explanation of the ancient and modern history touched on in the poem. Most of the items are the work of the editor, Ieronimo Ruscelli. However, some things are taken from other books (the life of Ariosto, for example, is from G. B. Pigna's *I Romanzi*, published in Venice in 1554), while others, though done for this edition, are the work of other men. To judge from the number of printings, this was the most popular edition of *Orlando Furioso* from the time of its appearance until 1580; in all, it went through more than two dozen printings.

that conclude the volume, for the annotations at the end of each canto often occupy a whole page, while the allegories rarely exceed six lines of type. Moreover, the allegories have to be seen from the point of view of book production. They were one of several features that made an edition of *Orlando Furioso* especially attractive or lavish. It is certainly true that most sixteenth-century editions of the poem contained allegories to each canto, but it is also true that these almost never appeared without handsome woodcuts illustrating one or more scenes from the canto. The sixteenth-century reader expected to have illustrations and "arguments" as well as allegories, and it would be difficult to make the case that he regarded the allegories with any special excitement or solemnity.

Allegorical interpretations of *Orlando Furioso* appeared both in editions of the poem,[4] and in a variety of moral and critical writings. Of the latter, the first and much the most important is Simon Fornari's *Spositione . . . sopra l'Orlando Furioso* (Florence, 1549; volume 2, 1550). The first volume of this is a bulky octavo of some 800 pages. After 75 pages that include a life of Ariosto (frequently reprinted in editions of *Orlando Furioso*), an "Apology" for the poem, and a discussion of some apparent contradictions in it (reprinted in Ruscelli's edition), Fornari settles down to a running commentary on the poem. This commentary is primarily a series of footnotes, giving the reader information on historical, mythological, scientific, and linguistic matters. But whenever Fornari comes upon an episode he considers allegorical, he gives a thorough exposition of it, and the

---

[4] There were scores of editions of *Orlando Furioso* in the sixteenth century, but all that concerns us is to identify the editors who provided allegorical annotations: (1) Lodovico Dolce first published an edition with allegories at the beginning of each canto (Venice, Gabriele Giolito, 1542). The allegories are always brief and strike one as casual and obvious. This edition was constantly reprinted during the next two decades. (2) Clemente Valvassori (Venice, Giovanni Andrea Valvassori, 1553) wrote fuller allegories than any other editor, but his edition went through many fewer printings than those of Dolce, Ruscelli, or Porcacchi. (3) Ruscelli (see note 3). This was much the most frequently printed edition for two decades. (4) Giuseppe Horologgio (Venice, Giorgio Varisco, 1563). The allegories are quite full and solemn, but they were reprinted only twice. (5) Tomasso Porcacchi (Venice, Guerra, 1568). The most frequently printed edition at the end of the century (more than a dozen printings between 1580 and 1600).

My account, here and in the text, is based on Giuseppe Agnelli and Giuseppe Ravegnani, *Annali delle Edizioni Ariostee*, Bologna, 1933, 2 vols.; on Giuseppe Fatini, *Bibliografia della Critica Ariostea (1510–1956)*, Florence, 1958; and on my work in the Houghton Library, Harvard, and the British Museum. A study of the allegorizations of Ariosto, by Peter Marinelli, is currently in preparation.

second volume of the *Spositione* is devoted to a separate exposition of the two major allegorical sequences in *Orlando Furioso*—first, Ruggiero's adventures on Alcina's island, his captivity by Alcina, his release by Melissa, and his journey to Logistilla (cantos 6–8, 10); second, the various conquests Astolfo achieves by means of the book and the magic horn given to him by Logistilla (cantos 15, 20, 22, 33). As in any criticism of this sort, Fornari assumes that the internal consistency of his exegesis proves its truth, and the single-mindedness with which he pursues his elected meanings can be wearying. Nevertheless, once one grants the kind of meaning he seeks, Fornari is lively and sensible in pointing out details in the poem or analogous details in other poets, and he maintains his responsibility both to the text of the poem and to his own argument. While we can look to the other allegorists only for their interpretation of specific details in *Orlando Furioso,* Fornari's allegories, both by their extent and their intelligence, give us an opportunity to investigate a whole process of reading and interpretation.

Orlando Furioso was the subject of a good deal of controversy in the sixteenth century, but the issues are preponderatingly formal; and when Ariosto's moral gravity is in question, the defense is characteristically in terms of the examples of Christian knighthood, moral justice, and Divine Providence in the narrative action.[5] To my knowledge, the only allegorical interpretation of any importance occurs in Giovan Battista Pigna's *I Romanzi* (Venice, 1554), in which a few pages are devoted to an allegorical exposition of Alcina, Logistilla, and the most important magical objects that Ariosto took over from Boiardo. In addition to theoretical and controversial writings, several books, though not exactly studies of *Orlando Furioso,* draw a great deal of material from it. Dolce's *Nuove osservazioni della lingua volgare* (Venice, 1568) and Ruscelli's *Del modo di comporre in versi nella lingua italiana* (Venice, 1558) are characteristic examples, while the most unusual is probably Levantio da Guidicciolo, *Antidoto della Gelosia . . . estratto da l'Ariosto* (Brescia, 1565)—an essay on jealousy, in which the many examples of jealous behavior and feeling are taken from *Orlando Furioso.* Guidicciolo gives an allegorical exposition of cantos 6 through 10, some of which was cited in the last chapter. Of all these writings, the one of most interest to us is Oratio Toscanella's *Bellezze del Furioso* (Venice, 1574). Toscanella's main

[5] For an account of the controversies, see Bernard Weinberg, *A History of Literary Criticism in the Italian Renaissance*, Chicago, 1961, 2, 954–1073.

interest, as he says in his preface, is in verbal graces and beauties, which he considers to have been rather neglected because of the attention given to allegorical interpretation. The book, like Fornari's, is simply a series of annotations and observations, but unlike Fornari, Toscanella does not make his allegorical interpretations part of the running commentary. Instead he provides, exactly as if it were an edition of the poem itself, an argument, a woodcut, and an allegory for each canto. The allegories follow the "In X we see Y" formula and are as dull as any of their predecessors. Toscanella also provides a prefatory list of characters, each of whom is given an allegorical meaning.

In comparing Spenser's actual use of several episodes in *Orlando Furioso* with the allegorists' versions of them, I have consulted all the allegories, despite the very slight interest of some of them. I have also consulted and will discuss Sir John Harington's commentary in his translation of *Orlando Furioso* (1591), which appeared the year after the first three books of *The Faerie Queene*. Harington's *Orlando Furioso* is rather different in format from the Italian editions. At the beginning of each canto is a full-page engraving in brass and an ottava rima argument, but no allegory. Unlike any Italian edition that I have seen, the canto itself has copious marginal annotations. At the end of the canto is a commentary, usually about half a page long, that is divided into four sections—moral, history, allegory, allusion—according to a four-fold scheme of allegory that Harington outlines in his prefatory "Apology for Poetry." In his "Apology" Harington exemplifies this scheme by applying it to the myth of Perseus, but nothing so rigorous or intensive is done in the commentaries to the poem itself.[6] These are, in effect, a combination of the *allegorie* (Harington's "moral" and "allegory") and the *annotationi* (Harington's "history" and "allusion") of the Italian editions. At the end of Harington's volume is "A Briefe and Svmmarie Allegorie of Orlando Fvrioso." This is an adaptation of the "Allegoria" by Gioseffo Bononome that introduced the handsome Ruscelli edition (Venice, Franceschi, 1584) in which first appeared the engravings that Harington had copied for his edition. Harington also included a life of Ariosto, taken from various Italian writers, and an index of the principal characters and their appearances.

---

[6] This fact is less surprising when we learn that Harington's interpretation of Perseus is translated word for word from Leone Ebreo's very popular *Dialoghi di Amore*, Venice, 1558, f. 61. See Robert Ellrodt, *Neoplatonism in the Poetry of Spenser*, Geneva, 1960, p. 183.

After his brief allegorical exposition of magical objects in *Orlando Furioso,* Pigna says, "We have been able to see up to this point how much morality there is underneath the devices of romance" ("Habbiam potuto vedere infino à questa parte quanta moralità sotto le Romanzerie si ritruoui").[7] One of the objects he moralizes, the enchanted shield that first belongs to Atlante and then to Ruggiero, becomes Arthur's shield of diamond in *The Faerie Queene.* There is a great deal of allegorical commentary on Atlante's shield, and it seems undeniable that Spenser is indebted to Fornari for an important suggestion about the way he could use it. Susannah McMurphy was the first to point this out, and her discussion is of interest because it reveals how misleadingly we can evaluate the facts of a case:

> This shield, according to Fornari, represents the light of Illuminating Grace—that is, when Ruggiero uses it to abash Alcina's huntsman, horse, dog, and hawk, this is its significance, but on other occasions it means fraud and deceit in a combat, or the bright, sparkling light of ladies' eyes! Perhaps if we knew all the "correspondences" of the Neoplatonist we could reconcile these explications, but we have lost the key, and Fornari does not enlighten us. As Spenser was wise enough to use these weapons only in the legends of Holiness and of Chastity, we are not confused by conflicting interpretations. In his story the shield apparently means the blinding light of purity and truth, which dashes pride, lust, and passion.[8]

Miss McMurphy conveys so strong a sense of the absurdity of Fornari's allegory that it is hardly any praise of Spenser to say he was wise enough to avoid conflicting meanings. Quite the reverse, by taking the interpretations seriously, he is implicated in their mindlessness. Miss McMurphy's feeling of bemused incredulity reappears in a comment by William Nelson, though he offers an opposite interpretation of the allegorists' influence:

[7] *I Romanzi,* p. 90.

[8] *Spenser's Use of Ariosto for Allegory,* Seattle, 1924, p. 30. The remark about Neoplatonic correspondences refers to the theory of allegory that Fornari presents in a brief introduction to the second volume of his commentary. See below, chap. 7, n. 9. Arthur does not in fact use his shield in the legend of Chastity (Book III). He uses it twice in Book V (8.37–41, 11.21, 26) and once, accidentally, in Book IV (8.42).

Sometimes Spenser seems almost perverse in the way he turns his borrowed matter upside down . . . Arthur's miraculous shield is another instance of imitation by reversal. It was originally the property of Atalanta, in the *Orlando Furioso*. Sir John Harington explains its principal significance: "In the shield, whose light amazed the lookers on, and made them fall down astonied, may be Allegorically meant the great pompes of the world, that make shining shewes in the bleared eyes of vaine people, and blind them, and make them to admire and fall downe before them . . . either else may be meant the flaring beauties of some gorgeous women that astonish the eyes of weake minded men." But in Spenser's version this trumpery shield becomes the divine power that destroys illusion:

> all that was not such, as seemd in sight,
> Before that shield did fade, and suddeine fall. (1.7.35)

That which hides the truth Spenser turns into that which reveals it.[9]

Again it is assumed that if Spenser borrows from *Orlando Furioso* for his own allegorical purposes, he must be working by means of the allegorists' commentaries. This is complicated by the assumption that an object is single and therefore has a single meaning, or allegorical identity. This assumption makes Miss McMurphy find Fornari's inconsistencies silly, and Nelson assume that Spenser is reversing a meaning that is as fixed and external a reality as the shield itself. But Arthur's shield, unlike Atlante's, is not even conceived as the kind of real object which, since it has specific properties and obeys certain rules, would be capable of carrying a fixed meaning. As we shall see, some statements about Arthur's shield are untrue if we take them as assertions about a single object. Hence if we begin by assuming that Spenser found in *Orlando Furioso* the allegorists' meanings in the form in which they appear in the commentaries, we are forced to the embarrassing conclusion that in trying to incorporate these meanings in *The Faerie Queene* he somehow botched the job. These problems, however, can be put aside for the moment. Arthur's shield does have an identifying characteristic, its blazing light, and everyone remembers it as the weapon with which Arthur defeats Orgoglio. We shall begin, then, by discussing the relationship of this episode to Ariosto's use of Atlante's shield.

[9] *The Poetry of Edmund Spenser*, New York, 1963, pp. 142–143. Harington's moralization is from the commentary to canto 2.

In *Orlando Furioso,* the shield whose light blinds and stuns the viewer is originally the property of the old magician Atlante, who uses it to conquer the knights whom he imprisons in his castle of steel (2.54–56). Bradamante, who seeks to liberate her lover Ruggiero, gains possession of Angelica's magic ring, which alone can resist the power of the shield (3.67–70). Bradamante defeats Atlante by pretending to be stunned by the shield; when Atlante dismounts from the hippogriff, his flying steed, to bind her, she suddenly seizes and captures him (4.21–26). Ruggiero is liberated, but through a stratagem of Atlante's is carried off by the hippogriff (4.42–46). When Atlante dismounted to bind Bradamante, he left the shield in its cover of silk (2.55) tied to the hippogriff's saddle (4.25, 42), and it thus passes into the hands of Ruggiero. However, Ruggiero refuses to use the shield when he first has an opportunity. In his battle with Alcina's troop of monsters, he scorns to unveil it, "because he wished to use strength and not deception" ("perché virtude usar vòlse, e non frodo," 6.67). Ruggiero does not use the shield until Melissa has released him from Alcina's enchantment and he is on his way once more to the kingdom of Logistilla, Alcina's virtuous sister. He has scarcely started out when he finds his way blocked by Alcina's huntsman and three fierce animals, a horse, a dog, and a hawk. Ruggiero knows he must hurry to escape Alcina, but he scorns to use his sword against animals and an unarmed man, so he uncovers the shield, stuns the beasts and the huntsman, and rides away (8.10–11). Two cantos later, when Ariosto returns to him, Ruggiero is in the last stages of his journey; he is being taken to Logistilla in a boat when Alcina and her navy catch up with him. Logistilla's boatman tells Ruggiero to uncover the shield, and by doing so he stuns his pursuers (10.50).

Here and in the earlier encounter with the huntsman, one is certainly encouraged to think that the *romanzeria* conceals *qualche moralità.* But sixty stanzas later the shield is once more simply a magical weapon. In an episode based on Perseus' rescue of Andromeda, Ruggiero rescues Angelica from the Orc by stunning it with the shield (10.107–110; the shield only stuns its victims, so that the Orc is not killed until Orlando rescues Olimpia in canto 11). Ruggiero uses the shield only once more, in his battle with Grifone, Aquilante, and Guidon Selvaggio—good knights who have been forced to impose Pinabello's wicked penalty on travelers. Ruggiero does not mean to use the shield, but its cover is accidentally torn off in a skirmish, and when he turns around to join battle again he finds that his enemies and their horses have all fallen senseless (22.84–87). Ruggiero is ashamed of such a victory and fears he might be accused of winning all his battles by enchantments and not by his own valor (22.90). Luckily he comes upon a deep well, into which he throws the shield (22.92). Fame with her trumpet quickly spreads the news that Ruggiero has thrown away so wonderful a weapon, but since she neglects to tell anyone where he threw it, the shield is lost forever (22.93–94).

It is easy to see why a single allegorical identification of the shield could not be sustained through all its appearances in *Orlando Furioso*. Fornari, who though very serious is not a fool, does not offer a Neoplatonic key, because he is perfectly aware that there could be none: "Thus we shall say that this word, 'shield,' is not single in meaning but is equivocal, that is, of many meanings. For that reason sometimes it will signify illuminating grace, other times a simple shield, and often it will denote fraud, as one sees in this passage [6.67, the battle with Alcina's monsters] and later, when Ruggiero plunges it into the well."[10] When the shield is simply a shield, it creates problems only because there is a feeling of trickery in Ariosto's reversion to mere romance. A greater problem is that the hero in whose hands the shield represents illuminating grace sometimes scorns the shield, and his valuation forces us to interpret it as something worthy of scorn. There is finally the difficulty, which Fornari does not mention in this note, that the shield was originally Atlante's and becomes involved in whatever meanings are discovered in his imprisoning brave knights and keeping them happy with all the delights they could have in the world outside (4.32). Fornari interprets "this tale of Atlante become a knight" as "Love's strange sports and playful enterprises with lovers," and the shield, which is simply one of many significant details, becomes "the shining eyes of beloved and beautiful women, who make their lovers mad and beside themselves."[11] We have the interesting phenomenon of a magical object retaining its identity as an object, but resisting a fixed allegorical meaning. The commentaries reflect this problem by giving the shield a bad significance in cantos 2 and 4 and omitting, for the most part, any mention of the shield in its victories over Alcina—just when the poem most allows the search for allegorical significance.[12] Valvassori alone makes an effort to accommodate an im-

---

[10] *Spositione*, 2, 76.   [11] *Ibid.*, 1, 181, 183.

[12] Ruscelli calls the shield "violence and deceits" in the allegory to canto 2 and does not mention it again until Ruggiero throws it into the well. Pigna's interpretation of the shield as Deceit (*I Romanzi*, p. 87) is based solely on cantos 2 and 4. Horologgio calls the shield "mortal beauty" in cantos 2 and 4 and, simply letting the inconsistency stand, "reason" in canto 8. Porcacchi and Toscanella give no allegorical interpretations of the shield, perhaps because

moral object to moral actions: "The shield's radiance, with which the four animals are dazzled, one interprets to mean that the passions of the spirit can be calmed when one deceives them by placing some object in the heart which is their opposite."[13]

This survey of interpretations may seem to confirm Miss McMurphy's account of Spenser's borrowing. It is not so easy as one might think to attach a precise significance to Arthur's shield, but "illuminating grace" is surely close to what Spenser has in mind, and it seems entirely reasonable to think that, in this instance at least, Spenser reads *Orlando Furioso* as Fornari does—treating the conquests of Alcina's huntsman and her navy as the two major actions of the shield and letting the other meanings arrange themselves as best they can. The first objection to this view will probably occur to most readers even before they look back to the text of Spenser's episode. One of the most memorable details in Arthur's battle with Orgoglio is that the blazing shield is uncovered "by chaunce" (1.8.19). Here Spenser was surely thinking of Ruggiero's final battle with the shield, and we find other indications that he had in mind instances in which neither he nor Fornari would have thought of identifying the shield with illuminating grace. Whenever the shield is in action, Ariosto mentions its blinding light, but when Spenser speaks of "the light . . . that heauens light did pas" and the "flashing beames of that sunshiny shield" (1.8.19, 20), one particular line has stayed in his mind. When Ruggiero uncovers the shield to stun the Orc, "it seems that he adds another sun to the sky."[14]

As soon as we read Spenser's episode in detail, we find that it has a relationship to *Orlando Furioso* that is very different from a detailed reading of the poem done in Fornari's manner. Here is Fornari on Ruggiero's encounter with the huntsman:

> But since it seems right to her [reason] to persuade the soul how cowardly it is to let itself be beaten by such obvious and base desires, it does not seem fitting to her to use the sword, that is the doctrines of theology, of which the Apostle says, "Divine speech is living and effective and more penetrating than any cutting blade."

---

they felt the soil had already been well worked. What is most remarkable is that none of the commentators, except Fornari, mentions the use of the shield to confound Alcina's pursuing ships. Perhaps taking his cue from this silence, Harington omits this incident in his translation.

[13] Allegory to canto 8.

[14] "E par ch'aggiunga un altro sole al cielo" (10.109). This is the only comparison of Atlante's shield to the sun.

Not wishing, therefore, to put sacred doctrine to work in order to prove things that are clear, she takes as her aid only the illuminating grace of God. This is what one can best understand here by the radiant shield, which one sees is of such strength that it dazzles the servant with the three animals and makes them fall to the ground. This signifies that the mind enlightened by God easily conquers all disturbances.[15]

Obviously Spenser would have found this an interesting and suggestive exposition, but that does not mean that it represents the way he read Ariosto. Fornari's interpretation of the shield is based not simply on its blazing light, but also on the dramatic action and the distinction it enforces between the sword and the shield. For Fornari, Ruggiero's decision to use the shield and not the sword is reason's acting on its awareness both of its obligations to itself and of the support it can rely on. The question is whether we should attribute a like significance to the fact that the uncovering of Arthur's shield is not a decision but an accident. Perhaps we should think of Spenser continuing the allegory into regions uncharted by Fornari, and elaborating to himself an explication of the accidental uncovering of the shield in Ruggiero's battle with Grifone and Aquilante. Or perhaps we should say that while Spenser would not have pretended to straighten out the use of the shield in *Orlando Furioso,* he nevertheless was conscious of reversing the significance of Ruggiero's deciding to use the shield—whatever, precisely, that reversal of meaning would be. These hypotheses may seem farfetched and literalistic, but they are quite consistent with the kind of reading Fornari gives *Orlando Furioso.* If we cannot accept these images of the way Spenser thought through Arthur's battle with Orgoglio, then we must seek a different way to describe his use of Atlante's shield and the way in which Fornari influenced him.

The two qualities emphasized in Arthur's battle with Orgoglio—the blinding light of the shield and its stunning effect on its victims—are those to which Ariosto draws attention whenever the shield appears. When Spenser says that Arthur's shield "Such blazing brightnesse through the aier threw, / That eye mote not the same endure to vew" (1.8.19), he is drawing not on a single passage of *Orlando Furioso,* but on the reiterated use of the word *splendor* and descriptions of the way the light of the shield strikes the eyes.[16] Simi-

[15] *Spositione,* 2, 157–158.
[16] See *OF* 2.56; 3.67; 7.76; 8.11; 10.50, 107, 110; 22.68, 81, 85, 89, 95.

larly, when he says Duessa's beast "became starke blind, and all his senses daz'd" (1.8.20), he is drawing on three recurrent words in Ariosto's descriptions of the shield—*cieco, abbarbagliare,* and *abbacinare.*[17] In the simile that concludes his rendering of the shield's effect—"As where th'Almighties lightning brond does light, / It dimmes the dazed eyen, and daunts the senses quight" (1.8.21)—he uses not only the complex of words and experiences we have already noted, but also the fact that Ariosto describes the shield as stunning other senses as well as the eyes.[18] The imaginative impact of Atlante's shield on Spenser is essentially what it would be on any reader. When we look at Spenser's use of the shield in this way, we find nothing mysterious in the fact that the accidental unveiling of the shield was actively available to him for use in his own poem, or that the line, "e par ch'aggiunga un altro sole al cielo," stuck in his mind.

We must beware here of the misconception that Spenser simply borrowed physical properties from Ariosto's description of the shield and endowed them with his own abstract meanings. In this case, even if he were not literally seeing *Orlando Furioso* through Fornari's eyes, he would certainly be reading it in the manner of Fornari. This way of understanding Spenser's borrowings is unacceptable, because in *The Faerie Queene* it is impossible to isolate the merely physical experience of being dazzled by the shield:

> At her so pitteous cry was much amoou'd,
> Her champion stout, and for to ayde his frend,
> Againe his wonted angry weapon proou'd:
> But all in vaine: for he has read his end
> In that bright shield, and all their forces spend
> Themselues in vaine: for since that glauncing sight,
> He hath no powre to hurt, nor to defend;
> As where th'Almighties lightning brond does light,
> It dimmes the dazed eyen, and daunts the senses quight.
>
> (1.8.21)

Compare the effect of the shield on Alcina's huntsman and her sailors:

> Fece l'effetto mille volte esperto
> il lume, ove a ferir negli occhi venne:
> resta dai sensi il cacciator deserto,

[17] See *OF* 2.55, 56; 3.68; 6.67; 7.76; 10.50, 107; 22.85, 86, 95.
[18] See *OF* 2.56; 3.67; 7.76; 8.11; 22.86, 95.

cade il cane e il ronzin, cadon le penne,
ch'in aria sostener l'augel non ponno.
Lieto Ruggier li lascia in preda al sonno.

As soon as it came to strike their eyes, the light caused the effect
tested a thousand times: the hunter lies bereft of his senses,
the dog and the horse fall down, the wings fall so they cannot
sustain the bird in the air. Ruggiero is happy to leave them a prey
to slumber. (8.11)

L'incantato splendor che ne sfavilla,
gli occhi degli aversari così offese,
che li fe' restar ciechi allora allora,
e cader chi da poppa e chi da prora.

The enchanted splendor that sparkles from it so harmed the eyes
of their enemies that it made them in an instant become blind
and fall, some from the poop and some from the prow. (10.50)

The difference between the experiences rendered by the two poets
can be seen most clearly by comparing the effect of verse movement
in the two lines beginning "cade il cane" and in Spenser's successive
enjambments, "end / In that bright shield" and "spend / Themselues
in vaine." Ariosto's repetition of the verb *cadere,* in the first passage,
and the moderately halting movement of the next line—which sug-
gests a failing effort to keep the bird aloft—are mimetic effects de-
signed to render a physical event external to the observer. Spenser's
enjambments, on the other hand, render a psychological experience
of losing strength, and the intimacy with which we follow the verse
makes us take this experience into ourselves, rather than looking at
it as the experience of a character outside ourselves. We can see
how Ariosto's verse is consistent with a notion of allegory that treats
narrative events as a physical surface that the observer, looking from
the outside in, must penetrate in order to discover the hidden mean-
ing. But Spenser forbids this separation into physical and abstract,
because the intimacy of the rendered experience is not a matter of felt
physical closeness or closeness of observation. The experience feels
intimate because Spenser involves in it all our capacities of response
and judgment, so that in lines like "all their forces spend / Themselues
in vaine" we cannot say how much of our response is physical ex-
perience and how much is moral awareness. Similarly, the intense
physical presence of the concluding simile also contains, in "th'Al-

173

mighties lightning brond," the most explicitly stated context of moral judgment in the stanza. These closing lines draw on the most immediate physical details in Ariosto's narrative, but Spenser transmutes these details into his own kind of *enargeia*. He increases the element of physical sensation not in order to render a physical event in the narrative, but to clinch the psychological experience of being overwhelmed. Spenser uses Ariosto here not by following allegorical translations, but by turning a lively and detailed reading of *Orlando Furioso* into his own kind of poetic narration.

But if the commentators did not give Spenser a way of reading Ariosto's poem, they did give him suggestions for his own. It seems entirely likely that Fornari's interpretation of Atlante's shield as illuminating grace gave Spenser the idea of using it in Book I. More interesting is the possibility that Fornari's explication of Ruggiero's conquest of the huntsman suggested or influenced the accidental uncovering of Arthur's shield. This detail is essential to the way the humbling of Orgoglio expresses man's experience of grace: it makes the purging, dazzling effect of illumination something that happens to and overwhelms us, not something our will can summon to conquer a separable part of ourselves. Fornari's explication of Ruggiero's victory surely could have influenced Spenser's handling of his materials here. Fornari very much appreciates the sense of decision and heroic independence in Ruggiero's action. It is this quality of experience—which Fornari has no way of making an explicit part of his allegorical translation—that Spenser can be thought to be reversing in his episode. Incidentally, we now see why Spenser could unabashedly use the accidental uncovering of Ruggiero's shield in the battle with Grifone and Aquilante. Ruggiero's shame comes precisely from his feeling that the accident has undermined his heroic independence. Spenser's use of the event is not only compatible with, but directly dependent on, his appreciation of its force in *Orlando Furioso*. It may well be argued that Spenser is taking the whole episode too seriously—that his valuation, as he reads it, is Ruggiero's rather than Ariosto's. But this does not alter the fact that we are dealing with his experience of and response to *Orlando Furioso* itself, and not to the commentators' interpretation of it.

Arthur's shield is first described in four stanzas that conclude the description of his armor (1.7.33–36). The passage is a grand and self-conscious example of the way in which Spenser uses Ariosto—turning a detailed reading of *Orlando Furioso* into his own kind of poetic narration. The second and third stanzas have the most interest for us (in the first, Spenser describes the shield's amazing durability and hardness):

> The same to wight he neuer wont disclose,
> But when as monsters huge he would dismay,
> Or daunt vnequall armies of his foes,
> Or when the flying heauens he would affray;
> For so exceeding shone his glistring ray,
> That *Phoebus* golden face it did attaint,
> As when a cloud his beames doth ouer-lay;
> And siluer *Cynthia* wexed pale and faint,
> As when her face is staynd with magicke arts constraint.
>
> No magicke arts hereof had any might,
> Nor bloudie wordes of bold Enchaunters call,
> But all that was not such, as seemd in sight,
> Before that shield did fade, and suddeine fall:
> And when him list the raskall routes appall,
> Men into stones therewith he could transmew,
> And stones to dust, and dust to nought at all;
> And when him list the prouder lookes subdew,
> He would them gazing blind, or turne to other hew.
>
> (1.7.34–35)

When we read these stanzas with *Orlando Furioso* in mind, they seem a sort of compendium of Atlante's shield. The occasions on which Arthur will disclose his shield are just those on which Ruggiero already has—to dismay the monstrous Orc and to defeat Alcina's navy. (It is not clear what "the flying heauens" are, but they might have some connection with the descriptions of Atlante traversing the sky on the hippogriff, *OF* 2.49–54, 4.4–6.) The rhetorical device of listing the occasions for using the shield was probably suggested by a very striking stanza in which Ariosto, just before Ruggiero clashes with Grifone and Aquilante, looks back over the three occasions of extreme danger in which Ruggiero had used the shield (*OF* 22.82). In the next stanza there are no direct recollections of Atlante's shield. But the power of Arthur's shield to turn men into stones recalls Medusa's head, which, it was generally agreed, Ariosto was imitating when he invented Atlante's shield.[19] And the power of the shield to make fade "all that was not such, as seemd in sight," though it has

---

[19] See Pigna, *I Romanzi*, p. 86; Toscanella, *Bellezze*, p. 30, note on 2.55–56; Harington, p. 13, marginalium to 2.56.

nothing to do with the shield in *Orlando Furioso*, is the essential power of Melissa's ring when it is used allegorically as reason (*OF* 8.1–2) to show Ruggiero the true ugliness hidden underneath Alcina's specious beauty (7.70–74)—the episode Spenser imitates in the disrobing of Duessa (1.8.46–49).

It is not at all certain that these stanzas are genuine allusions to Atlante's shield—that is, that the reader is supposed to think of Ariosto as he reads—but there is no doubt that Spenser was thinking of Ariosto as he composed the stanzas and that they represent a continual picking up of hints from *Orlando Furioso*. But to what purpose does Spenser do this? There would of course be nothing wrong in his turning two of Ariosto's magical objects into one of his own, but the fact is that the power to reveal the false, which Spenser takes from Melissa's ring, is not that shown by the shield when Arthur uses it. Orgoglio does not pretend to be anything he is not, in the way Duessa and Archimago do, and though Arthur deflates him to "an emptie bladder" (1.8.24), he does so by cutting off his head and making his breath pass from his body, not by stunning him with the shield. Statements like this in Spenser's poetry are not assertions about putative objects. In fact when we look at these stanzas, we find that most of what Spenser says proves not to be true. Arthur does not use the shield against "vnequall armies" or "raskall routes" and he does not turn anyone into stone or dust. The shield is accidentally uncovered in Arthur's fight with Corflambo (4.8.42), but all it does is stun Placidas and the dwarf; however, Arthur finally does dismay a monster with it in Book V (11.21, 26). Arthur's only major exploit with the shield after his defeat of Orgoglio is his conquest of the wicked Sultan (5.8.37–41)—certainly a case of subduing "the prouder lookes." But on this occasion the shield, though it still flashes brightly, does not stun anyone. Instead it terrifies the Sultan's horses, so that they run away with him. That is, it behaves like yet another of Ariosto's magical weapons, Astolfo's horn, which makes everyone who hears it flee (*OF* 15.14).

These stanzas, then, do not describe an object or state rules for its behavior and use. They do what Spenser's poetry always does—create and develop responses and attitudes in the reader. We can see this most readily in the conclusion of stanza 34:

> And siluer *Cynthia* wexed pale and faint,
> As when her face is staynd with magicke arts constraint.

It is puzzling to have the shield's effect compared to disturbing manifestations of magical power, especially since "magicke arts constraint" is the province of Archimago. But the point is precisely that Spenser wants us to feel puzzled, and he is not at all worried by implicit assertions about the nature or source of the shield's power. Looking back at the stanza, we find there is a progression of wonder and puzzlement at the shield. We first see this in "Or when the flying heauens he would affray," which is not the third in a series of equal exploits, but a quite unimaginable event even in the world of romance: the uncertain meaning of the line may not be verbal carelessness, but a deliberate avoidance of a formula that would specify a particular event. The expanded sense of amazement is continued in lines 5 and 6, and the seventh introduces a strong feeling of puzzlement. When we read "That *Phoebus* golden face it did attaint," we assume that this happens because of the shield's excessive brightness, and we may even take "attaint" to be a loose rhyme word, without its specific suggestions. But its specific meanings are very much drawn out by the next line, which prepares us for the comparison at the end of the stanza.

The puzzled involvement with the wonderful shield that Spenser creates at the end of this stanza is beautifully reversed in the beginning of the next. Just when it seems that the shield is being called a prime creation of magic, it turns out to be a dissolver of magic. We can see again how important it is in Spenser, as in any poet, to consider poetic statements in their poetic contexts, when we consider the effect this development has on the next lines:

> But all that was not such, as seemd in sight,
> Before that shield did fade, and suddeine fall.

If this were said about Melissa's ring, it would refer to man's power, through his reason, to strip away a false veneer and see the clearly discernible reality underneath. We recall that Melissa does not give Ruggiero the ring until, disguised as Atlante, she has shamed him for failing in his obligations as a knight (7.56–64). But for Spenser, at least in Book I, an enchantment has a much more pervasive and sinister power to capture a man;[20] conversely, when Spenser imitates the exposé of Alcina, Duessa's ugliness is revealed by a literal disrobing, not by the dissolution of an enchantment. By making our wonder here develop through a sense of puzzlement at magic, Spenser is able to put us in imaginative possession of the shield's powers without

[20] On this subject, see Robert M. Durling, "The Bower of Bliss and Armida's Palace," *Comparative Literature*, 6 (1954), 335–347.

therefore making us feel immune to "bloudie wordes of bold Enchaunters call." To put it another way, when Spenser clinches the first stanza by apparently commending to us "magicke arts constraint" and then completely reverses our expectations at the beginning of the next stanza, he puts us rather in the position of the shield's victims, and certainly *not* in the position of the person who wields the power of the shield.

But the surprises are not over. Here is the final stanza about Arthur's shield:

> Ne let it seeme, that credence this exceedes,
> For he that made the same, was knowne right well
> To haue done much more admirable deedes.
> It *Merlin* was, which whylome did excell
> All liuing wightes in might of magicke spell:
> Both shield, and sword, and armour all he wrought
> For this young Prince, when first to armes he fell;
> But when he dyde, the Faerie Queene it brought
> To Faerie lond, where yet it may be seene, if sought.
>
> (1.7.36)

Once again, we can mention in passing, these are not statements about an object: no one, reading Arthur's battle with Orgoglio in the next canto, is supposed to think that Merlin has made the shield whose power is like that of the Almighty's lightning. A narration of the past history of an object—Spenser may again be thinking of Ariosto, for it occurs several times in *Orlando Furioso*[21]—is not the kind of stanza that permits Spenser's types of verbal richness and life. Nevertheless, the preceding stanzas are enough to make us charmed and interested by a stanza that purports to tell us that everything is believable, and then conducts its explanation by a series of statements which require fresh suspensions of disbelief, like accepting the sudden introduction of Merlin. The tempered sense of wonder—the kind appropriate to romance events, rather than romance marvels— is closely connected with Spenser's introduction of a good magician here. He is trying to give some kind of tentative resolution to the issues of human power that are raised by the appearance of the hero of his poem and his magical weapon.

Any questions about human heroism in *The Faerie Queene* are questions about the reader. The greatest single wonder in this stanza

[21] E.g. *OF* 4.18–19, 19.37–39.

is in the final line, which suddenly makes us actively assent to the reality of the shield. In isolation this line would seem to assert that a putative object exists in a putative world. But the reader of Spenser should know that the assertion lies not in an implied "it is," but in the stated "it may be seene, if sought." In saying this, Spenser reminds us that this figment of romance, this creation of magicians, is something whose reality lies—not in ourselves precisely, but in the exploring and responding activity of our reading the poem. And as Spenser makes this explicit in the final lines, we become aware that what he has done in these stanzas—what explains so energetic a reviving of Ariosto's materials—is to show us, in his own mode of narration, "quanta moralità sotto le Romanzerie si ritruoui"—how much morality there is underneath the devices of romance.

I I I

In the rest of this chapter we shall examine Spenser's other major borrowings from Ariosto. We begin with another instance in which, as Graham Hough points out, he undoubtedly got a suggestion from the allegories: "Atlante the enchanter, from whose castle Bradamante liberates prisoners as Britomart liberates Amoret, represents Lust for Fornari, Love for Toscanella and Porcacchi—and for Porcacchi, love described specifically as an *appetito*. Here we have clearly the origin of Busirane and his house."[22] This is an accurate summary of the commentaries, but it does not tell us much of importance about the way Spenser read Ariosto. In the first place, what Spenser chooses to use for his purposes is not what the commentators regard as important for the allegory of the episode. Fornari, who does a characteristically alert and very thorough job on this episode, pays a great deal of attention to the rough and steep path leading to Atlante's castle, which symbolizes, to use Harington's version of it, the "craggie, headlong, and unpleasant . . . wayes of that passion [love]."[23] But Spenser does not use this detail at all, nor does he give Busyrane's palace the smoking jars that lie under Atlante's threshold (4.38) and that engage

---

[22] *A Preface to "The Faerie Queene,"* p. 120.

[23] Harington's long allegory to canto 4 is all cribbed, including the quotations from other poets, from Fornari, *Spositione,* 1, 181–184. However, Harington gives up trying to transcribe all of Fornari's tireless and detailed exposition, and he dismisses more than half of it by saying, "Finally, the fortification of the castle, the fuming pots of stone, the scituation and height, and euery thing that is said of the man, the horse, the house, the shield, are so easie to vnderstand in allegoricall sence, as I thinke it needlesse to proceede anie furder in this matter" (p. 30).

179

the attention of both Fornari, who calls them "ardent sighs that issue from [lovers'] scorched hearts,"[24] and Valvassori, who devotes a separate sentence to them and calls them disturbances of the mind. On the other hand, one of Spenser's debts to Ariosto is for the scene in which Britomart discovers Scudamour lamenting by a fountain (*FQ* 3.11.7–20). This adapts Bradamante's discovery of Pinabello, who is also discovered by a fountain and who is also lamenting the loss of his lady to the wicked magician (*OF* 2.34ff.). The commentators say nothing about this scene in connection with Atlante's castle, though they do treat Pinabello as a representation of treachery and deceit, which are certainly exemplified by his attempt to kill Bradamante (2.66ff.). It is true that Spenser gets an important suggestion from the identification of Atlante as love. But it seems silly to think that he saw Ariosto through the eyes of the commentators, when we consider that he uses Bradamante's discovery of Pinabello, changes the wicked Pinabello to the sympathetic Scudamour, and takes him and Britomart to a castle that is surrounded by a wall of flames from *Gerusalemme Liberata* (13.32–37). Obviously Spenser feels and has complete freedom with the materials he borrows, and his use of them is to be explained only in terms of what his own poetry makes of them, not in terms of someone else's prose.

Even more important than the signs of Spenser's freedom in using *Orlando Furioso* is the evidence that he was a superb reader of the poem—even of episodes that our traditional notions of "sage and serious" Spenser tell us he could not have properly enjoyed. Critics tend to exaggerate the bawdy element in *Orlando Furioso,* but it is indubitably present in the story of Ricciardetto and Fiordispina (25.26–70). Harington says, "I must confesse my author sheweth in the tale, rather pleasant wit, then any sober grauitie, and the best I can say is this, that it is a bad matter not verie ill handled."[25] Ricciardetto, the twin brother of Bradamante (the model for Britomart), tells Ruggiero the story after Ruggiero has rescued him from being burned at the stake. Fiordispina, a Spanish Saracen, is out hunting in the woods when she comes upon Bradamante armed from head to toe. She takes Bradamante to be a man and falls violently in love with her. Even when Bradamante reveals that she is a woman, Fiordispina cannot tame her passion, which indeed torments her more because it cannot be fulfilled. On returning home, Bradamante tells this story to Ricciardetto, who, after some brief scruples about taking advantage

[24] *Spositione*, 1, 183.
[25] "Moral" to canto 25, p. 204.

of Fiordispina's desire for his twin, gallops off to her. Pretending to be his sister, he says that he has been transformed into a man by the nymph of a local stream, and he and Fiordispina spend many months living together in the midst of the court—for Bradamante, when she was there, had her hair cropped and everyone thinks Ricciardetto is she. At last the lovers are discovered and sentenced to the stake. Ruggiero rescues Ricciardetto, and we never learn what happens to Fiordispina.

This may or may not be "a bad matter," but the reader will recognize that the part of the story that concerns Bradamante and Fiordispina is the source of the story of Britomart and Malecasta in the first canto of Book III. Spenser is indebted to Ariosto not only for the situation, but also for some hints about the setting in a sophisticated court (see *OF* 25.56–58), details like Britomart's peaceful and Malecasta's restless sleeping (compare *OF* 25.42–43 with *FQ* 3.1. 58–59), and, most important, the rendering of Malecasta's passion as a raging internal fire (see *OF* 25.29, 32, 42 and *FQ* 3.1.47, 50, 53, 55). As for the commentaries, the situation here is the opposite of what it was with Atlante's shield. Instead of an abundance of interpretive material on Fiordispina, there is only Toscanella's identifying her as *impudicitia* in his index of characters. It is possible, obviously, that this suggested the transformation of Fiordispina into Malecasta, and while one word does not constitute a reading of an episode, we can certainly imagine a reading that begins with Toscanella's label and continues in the moralistic vein of Fornari's comment on the episode: "One sees that love's deceits, which for a time please and suit the lovers, in the end become their downfall because of fortune's various changes and because of the always eager curiosity of men."[26]

However, Spenser's use of the episode makes it impossible for us to think that his reading of it was simply moralistic—that is, that he regarded Fiordispina merely as an example of bad conduct or as an embodiment of an evil passion. One of his most important borrowings is not for Malecasta, but for Britomart's scene with Glauce when she confesses her love for Artegall (3.2.30–47). Glauce encourages Britomart by saying that at least her love is not unnatural like the loves of Myrrha, Byblis, and Pasiphae (3.2.41). But Britomart replies:

> Beldame, your words doe worke me litle ease;
> For though my loue be not so lewdly bent,

---

[26] *Spositione*, 1, 439.

As those ye blame, yet may it nought appease
My raging smart, ne ought my flame relent,
But rather doth my helpelesse griefe augment.
For they, how euer shamefull and vnkind,
Yet did possesse their horrible intent:
Short end of sorrowes they thereby did find;
So was their fortune good, though wicked were their
    mind.

But wicked fortune mine, though mind be good,
Can haue no end, nor hope of my desire,
But feed on shadowes, whiles I die for food.

                       (3.2.43–44)

This exchange adapts the lament in which Fiordispina accuses love
of tormenting her more harshly than any other lover:

        D'ogn'altro amore, o scelerato o santo,
        il desïato fin sperar potrei;
        saprei partir la rosa da le spine:
        solo il mio desiderio è senza fine!

In every other love, whether wicked or holy, I could hope for the
outcome I desire; I would know how to part the rose from the
thorns; my desire only has no fulfillment. (25.34)

She then cites, by way of contrast, three ancient instances of wicked
lovers (two of whom are Myrrha and Pasiphae) who did achieve their
ends, unnatural as they were.[27] None of this means that Spenser sym-
pathizes with Fiordispina as a character, in the sense that he likes and
admires her as he does Bradamante and Britomart. It only means that
his reading of the episode was sufficiently unhampered to enable him
to have Fiordispina's unusual love complaint available as material
with which he could express Britomart's equally unusual love woes.
When we ask why and how Spenser uses Fiordispina's lament, we
discover a great deal about the way in which he read the episode. It is
quite clear that in canto 2 of Book III, Britomart, suffering the raging

[27] Both the fact that three women are named (two of whom occur in both
passages) and the point about unattainable love make this closer to Spenser
than the passage in the pseudo-Virgilian *Ciris*, lines 237–249, that is the source
of the whole episode (see *The Works of Edmund Spenser: A Variorum Edition*,
ed. Edwin Greenlaw, et al., Baltimore, 1932–1947, Book III, p. 335). There
the nurse mentions only Myrrha, and the love in question is merely dishonor-
able, not sexually unnatural or impossible. Spenser is also closer to Ariosto
than to Ovid, *Metamorphoses* 9.726ff., which is one of Ariosto's sources. See
Pio Rajna, *Le Fonti dell' Orlando Furioso*, 2nd edn., Florence, 1900, p. 369.

fire of love (see 3.2.32, 37, 42, 43) and fixing her desires on an unattainable object, is a version of Malecasta—but one whose love we feel, for various reasons, to be natural and good. Spenser's use of Fiordispina for the portrayal of both Britomart and Malecasta has a real point to it, and it shows us that he could not have thought of Fiordispina as a character who stands for *impudicitia* or any other vice (or virtue, for that matter). To use the episode as he did, Spenser must have read it as it ought to be read—a situation whose dramatic workings bring out a bizarre variant of love's dealings with men. This episode, just like the very different story of Ariodante and Ginevra, gets its poetic force less from characterization than from a full dramatic playing out of a situation that entangles more or less conventional knights and ladies.

In addition to being an intelligent reader of the story of Ricciardetto and Fiordispina, Spenser was also a responsive one. The main reason we feel that Britomart's love pangs are natural and good is that Spenser treats them in a benign and comic manner. Britomart feels her torments to be horrible, because she feels only them. We, on the other hand, see beyond them in many ways—by our awareness of the universal power of "Imperious Loue" (3.2.23) and our sophisticated smiling at Britomart's plight (3.2.26, 27); by our amusement at Britomart's girlish impetuousness whenever she appears and at the lies with which she gets the Red Cross Knight to praise Artegall; by our appreciative enjoyment of Glauce, who, like the nurse in *Romeo and Juliet,* expresses a kind of wisdom and is also a figure of fun. The point of view Spenser gives us in this canto is genial, easy, and confident; we feel certain, before we hear a word from Merlin about Britomart's offspring, that, to use Glauce's image (3.2.45), Britomart will find the body with whose shadow she has fallen in love. The canto is full of comic moments, and one of the finest is the beginning of the speech in which Glauce encouragingly tells Britomart that she is not like Myrrha, Byblis, and Pasiphae. She replies to a speech in which Britomart characterizes her love in terms that remind us of Malecasta:

> Sithens it hath infixed faster hold
> Within my bleeding bowels, and so sore
> Now ranckleth in this same fraile fleshly mould,
> That all mine entrailes flow with poysnous gore,
> And th'vlcer groweth daily more and more.
>
> (3.2.39)

Glauce replies:

> Daughter (said she) what need ye be dismayd,
> Or why make ye such Monster of your mind?
>
> (3.2.40)

This is great comedy because the phrase Glauce produces has so much resonance. Britomart has indeed been making a monster of her mind, but just at the moment in which we recognize the truth of the phrase, the tone in which Glauce says it gives us a new perspective on its meaning. Glauce's down-to-earth ease makes us feel less that Britomart's mind is monstrous than that her love pangs are merely imaginary, "of the mind." The phrase opens up, by means of our enjoyment of Glauce, a relaxed and genial attitude towards Britomart's sufferings, while at the same time it retains full possession of the awareness that there is such a thing, as we have seen in Malecasta, as making a monster of one's mind.

In Ariosto's episode, the assurance that Fiordispina's love will reach "il desïato fin" comes largely from the first two facts that are told us—that Ricciardetto is Bradamante's twin and that at the time all this happened, Bradamante had her hair cropped (*OF* 25.24, 26). But comic perspective lies in more than a knowledge of facts, and it is wonderfully registered in the stanza that precedes Fiordispina's lament:

> Per questo non le par men bello il viso,
> men bel lo sguardo e men belli i costumi;
> per ciò non torna il cor, che già diviso
> da lei, godea dentro gli amati lumi.
> Vedendola in quell'abito, l'è aviso
> che può far che 'l desir non la consumi;
> e quando, ch'ella è pur femina, pensa,
> sospira e piange e mostra doglia immensa.

The face of Bradamant does not for that reason [knowing she is a woman] seem less beautiful to her, her expression less beautiful and her manners less beautiful; her heart, already taken away from her, which was rejoicing within the eyes she loved, does not for this return to her. Seeing her in this costume [her armor], she believes it can be that her desire will not consume her, but when she remembers she is only a female, she sighs and weeps and shows immense grief. (25.33)

Though one might expect that the last four lines would register the exposure of a delusion by the truth, Ariosto makes us see both the hope produced by Bradamante and the recognition that she is a woman as actions of poor Fiordispina's mind. Rather than presenting her as suffering a special fate because of the circumstances of her case, he presents these circumstances as if they were part of the oscillations of hope and despair that occur in any of love's victims: the sixth and eighth lines could describe the miseries of any lover. Our perspective on this love anguish comes from Ariosto's delicacy in evenly poising the two alternatives and in his being satisfied with narrating them as dramatic imaginings. A broader instance of our comic perspective occurs when Fiordispina dreams that her desires are satisfied and wakes to find it an empty dream (*OF* 25.43):

> Quanti prieghi la notte, quanti voti,
> offerse al suo Macone e a tutti i dèi,
> che con miracoli apparenti e noti
> mutassero in miglior sesso costei!

How many prayers, how many vows she offered in the night to her Mahound and to all the gods, that with clear and evident miracles they would change that woman to the better sex! (25.44)

The prayer is answered by Ricciardetto's cock-and-bull story about his transformation by the local nymph. No one would claim that Spenser was writing *in* the spirit of Ariosto's episode, but he certainly could not have written as he did without a just appreciation *of* Ariosto's spirit. We shall never understand Spenser's use of Ariosto, much less *The Faerie Queene* itself, if we think that such episodes show "how he could read his own steadfast idealism into the most openly licentious passages of the *Furioso*."[28]

We now turn to perhaps the most remarkable of Spenser's borrowings from Ariosto—his transformation of the pastoral idyll of Angelica and Medoro (*OF* 19.17–42). In this episode Ariosto returns, after a silence of seven cantos, to the beautiful Eastern princess Angelica, with whom all the knights in *Orlando Furioso* are in love and for whom Orlando will lose his wits. Angelica has recovered the magic ring that was originally hers and that in the hands of Bradamante and Melissa had been turned to moral and allegorical purposes. With the ring she no longer needs the protection that she formerly secured by

---

28 R. E. Neil Dodge, "Spenser's Imitations from Ariosto," PMLA, 12 (1897), 183. This is the pioneer article on Spenser's use of Ariosto.

stringing along her various lovers, and she grows intolerably proud. In order to punish her, Love lies in ambush where the beautiful Saracen foot-soldier, Medoro, lies dying of the wound he received in attempting to bury the body of his commander, Dardinello. When Angelica sees him she is struck with pity and, remembering the medicinal arts she learned in India, goes in search of herbs. She meets a shepherd who returns to Medoro with her; after Angelica treats Medoro's wound, he is put on a horse and taken to the shepherd's cottage. There, while he is recovering, Angelica receives from his eyes a wound of love that is deadlier than his physical wound and that grows more and more severe as his wound heals. Angelica finally confesses her love, and she and Medoro celebrate their marriage under the shepherd's humble roof. They remain for a month, enjoying each other's love in fields, in groves, and in caves, and wherever they can they write or carve their names—not only on trees and the softer rocks, but also on the walls of the cottage. Finally Angelica and Medoro set out for her kingdom in Cathay, and except for a brief encounter (29.57ff.) with the mad Orlando (driven mad when he comes upon the lovers' pastoral paradise and discovers "Angelica and Medoro" written everywhere) this is the last we see of them (see 30.16).

The reader will recognize that Spenser adapts this episode in Book III, canto 5, when Belphoebe discovers the wounded Timias and, while curing him in her pastoral grove, inflicts a deadlier wound of love. Timias, in his role of the faithful squire, is clearly modeled on Medoro, while Belphoebe shares with Angelica not only her beauty and self-sufficiency, but also her knowledge of herbs and simples. If there is less sense of a necessary connection between Ariosto's episode and Spenser's in this case than in others, it is because nothing in Ariosto can be thought to dictate or suggest Spenser's two major changes in the episode: he transfers Angelica's role as the love-stricken one to Timias and makes the love an unrealized one. The reasons for these changes must be sought outside Ariosto, and they are not simply political. Belphoebe is a figure of Diana as well as of Queen Elizabeth, and one would particularly expect Spenser, who praises married love as chastity, to explore the relationship of heroic virginity to erotic desire. It is impossible to decide whether Spenser got the idea for this episode while reading or thinking about *Orlando Furioso,* or whether he had worked out something like this episode and then thought to make it a version of Angelica and Medoro. Whichever is true, the relationship here is one of the fullest and most interesting of all those that exist between the two poems. In any case, it has nothing to do with the commentaries, which are particularly ludicrous in dealing with this episode. Their predominating characteristic is antagonism to Angelica, and their tone can be seen in Harington's version of Bononome's interpretation, in his allegory to the whole poem: "In *Angellyca,* the excellentnesse of her bewtie bred such an exceeding pride, that disdayning the greatest and worthyest Princes that liued in that age, she cast her selfe away at last vpon a poore seruing-man, for a iust recompence of her to haughtie conceipt."[29]

The first thing to note is that not all of Angelica's role is transferred to Timias. At her first appearance, Angelica sounds very much like Belphoebe:

> Gli sopravenne a caso una donzella,
> avolta in pastorale et umil veste,
> ma di real presenzia e in viso bella,
> d'alte maniere e accortamente oneste.

---

[29] Harington, pp. 410–411. This follows Bononome in the edition of 1584, f. **8, except for the last phrase, which in the original is nastier: "a servant, because she saw him with his cheek scrubbed a bit."
Fornari gives Angelica's proud self-sufficiency at the beginning of the episode a rather dignified interpretation—it signifies some ladies' excessive confidence in their own prudence—because he insists, characteristically, on retaining the allegorical identification of the ring as reason. It is even possible that Belphoebe's disavowal of Timias' worship and her claim to be only a "mortall wight" who is "bound with commun bond of frailtee" (3.5.36) owes something to the conclusion of Fornari's discussion of *OF* 19.18–19: "[It is] as if this Deity of Love, Nemesis rather, does not wish that man go exempt from human law and that he go proudly as if freed from his mortal condition, without paying the penalty" (*Spositione*, 1, 390). Later in the episode, however, Fornari finds plenty of opportunities to be harsh with Angelica. He even interprets her eagerness to carve their names in trees as "the rage and wicked mind of a woman who after long honesty is taken and made prisoner by love" (1, 392).
Of the other allegorists, only Ruscelli does not say that the point of the episode is Angelica's just humiliation. He says it shows that well doing (Medoro's faithfulness) is always rewarded and that love is more a matter of destiny than of choice. These interpretations at least show an understanding of the general character of the episode. Of all the attempts to make something moral, in the commentators' sense, out of this episode, the most notorious is probably the allegory Harington invented: "In *Angelicas* wedding of *Medore* I gather this Allegorie, *Angelica* is taken for honor, which braue men hunt after, by blood, and battells, and many hardie feats, and misse it: but a good seruant with faith and gratefulnesse to his Lord gets it" ("allegory" to canto 19, p. 151). This is sometimes cited as a particularly absurd example of the attempt to allegorize Ariosto, but it is at least in the spirit of the episode.

By chance there came upon him a maiden, clad in humble shepherd's dress, but of regal presence and beautiful in face, with manners noble and of courtly dignity. (19.17)

The commentators speak so harshly about Angelica because they fail to see that the context of her marriage to Medoro is not the just punishment of a proud character. It is rather the compatibility of the grand and the humble, which is stated here at the beginning by the fact that Angelica's rustic garb in no way diminishes her genuine regality. Even though the episode begins as Love's punishment, it ends as an idyll and a celebration, and though Angelica's humbling involves her being a shepherdess, the final transformation is of Medoro into a prince. Spenser is equally conscious of reconciling the grand and the humble, and in introducing the contrast, he gives it the broadest possible terms of reference. Timias awakens to see "The goodly Mayd full of diuinities, / And gifts of heauenly grace" (3.5.34), and in the next two stanzas Spenser fully plays out the possible meanings of these phrases:

> Mercy deare Lord (said he) what grace is this,
> That thou hast shewed to me sinfull wight,
> To send thine Angell from her bowre of blis,
> To comfort me in my distressed plight?
> Angell, or Goddesse do I call thee right?
> What seruice may I do vnto thee meete,
> That hast from darkenesse me returnd to light,
> And with thy heauenly salues and med'cines sweete,
> Hast drest my sinfull wounds? I kisse thy blessed
>   feete.

> Thereat she blushing said, Ah gentle Squire,
> Nor Goddesse I, nor Angell, but the Mayd,
> And daughter of a woody Nymphe, desire
> No seruice, but thy safety and ayd;
> Which if thou gaine, I shalbe well apayd.
> We mortall wights, whose liues and fortunes bee
> To commun accidents still open layd,
> Are bound with commun bond of frailtee,
> To succour wretched wights, whom we captiued see.

> (3.5.35–36)

This contrast of angel and simple nymph continues throughout the episode. Timias constantly thinks of Belphoebe as divine, and he be-

moans, like a self-conscious Medoro, his lowly estate (3.5.44, 47).
Belphoebe meanwhile remains the simple country girl: she keeps on
applying her medicines and wonders why Timias does not get better
(3.5.49–50). The two attitudes towards Belphoebe can be very funny
when juxtaposed—for example, "Still whenas he beheld the heauenly
Mayd, / Whiles dayly plaisters to his wound she layd" (3.5.43). But
to genuinely reconcile them is an imaginative effort of greater magni-
tude than that of presenting a princess in pastoral disguise. The
reconciliation of the grand and the humble occurs in this episode only
when Spenser detaches Belphoebe from her dramatic situation and
presents her as an exemplary figure, whose "existence" lies in the
reader's awareness of a virtue and whose presentation is the climax
of a direct address to the female readers of the poem:

> In so great prayse of stedfast chastity,
> Nathlesse she was so curteous and kind,
> Tempred with grace, and goodly modesty,
> That seemed those two vertues stroue to find
> The higher place in her Heroick mind:
> So striuing each did other more augment,
> And both encreast the prayse of woman kind,
> And both encreast her beautie excellent;
> So all did make in her a perfect complement.
>
> (3.5.55)

Spenser achieves his reconciliation of the grand and the humble by
adapting Ariosto's pastoralism, which has a similar function in his
episode. The pastoralism of Angelica's story is at first dominated by
rusticity, of which the most decisive stroke is at the "marriage" of the
lovers:

> Per adombrar, per onestar la cosa,
> si celebrò con cerimonie sante
> il matrimonio, ch'auspice ebbe Amore,
> e pronuba la moglie del pastore.

To cover up the affair, to make it honorable, they celebrated
matrimony with holy ceremonies, having Love as the groomsman
and the wife of the shepherd as the bridesmaid. (19.33)

To make the shepherd's wife the other attendant at a marriage whose
patron is the god of Love himself perfectly suggests that the beauty
we find in this match is not dependent on awesomeness. But the rustic

detail, by increasing the charm of the event, serves to increase, rather than undercut, our readiness to believe in the presence of a genuine attending deity. After this point the pastoralism of the episode becomes a matter of idyllic landscape. The richest expression of the harmony of the grand and the humble occurs in the account of the lovers' month in the country:

> Se stava all'ombra o se del tetto usciva,
> avea dì e notte il bel giovine a lato:
> matino e sera or questa or quella riva
> cercando andava, o qualche verde prato:
> nel mezzo giorno un antro li copriva,
> forse non men di quel commodo e grato,
> ch'ebber, fuggendo l'acque, Enea e Dido,
> de' lor secreti testimonio fido.

Whether she rested in the shade or went out of the house, day and night she had the handsome youth by her side. Morning and evening she went straying now by this stream now by that, or in some green meadow. In the middle of the day a cave sheltered them, perhaps not less fit and pleasing than that which Aeneas and Dido had as the faithful witness of their secrets when they fled from the waters. (19.35)

Ariosto's unassertive way of equating this cave with that of Dido and Aeneas enables him to hold in poise two divergent suggestions. On the one hand, the equation of the lovers with Dido and Aeneas suggests that they are dignified and heroic. On the other hand, to say that their cave was no less "commodo e grato" means simply that it served equally well the purposes of love. The humble cave is praised for being as good as the heroic one, and this tactic carries a suggestion that it is in some ways better. Just as the phrase "fuggendo l'acque," sharply distinguishes the purpose of Dido's cave from the normal pastoral function (providing shade at noontime) of Angelica's, so one feels that Angelica's fate in love is distinguished from Dido's.

In Spenser's episode, the pastoralism is almost entirely that of the idyllic landscape. Though its specific character has changed, its poetic role is the same as it is in Ariosto:

> Into that forest farre they thence him led,
> Where was their dwelling, in a pleasant glade,
> With mountaines round about enuironed,
> And mighty woods, which did the valley shade,

And like a stately Theatre it made,
Spreading it selfe into a spatious plaine.
And in the midst a little riuer plaide
Emongst the pumy stones, which seemd to plaine
With gentle murmure, that his course they did
    restraine.

Beside the same a dainty place there lay,
Planted with mirtle trees and laurels greene,
In which the birds song many a louely lay
Of gods high prayse, and of their loues sweet teene,
As it an earthly Paradize had beene:
In whose enclosed shadow there was pight
A faire Pauilion, scarcely to be seene,
The which was all within most richly dight,
That greatest Princes liuing it mote well delight.

(3.5.39–40)

Ariosto provides sufficient authority for this kind of description, especially if we look ahead to Orlando's arrival at the scene of Angelica's and Medoro's lovemaking (*OF* 23.100–101, 105–106, 108–109). But even what is distinctly Spenser's in this passage—the numerous indications of stateliness—is in harmony with his imitation. These details are introduced (as we see most clearly in the birds' songs of praise and love) not simply to make the landscape noble, but to make us feel that it harmonizes sweetness and nobility, the humble and the august. Spenser's adaptation turns the landscape fit for love into a fit home for Belphoebe.

Spenser's adaptation of Ariosto's pastoralism enables him to turn to his own account one of the major poetic moments in *Orlando Furioso*. When Angelica drops all shame and confesses her love to Medoro, Ariosto interrupts with an apostrophe to the great knights whom Angelica spurned:

> O conte Orlando, o re di Circassia,
> vostra inclita virtù, dite, che giova?
> Vostro alto onor dite in che prezzo sia,
> o che mercé vostro servir ritruova.

O Count Orlando, O King of Circassia, tell me, how does your famous courage help you? Tell me what value is set on your high honor and what thanks your service gains. (19.31)

After two stanzas in which he summons up the heroes of his poem
(in a tone which could be either heroic outrage or gentle mockery,
depending on the extent to which the speaker identifies himself with
the warriors addressed), Ariosto narrates the event that has been
awaited since the beginning of the poem:

> Angelica a Medor la prima rosa
> coglier lasciò, non ancor tocca inante:
> né persona fu mai sì aventurosa,
> ch'in quel giardin potesse por le piante.

Angelica let Medoro gather the first rose, untouched before; for
no one had been so fortunate that he could set foot in that gar-
den. (19.33)

The image of the rose is a poetic climax in Spenser's episode too, and
Spenser turns it to his purposes by a marvelous adaptation of yet
another feature of Ariosto's pastoralism. We recall that at the end of
his address to the ladies, Spenser produces Belphoebe as an exem-
plary figure who reconciles heroic chastity with graciousness. How-
ever, when Belphoebe is a dramatic figure, in her treatment of Timias,
the graciousness that goes with her virginity is incompatible with the
grace a lover seeks from his lady—by which I mean not primarily
sexual relief, but simply the recognition of the lover's feelings and a
correspondingly loving regard for them. Belphoebe is simply unaware
of the nature of Timias' suffering:

> She gracious Lady, yet no paines did spare,
> To do him ease, or do him remedy:
> Many Restoratiues of vertues rare,
> And costly Cordialles she did apply,
> To mitigate his stubborne mallady:
> But that sweet Cordiall, which can restore
> A loue-sick hart, she did to him enuy;
> To him, and to all th'vnworthy world forlore
> She did enuy that soueraigne salue, in secret store.
>
> (3.5.50)

The ample terms at the beginning of this stanza amount to nothing
more, in narrative action, than the application of more medicines. At
the same time, when Belphoebe's "costly Cordialles" become a meta-
phor of love poetry, they take on an interest and attractiveness that
balance the sense of self-absorption that we find in Belphoebe's dra-

matic behavior. Spenser can count on both these attitudes coming into play because behind this stanza lies Belphoebe's first medical treatment of Timias. There the language is so frank and simple in its sensuousness that it simply holds in solution any potentially incompatible attitudes.

> The soueraigne weede betwixt two marbles plaine
> She pownded small, and did in peeces bruze,
> And then atweene her lilly handes twaine,
> Into his wound the iuyce thereof did scruze,
> And round about, as she could well it vze,
> The flesh therewith she suppled and did steepe.
>
> (3.5.33)

This stanza is a very close imitation of *OF* 19.24, but even so Spenser transmutes it to his mode and for his purposes. Thus where Ariosto mentions Angelica's white hands because she is a princess who has turned to a humble task, Belphoebe's "lilly handes twaine" seem the natural instruments to perform so richly detailed a task as Spenser makes this. On the basis of lines like these, Spenser can exploit both the attractive and the cloistered aspects of Belphoebe's pastoralism, and this double awareness reaches its climax in the image of the rose, in the stanza that follows the translation of Belphoebe's cordials into a metaphor for her chastity:

> That dainty Rose, the daughter of her Morne,
> More deare then life she tendered, whose flowre
> The girlond of her honour did adorne:
> Ne suffred she the Middayes scorching powre,
> Ne the sharp Northerne wind thereon to showre,
> But lapped vp her silken leaues most chaire,
> When so the froward skye began to lowre:
> But soone as calmed was the Christall aire,
> She did it faire dispred, and let to florish faire.
>
> (3.5.51)

In this brilliant assimilation of Ariosto's image, Spenser most fully presents and evaluates the form of chastity Belphoebe embodies. We feel very keenly the attractiveness and naturalness of the rose as part of a pastoral garden of love, and when the rose becomes frankly metaphoric in the subsequent address to the ladies, it gets its strength from these feelings. At the same time, when we pay attention to Bel-

phoebe's dramatic relation to the flower of her chastity, we sense the
limitation of this rose as an expression of human personality.[30]

None of Spenser's other imitations of Ariosto requires extended
analysis. We can survey his other borrowings in the course of dis-
cussing two phenomena that show how full, direct, and understand-
ing was his reading of *Orlando Furioso*. We have remarked in passing
that Spenser usually (and rightly, given the nature of *Orlando Fu-
rioso*) adapts dramatic situations rather than characters. The com-
mentators give an exaggerated emphasis to character, because they
assume that the personages of the poem exemplify certain vices or
virtues. Even when they moralize dramatic situations, they usually
do so from the standpoint of character—what the good person
ought to do or avoid doing in a given situation, or what a given situ-
ation shows about the tendencies of human behavior. A decisive indi-
cation of this tendency in the commentaries is their treatment of the
story of Ariodante and Ginevra. The force of the episode, as Spenser
recognizes by the nature of his adaptation, lies in the cumulative inter-
locking of erotic and chivalric desires and the resultant sense that
everyone is involved in the illusions of love. But the commentaries
split up their interpretations into separate morals for each character,
and they even moralize separate actions of the characters.[31]

Our discussions of both Angelica and Fiordispina suggest that
when Spenser borrows a character from Ariosto, he is interested in a
more or less conventional figure who is in a poetically interesting situ-
ation, as opposed to an individual with a unique moral nature. (The
exception to this rule is his using Bradamante as the model for Brito-
mart.) This explains a fact that has long puzzled modern critics—
Spenser's basing Florimell on Angelica. The assumption is that Spen-
ser would have to fly in the face of the poem and accept an interpre-
tation that makes Angelica a virtuous person or the embodiment of a
virtue before he could use her as the model for the virtuous Florimell.
But Spenser is interested not in a character, but in the beautiful
maiden who arouses erotic desire and is constantly being pursued;
this dramatic situation stimulates some of his most interesting poetry

---

[30] See below, p. 390.

[31] See Harington's "moral" to canto 5, which is based on Valvassori: "You
may note in *Polynesso* an enuious and trecherous minde: in *Ariodant* the hurt
of a credulous ielousie: in *Lurcanio* the vehemencie of a wrong surmise. In
Polynessos entent to kill *Dalinda*, you may obserue how wicked men often
bewray their owne misdeeds, with seeking to hide them. In *Geneuras* accusa-
tion and deliuerie, how God euer defends the innocent. And lastly in *Polynessos*
death, how wickednesse ruines it selfe" (p. 39).

about human desire.[32] The most striking illustration of the point we are making is Spenser's use of some situations which involve a maiden in distress. Spenser's episodes of Sansloy's assault on Una (1.6.3–7) and the old fisherman's on Florimell (3.8.20–31) are modeled, respectively, on Odorico's assault on Isabella (*OF* 13.26–29) and the old hermit's attempt to rape Angelica (*OF* 8.30–50).[33] For Spenser the parts of these and other episodes are to some extent interchangeable, and he feels no impediment in the fact that some details concern Isabella, the model of chastity, and others Angelica, the arch-flirt. Angelica is rescued from the hermit by the sailors of Ebuda, who take her off to be sacrificed to the Orc. This sequence of events suggests Florimell's falling from the frying pan into the fire when Proteus rescues her.[34] But of the three stanzas in which Ariosto laments Angelica's cruel fate, Spenser transfers the first (*OF* 8.66) to the Una-Sansloy episode;[35] he does not use the last (the wish that the lady's knights were present, 8.68) in the episode with Proteus, but instead uses it at the climax of his outcry when the fisherman assaults Florimell (3.8.27–28).[36] His major rhetorical outburst in the episode with Proteus, the praise of Florimell's chastity (3.8.42–43), is in its turn taken from Ariosto's praise of Isabella's chastity (*OF* 29.26–27) when, rather than give herself to Rodomonte, she tricks him into killing her.

These last examples indicate not only how well Spenser read

[32] See below, pp. 394–396. Miss McMurphy discusses Spenser's use of Angelica for three figures—Florimell, the false Florimell, and Belphoebe—and what she says is perfectly sensible as a description of what Spenser does. But she considers that "this splitting of the character of Angelica into three distinct units" is done "to supply each lady with just those features from Ariosto's storehouse that remodel her into a consistent character" (p. 39).

[33] For Spenser's use of the Odorico-Isabella episode, see chapter 1. In addition to taking the basic situation of Florimell and the fisherman from Ariosto, Spenser is indebted to him for specific details in 3.8.22 (cf. *OF* 8.48), 23 and 25 (cf. 8.31), and 25 (cf. 8.47).

[34] Spenser probably got from Ariosto the idea of having Proteus rescue Florimell. In explaining how the people of Ebuda came to scour the coasts for beautiful women, Ariosto tells of their offending Proteus, who sent the Orc in vengeance. Spenser's "*Proteus* is Shepheard of the seas of yore, / And hath the charge of *Neptunes* mightie heard" (3.8.30) is almost a direct translation of Ariosto's, "Proteo marin, che pasce il fiero armento / di Nettunno che l'onda tutta regge" ("Proteus of the sea, who tends the fierce herd of Neptune, who rules all the water," 8.54).

[35] See above, pp. 28–29.

[36] Robert M. Durling notices Spenser's multiple use of single passages in Ariosto and points out that *OF* 8.66–67 is also echoed in *FQ* 3.8.1 and 4.11.1. *The Figure of the Poet in Renaissance Epic*, Cambridge, Mass., 1965, pp. 212–213.

Ariosto's poem, but how intimately he knew it. The major sign that *Orlando Furioso* was continually present in Spenser's mind is that episodes that are important to him characteristically appear in more than one episode of *The Faerie Queene*. Thus the Red Cross Knight's disarming by the fountain (1.7.2–4) comes from Ruggiero's refreshing himself in Alcina's grove (*OF* 6.20–25), but the narration of Astolfo turned into a tree, which immediately follows in *Orlando Furioso* (6.26–53), is used much earlier in Book I in the story of Fradubio (2.30–44). Alcina, the enchantress who transforms men to beasts, is a characteristic Renaissance version of Circe, and in this respect is like Spenser's Acrasia. But the unveiling of her ugliness (*OF* 7.70–74) produces the disrobing of Duessa (1.8.46–49), while in a particularly skillful adaptation, Ruggiero's nervous waiting for Alcina (*OF* 7.23–26) becomes Malecasta's agitated creeping to Britomart's bed (3.1.58–61). In Astolfo's first victory with his magic horn, his conquest of the giant Caligorante (*OF* 15.10–62), the description of Caligorante's lair and the country around it (*OF* 15.49–50) suggests the dwelling of Despair and other Spenserian monsters; the description of Caligorante's subtly woven net (*OF* 15.56), with which he captures his victims and into which Astolfo makes him fall, is adapted by Spenser in his description of the net in which the Palmer catches Acrasia (2.12.81); and the binding of Caligorante and Astolfo's leading him into Cairo to the amazement of the townspeople (*OF* 15.59–62) produce Calidore's taming the Blatant Beast (6.12. 36) and leading him about to the admiration of "all the people where so he did go" (6.12.37). Bradamante's defeat of Atlante not only supplies materials for the final cantos of Book III, it also provides one of the most striking touches in Book I. The moment when Sansloy unlaces the helmet of the knight he thinks is the Red Cross Knight and uncovers the "hoarie head of *Archimago* old" (1.3.38) is directly taken from Bradamante's catching sight of Atlante's face when she is about to kill him (*OF* 4.27).

Spenser's use of the episode in the Castle of Tristran (*OF* 32.64–110) is especially interesting. He uses the first half in Book III and reserves the second half for Book IV, where it provides the first of a series of episodes that belong specifically to the Book of Friendship —episodes in which the conflicting desires of good knights and ladies are turned into a harmony. In the first half of her adventure, Bradamante gains the right to shelter from a storm by defeating three knights outside the castle; this is the source for the entry of Britomart, Paridell, and their companions into the castle of Malbecco and Hellenore (3.9.1–18). (The special rule that makes a knight gain his entrance into the Castle of Tristran is due to the jealousy and inhospitality of its original owner—*OF* 32.83–94—and this may have suggested to Spenser Malbecco's barring the gates because of his jealousy.) When it is discovered inside the castle that Bradamante is a woman, she is declared subject to the second half of the rule of the Castle of Tristran, which requires that only the woman judged to be the fairest can stay inside the castle. Ullania, who was already inside the castle, is less beautiful than Bradamante. She is about to be sent out into the storm, when Bradamante announces that she cannot be subject to the rules for both sexes, and she states that for the night she is to be considered a warrior, not a woman (*OF* 32.101–106).

In the opening canto of Book IV, Spenser borrows this device of the female warrior resolving, by her paradoxical nature, a problem created by special rules of hospitality. Britomart and Amoret come to a castle whose rule is that no knight who does not have a lady can stay within. A solitary knight challenges Britomart for Amoret's hand, but after defeating him, Britomart, "that no lesse was courteous then stout" (4.1.11), devises a way to allow him to stay. After getting Amoret secured to her as a knight, she reveals her sex and offers herself to the stranger knight as a lady (4.1.12). Britomart's behavior is based on Bradamante's solicitude for Ullania, and her resolution of the dilemma by letting down her hair (4.1.13) turns a striking dramatic moment in Ariosto's narration into a climactic moment in Spenser's rhetorical mode. It is at this point in Spenser's borrowings that the two halves of Ariosto's episode overlap. This stanza and its analogue in the Malbecco episode (3.9.20) are both imitations of the stanza in which Bradamante lets down her hair in the Castle of Tristran (*OF* 32.79–80). Spenser remembered this episode in yet another book of *The Faerie Queene*. In describing Irena's joy when Artegall rescues her (5.12.13), he borrows the simile with which Ariosto rendered Ullania's happiness at being allowed to stay in the castle (*OF* 32.108).

If we start with a single episode in *The Faerie Queene* and seek out its Ariostan sources, we will often get the impression that Spenser's use of Ariosto is capricious and superficial. On the other hand, if we start with an episode in *Orlando Furioso* and ask what it produces, influences, or suggests in *The Faerie Queene,* we will get a truer sense of Spenser's familiarity with Ariosto's poem and the ease with which he could draw on it for his own. The best way to understand Spenser's use of Ariosto is simply to read the first dozen or so cantos of *Orlando Furioso* and notice how many things appear in *The Faerie Queene*. It seems absurd to start with Archimago's meeting the Red Cross Knight and Una (1.1.29–30) and point back to Angelica's meeting with the hermit (who also turns out to be a magician, *OF* 2.12–13), as if there were some exciting relation between the two incidents taken in isolation. But when we are reading *Orlando Furioso,* we see that Spenser's adaptation of the incident is precisely not an occasion for excitement, but simply one more sign that he had the whole poem at his fingertips. Critics have often poked fun at Spenser for taking seriously the ironic stanza that begins "Oh gran bontà de' cavallieri antiqui!" (*OF* 1.22; cf. *FQ* 3.1.13). Spenser appears so simple-minded here, because we assume that he solemnly sought out this individual stanza and used it as humorlessly as possible. But the opening canto of *Orlando Furioso,* in which this stanza occurs, is one Spenser must have known almost by heart and on which he draws time and again in *The Faerie Queene.* If his use of the stanza is part of a lively and immediate contact with Ariosto's poem, then it seems more likely than not that he was conscious of changing Ariosto's tone, and that his failure to reproduce it is not a sign that he mistook it.

As many Renaissance writers said, imitation is digestion and absorption, not passive copying. When a major poet is profoundly influenced by another major poet, he undoubtedly puts his own stamp on what he borrows. But we have assumed hitherto that Spenser's use of Ariosto is narrow-minded and inappropriate, like the Christian moralization of Ovid. The proper analogy is to Ben Jonson's use of Horace, Dryden's use of Virgil, Wordsworth's use of Milton, Melville's use of Shakespeare, or Eliot's use of Dante. In each case, the poet's use of his predecessor involves an unmistakable transmutation, emphasis of some qualities at the expense of others. But at the same time the borrowings of poets like these characteristically reveal a full and intelligent awareness of the poet imitated. Yet even when we have seen how well Spenser knew and understood *Orlando Furioso,* we may still wonder whether there was a temperamental affinity between him and Ariosto of the sort that we expect to find in so major a case of influence and imitation. Our accepted notions of the two poets—frivolous and ironic Ariosto, sage and serious Spenser—of course suggest that no such affinity could exist. Yet once we clear our minds of these clichés and the attendant simplistic notions of morality and irony, seriousness and play of mind, we have no trouble in seeing why Spenser felt close to *Orlando Furioso*. Are not some of his most notable and precious characteristics as a poet—his moral generosity, the poise and lucidity of his intelligence, his geniality, affectionateness, and humanity—qualities that he would have found preeminently in Ariosto?

Chapter Seven

Iconography in *The Faerie Queene*

I

No English poem would seem more susceptible to iconographic analysis than *The Faerie Queene*.[1] It is full of emblematic characters and personifications of the type found in Ripa's *Iconologia*. Spenser's use of classical mythology is obviously a product of the tradition of allegorical interpretation that is represented, in the sixteenth century, by such handbooks as Cartari's *Gli Imagini de i Dei* and Natalis Comes' *Mythologia*. The proliferation of pictorial details is a sign of the fact that emblem books were an important intellectual fad in the sixteenth century. On the face of it, Spenser, in Frank Kermode's words, "seems to be assuming a special kind of reader, or rather a special kind of information."[2] Yet if we look at some passages in which Spenser seems to use and expect this kind of information, we find that his attitude towards it is considerably less strict than that of many of his contemporaries and of many modern scholars. Spenser does not treat conventional symbolic identifications as an established code to which he as a poet has special obligations. This is partly a matter of intellectual temper: Spenser's use of iconographic materials bears out Robert Ellrodt's demonstration that his Platonism is neither esoteric nor intellectually elaborate. But it is also a matter of Spenser's sense

---

[1] The following works are mentioned frequently in this chapter and will be cited by the authors' names:

Andrea Alciati, *Omnia Emblemata, cum commentariis . . . per Claudium Minoem*, Antwerp, 1577.

Cesare Ripa, *Iconologia*, Rome, 1603. For our purposes, Ripa is simply a convenient collection of traditional materials and a representative of an important mode of thought. Spenser could not have used the *Iconologia* for *FQ* I–III. It was first published in 1593 without figures; this is the first illustrated edition.

Giovanni Piero Valeriano, *Hieroglyphica*, Basel, 1575.

Otto van Veen, *Quinti Horatii Flacci Emblemata*, Antwerp, 1612.

Geoffrey Whitney, *A Choice of Emblemes* (1586), facsimile reprint, ed. Henry Green, London, 1866.

Erwin Panofsky, *Studies in Iconology*, New York, 1939.

Mario Praz, *Studies in Seventeenth-Century Imagery*, vol. 1, London, 1939; vol. 2: A Bibliography of Emblem Books, London, 1947.

Edgar Wind, *Pagan Mysteries in the Renaissance*, London, 1958.

[2] "The Cave of Mammon," in *Elizabethan Poetry*, ed. John Russell Brown and Bernard Harris, London, 1960, p. 151.

of the reality his poem has and the way in which it expresses moral meanings. The first requirement for our understanding Spenser's interest in and use of iconographic materials is not that we postulate a "sixteenth-century reader," but that we ourselves be good readers of *The Faerie Queene*. As we shall see, there is no justification for assuming, as Kermode claims, that "the marrow of a Spenserian allegory is designed to be extracted by the same enlightened method as that of an Orphic mystery, an Egyptian hieroglyph, [or] a Renaissance emblem."[3] Instead we should take our cue from Sir Kenelm Digby, who begins his *Observations* (1644) on the mystical numerology of *FQ* 2.9.22 by making it clear that this stanza is exceptional, perhaps unique, in *The Faerie Queene:*

> In this Staffe the Author seemes to me to proceed in a different manner from what he doth elsewhere generally through his whole Book. For in other places, although the beginning of his Allegory or mysticall sense, may be obscure, yet in the processe of it, he doth himself declare his own conceptions in such sort as they are obvious to any ordinary capacitie.[4]

Iconography is essentially a means of interpreting visual images. Any painting may be susceptible to iconographic interpretation simply because it is a painting, but in a poem we must first determine whether the equivalent of a visual image is being presented. For example, in canto 42 of *Orlando Furioso,* Rinaldo learns that Angelica has given herself to Medoro, and tormented by his love, he sets out to find her. As he travels through the Forest of Ardennes, he sees "a strange monster in female form" come out of a cave:

> Mill'occhi in capo avea senza palpèbre;
> non può serrarli, e non credo che dorma:
> non men che gli occhi, avea l'orecchie crebre;
> avea in loco de crin serpi a gran torma.
> Fuor de le diaboliche tenèbre
> nel mondo uscì la spaventevol forma.
> Un fiero e maggior serpe ha per la coda,
> che pel petto si gira e che l'annoda.

She had in her head a thousand lidless eyes; she is not able to shut them and I do not believe she sleeps; her ears were not less

---

[3] *Ibid.*, p. 155. In the next chapter I discuss the interpretation of the Cave of Mammon that Kermode develops from this assumption.

[4] In *The Works of Edmund Spenser: A Variorum Edition*, ed. Edwin Greenlaw, et al., Baltimore, 1932–1957, Book II, p. 472.

thickset than her eyes; in place of hair she had serpents in a great swarm. Out of the shades of hell her terror-raising form came into the world. She has for a tail a larger fierce serpent that curls on her breast and knots around her. (*OF* 42.47)

This monster, as all the sixteenth-century commentators point out, is Jealousy. Ariosto does not name her; we must identify her by her attributes. We are expected to be able to do this, because we have formerly encountered Ovid's hag Invidia in her cave (*Metamorphoses* 2.760–782) or her snaky-headed descendant in the emblem books.[5] Hence Harington says, "It is so plaine in the verse it needs no exposition."[6] Most readers, I think, assume that Spenser presents allegorical figures and settings in this way, and that without the key provided by emblem books and the like, the reader would not recognize the significance of physical attributes and descriptive details. But in fact Spenser's practice is invariably to identify allegorical figures.[7] Thus when Artegall encounters Envy (the same figure as Ariosto's monster, though the snaky head has been replaced by the equally familiar detail of her gnawing on a snake), Spenser names her in the stanza that follows his description (5.12.31). Spenser's handling of an emblematic attribute is exemplified by his description of the caduceus carried by Canacee when she comes to stop the battle between Cambel and Triamond:

> In her right hand a rod of peace shee bore,
> About the which two Serpents weren wound,
> Entrayled mutually in louely lore,
> And by the tailes together firmely bound,
> And both were with one oliue garland crownd,

[5] See, for example, Alciati, no. 71, pp. 271–273; Whitney, p. 94; van Veen, p. 96, with the plate on p. 99.

[6] Sir John Harington, *Orlando Furioso in English Heroical Verse*, London, 1591, p. 357.

[7] Under certain circumstances, Ariosto identifies allegorical figures. In the consciously epic context of canto 14, when God intervenes in the siege of Paris, St. Michael seeks out Discordia and Fraude (14.79ff.; see also 18.26ff., 27.34ff.). After Rinaldo drinks from the fountain that purges him of love for Angelica, the knight who has rescued him reveals that he is Sdegno (42.64): presumably the gesture suggests that Rinaldo has come to his moral senses and now knows himself. Allegories and emblems are explained to Astolfo when he goes to the Earthly Paradise (34.73ff., 35.11ff.). However, the fact that Ariosto identifies some figures does not make it any less striking that Spenser, writing "a continued Allegory, or darke conceit," leaves no major figure unidentified, as Ariosto does Jealousy or the Beast of Avarice (*OF* 26.31–36).

Like to the rod which *Maias* sonne doth wield,
Wherewith the hellish fiends he doth confound.

(4.3.42)

The caduceus is a symbol of concord, and Spenser, far from confin-
ing himself to physical description, frankly declares moral meanings.[8]
A writer like Ariosto would treat the line, "And by the tailes to-
gether firmly bound" as a visual fact that has a spiritual significance.
In Spenser's verse the opening formula, "rod of peace," and the line,
"Entrayled mutually in louely lore," give the force of a direct moral
formula to "together firmly bound." Similarly the detail of the olive
garland, which in Ariosto would be part of a consistently visual de-
scription, has the effect, in Spenser's stanza, of *returning* us to the
physical surface of the object seen. What we are observing here is by
now perfectly familiar to us. Spenser does not describe "objects" in
his poem as if they were objects in an external world, and physical
and moral formulas have equivalent status in the verbal reality of his
poem. What we must now consider is the bearing these facts have on
Spenser's use of iconographic materials.

Iconographic analysis assumes that objects and personages are
constituted by the poet and perceived by the reader as if they were
like objects and persons in the real world. In discovering symbolic
meanings, Renaissance writers appealed to the traditional image of
the universe as divided into sublunary, celestial, and supercelestial
worlds. In the words of Pico della Mirandola: "For euen as the . . .
three worlds being girt and buckled with the bands of concord doe
by reciprocall libertie, interchange their natures; the like do they also
by their appellations. And this is the principle from whence springeth
and groweth the discipline of allegoricall sense. For it is certaine that
the ancient fathers could not conueniently haue represented one thing
by other figures, but that they had first learned the secret amity and

[8] For the caduceus, see Wind, pp. 91, 163; Valeriano, f. 115 verso. An excep-
tion that proves this rule is 4.10.40, in which Spenser does not state the sig-
nificance of the snake that enwraps the legs of the statue of Venus. However,
in the next stanza, Spenser makes it an explicit point that this is a mystery:

> The cause why she was couered with a vele,
> Was hard to know, for that her Priests the same
> From peoples knowledge labour'd to concele.

(4.10.41)

Thomas P. Roche, Jr. gives some details of the iconography of the serpent and
suggests that Spenser's conception is all-inclusive here. *The Kindly Flame*,
Princeton, 1964, p. 132.

affinitie of all nature."[9] This view treats spiritual meanings as inherent in physical objects, which thus have fixed symbolic identities. "Otherwise," as Pico says in the next sentence, "there could bee no reason, why they should represent this thing by this forme, and that by that, rather then otherwise." Note, however, that this view does not reject symbolic meanings that are found in the writings of men rather than in natural analogies. Pico would be displeased to find Panofsky (pp. 3–17) calling mythographic and emblematic interpretations "conventional," but only because that word implies that the truth of these interpretations lies solely in the agreement of particular men at a particular time. Renaissance writers would justify the truth of their writings and of the wisdom of the ancients by appealing to the nature of the universe.[10] But as a practical matter, their attitude is expressed by what Panofsky means by convention—the acceptance as true of a variety of symbolic meanings transmitted in a variety of ways.

When we consider the solemnity with which Renaissance exegetes, not to mention modern scholars, regard traditional symbolic correspondences, it is rather astonishing to find that Spenser can treat them with genuine carelessness. A striking example occurs when Maleger's army assaults the five bulwarks, corresponding to the senses, of Alma's castle. In accordance with a long tradition of associating various animals with the senses, Spenser assigns symbolic animals to each of Maleger's troops. But in at least one instance he simply makes a mistake:

> Likewise that same third Fort, that is the *Smell*
> Of that third troupe was cruelly assayd:
> Whose hideous shapes were like to feends of hell,
> Some like to hounds, some like to Apes, dismayd,
> Some like to Puttockes, all in plumes arayd.

(2.11.11)

[9] Introduction to the *Heptaplus*, in *De Hominis Dignitate, Heptaplus, De Ente et Uno*, ed. Eugenio Garin, Florence, 1942, p. 192. The passage is quoted by Roche (*The Kindly Flame*, pp. 7–8), who makes it the starting point of his analysis of *The Faerie Queene*. Roche quotes the English translation of Pierre de la Primaudaye, *The French Academie*, London, 1618, p. 671. De la Primaudaye simply translates Pico. Roche points out that the passage also occurs in the theoretical preface that Simon Fornari wrote for the volume in which he addressed himself to the major allegorical passages in *Orlando Furioso—La Spositione . . . sopra l'Orlando Furioso*, Florence, vol. 2, 1550, 3.

[10] On this point see E. H. Gombrich, "*Icones Symbolicae*: The Visual Image in Neo-Platonic Thought," *JWCI*, 11 (1948), 163–192.

While the hound and vulture are associated with smell, the ape is consistently associated with taste, and nowhere else, to my knowledge, with the sense of smell.[11] Hence Thomas Tomkis corrected the iconography when he used Spenser's passage in his comedy *Lingua: or The Combat of the Tongue, And the five Senses for Superiority* (1607). The army of Olfactus is accompanied by hounds and vultures, while the ape is transferred to the army of Gustus.[12] Spenser's mistake here may certainly be considered a case of Homer nodding. But if the poet nods at this point in this context, his attitude towards iconographic materials is more casual than we have supposed.

This first example makes an important negative point. In our next example, Spenser's ignoring an accepted iconographic meaning directly plays a part in his poetic achievement. After touring Alma's castle, Guyon and Arthur are brought into a "goodly Parlour" in which "A lovely bevy of faire Ladies sate" (2.9.33–34).

> Whom when the knights beheld, they gan dispose
> Themselues to court, and each a Damsell chose:
> The Prince by chaunce did on a Lady light,
> That was right faire and fresh as morning rose,
> But somwhat sad, and solemne eke in sight,
> As if some pensiue thought constraind her
>   gentle spright.
>
> In a long purple pall, whose skirt with gold
> Was fretted all about, she was arayd;
> And in her hand a Poplar braunch did hold.
>
> (2.9.36–37)

This poplar branch is the damsel's identifying characteristic: two stanzas later, Arthur asks "what wight she was, that Poplar braunch did hold." He is told that "her name was *Prays-desire,* / That by well doing sought to honour to aspire" (2.9.39), and we naturally assume that this is the emblematic significance of the poplar. The poplar does have a well-established symbolic identity, but it has

---

[11] See H. W. Janson, *Apes and Ape Lore*, London, 1952, pp. 239–241. For a representative list of associations of animals with senses, including the ape with taste, see Gabriel Harvey's *Speculum Tuscanismi*, a satiric poem that appears in the fifth Spenser-Harvey letter (*Variorum*, Prose Works, p. 467). See also Ripa, p. 449, s.v. *Sensi.*

[12] *Lingua*, London, 1607, sig. E2 verso. For Tomkis' indebtedness to Spenser, see M. P. Tilley, "The Comedy *Lingua* and the *Faerie Queene*," *MLN*, 42 (1927), 150–157.

nothing to do with the desire for glory or honor. In Alciati, Valeriano, Cartari—any of the writings the sixteenth-century reader might bring to bear on this passage—the poplar is identified with time, because its leaves are white (symbolizing day) on one side and black (symbolizing night) on the other.[13] Obviously the poplar does not stand for time whenever it is mentioned, and as Hercules' tree it has a clear relevance to the desire for glory. Nevertheless, the difficulty in the passage remains. Although the poplar suggests the rewards of heroism (which could include praise), the problem is one of specifically identifying the desire for praise.

We can understand what Spenser is up to by looking at the whole passage:

> In a long purple pall, whose skirt with gold
> Was fretted all about, she was arayd;
> And in her hand a Poplar braunch did hold:
> To whom the Prince in curteous manner said;
> Gentle Madame, why beene ye thus dismaid,
> And your faire beautie do with sadnesse spill?
> Liues any, that you hath thus ill apaid?
> Or doen you loue, or doen you lacke your will?
> What euer be the cause, it sure beseemes you ill.

> Faire Sir, (said she halfe in disdainefull wise,)
> How is it, that this mood in me ye blame,
> And in your selfe do not the same aduise?
> Him ill beseemes, anothers fault to name,
> That may vnwares be blotted with the same:
> Pensiue I yeeld I am, and sad in mind,
> Through great desire of glory and of fame;
> Ne ought I weene are ye therein behind,
> That haue twelue moneths sought one, yet no
> where can her find.

> The Prince was inly moued at her speach,
> Well weeting trew, what she had rashly told;

[13] Alciati, no. 211 (misnumbered 213), pp. 670–671; Valeriano, f. 381 verso; Vincenzo Cartari, *Gli Imagini de i Dei*, Venice, 1580, p. 350. See also G. C. Capaccio, *Delle Imprese*, Naples, 1592, book 2, f. 133. A secondary significance of the poplar, found for example in Valeriano and Capaccio, is that it is a funeral tree.

Yet with faire semblaunt sought to hide the breach,
Which chaunge of colour did perforce vnfold,
Now seeming flaming whot, now stony cold.
Tho turning soft aside, he did inquire,
What wight she was, that Poplar braunch did hold:
It answered was, her name was *Prays-desire,*
That by well doing sought to honour to aspire.

(2.9.37–39)

Prays-desire is simply herself, but for Arthur to "be himself" he must acknowledge the force of "desire for praise" within himself, and at the same time behave courteously, as a knight ought. The point of the passage lies in the confrontation of a complex human being, composed of many qualities, with the personification of one of those qualities. In the next few stanzas, Spenser makes this the basis of a comedy of self-knowledge. Guyon finds himself with a lovely maiden who keeps her eyes to the ground and constantly blushes. Guyon tries to make her speak—exactly as if he were making conversation with a shy stranger at a party—until finally Alma says:

> Why wonder yee
> Faire Sir at that, which ye so much embrace?
> She is the fountaine of your modestee;
> You shamefast are, but *Shamefastnesse* it selfe
> is shee. (2.9.43)

Both this and Arthur's encounter would be pointless if it were not clear that the two "persons" who meet are not beings of the same kind. Hence Spenser endows Prays-desire with a prop that makes it clear that she is a personification.

However, we must still explain why Spenser has not given Prays-desire an attribute that would truly identify her. The best way to understand this is to consider Ripa's description of Emulatione:

A beautiful young woman with bare arms and blond, curly hair . . . She will be in the act of running, having winged feet, and with the right hand gracefully hold a spur or a bundle of thorns.

According to Aristotle, *Rhetoric,* book 2, Emulation is a painful feeling (*un dolore*) that makes us see, in those like us in nature, some good that is honored and still possible to obtain; and this painful feeling arises not because someone else has that good, but because we too would like to have it, and we do not have it. . . .

She is given a spur, in accordance with what Cavalcanti says in his *Rhetoric,* book 4: Emulation is a spur that pricks strongly, and arouses not only bad men to desire and act against the good of others, in envy of them, but arouses good and great-hearted men to pursue for themselves that which they see in others and know that they themselves lack. Apropos of this it is said, *Stimulos dedit aemula virtus.*[14]

The interest of emulation lies in the disparity between a simple, worthy end and the complexity of feeling that impels a man to seek it. Similarly Spenser's portrayal of Prays-desire is based on the mild paradox that a noble end, which presumably would create noble feelings in the hero, in fact provokes emotional distress. If Spenser had sought a true emblematic prop for Prays-desire, a spur would have been a perfect choice. On the other hand, as a direct equivalent for the distress of emulation, it would simply repeat what is brought out by Prays-desire's behavior, while the poplar branch evokes additional notions of heroism and its reward. By ignoring accepted iconography, Spenser is able to make his figure express the full interest and human complexity of the emotion she personifies.

However, there is more to be said than this. As a physical object the spur suggests painful incitement, but it is at the same time a common metaphor for the arousing of noble desires. Thus in itself it perfectly well suggests the double aspect of emulation. But there is another reason why Spenser avoids the spur or anything like it in this passage. If Prays-desire had a true emblematic prop, the reader would be able to identify her immediately; at the very least he would not be puzzled at her reply to Arthur's question about her sullen behavior. Instead, Spenser makes our knowledge of Prays-desire occur through Arthur's experience. When Arthur replies to her speech (2.9.39), we do not laugh at him for not knowing who his companion is. Rather we share his mixed feelings, and through them we come to identify the mixed emotion, "praise-desire." Once again we see that knowledge in *The Faerie Queene* is inseparable from the process of reading. In the more openly comic scene between Guyon and Shamefast-nesse—in which to some extent we laugh at the hero—Spenser gives his allegorical figure a true emblematic prop, the turtledove. But he still keeps us close to the verse by identifying the bird not by its name, but by a circumlocution:

[14] P. 129. I have not been able to find in Ripa or anywhere else a personification with a name that is close to "Prays-desire."

Vpon her fist the bird, which shonneth vew,
And keepes in couerts close from liuing wight,
Did sit, as yet ashamd, how rude *Pan* did her dight.

(2.9.40)[15]

Spenser's interest in personifications, emblems, and the like did not at all entail adherence or obligation to conventional meanings and modes of representation. By the same token, the reader is not expected to bring to the poem the elaborate iconographic apparatus that is sometimes recommended to him, and when he uses his knowledge of emblem books and mythographies it is in a more flexible, a less predetermined way than we have thought. Spenser's freedom in using iconographic materials remains even when a traditional emblem plays an important role. In the fourth canto of Book II, Guyon and the Palmer come upon a madman who is beating a youth and dragging him along the ground. Another figure follows:

And him behind, a wicked Hag did stalke,
In ragged robes, and filthy disaray,
Her other leg was lame, that she no'te walke,
But on a staffe her feeble steps did stay;
Her lockes, that loathly were and hoarie gray,
Grew all afore, and loosely hong vnrold,
But all behind was bald, and worne away,
That none thereof could euer taken hold,
And eke her face ill fauourd, full of wrinckles old.

(2.4.4)

This hag is later identified as Occasion, and we recognize her most common emblematic attribute, the forelock. But Occasion has taken a form in which no reader of Spenser's had seen her before. In the emblem books, Occasio is always a young woman. Her feet are winged, she has a long forelock (the back of her head being bald), she stands on a ball or a wheel, often in the midst of the sea, and she often holds a razor in her hand.[16] The main features of this figure

---

[15] Commentators thought this bird was an owl until Alastair Fowler pointed out its true identity in *Essays in Criticism*, 11 (1961), 236. Fowler cites Ripa, p. 420, s.v. *Pudicitia*, and Valeriano, f. 161. See also *Batman uppon Bartholome*, London, 1582, f. 188. No one has explained the reference to Pan, which has no apparent connection with the turtledove.

[16] The discrepancy between this figure and Spenser's Occasion was long ago pointed out by James G. McManaway, " 'Occasion,' *FQ* II.iv.4–5," *MLN*, 49 (1934), 391–393. For examples of this emblem, see Alciati, no. 121, pp. 415–417, and Whitney, p. 181.

come from a Greek statue of a young man named Kairos—a word which means "opportune moment" and which is translated in Latin by *occasio*.[17] Some details, like the wheel and the sea, and the change in sex come from a later association of this classical figure with Fortuna.[18] The change in Spenser's description of the figure corresponds to an equally distinct change in its meaning. *Occasio* is at various times equivalent to *kairos, fortuna* or simply *tempus,* but in each case it refers to some aspect of the external world in which man lives. But Spenser's Occasion is "the root of all wrath and despight" (2.4.10) because she is a dangerous psychological force: she is the mother of Furor, whom she constantly incites. With this change in conception, it is natural for Spenser to transform Occasion from an attractive—often a deceptively attractive—woman to a hag who resembles a Fury or a figure like the Envy of the emblem books. Similarly, taking hold of her forelock, which traditionally means "Seize the advantageous moment when it offers itself," now expresses mastery of a psychological force. When Guyon has been told who and what Occasion is, he is able to seize her forelock and throw her to the ground (2.4.12). The moral is no longer "Know the nature of things," but "Know thyself."

The nature and point of Spenser's changes in depicting Occasion are perfectly clear when we look at the whole episode. But our interest is in what the reader makes of emblematic descriptions when he encounters them, and I think that the sixteenth-century reader would have been rather puzzled by the initial description of Occasion. No figure the reader might know answers to the description of an old woman, lame in one leg and using a staff, and bald except for a forelock. If the forelock unequivocally identified the figure as Occasion, the reader might grasp what Spenser has done. But Fortune too is depicted with a forelock,[19] and old age and lameness would be more easily associated for the nonce with her—since she is an ubiquitous

[17] For a history of the figure, see Panofsky, pp. 71–72, and John E. Matzke, "On the Source of . . . 'To Take Time by the Forelock,' " *PMLA,* 8 (1893), 303–334. There are useful addenda and corrections to Matzke in G. L. Kittredge, " 'To Take Time by the Forelock,' " *MLN,* 8 (1893), 230–235.

[18] See Howard R. Patch, *The Goddess Fortuna in Medieval Literature,* Cambridge, Mass., 1927, pp. 115–117. The change in sex is also due to the fact that *occasio,* unlike *kairos,* is a feminine noun. See Matzke, pp. 317–318.

[19] See Joannes Sambucus, *Emblemata,* Antwerp, 1584, p. 214. In Achilles Bocchi, *Symbolicarum Quaestionum . . . libri quinque,* Bologna, 1574, the young woman with a forelock appears as both Fortune (emblem 51, p. 110) and Occasion (emblem 71, p. 152). See also Wind, p. 91, n. 5, and Tasso, *Amore Fuggitivo,* lines 87–92 (sometimes printed as the epilogue to *Aminta*).

figure who could include a range of meanings—than with the quite limited figure of Occasion. Or if the reader took the hag's lameness and staff as his initial clue, he might think of the figure of Time, who has a crutch or staff as a regular attribute.[20] So far as I can discover, Time does not appear with a forelock in the emblem books, but we do find him described this way in literary sources.[21] Time, too, is old; indeed if this figure were a man and not a woman, he would be identified as Time.

The next stanza makes it clear that Spenser did not intend us to identify Occasion at this point:

> And euer as she went, her tongue did walke
> In foule reproch, and termes of vile despight,
> Prouoking him by her outrageous talke,
> To heape more vengeance on that wretched wight;
> Sometimes she raught him stones, wherwith to smite,
> Sometimes her staffe, though it her one leg were,
> Withouten which she could not go vpright;
> Ne any euill meanes she did forbeare,
> That might him moue to wrath, and indignation reare.
>
> (2.4.5)

Spenser does not exploit (and thus help us make sense of) the one decisive attribute, the forelock. Alternatively, he could have committed us to the word "occasion," which must be somewhere in our minds at this point, by depicting an action that would provide the verb in a sentence of which "occasion" is the subject. But "occasion provokes wrath" does not impose itself as a moral dictum, and if it has a clear meaning it is the wrong one. Whatever specific definition we give "occasion" the sentence suggests that anger is aroused by something that acts on us from outside. In addition to not helping us make a specific interpretation of the figure, this second stanza adds a new complication. It disappoints our expectation that the descriptive de-

[20] See Panofsky, pp. 77–80 and figs. 48, 49, 52, 54, 55, 56, 60; van Veen, p. 46. Compare *Much Ado about Nothing*, 2.1.373: "Time goes on crutches till love have all his rites." Envy traditionally has a staff, but it is a weapon, not a support for lameness.

[21] E.g., Robert Southwell, "Loss in Delay," cited by Karl Pietsch, "On the Source of . . . 'To Take Time by the Forelock,'" *MLN*, 8 (1893), 235–238. See also *Orlando Furioso*, 38.47. Passages like these presumably derive from Phaedrus, *Fables* 5.8, where the statue of Kairos is called Tempus. The expression "to take time by the forelock" is well established in Elizabethan English, though "to take occasion by the forelock" is the more common form of the saying. See *Oxford Dictionary of Proverbs*, which cites, e.g., *Amoretti* 70.

tails in the preceding stanza are genuinely emblematic. The staff, which seemed to be a symbol of feebleness, is now simply a weapon; meanwhile the forelock has disappeared, not to be mentioned again until Occasion has been identified. On the basis of this stanza, it would seem appropriate to treat the figure as a rather general allegorical hag, who suggests discord, outrage, and the like, but has no really specific identity.[22] But the preceding stanza is too decisively emblematic to permit our accepting this solution. We still feel that at least the forelock requires a specific symbolic identification.

The purposes served by Spenser's handling of Occasion are very much like those that determined his treatment of Prays-desire and Shamefastnesse. Once again he depicts his hero learning the nature of a personification by first attempting to deal with it as a human being. Guyon attempts to do actual battle with Furor until the Palmer cries out:

> Not so, O *Guyon,* neuer thinke that so
> That Monster can be maistred or destroyd:
> He is not, ah, he is not such a foe,
> As steele can wound, or strength can ouerthroe.
>
> (2.4.10)

And he concludes by naming first Furor and then Occasion. The reader's initial inability to identify Occasion means that he does not see this episode from the vantage point of the Palmer, but to some extent comes to his knowledge by participating in Guyon's experience.

However, in saying "to some extent" we raise a broader question: does a knowledge of contemporary iconography make *any* difference to the reader of this passage? At the simplest level, the answer is no. An ignorant viewer will simply not know what Bronzino's "Venus, Cupid, Folly, and Time" or Titian's misnamed "Sacred and Profane Love" are about.[23] Nevertheless, he will recognize that these paintings are allegorical, and such an elementary awareness of allegory

---

[22] McManaway suggested that figures of Discord may have provided some details in the portrayal of Occasion, and a fusion of the two figures would certainly have been appropriate here. But no reader could have recognized such a fusion, because none of the identifying characteristics of Discord are present. Ariosto's St. Michael, told to find Discordia, recognizes her by attributes that directly suggest discord—multicolored, unevenly cut clothes, even multicolored hair (*OF* 14.83). Similarly, Spenser's Ate has "squinted eyes contrarie ways intended," a divided tongue, and mismatched ears, hands, and feet (4.1.27–29). See also Ripa, s.v. *Discordia.*

[23] For the Bronzino, see Panofsky, pp. 86–91; for the Titian, see Panofsky, pp. 150–160, and Wind, pp. 121–128.

(for example, knowing that such things as personifications exist) is all that is indispensable for a grasp of Spenser's episode. On the other hand, it is unquestionable that a knowledge of the iconography of Occasion makes one a better reader of this passage. An ignorant reader will be baffled by the first description of Occasion, whereas the knowing reader's attempt to identify the figure will make him feel entertained by a puzzle. He will have a direct sense of Spenser's handling a familiar type of figure, so that in the second stanza he will not helplessly look for clues, but will recognize an alternative way of exploiting such a figure. Our understanding of the episode changes significantly if we engage from the beginning in the play of Spenser's mind. Guyon's role is a partial expression of our psychological experience, but to the extent that we know that "something is up," we can see him as the victim of his not knowing what he is combatting. The ignorant reader's knowledge of Occasion will come almost entirely through Guyon's experience; for him the Palmer's speech will be a voice intervening from outside with a piece of information. But for the reader versed in iconography the identification of the hag as Occasion is not information, but a recognition. For such a reader, the Palmer serves not as a moral *deus ex machina,* but as a part of his own mind. When the reader participates in the episode in this way, the final event becomes fully and naturally allegorical. Guyon's binding Occasion and Furor is not meant to be an external action that one character learns from another, but is an expression of the clarity and strength with which the mind can deal with the forces within itself.

The question, "Did the poet really intend all this?" is often irrelevant or misleading, but it is much less so when we are assessing the use of iconographic materials. We ought to be able to give a plausible account of the way Spenser created his figure of Occasion. The primary point we can establish is that Spenser did not intend his initial description to convey to the reader the abstract noun "occasion." In terms of the creative process this means that Spenser did not start with a verbal formula, which he then translated into visual terms. This is the essential way in which emblems are created—a large number of Alciati's emblems are graphic renderings of epigrams from the Greek anthology[24]—and it is well exemplified by the few appearances in the emblem books of lame women. Alciati shows three old women, two walking with staffs, in an emblem based on Homer's

[24] Praz, 1, 20–22.

description of prayers as lame.[25] Otto van Veen depicts Poena with a wooden leg because Horace speaks of *pede poena claudo*.[26] The lameness of these personifications is a metaphor for the slowness with which, respectively, prayers and punishment take effect. But the lameness of Spenser's hag (which is not mentioned after the opening stanzas) has no conceptual equivalent, and we therefore cannot assume that the formula "Occasion is lame" produced this part of Spenser's description.

More broadly, no meaning of "occasion" can be thought to have produced Spenser's personification. The word always refers to external circumstances or forces, and the most we can find in *OED* are meanings (numbers 2 and 3), more or less synonymous with "cause," that are compatible with or permit giving this name to this figure. The identification of Occasion as a psychological force directly depends on Spenser's portrayal of her and her actions. It seems to me plausible that Spenser first imagined an allegorical hag who provoked wrath; that he then thought of giving her Occasion's forelock as a means of making a point about dealing with psychological forces; and that he realized the compatibility of the word "occasion" with this figure. The last two steps, I would imagine, took place more or less simultaneously, as part of the same creative decision. Of course, this kind of reconstruction is conjectural. However, I think we can be sure that the "cause" of the figure was partly dramatic (the hag's provoking Furor), partly visual and emblematic (the forelock), and partly verbal, and that we cannot find grounds for separating these elements or giving priority to one of them. In the usual emblem the visual and the conceptual are separate and interchangeable—a point made by Renaissance writers in distinguishing emblems from devices.[27] But in Spenser's portrayal of Occasion, the emblematic, the dramatic, and the verbal are not convertible into each other. Each is indispensable not simply to expression, but to the very conception of "occasion" in this episode. Hence, though we know from the opening stanza that something is up, we know nothing decisively until the Palmer identifies Occasion and her role.

[25] *Iliad*, 9.502ff. See Alciati, no. 130, pp. 441–445.

[26] *Odes*, 3.2. See van Veen, p. 180 and p. 26.

[27] William Drummond says, "The Words of the Emblem are only placed to declare the Figures of the Emblem; whereas, in an Impresa, the Figures express and illustrate the one part of the Author's intention, and the Word the other." "A Short Discourse upon Impresa's and Anagrams," *Works*, 1711, p. 228. Similarly, Stefano Guazzo snubs the emblem on the grounds that "when you have read the verses under the emblems, the pictures are useless and superfluous, and serve only as a pastime for children like the pictures in Aesop's fables." Quoted by Praz, 1, 73.

II

Encounters with figures like Occasion and Prays-desire are not the
only instances in which iconographic questions arise in *The Faerie
Queene*. In one of the best known passages in the poem, the old
miser and cuckold Malbecco is transformed into the monster Jealousy,
and it seems natural to ask what relationship this creature has to tra-
ditional figures of Jealousy. Much of the material that follows was
discovered by trying to answer this question. But we should begin by
observing that Spenser turns the Ovidian metamorphosis into his own
kind of poetic narration, even in a stanza that exploits an Ovidian
device:

> But through long anguish, and selfe-murdring thought
> He was so wasted and forpined quight,
> That all his substance was consum'd to nought,
> And nothing left, but like an aery Spright,
> That on the rockes he fell so flit and light,
> That he thereby receiu'd no hurt at all,
> But chaunced on a craggy cliff to light;
> Whence he with crooked clawes so long did crall,
> That at the last he found a caue with entrance small.
>
> (3.10.57)

The sudden producing of Malbecco's "crooked clawes" is a trick
learned from Ovid, yet even this touch is in the Spenserian mode. Our
sense of sudden change comes when Spenser introduces the harsh
alliterative formula, "craggy cliff." Instead of seeing Malbecco un-
dergo a change, we experience a shift of diction, and it is this that
enforces the reality of "crooked clawes."

Despite this, the stanza, taken by itself, could pass for true fic-
tional narration. But in its context it engages our attention in ways
that show that it exemplifies Spenser's characteristic transformation
of narrative materials. In the preceding stanza we see Malbecco's
flight and his leap:

> Still fled he forward, looking backward still,
> Ne stayd his flight, nor fearefull agony,
> Till that he came vnto a rockie hill,
> Ouer the sea, suspended dreadfully,
> That liuing creature it would terrify,
> To looke adowne, or vpward to the hight:

From thence he threw himselfe dispiteously,
All desperate of his fore-damned spright,
That seem'd no helpe for him was left in liuing sight.

(3.10.56)

This stanza makes us aware how active our minds are in the stanza that follows. For example, the phrase "selfe-murdring thought," which in isolation may seem uncomplicated, becomes a genuine play on words when it follows the description of Malbecco's suicidal leap. More broadly, we see that the "so . . . that" constructions in stanza 57 (lines 2–3, 5–6) do not simply mirror external reality. When we have read stanza 56, with its explicit straining of the human imagination, it is clear that these constructions are meant to create a sense of wonder. Each time the word "That" is used at the beginning of a line, it engages the reader's mind—partly through his sense of awe, partly through his acknowledging the consequences of what has occurred in the preceding line. Recognizing and responding to this verbal trick is essential to understanding the concluding lines. The "so . . . that" construction there does not control the most important words, but the force given to the initial "That" by its previous occurrences makes us feel that the last line is a consequence of Malbecco's "crooked clawes" as well as of his crawling. However, the consequentiality has no ready explanation (as it does in lines 2–3 and 5–6), just as there is no explanation of the firm connection made by alliteration between "craggy cliff" and "crooked clawes." With the loss of clear explanations, our earlier sense of wonder turns into something like curiosity or expectancy. Spenser uses this stanza to transform our relationship to Malbecco. In the preceding stanza we observed a being separate from us—a "fore-damned spright" as opposed to a "liuing creature"—and, as the alexandrine brings out, we felt that Malbecco was undergoing experiences quite different from ours. By the end of stanza 57, there is no question that we are involved, in an as yet undefined way, in Malbecco's transformation.

The change this stanza has brought about becomes clear in the next:

Into the same he creepes, and thenceforth there
Resolu'd to build his balefull mansion,
In drery darkenesse, and continuall feare
Of that rockes fall, which euer and anon
Threates with huge ruine him to fall vpon,
That he dare neuer sleepe, but that one eye

Still ope he keepes for that occasion;
Ne euer rests he in tranquillity,
The roring billowes beat his bowre so boystrously.

(3.10.58)

The word "mansion" makes explicit the connection we felt between "cliff," "clawes," and "caue": this is an allegorical habitat, in which every detail expresses a single spiritual reality. Because of our sympathetic participation—which Spenser ensures by continuing, in "creepes," the alliterative patterns at the end of the last stanza—we find ourselves, as it were, inside this habitat. We share Malbecco's fear and look up at the rock with him; the onomatopoeia in the alexandrine recreates in our minds his sense of being assaulted on all sides. Characteristically, Spenser makes our knowledge of a spiritual phenomenon involve our participation in it as a psychological experience.

We can now understand the way iconographic materials are used in the seven stanzas of this passage. If Spenser described a true fictional transformation, his notions of iconography would be the same as the ones we find in the concluding passage of Tasso's *Discorso della Gelosia:*

It remains for me to bring before you, like a little picture, the description of Jealousy found in Boccaccio's Filocolo, a description by which many of the properties of jealousy can be known. He says that Jealousy's home is in one of the highest cliffs of the Apennines, in a dark cave surrounded on every side by snow, battered by the wind, and where two huge dogs, always watchful, are on guard; that she is dressed in brown; that she is female, old, ashen in color, and emaciated; that she was warming herself at a fire where two almost extinguished logs were glowing; that she slept on her threshold between her two dogs. From this description, many of her properties can easily be understood. Her home is said to be on mountains in the midst of snow, to indicate the coldness of her nature; since jealousy is fear, it ought to be cold, since every fear is cold, because the blood collects and thus causes a chill around the heart. . . . The cave where she lives is depicted as dark to show the sadness of those breasts in which she makes her home. The dogs who guard the house and the sleeping between these two animals, which she does on the threshold, make us see her watchfulness; because as dogs are watchful by nature, so

217

jealous men are extremely watchful and are always awake to spy upon all the thoughts and actions of the beloved. She is said to warm herself at a nearly extinguished fire, because jealousy at its peak, heading towards despair, continually extinguishes the fire of love. She is said to be female, not so much with regard to the word [i.e., its gender], as to the nature of women—who, having bodies cold in temperature and with more refined spirits, are therefore more subject to fear and consequently to jealousy. She is made old, because age makes people more suspicious, both because of their experience of the deceptions of the world and because of the chilling of the blood and of the spirits. She is said to be ashen in color and emaciated because jealousy produces these miseries in its victims. She is dressed in brown, because this clothing is suitable for those who are grieving."[28]

Tasso assumes that knowing a moral phenomenon is like seeing a physical object. Jealousy is a definable reality, external to us, and we know it by a set of characteristics that can be expressed by physical properties. If Spenser shared these assumptions, the metamorphosis of Malbecco would be in the Ovidian manner, and the monster Jealousy would emerge, like Ariosto's hag, as a figure composed of traditional and recognizable attributes. But for Spenser the mode of knowledge is not physical vision but psychological experience. We know fear as a defining characteristic of jealousy by sharing Malbecco's terror, not by observing and interpreting his physical attributes and those of his environment.

Spenser's sense of moral knowledge determines the way he uses the traditional attributes of jealousy:

> Ne stayd he, till he came vnto the place,
> Where late his treasure he entombed had,
> Where when he found it not (for *Trompart* bace
> Had it purloyned for his maister bad:)
> With extreme fury he became quite mad,
> And ran away, ran with himselfe away:
> That who so straungely had him seene bestad,
> With vpstart haire, and staring eyes dismay,
> From Limbo lake him late escaped sure would say.

[28] Torquato Tasso, *Prose diverse*, ed. Cesare Guasti, Florence, 1875, 2, 183–184. Boccaccio's description occurs in Book III of *Il Filocolo*, ed. Salvatore Battaglia, Bari, 1938, pp. 214–216.

High ouer hilles and ouer dales he fled,
As if the wind him on his winges had borne,
Ne banck nor bush could stay him, when he sped
His nimble feet, as treading still on thorne:
Griefe, and despight, and gealosie, and scorne
Did all the way him follow hard behind,
And he himselfe himselfe loath'd so forlorne,
So shamefully forlorne of womankind;
That as a Snake, still lurked in his wounded mind.

(3.10.54–55)

In these stanzas there are three features that a sixteenth-century reader might expect to find in a portrait of Jealousy—its representation as an infernal fury, the thorns (which do not always appear underfoot), and, the most familiar attribute, the snake.[29] But we notice that these are not details in a portrait. Quite the contrary, the last two are stated as similes, not descriptions, and the first, far from rendering a fixed and observable figure, is explicitly an effort of the observer's mind to express the amazement registered in "And ran away, ran with himselfe away." Moreover, this amazement is not merely the response to something external; the energetic tone of voice and the play on words show the mind actively projecting the possibility that a human personality can transform itself. The next stanza continues to render the mind's activity in understanding a psychological phenomenon, and it calls on mental energies similar to those in the preceding stanza. The snake, the definitive emblem of jealousy, emerges as the climax of the sustained amazement in the last five lines. And at the center of the stanza Spenser again engages us in a verbal puzzle, which again produces the central issue of the episode. The possibility that "Griefe, and despight, and gealosie, and scorne" are personifications[30] directly raises the possibility that the mind af-

[29] For Jealousy as a creature who comes from hell, see *Orlando Furioso*, 31.4, 42.47 (quoted above) and 50, and Fornari's comments, *Spositione*, 1, 483, and 2, 325, 327. See also *The Blazon of Iealousie*, London, 1615, pp. 41–42. This work is a translation by Robert Tofte of Benedetto Varchi's *Lezzione sopra la Gelosia*, an academic discourse, delivered in 1545, on Giovanni della Casa's sonnet, "Cura, che di timor ti nutri, e cresci." Cited hereafter as Tofte.

A staff of thorns is a common attribute of Envy. See Ovid, *Metamorphoses* 2.789–790; Alciati, no. 71, pp. 271–273; Whitney, p. 94. Cf. Ripa, pp. 181–182, s.v. *Gelosia*, and *FQ* 4.5.31. Two passages in Sidney are especially close to Spenser's description here: *Astrophel and Stella* 78 and *Arcadia* 2.25, in *Works*, ed. A. Feuillerat, Cambridge, 1912, 1, 308. For the snake, see above, n. 5.

[30] Upton in the eighteenth century noticed this ambiguity. See the *Variorum* note on the passage.

flicted by passions can become the allegorical representation of itself. It is clear that in these stanzas conventional attributes of Jealousy are conceived as part of the reader's mental equipment and not as part of a reality external to him. The traditional attributes are not the end point reached in Malbecco's transformation, but, in the form of similes, render the mind's initial efforts to understand it.

As the passage goes on, in the three stanzas we have already examined, Spenser shifts to iconographic details that, while entirely appropriate to jealousy, are not exclusively or primarily indicative of it. The leap from a cliff, though it is sometimes caused by jealousy (as it is in Ariosto's Ariodante), is often an expression of the love-despair caused by a chaste mistress.[31] Claws can be connected with jealousy, but they are so common a sign of monstrosity that they could hardly, by themselves, serve as a defining characteristic for any individual sin.[32] Finally, the most interesting iconographic detail in these stanzas is the rock that threatens to fall on Malbecco. Spenser took this image not from allegorical representations of Jealousy, but from classical mythology. It is one of Tantalus' punishments in hell—sometimes alone, sometimes in conjunction with the more familiar torment of the fleeing food and drink. It has no traditional connection with jealousy, and its relevance to this passage is indicated by the source from which Spenser probably took it:

> What again is not only more wretched but more degraded and hideous than a man, depressed, enfeebled and prostrate with distress? And to this state of wretchedness that man comes nearest who is in fear of the approach of some evil, and whose soul is paralyzed with suspense. And it is as a symbol of this power of evil that the poets imagine the rock hanging over Tantalus.

> Punishing his sin and want of self-control and
> boastful tongue.

[31] As in Sannazaro, *Arcadia*, 1504, prose 8, and Tasso, *Aminta*, 4.2.191–250. In his edition of *Aminta*, Milan, 1952, Bruno Maier cites Theocritus, 3.25–26, and Vergil, *Eclogues* 8.59–60, as the prototypes of passages like these.

[32] Spenser's Envy (5.12.30) has "long nayles ouer raught, / Like puttocks clawes." But claws commonly appear on representatives of other sins. For lechery, see the examples cited by Samuel C. Chew, "Spenser's Pageant of the Seven Deadly Sins," in *Studies in Art and Literature for Belle da Costa Greene*, ed. Dorothy Miner, Princeton, 1954, pp. 48–49. As Chew notes, figures of Avarice are also presented with claws; hence Spenser says that Mammon's "nayles like clawes appeard" (2.7.3).

Such is the general penalty of folly; for in all cases where the mind recoils from reason there is always some such kind of overhanging dread.[33]

This passage directly makes our point about the way in which Spenser has used his iconographic materials. Fear is one of the identifying characteristics of jealousy,[34] but Spenser's image, unlike the coldness of Boccaccio's Gelosia and her abode, is not chosen to impress that fact on us. Rather it makes us share a broad and general fear, one that could hardly be attached to or identified with a specific passion. It is entirely appropriate that the image that clinches the stanza is the sea—the image that more than any other reminds us of the distresses of all human life and all human love.

The iconography of the passage, as well as its rhetorical management, shows how untenable is the view of it advanced by Northrop Frye: "Sometimes the fiction writer clashes with the moralist in Spenser, though never for long. When Malbecco offers to take Hellenore back from the satyrs, he becomes a figure of some dignity as well as pathos; but Spenser cannot let his dramatic sympathy with Malbecco evolve. Complicated behaviour, mixed motives, or the kind of driving energy of character which makes moral considerations seem less important, as it does in all Shakespeare's heroes, and even in Milton's Satan—none of this could be contained in Spenser's framework."[35] Frye's view of Spenser's "framework" is as oversimplified as his view of "moral considerations." As we read this passage, Spenser makes it impossible for us to feel that jealousy is a delimited moral monstrosity that we can know as a thing external to us. Quite the contrary, he brings the phenomenon of jealousy directly into our minds, and as he

[33] Cicero, *Tusculan Disputations*, 4.16, tr. J. E. King, London: Loeb Classical Library, 1927. The passage is quoted by Natalis Comes, *Mythologia*, Frankfort, 1581, 6.18, p. 635. Comes, p. 638 cites, as a passage similar to Cicero's, Lucretius, *De Rerum Natura*, 3.978–983. For a complete list of classical references, see the note on Pausanias, *Description of Greece*, 10.31.12, in J. G. Frazer's commentary, London, 1898, 6 vols.

William Nelson has suggested that Malbecco's rock comes from Gascoigne's *Adventures of Master F. J.* in "A Source for Spenser's Malbecco," *MLN*, 68 (1953), 226–229. But as Waldo McNeir has pointed out, neither Gascoigne nor his source (Ariosto, *Cinque Canti*, 2.18) describes an overhanging rock; rather the allegorical figure of Sospetto lives on a cliff high above the sea, and it is the cliff itself that threatens to fall. "Ariosto's Sospetto, Gascoigne's Suspicion, and Spenser's Malbecco," in *Festschrift für Walther Fischer*, Heidelberg, 1959, p. 44.

[34] See Tofte, pp. 18, 22 (i.e. 23), 25, 38, 50, and Tasso, *Prose*, 2, 173ff.

[35] "The Structure of Imagery in *The Faerie Queene*," in *Fables of Identity*, New York, 1963, p. 74.

does so his iconography becomes more humanly inclusive. Our sense of kinship with Malbecco is not denied, but rather broadened and intensified as the passage develops.

The stanza that follows the depiction of Malbecco in his cave seems at first to be a direct contradiction of all that we have said:

> Ne euer is he wont on ought to feed,
> But toades and frogs, his pasture poysonous,
> Which in his cold complexion do breed
> A filthy bloud, or humour rancorous,
> Matter of doubt and dread suspitious,
> That doth with curelesse care consume the hart,
> Corrupts the stomacke with gall vitious,
> Croscuts the liuer with internall smart,
> And doth transfixe the soule with deathes eternall
> dart.   (3.10.59)

This stanza seems to do in physiological terms what a description of a monster of Jealousy does in emblematic terms: it appears to treat jealousy as a specific and isolatable condition, with disease replacing monstrosity as the underlying metaphor. Just as one at first assumes that the iconography in earlier stanzas is orthodox,[36] so one here assumes that Spenser is following a more or less standard account of the physiological symptoms of jealousy. But no such account exists. We go, for example, to *The Anatomy of Melancholy,* and we find that Burton's long discussion of jealousy (part 3, section 3) is written entirely as a moral essay, without a word of physiology or humors or even faculty psychology. As Lawrence Babb says, commenting on the fact that Burton cites practically no medical authorities in this part of the *Anatomy,* "the concept of melancholy jealousy is popular rather than scientific."[37]

Theoretically, one ought to be able to give a physiological account of jealousy. It was one of the passions, and a passion by definition caused some change in the body.[38] But some passions (like choler)

---

[36] We should note that the frogs and toads that we find in this stanza are not commonly identified with jealousy or envy. In the procession of the Seven Deadly Sins, Envy gnaws on a toad (1.4.30) instead of the more usual snake or heart. But Samuel Chew, "Spenser's Pageant of the Seven Deadly Sins," p. 51, can cite only one analogue to this detail, and it is a description of Envy with garments "speckled" with toads. Presumably Spenser uses the toad in these passages because it was thought to be poisonous. See *Batman uppon Bartholome,* London, 1582, f. 351.

[37] *The Elizabethan Malady,* East Lansing, Mich., 1951, p. 141.

[38] See J. B. Bamborough, *The Little World of Man,* London, 1952, pp. 119ff.

are easier to describe physiologically than are others. There seems, for example, to have been no physiological account of such phenomena of jealousy as suspicion and possessiveness. Moreover, jealousy includes a variety of feelings, some of which are physiologically incompatible with each other. This problem can best be understood by considering the way in which the physician Jacques Ferrand worries about an analogous problem concerning, as the chapter title has it, "the internall causes of love melancholy":

> *Aristotle* in his Problems saies, that those that are Melancholy are most subject to this malady [love]. . . . Which conclusion of his would be most Absurd, if so be he meant here those that are Melancholy by reason of the aboundance of their naturall Melancholy [i.e. the humour known as melancholy, or black bile]; which of it selfe is extreame cold and dry, and by consequence cleane repugnant to the heat required in this disease. Otherwise, Old men, who abound chiefly with this Humor, should oftner fall in Love, then young; and his unruly Desires, increase with his yeares. . . . But those that are Melancholy, by reason of the Adustion [i.e. physiological heating] of Humours, . . . these are Hot and Dry, and apt to have ingendred within them a certain kind of Flatulent vapour, that tickles them extreamely, and by consequent, makes them beyond measure lascivious.[39]

As Tasso says in explaining Boccaccio's personification, jealousy was considered to be "cold" in nature because it is based on fear—hence Malbecco's "cold complexion." But if this fact were regarded with Ferrand's medical strictness, one would be obliged to ignore phenomena that are caused by hot blood, such as the notorious jealousy of Italians and Spaniards.[40]

Spenser, of course, is writing only about the old man Malbecco with his "cold complexion," and he could have given a physiologically coherent description of his internal condition. However, he does not at all seem to have had this in mind. The one humor he specifies, gall (or choler), is the hottest of the four, and "vitious" may mean that it is adust.[41] The "internall smart" of the liver would involve blood,

[39] *Erotomania*, tr. Edmund Chilmead, Oxford, 1640, pp. 64–66. First French edition, 1612.
[40] See Robert Burton, *Anatomy of Melancholy* 3.3.1.2, ed. A. R. Shilleto, London, 1896, 3, 303–304. Also Tofte, pp. 21–22, 29.
[41] "Vicious" can mean "foul, impure, noxious, morbid" (*OED* 7), and the examples in *OED* indicate that the word specifically refers to a natural condition.

the other hot humor, and the liver is mentioned in this context presumably because it is the seat of lust. Moreover, Spenser would not say that the stomach and the liver were the organs affected if he were trying to make his description conform to scientific theories. If we take Spenser's stanza to be a true medical description, it describes a case of what was called hypochondriacal (i.e., visceral) melancholy. Jealousy, on the other hand, was a subdivision of love melancholy, which was usually considered (as it is by Burton) to belong to the type of melancholy that affected the head.[42] Ferrand (uniquely to my knowledge) argued that love melancholy was a form of hypochondriacal melancholy, "seeing that the parts affected in it are principally the Liver, and the parts adjoyning, from whence those black Fuliginous vapours doe arise, which ascending up to the braine, doe hinder, and pervert the principall faculties thereof."[43] But even he regards jealousy as an affliction of the heart and brain.[44] No reader would have thought that Spenser was indicating the physiological symptoms of jealousy in the line, "Corrupts the stomacke with gall vitious." Medically it describes nothing more interesting than a case of acid indigestion.

For all its scientific appearance, the stanza makes sense only as poetic discourse. As it proceeds, it moves from a physiological to a moral account of Malbecco's condition. The shift first occurs in the line, "A filthy bloud, or humour rancorous." "Filthy bloud" (like "cold complexion") is a straightforward medical description; it indicates a general condition of disease, "the presence of excess or corrupt humour in the blood."[45] "Humour rancorous," on the other hand, deliberately straddles medical and moral meanings—not only in the double reference of "humour," but also in "rancorous," the meanings of which are predominantly moral and emotional.[46] In the next line,

---

[42] The third major type of melancholy was that which affected the whole body. For an account of the three types, see Burton, *Anatomy*, 1.1.3.4, ed. Shilleto, 1, 199–202.

[43] *Erotomania*, p. 26.

[44] *Ibid.*, pp. 203–204.

[45] Bamborough, p. 70.

[46] This was a new word in 1590. *OED* gives as the first uses *FQ* 1.11.14 ("rancorous yre"), *Comedy of Errors*, 1.1.6 ("the rancorous outrage of your duke"), *Richard III*, 1.3.50 ("a rancorous enemy"), and Marlowe's *Edward II*, 2.2 ("rancorous minds"). See also *FQ* 2.7.22 ("rancorous Despight"). *OED* gives no physical meanings of "rancorous" earlier than 1660 ("Of a wound or sore: festering, inflamed"). However, it cites an obsolete meaning of "rancor," "rancid smell; rancidity; rankness," of which the last example is dated 1567. And compare Camden, *Remaines*, 1605: "Through the rancor of the poyson, the wound was iudged incurable."

"Matter of doubt and dread suspitious," a specifically physiological significance is maintained only through the double meaning of "matter." And in "That doth with curelesse care consume the hart," Spenser has completed the shift from the language of physicians to the language of poets. A sixteenth-century reader would have considered that this line states a medical truth, but he would equally have recognized that Spenser was employing a common poetic locution, and he would be conscious of the large amount of verbal play in the line—the pun ("curelesse care") on *cura* and the allusion to its supposed derivation from *cor* and *uro*.[47]

We are now in a position to understand how the line, "Corrupts the stomacke with gall vitious," can make poetic sense despite the irrelevance of its physiology. It is a commonplace that jealousy is "galling" in a loose or metaphoric sense. Pierre Charron calls it "the Gaule that corrupteth all the Hony of our life: it is commonly mingled with the sweetest and pleasantst actions, which it maketh so sharpe and sower as nothing more: it changeth love into hate, respect into disdaine, assurance into diffidence."[48] Tofte (see note 29) uses the verb "to gall" to render the torments and vexations of jealousy: thus, he translates a phrase from Della Casa's sonnet, "Ivi, a te stessa incresci" as "There, vexe, torment, and gawle thine inward selfe."[49] The usual physical embodiment of this commonplace is in the emblematic portraits of Envy, who is depicted as gnawing on either a poisonous snake or (less commonly) her heart. When Spenser says that Malbecco's humour "corrupts the stomacke with gall vitious," he is giving a physiological equivalent to this emblem. The line is a vivid rendering of what it is like to eat gall, and it is to be understood as a rhetorical intensification—analogous to Spenser's use of pictorial diction—and not as a medical description. It is entirely in keeping with this line and with the rest of the stanza that the next detail we are given is

[47] We should note that in discussing this kind of phenomenon, Renaissance medicine is largely moral and poetic:

"The common etymology will evince it, *cura quasi cor uro; dementes curae, insomnes curae, damnosae curae, tristes, mordaces, carnifices,* &c.—biting, eating, gnawing, cruel, bitter, sick, sad, unquiet, pale, tetrick, miserable, intolerable cares, as the Poets call them, worldly cares, and are as many in number as the sea sands. Galen, Fernelius, Felix Plater, Valescus de Taranta, &c., reckon afflictions, miseries, even all these contentions, and vexations of the mind, as principal causes, in that they take away sleep, hinder concoction, dry up the body, and consume the substance of it." Burton, *Anatomy,* 1.2.3.10, ed. Shilleto, 1, 313. Burton continues with a long disquisition on the miseries of human life.

[48] *Of Wisdome,* tr. Samson Lennard, London [1606], p. 92. Cf. Burton, *Anatomy,* 3.3.2, ed. Shilleto, 3, 321, and Tofte, p. 40.

[49] Tofte, p. 8. See also pp. 23 (i.e. 22), 26, 47, and *FQ* 4.5.31.

a piece of purely poetic medicine—for "Croscuts the liuer with in-ternall smart" is quite vague as scientific description—and that the concluding alexandrine could have come only from the poet's store of images.

Up to this point we have discussed this passage simply as a trans-mutation of Ovidian metamorphosis and emblematic description into the rhetorical mode of narration that we find throughout *The Faerie Queene*. But in the stanza we have just discussed it becomes clear, if it was not already, that the passage is rhetorical in the narrower and more usual sense. Particularly in the accumulation of parallel verbs in the last four lines, we become conscious of a voice addressing us. The stanza thus brings us to recognize the presence throughout this pas-sage of a type of poem that is not at all narrative—the complaint or invective against jealousy. Poems or passages of this type appear throughout Renaissance poetry. The best-known example, which one finds constantly cited in sixteenth-century writings, is the six stanzas that begin canto 31 of *Orlando Furioso*. Gascoigne translates this passage as the lament of the jealous Ferdinando,[50] and Spenser imi-tates it at the beginning of the canto that follows Malbecco's trans-formation. Other examples are the sonnet of Della Casa on which Varchi wrote his discourse; stanzas from Drayton's *Mortimeriados* and Daniel's *Complaint of Rosamond*, both quoted in *The Anatomy of Melancholy;*[51] a sonnet by Luigi Tansillo, "O d'invidia e d'amor figlia sí ria," that is cited by both Tasso and Bruno;[52] and a stanza in Spenser's *Hymne in Honour of Love:*

> Yet is there one [evil] more cursed then they all,
> That cancker worme, that monster Gelosie,
> Which eates the hart, and feedes vpon the gall,
> Turning all loues delight to miserie,
> Through feare of loosing his felicitie.
> Ah Gods, that euer ye that monster placed
> In gentle loue, that all his ioyes defaced.

(266–272)

The presence of this type of passage in the transformation of Mal-becco can be seen both in the active presence of Spenser's voice and

[50] George Gascoigne, *The Adventures of Master F. J.*, in *The Posies*, ed. John W. Cunliffe, Cambridge, 1907, pp. 424–426.

[51] 3.3.1.2 and 3.3.2, ed. Shilleto, 3, 305, 322.

[52] Tasso, *Prose*, 2, 172; Giordano Bruno, *De Gli Eroici Furori*, 1.1, in *Dialoghi Italiani*, ed. G. Gentile and G. Aquilecchia, Florence, 1958, p. 966.

mind and in the relationship of the speaker to the phenomenon of jealousy. In the invective against jealousy, the speaker is not observing a bizarre event or figure, but is a man among men, speaking of something that may happen and in some cases (as in Della Casa's sonnet) has happened to him. There is a wonderful manifestation of this relationship to jealousy in the description of Malbecco's rock:

> Into the same he creepes, and thenceforth there
> Resolu'd to build his balefull mansion,
> In drery darkenesse, and continuall feare
> Of that rockes fall, which euer and anon
> Threates with huge ruine him to fall vpon.
>
> (3.10.58)

"*That* rockes fall"—as if to say that we know what this experience is, whether through our own experience, or our knowledge of men, or our knowledge of books. Combining sympathetic experience of a feeling with clear-sighted observation of it is so essential a Spenserian achievement that one can hardly claim that its presence in this passage represents a specific indebtedness to the invective poem against jealousy. But there is no doubt that the passage concludes in the mode of these poems. Whereas Malbecco's suicide leap and the description of his cave could pass for Ovidian narrative, the physiological stanza that follows could not. There we are primarily conscious of the poet's voice addressing us and expressing something like what Varchi found in Della Casa's sonnet—"a kinde of religious and compassionate Indignation and Anger."[53]

Nowhere is the rhetorical mode of the passage more important for us to recognize than in the final stanza, in which the transformation of Malbecco is finally accomplished:

> Yet can he neuer dye, but dying liues,
> And doth himselfe with sorrow new sustaine,
> That death and life attonce vnto him giues,
> And painefull pleasure turnes to pleasing paine.
> There dwels he euer, miserable swaine,
> Hatefull both to him selfe, and euery wight;
> Where he through priuy griefe, and horrour vaine,
> Is woxen so deform'd, that he has quight
> Forgot he was a man, and *Gealosie* is hight.
>
> (3.10.60)

[53] Tofte, p. 9. This translates "una dogliosa, e compassionevole indignazione."

Taken by themselves, the last five lines seem to describe a figure like Boccaccio's, and the terms in which Spenser speaks seem to confirm the notion of moral monstrosity—something literally beyond the pale of normal humanity. Yet our sense of these lines and their import is completely changed when we read them in the context of what precedes them, and particularly in the light of the first four lines of the stanza. In these lines, the drastic suffering of the preceding stanza is turned into what we recognize as the normal experience of love: for the poetic commonplaces with which Spenser addresses us are the paradoxes of love, not of jealousy. Spenser makes us aware, with a fresh recognition, how truly painful is the painfulness of love, and conversely he makes us see jealousy under the aspect of normal love. Our human kinship with Malbecco is as firmly expressed here as anywhere else in the passage. Hence when we go on to the final lines, we find ourselves unable to adopt a punitive tone in calling Malbecco a "miserable swaine." The gravity with which that epithet must be said registers our awareness that the transformation wrought by jealousy is a terrible potentiality of human love.

We can now understand an odd fact about this stanza: the statement that Malbecco is "woxen so deform'd" is not supported by any visual description. Malbecco's transformation is directly stated as a change of human feeling and is rendered by the shift from the formulas of normal love to "Hatefull both to him selfe, and euery wight," "priuy griefe," and "horrour vaine." The final line, far from rendering a fixed monstrosity, directly reminds us that the moral deformity we see is a transformation of human feeling, and the phrase "forgot he was a man" expresses something genuinely tragic. While it reminds us of the humanity we shared with Malbecco, it conveys the finality of the change that has occurred within him. Our feelings here are much more than a response to an external reality. By this point in the passage, the notion of metamorphosis, of change of being, lies entirely in the speaker's and reader's awareness that something drastic and irreversible has occurred. The completion of Malbecco's transformation is expressed not in a description or depicted action, but by the poet's act of renaming him and the awesome recognition it produces that the name of a passion has become the name of a creature.

III

The mode of Spenser's narration and the fact that the reality of his poem is not analogous to that of the world account for his not using

iconographic materials in the way we might have expected him to
have done. Clearly, however, this does not mean that Spenser was
not interested in iconography and its traditions. For one thing, we
have seen how continuously he is interested in the nature of symbolic
figures, in what they tell us about human personality, and in the vari-
ety of ways in which they do so. Another sign of Spenser's interest in
iconography is his assumption that there is something especially vivid
and expressive about pictorial language. Moreover, it would be wrong
to think that Spenser's use of iconographic materials always involves
so extraordinary a transmutation as the stanzas about Malbecco. He
can employ a perfectly conventional mode of emblematic portraiture
and still turn it to his own poetic uses. After Guyon masters and
binds Occasion, he seizes and ties up Furor:

> With hundred yron chaines he did him bind,
> And hundred knots that did him sore constraine:
> Yet his great yron teeth he still did grind,
> And grimly gnash, threatning reuenge in vaine;
> His burning eyen, whom bloudie strakes did staine,
> Stared full wide, and threw forth sparkes of fire,
> And more for ranck despight, then for great paine,
> Shakt his long lockes, colourd like copper-wire,
> And bit his tawny beard to shew his raging ire.
>
> (2.4.15)

The verbal intensity here is rather simple and single-minded, but it
nevertheless serves a real purpose. Coming after the mastering of Oc-
casion and Furor, this stanza, through the unremitting vividness of its
details, makes us feel that rage is still a psychological force. To con-
trol its energies, we see, is not to eliminate them.

A great deal of work remains to be done on the iconography of
The Faerie Queene. Unfortunately much of what has been done is
hampered by the imposition of inappropriate assumptions and expec-
tations on the poem, and by a failure to make iconographic analysis
answerable to the literary experience of reading the poem.[54] It is one

---

[54] These seem to me especially serious faults in the work of Alastair Fowler,
who knows more about Renaissance iconography than any other student of
Spenser. (Among other things, we owe to him the explanation of Guyon's
name: see "The River Guyon," MLN, 75 (1960), 289–292.) Fowler constantly
makes the poem serve his learning and his theories, rather than the reverse.
His numerological and astrological study, *Spenser and the Numbers of Time*,
London, 1964, is full of what Huck Finn calls "stretchers." See the reviews by
David Kalstone, *Essays in Criticism*, 15 (1965), 446–452, and by William

thing to discover that Spenser uses or modifies a traditional emblem or symbolic attribute. It is quite another thing to assume that the relevant passage from Valeriano or Mignault's commentary on Alciati is a statement of Spenser's meaning.[55] In interpreting Spenser's use of

---

Nelson, *Ren News*, 18 (1965), 52–57. Even in work that seems more promising and sounds more persuasive than does this book, Fowler tends to spin his own cocoon and lose sight of *The Faerie Queene*. The reader should of course read Fowler's articles and decide for himself. But an example of his method is the argument that the fountain by which Mortdant and Amavia die is a symbol of both spiritual repentance and baptismal regeneration—"The Image of Mortality: *The Faerie Queene*, II.i–ii," HLQ, 24 (1961), 96–97. Fowler's argument may carry us along as we read it, but when we turn back to *FQ* 2.2.5–9, we feel that this cannot be the poem he is talking about: it broaches problems of spiritual purity by means of consciously Ovidian mythologizing and not by theological allegory. Then we realize that Fowler's main evidence comes from a Jesuit emblem book first published in 1624, and that a crux of his argument is a visual detail—water streaming from the petrified nymph's hands (suggesting the image of Christ in "The Fountain of Life")—that appears in the Jesuit emblem, but not in *The Faerie Queene*.

Fowler's other important articles are "Emblems of Temperance in *The Faerie Queene*, Book II," RES, n.s., 11 (1960), 143–149, and "Six Knights at Castle Joyous," SP, 56 (1959), 583–599.

[55] There are two aspects of this problem, both of which are illustrated in articles by John Steadman. "Spenser's House of Care: A Reinterpretation," *SRen*, 7 (1960), 207–224, is a commentary on *FQ* 4.5.30–46. As Steadman says, "Spenser has made the meaning of his 'darke conceit' extremely clear" (p. 207), and he devotes his article to suggesting sources and expanding and refining annotations. Most of the material is really interesting and helpful—the most striking point being the explanation of the symbolism of Care's hammers by the common use in sixteenth-century Italian of *martello* (hammer) as a metaphor for jealousy. But surely a "reinterpretation" should not only provide notes and sources but should use them to say something about the quality of experience and moral awareness in the episode.

When, on the other hand, Steadman does offer a real interpretation, he is too ready to allow the iconographic sources to speak for Spenser. In "Spenser's *Errour* and the Renaissance Allegorical Tradition," *Neuphilologische Mitteilungen*, 67 (1961), 22–38, he begins by associating the monster whom the Red Cross Knight encounters with Hesiod's Echidna: "There is . . . a distinct resemblance between the allegorical significance of Spenser's monster and the meaning which Renaissance commentators found in Hesiod's serpent-woman. In their conception of Echidna as 'variam multiformemque mentis vim, & multiplicibus implicitam spiris artem,' Spenser could have found a suggestion for representing in 'Errours endless traine' the subtle but specious arguments which (except for faith) would enmesh the Christian wayfarer in fallacy and falsehood" (p. 24).

But when we look at the passage, particularly at the stanza from which Steadman quotes (1.1.18), we find that Spenser uses the monster's coils to express a feeling of struggle and oppression in the mind and not an intellectual experience of sophistic argument. Hence there is no justification for imposing these commentaries on the poem, however likely it is that the Echidna was one of Spenser's sources. In the next four pages Steadman marshals a host of com-

traditional materials, we must always pay attention to the way meanings are expressed in the verse of *The Faerie Queene*. To see this, let us complete our account of the way Spenser develops the meaning of "occasion" in Book II, canto 4. When Phedon has been released from Furor's clutches, he begins to tell Guyon his story:

> With hart then throbbing, and with watry eyes,
> Faire Sir (quoth he) what man can shun the hap,
> That hidden lyes vnwares him to surpryse?
> Misfortune waites aduantage to entrap
> The man most warie in her whelming lap.
> So me weake wretch, of many weakest one,
> Vnweeting, and vnware of such mishap,
> She brought to mischiefe through occasion,
> Where this same wicked villein did me light vpon.
>
> (2.4.17)

What Phedon means by "occasion" is the traditional meaning that Spenser had ignored: occasion is one of the uncertain forces in the world, closely related to chance or fortune. What is distinctively Spenserian here is the way this notion becomes part of the meaning of "occasion" in the canto. In the simplest sense, the idea is rejected. It becomes abundantly clear that Phedon cannot so easily disavow moral responsibility and blame external circumstances. And yet in the final, and most potent, use of the word, we see that there was an important truth in what Phedon said. The Palmer speaks to Atin, whom Pyrochles has sent "to seeke *Occasion,* where so she bee" (2.4.43):

> Madman (said then the Palmer) that does seeke
> *Occasion* to wrath, and cause of strife;
> She comes vnsought, and shonned followes eke.
> Happy, who can abstaine, when Rancour rife
> Kindles Reuenge, and threats his rusty knife;
> Woe neuer wants, where euery cause is caught,
> And rash *Occasion* makes vnquiet life.
>
> (2.4.44)

"Seeke occasion to wrath" would unequivocally mean "seek the external circumstances that allow an expression of anger," and because

---

mentators who say that the Chimaera, the daughter of Echidna, symbolizes rhetoric. But this is relevant only if we accept the initial interpretation. Meanwhile, in these four pages, only one line from *The Faerie Queene* is cited—the notorious detail of Errour's vomiting books and papers (1.1.20).

of the syntax this remains the main meaning of the phrase as we read it. But by italicizing *"Occasion"* and thus making it the name of the hag, Spenser makes us recognize that the phrase can also mean, "encourage the forces of anger within yourself." Hence "she comes vnsought" includes both provoking events outside us and the unexpected wellings up of feeling within. Similarly, it is impossible to tell whether the psychological allegory in the next two lines recounts internal or external events. It is these double meanings—so characteristically lucid and unforced in their inclusiveness—that give resonance to "where euery cause is caught." In that phrase, our double awareness takes the form of a perception about dramatic behavior—that the rash man catches at causes not because of what they are, but because of what he is. When we reach the Palmer's final words, we can hardly discriminate the two meanings of "occasion": being the victim of one's passions becomes fused with being victimized by external circumstances. The stanza recapitulates and, as it were, joins forces with the story of Phedon to make us now see that man's susceptibility to anger is itself part of the uncertainty of his existence.

Anyone who knows the iconographic background of a passage like this will be a better reader of it than one who does not. At the very least, he will experience incidental pleasures like recognizing in "where euery cause is caught" a fine transmutation of the traditional moral of Occasion and her forelock. And I have already suggested that some iconographic knowledge is essential for an adequate understanding of the first episode involving Occasion. Still, it is difficult to say when this kind of knowledge is essential or important and when it is not. It certainly increases our pleasure in and admiration of the Malbecco passage, but surely the major effect of what we now know about that passage is to clear away false expectations and to encourage us to trust Spenser's verse. We began this chapter by observing how frankly Spenser declares iconographic meanings, so that symbolic identification, as we usually think of it, is a relatively simple matter. This phenomenon is an inevitable result of the way in which Spenser transforms the materials of a fictional world into the verbal formulas that constitute the reality of his poem. The stanza last discussed is iconographically complex, but this complexity is entirely expressed by verbal phenomena like the double meanings of *"Occasion"* and the inclusiveness of Spenser's formulas. Hence an ignorant reader is much less seriously handicapped than he would be at a moment of analogous complexity in *The Divine Comedy*. There is an important truth in the tradition that begins with Hazlitt's remark that Spenser's allegory is a painted dragon:

> Some people will say that all this may be very fine, but that they cannot understand it on account of the allegory. They are afraid of the allegory, as if they thought it would bite them: they look at it as a child looks at a painted dragon, and think it will strangle them in its shining folds. This is very idle. If they do not meddle with the allegory, the allegory will not meddle with them. Without minding it at all, the whole is as plain as a pike-staff.[56]

The most important modern champion of this view is C. S. Lewis:

> Allegory is not a puzzle. The worst thing we can do is to read it with our eyes skinned for clues, as we read a detective story. If the reader has some familiarity with the allegorical method in general and an ordinary measure both of sensibility and adult experience, then he may be assured that any *significacio* which does not seem natural to him after a second reading of the poem, is erroneous.[57]

> The allegory that really matters is usually unmistakable. Hazlitt can hardly have meant what he said on that subject. Few poets are so radically allegorical as Spenser. . . . But it is not impossible that many who thought they were obeying Hazlitt have read the poetry aright. They receive the allegory so easily that they forget they have done so, as a man in health is unaware of breathing.[58]

No doubt these remarks have too much an air that ignorance is bliss, but they are much closer to the realities of *The Faerie Queene* than are reactions against them like Alastair Fowler's view of the poem as a shrine of numerology and astrological arcana. What Lewis saw was the extraordinary degree to which the meanings of *The Faerie Queene* lie on its surface, and this aesthetic fact is not at all dependent on Lewis' own neoromantic interpretations of it.

Because Spenser does not purport to imitate a symbolic world, the emotional and moral complexities of his verse are compatible with relatively simple iconography. The Cave of Mammon, as we shall see in the next chapter, is a large-scale illustration of this fact. Conversely, when Spenser writes in traditional iconographic modes, his verse is

[56] *Lectures on the English Poets*, in William Hazlitt, *Works*, ed. P. P. Howe, London, 1930–1934, 5, 38.

[57] *The Allegory of Love*, Oxford, 1936, p. 333.

[58] *English Literature in the Sixteenth Century*, Oxford, 1954, p. 388.

often less interesting than when he is writing his own kind of poetic narration. The most important examples are provided by one of the best known phenomena in *The Faerie Queene*—the allegorical pageants. The lavish praise of these pageants is a heritage of the romantics, who overvalued Spenser's pictorialism because it was the antithesis of abstractions, ideas, and allegory in the bad sense. I know that it seems a betrayal of true Spenserianism to say that these pageants are relatively uninteresting. But compare the processions of the Seven Deadly Sins (1.4.18–35) or of the seasons and the months (7.7.28–46) with the equivalent number of stanzas in the Bower of Bliss or the Garden of Adonis. Or compare the processional part of the Masque of Cupid (3.12.7–18, i.e., up until the appearance of Amoret) with the description of Busyrane's tapestries (3.11.28–46). Or compare the marriage of the Thames and the Medway (4.11) with the Temple of Venus (4.10). When Spenser describes a procession, he accepts a mode that inherently prohibits the flexibility and richness of a passage like Malbecco's transformation. Moreover, he accepts the necessity of writing in this mode for whatever number of stanzas is required to complete the procession. The marriage of the Thames and the Medway is so interesting and sustains itself for so long precisely because Spenser is continually intervening and assimilating the pageant to the activity of his mind (see 4.11.10, 17, 22, 26, 28, 34, 38, 40, 43). It seems to me unnecessary to quarrel about whether the processions are more or (as I find them) less rewarding than, say, the story of Phedon, the canto devoted to Phaedria's island, or the episode of Hellenore among the satyrs. But I think we can say that the processions are not, as has been thought, a *definitive* excellence of Spenser's poetry, but are rather a specialized kind of poetic performance. Spenser does them wonderfully, but they impose limitations on his verse that most of the other modes of narration in *The Faerie Queene* do not.

Chapter Eight

Interpreting the Cave of Mammon

I

In this chapter we shall use the interpretation of a major episode in *The Faerie Queene* as a way of raising again the problems with which we have been concerned—the kind of meaning *The Faerie Queene* has, the relation between historical and critical understanding, and the kind of mental equipment and capacities Spenser expects in his reader. In recent years, the Cave of Mammon has attracted a great deal of attention, and I would like to conduct our discussion of it by examining two especially interesting analyses—Harry Berger, Jr.'s "The Hero Faints: A Critical Misadventure"[1] and Frank Kermode's "The Cave of Mammon."[2] Berger and Kermode are two of the liveliest and most intelligent critics of Spenser, and their essays are of particular interest to us, because each uses the Cave of Mammon as an opportunity for defining the nature of Spenser's allegory and the way in which *The Faerie Queene* should be read. In addition, the two essays illustrate what might be considered the Scylla and Charybdis of understanding literary works "historically"—a failure of historical imagination, on Berger's part, and on Kermode's a self-conscious historicism that results in the a priori assumption that one kind of scholarly knowledge is essential to understanding the poem. Moreover, the difficulties in which both men find themselves are in large part produced by the assumption that *The Faerie Queene* is essentially a fictional narration. The two essays, then, pretty well map out the ways in which an intelligent and sympathetic interpretation of *The Faerie Queene* can go wrong.

Berger's remark that "Canto 7 is a complex-looking episode poetically and a very simple discourse ethically" (p. 32) indicates what is perhaps the fundamental aim of both his essay and Kermode's. Each rightly seeks to make the poetic complexity of the Cave of Mammon part of its meaning, instead of treating it as mere decoration around a simple core like "Guyon refuses the enticements of wealth and

[1] This is the first chapter of *The Allegorical Temper*, New Haven, 1957, pp. 3–38.
[2] In *Elizabethan Poetry*, ed. John Russell Brown and Bernard Harris, London, 1960, pp. 151–173.

honor." Kermode argues that the complexity of the canto is primarily iconographic, and his theories, though they seem to me wrong, will help us define the way in which we should deal with individual passages and with the canto as a whole. He says that the canto is not a "face-value" allegory (p. 151), but is rather "a mystery of the sort that labours to be shadowed with obscurity" (p. 172). Spenser, he says, "seems to be assuming a special kind of reader, or rather a special kind of information, and he may also be held to believe that even this community of information will not, however complete and subtle, provide absolute explanations, full translations of image into discourse" (pp. 151–152). Later he explains that a Renaissance poet "would *invent,* though in the Renaissance sense of the word; he would create new figures and new meanings by adapting and re-combining any fragmentary or scattered evidence he could find. He would make new mysteries, and . . . their meaning would be of universal import because, in so far as they were authentic, truth lay enigmatically within them. . . . The material may derive from well-thumbed manuals, the contributory themes from the allegorical fantasies of Platonic academists; but the result will be an enigma calling for explication by adepts. . . . My assumption is that the Cave of Mammon had such a programme and that it is similarly enigmatic; that it is an invention of this kind, requiring the sort of attention given by art-historians to the *Primavera* [of Botticelli]" (pp. 154–155).[3]

Nothing would seem to illustrate the creation of an enigmatic image more handsomely than the golden chain in Philotime's throne room:

> There, as in glistring glory she did sit,
> She held a great gold chaine ylincked well,
> Whose vpper end to highest heauen was knit,
> And lower part did reach to lowest Hell;
> And all that preace did round about her swell,
> To catchen hold of that long chaine, thereby
> To clime aloft, and others to excell.
>
> (46)

This chain is mentioned in the *Iliad* (8.18–27) and was subjected to a great deal of allegorical interpretation in both antiquity and the

---

[3] Kermode has reiterated his view that "Spenser is, in his way, an esoteric poet" in "Spenser and the Allegorists," *Proceedings of the British Academy,* **48** (1962), 261–279, and in *"The Faerie Queene,* I and V," *Bulletin of the John Rylands Library,* 47 (1964), 123–150.

Renaissance. Natalis Comes says that the chain "is sometimes avarice and sometimes ambition," because just as the other gods could not dislodge Zeus from the heavens by pulling on the chain, so "the man who is truly good is moved from his place neither by avarice nor by any ambition."[4] Comes' commentary would in itself explain Spenser's use of the golden chain here, but the stanza is enriched by other traditional meanings. From antiquity the chain was commonly considered a symbol of cosmic order (as in *FQ* 4.1.30), and this meaning has direct relevance to the Cave of Mammon: it puts into perspective Mammon's claim to be "God of the world and worldlings" and the source of all worldly good. In addition, the golden chain was considered a symbol of the bond that exists between gods and men. A passage in Ripa shows the richness of meaning it might have for a Renaissance reader:

> It signifies, according to what Macrobius and Lucian say, the joining and binding together of human things with divine, and a bond connecting the human race with its great creator, who, when he pleases, draws men to himself and elevates our minds to the highest heaven, to which otherwise we could never attain by our earthly effort; therefore the divine Plato maintained that this chain was the force of the divine spirit and of its heavenly fervor, by which spirits of great worth are often inspired to notable undertakings.[5]

Some of these meanings at least are relevant to the passage. Philotime's hall is guarded by Disdain, who is seen "striding stiffe and bold, / As if that highest God defie he would" (40) and who is compared to a Titan (41); Philotime herself, whom Mammon calls "worthy of heauen and hye felicitie," has been thrust from heaven by the gods (49). Spenser's golden chain, then, is partly a symbol of the sins embodied in the Cave of Mammon and partly a parody of the true golden chain. It seems to answer exactly to Kermode's description of an enigmatic image. It combines old meanings into a new myth, and it coalesces so many meanings that it would seem impossible to translate image into discourse. Yet that is exactly what Spenser proceeds to do in the last two lines of the stanza:

> That was *Ambition*, rash desire to sty,
> And euery lincke thereof a step of dignity.

[4] *Mythologia*, 2.4, Frankfurt, 1581, p. 142.
[5] *Iconologia*, Rome, 1603, p. 146, s.v. *Fato*.

By naming the chain Ambition, Spenser seems intent on making this a "face-value allegory"; he seems not even to want us to entertain Comes' alternatives, ambition or avarice. If he is exploiting the meanings available to him, it is in a very different way from the one Kermode describes.

Kermode cites Erasmus' remark that "a pagan fable, allegorically interpreted, might be more valuable than scripture read literally (*si consistas in cortice*)" (p. 153), and he pays particular attention to Erasmus' use of the traditional metaphor of rind and pith for a fable and its meaning. According to Kermode, Spenser's poetry is calculated to have a double appeal—to the large number of ignorant readers, who see only the outer surface, and to the few adepts, who can penetrate to the core of its true meaning (pp. 153, 155). But this metaphor of rind and pith, or skin and marrow, depends on treating the poem, or parts of it, as a physical object. It would make sense to talk this way if Spenser really did present us solely with a visual image of a golden chain. An ignorant reader might then grasp little more than the connection of gold and Mammon, whereas the adept would see the full range of Spenser's meanings. But the rind, the surface, of Spenser's poem is not the verbal equivalent of a painter's image; it consists of formulas that in themselves bring to life and organize anew the meanings that are traditionally associated with the golden chain. Undoubtedly Spenser expects his reader to recognize this as Homer's golden chain, but in the sixteenth century this would be what every schoolboy knows and not esoteric knowledge. In any case, Spenser labors to declare, not conceal, the meanings of the chain. The word "gold" speaks for itself at this point in the canto, and the meaning "ambition" is indicated by the crowd's behavior—note the going beyond the physical surface in the phrase, "others to excell." Not only is the chain described as running from heaven to hell, the sense of order is conveyed by "ylincked well" and "knit," and the violation of order by the language of the second block of verse, beginning "And all that preace did round about her swell."

More important than the fact that Spenser makes traditional meanings plain is the fact that we apprehend their relevance and their organization into new meanings not through searching our minds for iconographic knowledge, but by being attentive to the language of the poem. When the stanza is taken by itself, "glistring" seems merely to reinforce "gold." But this is the third use of the word in ten stanzas, and the first two times it is used not of Mammon's gold, but of Guyon's armor:

> But when as earthly wight they present saw,
> Glistring in armes and battailous aray.
>
> (37)
>
> Soone as those glitterand armes he did espye,
> That with their brightnesse made that darknesse light,
> His harmefull club he gan to hurtle hye.
>
> (42)

The phrase "glistring glory" has heroic associations for us, so that applying it to Philotime is neither mere physical description nor moral tagging. It reminds us of the problematic nature of earthly glory—the more so since the preceding stanza is pointedly problematic, with Philotime's face illuminating the dark in the manner of Guyon's armor and with the puzzle about her "natiue hew" producing a mythic analogue to the fall of man (45).

When we understand the force of this first line, we can see that lines 1–4 are the broadest and most challenging version we have encountered of a claim that Mammon makes throughout the canto—that he is the god of this world and that the world obeys his laws. Instead of Mammon's brusque "Thou that doest liue in later times, must wage / Thy workes for wealth, and life for gold engage" (18), we have his element, gold, in one of the grandest and most honored forms it has taken in the human imagination. The next three lines are a sharp contrast, giving what we might call the human uses of this golden chain, and the double perspective of the stanza is recapitulated in the clash between what is suggested by each of the final lines:

> That was *Ambition,* rash desire to sty,
> And euery lincke thereof a step of dignity.

The effect of naming Ambition is precisely to make us pay attention to the surface of the verse, and we are amply rewarded. With the word "lincke," the final line translates the image of cosmic harmony into an image of human society. But we are made aware how problematic is man's potential nobility by the juxtaposition with another undeniable human reality, "rash desire." On Kermode's reading, these lines should be either dull, because they declare what would best be left hidden, or feeble, because they attempt to declare inexpressible meanings. Yet they are at least as vivid and interesting as the rest of the stanza, and the phrase that most declares meanings, "step of dignity," is the richest of all. With the support it gets from "lincke" and the image of the chain, it is a valid expression of true human worth, and at the same time it reminds us of earthly rewards, dignities, and their problematic relation to human worth. Kermode's notion of a poetry that creates new wisdom by using old materials applies very well to this stanza and to these lines. But you will only see what Spenser has done and grasp the meanings he creates, *si consistas in cortice.*

Kermode's interpretation of the Garden of Proserpina gives us a full view of his methods, because it combines local uses of mythography and iconography with an analysis of the organization and meaning of the whole canto. Turning from pagan mysteries to biblical commentary, Kermode proposes that "Guyon undergoes . . . a *total* temptation parallel to that of Christ in the wilderness" (p. 159). He bases his analysis on St. Augustine's commentary on 1 John 2:16: "Love not the World: for all that is in the world is the lust of the flesh, and the lust of the eyes, and the pride of life." Concupiscence of the flesh, Kermode says, is treated in the Phaedria episode; Mammon's offers, up to and including Philotime, are an appeal to the pride of life. Then, having cited the analogous series of temptations in *Paradise Regained,* Kermode deduces that the Cave of Mammon concludes with "a temptation to vain learning," and this, he argues, explains the Garden of Proserpina (p. 161).

It is remarkable how little justification there is for the case Kermode makes. If the Garden of Proserpina is a temptation, it seems odd that Mammon does not offer it to Guyon in the way he offers the riches and honors of the world. The Garden is simply a place Guyon looks at, and not until he has looked into Hell and seen Tantalus and Pilate does Mammon tempt him. Moreover, what Mammon offers is food and rest (63), the satisfaction of the simplest human needs. Surely the analogy is with Satan's tempting Christ to turn stones into bread when He was hungry—the episode that symbolizes the lust of the flesh. The analogy with the temptation in the wilderness unquestionably enlarges the reader's understanding of Guyon's ordeal, but it is quite another thing to make Christ's temptation a controlling structural reality that determines the organization and details of the whole canto.[6]

---

[6] It seems to me that the same things are to be said of Kermode's handling of the Cave of Mammon as Rosemond Tuve says of rigid modern interpretations of medieval romances, even those that are unquestionably allegorical: "We find the tight relations and complex networks of equivalents to be characteristics of modern interpretation but *not* of mediaeval presentation; this is not, therefore, what we expect a sixteenth-century reader to have learned about the mode from its earlier practitioners. Historically, the vast development of allegory was concerned to let story point to doctrine, not to make story re-tell

Nor is Kermode's iconographic evidence more convincing. Here is his account of the golden apples that grow in Proserpina's garden:

> Whatever they signify it is not avarice, as the commentators say; we have left that behind. The apples of the Hesperides were emblems of astronomical knowledge. The story of Atalanta was sometimes interpreted as a warning against blasphemy, since she desecrated the shrine of the Great Mother. . . . Comes says that the apple offered by Discord to the goddesses was the symbol of an insane contempt for the divine wisdom. . . . For the apple of Acontius [*Heroides* 21.103–124] I can find no mythographical source; this may be one that Spenser made up himself. Acontius, enamoured of Cydippe, won her by a trick. He wrote on an apple, "I swear by Artemis that I will marry Acontius" and threw it in the girl's way. She picked it up and read the message aloud; and as she did so in the precincts of the temple of Artemis the words had the force of a solemn oath. Attempts to marry her to another man were thwarted by the gods, and in the end she married Acontius. It may be this trifling with an oath that made the story seem to Spenser another illustration of the danger of blasphemy; certainly the apple-stories all indicate intemperance of mind not body (pp. 162–163).

It seems to me that Kermode is simply making a case for a conclusion previously determined—rather in the manner of the allegorists who had to find, as best they could, Christian meanings in pagan tales. The discussion of Acontius is a clear instance of this process and so, less obviously, is the meaning assigned to Atalanta. In Comes, who is Kermode's authority here, it is an interpretation of her metamorphosis into a lion,[7] so that Spenser's referring to the race with the golden apples would hardly prompt us to recognize this meaning unless we were already looking for it. The problem of what the reader expects causes one to object even to a stronger piece of evidence—the fact that "the apples of the Hesperides were emblems of astronomical knowledge." So they were, but Comes also says, "Just as those serpents guard the golden apples, there are certain men who cannot sleep

---

Christ's history. . . . What we observe in the text itself is not a re-telling through a code of equivalents but instead, a loose juxtaposition that makes us connect the story we read with significances more universal because we see that it shadows a greater story in general drift of meaning." *Allegorical Imagery*, Princeton, 1966, p. 408.

[7] *Mythologia*, 7.8, p. 738.

securely because of avarice; wherefore it is excellently said by wise men, that riches are a sort of touchstone of the soul."[8] When Spenser begins by saying, "Their fruit were golden apples glistring bright, / That goodly was their glory to behold" (42), most of our attention will be given to the repetition of the language with which, eight stanzas earlier, Philotime and the golden chain were described. But if the reader, conscious that Spenser is recasting familiar myths, seeks out a mythographic interpretation, the association of the golden apples with avarice will surely seem more natural and relevant here than the association with astronomical knowledge.

Kermode's attempts to unearth mysteries consistently prevent him from discerning the meanings, the rich and complex meanings, that lie on the surface of the poem. The most important argument against him here is that he ignores the verbal and thematic emphases of the stanzas about the golden apples:

> Their fruit were golden apples glistring bright,
> That goodly was their glory to behold,
> On earth like neuer grew, ne liuing wight
> Like euer saw, but they from hence were sold;
> For those, which *Hercules* with conquest bold
> Got from great *Atlas* daughters, hence began,
> And planted there, did bring forth fruit of gold:
> And those with which th'*Eubœan* young man wan
> Swift *Atalanta,* when through craft he her out ran.

> Here also sprong that goodly golden fruit,
> With which *Acontius* got his louer trew,
> Whom he had long time sought with fruitlesse suit:
> Here eke that famous golden Apple grew,
> The which emongst the gods false *Ate* threw;
> For which th'*Idœan* Ladies disagreed,
> Till partiall *Paris* dempt it *Venus* dew,
> And had of her, faire *Helen* for his meed,
> That many noble *Greekes* and *Troians* made to bleed.
>
> (54–55)

When we read the stanzas, it is clear that what unites these myths is not a common symbolic referent, but the fact that each involves golden fruit. As we have already observed, the first two lines recall

[8] *Ibid.,* 7.7, p. 736.

the description of Philotime and the golden chain, but this connection is complicated by the lines that immediately precede them:

> Next thereunto did grow a goodly tree,
> With braunches broad dispred and body great,
> Clothed with leaues, that none the wood mote see
> And loaden all with fruit as thicke as it might bee.
>
> (53)

Coming after the description of the deadly black fruits in the garden (51–52), this indeed seems to us "a goodly tree." Our sense that its abundance is natural is supported by lines in which Spenser had conveyed the unnaturalness of the black fruit: "Not such, as earth out of her fruitfull woomb / Throwes forth to men, sweet and well sauoured" (51). We are prepared to accept the golden apples as genuine fruit and to acknowledge that "goodly was their glory to behold." Instead of unequivocally identifying the apples with Philotime's "glistring glory," Spenser holds out the possibility that they might present a genuine human good.

The next two lines—"On earth like neuer grew, ne liuing wight / Like euer saw, but they from hence were sold"—again expand the possible significance of words that we might have thought were clear in their moral implications. These lines adapt a formula that is used of Mammon's first two offers:

> And shewd of richesse such exceeding store,
> As eye of man did neuer see before.
>
> (31)

> Behold, thou Faeries sonne, with mortall eye,
> That liuing eye before did neuer see.
>
> (38)

A similar notion is used to express wonder at Disdain ("Far passing th'hight of men terrestriall," 41) and Philotime ("neuer earthly Prince in such aray," 44). All these lines appear in some connection with excessive size or quantity, and Spenser uses them to suggest the moral and emotional strain of contemplating material goods that exceed human imagination, much less human need. Thus Mammon, at the beginning of the canto, appeals to Guyon's "great mind, or greedy vew" and Guyon counters by rejecting "such eye-glutting gaine" (9). Spenser's saying that the black fruits were those "whose kinds mote not

243

be red" (51) would seem to confirm the moral suggestions of "On earth like neuer grew, ne liuing wight / Like euer saw" in reference to the golden apples. Yet when we go on to read "but they from hence were sold," the implications change entirely. These *are* apples that can be seen on earth, and the formula suggests that if there are any true earthly wonders, they are these fruits. Hence in the next lines Spenser can make Hercules' "conquest bold" a genuine expression of heroic worth, and we feel more firmly than in the opening lines that the "fruit of gold" is a natural growth. Yet this is not the note on which the stanza ends. Having persuaded us to enter imaginatively the world of heroic endeavor, Spenser reminds us that it depends on human qualities—"when through craft he her out ran." A similar pattern occurs in the next stanza. Spenser begins by eliciting our full assent to the mythological world of these stanzas and to the naturalness of the "goodly golden fruit." Here a "fruitlesse suit" is indeed one that is attempted without the help of the golden apples. But the story of a man who gets his "louer trew" is followed by the Judgment of Paris and a full rendering of its consequences.

The way to read Spenser's verse, here and everywhere, is to pay the fullest and most detailed attention to the surface of the verse. But in showing this, we have not fully answered some questions Kermode raises about the organization and development of the whole canto. He is rightly concerned with the way in which Guyon's encounter with Mammon gets broader and more complex meanings as the canto progresses. To understand this, we must first determine what kinds of simple, even simple-minded, understanding Spenser expected of his reader. Kermode would say that the reader's basic grasp of the canto and its parts takes the form of narrative action—in the manner, say, of the arguments to the cantos. But there is a nonnarrative equivalent to a summary statement of action, in the form of a simple grasp of themes and issues. Thus in the Garden of Proserpina, the initial description of the "hearbs and fruits" that are "direfull deadly blacke" (51) and the subsequent dwelling on golden fruit make us see this garden as an unnatural place and to connect it with the unnaturalness of Mammon. These awarenesses can be held in the loosest and simplest way, and yet they are continuous with an intense and sophisticated reading. As one learns the passage better and pays closer attention to the verse, the simple awareness becomes fuller, more complex, and more precisely organized. A simple narrative grasp of this passage would be impossible, since there is no action. But even where it is possible and justifiable, such a grasp tends to be a dead end. In the Philotime passage, for example, narration and theme are practically identical in their simplest form. But if our simple grasp of the passage takes the form of "This is about worldly honors and the desire for them," we will find a fuller acquaintance with the passage natural and plausible. On the other hand, if our basic grasp of the passage takes the form "Mammon offers Guyon Philotime as his wife," we will find details and emphases puzzling and unhelpful—even in the stanza in which Mammon makes his offer:

> And faire *Philotime* she rightly hight,
> The fairest wight that wonneth vnder skye,
> But that this darksome neather world her light
> Doth dim with horrour and deformitie,
> Worthy of heauen and hye felicitie,
> From whence the gods haue her for enuy thrust:
> But sith thou hast found fauour in mine eye,
> Thy spouse I will her make, if that thou lust,
> That she may thee aduaunce for workes and merites iust.
>
> (49)

It would be difficult to regard the first six lines as an attempt to persuade Guyon to take Philotime's hand. Rather the speech is a means of broaching essential problems about man's nature and his deserts; in the context of Philotime's court, the last line is a pointed challenge to the notion of Christian heroism.

If we ask what is the simple, obvious point of each episode, we find that the canto is rather static and repetitive. Each of Mammon's first three offers (5–9, 31–32, 36–38) is a vision, simultaneously impressive and repugnant, of abundant riches, and each challenges us to accept wealth and its benefits as human goods. The Philotime passage seems to expand the canto's terms of reference, but the Garden of Proserpina again presents us with a new image of an old reality— abundant gold and the problem of its naturalness and desirability. The repetitive aspect of the canto is made clear when we get to Tantalus. Kermode's interpretation is a resolute attempt to absolve Spenser of an uninterestingly close adherence to his ostensible subject, the use and abuse of riches. Tantalus, Kermode says, "is normally taken as a type of avarice, not without support from the mythographers; but he is much more certainly a type of blasphemous or intemperate knowledge" (p. 163). But almost none of the evidence Kermode presents enters into Spenser's portrayal of Tantalus. We hear nothing of the fact that, as Comes says, Tantalus was "a man deeply versed in di-

245

vine and natural knowledge," or that he was punished "for his loquacity, in that he revealed to mortals the secrets of the Gods."[9] Moreover, Kermode has no warrant for his confidence that the interpretation he favors is "much more certainly" the prevailing one in the Renaissance. The punishment Spenser depicts, Tantalus reaching for the fleeing fruit and water, was repeatedly interpreted as a representation of the spiritual state of a miser—by Erasmus, for example, in the very passage in which he urges the reader to look beneath the surface of ancient fables.[10] The classical authority for this interpretation is a passage in which Horace addresses a covetous man:

> Tantalus a labris sitiens fugientia captat
> flumina—quid rides? mutato nomine de te
> fabula narratur: congestis undique saccis
> indormis inhians, et tamquam parcere sacris
> cogeris aut pictis tamquam gaudere tabellis.
> nescis quo valeat nummus, quem praebeat usum?

Tantalus, thirsty soul, catches at the streams that fly from his lips —why laugh? Change but the name, and the tale is told of you. You sleep with open mouth on money-bags piled up from all sides, and must perforce keep hands off as if they were hallowed, or take delight in them as if painted pictures. Don't you know what money is for, what end it serves?[11]

Alciati based his emblem 84 (Avaritia) on this passage, and his woodcut depicting Tantalus' torment reappears in Whitney's *Choice of Emblemes* with verses based on Horace.[12] Harington quotes Horace's lines to show that a tale can contain a moral truth,[13] and Sidney adapts the tale and its moral to attack Stella's husband (*Astrophel and Stella* 24, "Rich fooles there be"). It seems unquestionable that when Spenser shows us Tantalus at the end of our journey through Mammon's realm, he expects us to recognize him as an emblem of

---

[9] *Mythologia*, 6.18, p. 637; cf. Ovid, *Amores* 2.2.43–44.

[10] Desiderius Erasmus, *Enchiridion*, Cologne, 1519, f. 41.

[11] *Satires*, 1.1.68–73. *Satires, Epistles and Ars Poetica*, tr. H. Rushton Fairclough, London: Loeb Classical Library, 1929. There is a similar passage in Petronius, *Satyricon* 6, which is cited by Alciati, Ripa (s.v. *avaritia*), and other Renaissance writers.

[12] Andrea Alciati, *Omnia Emblemata cum commentariis . . . per Claudium Minoem*, Antwerp, 1577, pp. 306–308. Geoffrey Whitney, *A Choice of Emblemes* (1586), facsimile reprint, ed. Henry Greene, London, 1866, p. 74.

[13] Sir John Harington, "A Brief Apology for Poetry," in *Elizabethan Critical Essays*, ed. G. Gregory Smith, Oxford, 1904, 2, 208.

avarice. It is true, as Kermode says, that Guyon calls Tantalus an "ensample . . . of mind intemperate," but Kermode does not mention that this speech begins with Guyon addressing him as "thou greedie *Tantalus*" (60).

On a simple reading the canto seems static and repetitive. We are of course interested in more than a simple reading, but it is surely desirable to specify, as best we can, what Spenser would have regarded as a minimal understanding of the canto. And we are now in a better position to discern what elements make for the dynamics of the canto, its changes and complications. Perhaps the major difficulty in treating the canto as a series of temptations is that a temptation involves an intrinsic dramatic relation between the thing presented and the human reaction to it. As the dramatic narration of temptations, the canto can seem repetitious in a bad sense, because similar offers entail similar responses on the part of the hero. But in fact there are more significant changes in Guyon's responses to Mammon's offers than there are in the offers themselves. Philotime and her court essentially spell out the implications of the first two offers of gold, but Guyon's reaction to her is the exact opposite of the heroic self-confidence with which he rejected those offers (33, 39):

> Gramercy *Mammon* (said the gentle knight)
> For so great grace and offred high estate;
> But I, that am fraile flesh and earthly wight,
> Vnworthy match for such immortall mate
> My selfe well wote, and mine vnequall fate.
>
> (50)

Even more revealing than the change in Guyon's reactions is Spenser's evident interest in problems of the heroic personality, quite apart from their connection with Mammon's offers. Two of the most puzzling passages in the canto—Guyon's encounter with Disdain (40–42) and the vision of Pilate, the unjust judge (61–62)—make perfect initial sense once we cease to worry about their lack of connection with riches and recognize that Spenser is directly concerned with heroic psychology and attitude.[14] These passages make explicit and

---

[14] Pilate, of course, traditionally exemplifies injustice. The only instances I have found in which he is presented as covetous are two passages in the Towneley plays that are cited by Arnold Williams, *The Characterization of Pilate in the Towneley Plays*, East Lansing, Mich., 1950, p. 44. These two examples are the only ones mentioned in John A. Yunck, *The Lineage of Lady Meed*, Notre Dame, 1963.

independent Spenser's central concern in the Cave of Mammon. It is his interest in human heroism, not in problems of riches alone, that explains the development and dynamics of the canto and gives life and interest to the details of the verse. To see how the subjects of heroism and riches are connected, and to understand the form in which the subject of heroism enters the canto, we must return to the beginning of the canto and Berger's interpretation of it.

II

Berger focuses his essay on some problems that have often been recognized, but have never been coherently explained. Why does Guyon faint after so heroically resisting Mammon? How do we explain the fact that Guyon is obviously untempted by Mammon's offers? Are we to think that Guyon's rather chilly self-assurance is a model of the way men do or should deal with the spiritual terrors revealed in Mammon's abode? Berger pinpoints these questions extremely well, and he rightly considers them to be problems of critical interpretation, and not, say, of intellectual history. He claims that our confusions come from failing to heed the distinction between the experience of the fictional hero in the world of the poem and the experience of the human reader as he reads. Guyon, Berger argues, is naturally and instinctively virtuous: what would be tempting or terrifying to ordinary, fallen mortals is not so to him (p. 37). We can thus see that his priggishness, his confidence in his brief pieties, is not an aesthetic blemish to be explained away; rather, we miss Spenser's meaning if we do not respond to this quality in Guyon's behavior.

Berger's theories and interpretations are to a great extent determined by the assumption that "poetic" and "fictional" are synonymous in *The Faerie Queene*. He complains of one critic that he "never . . . speaks of Guyon as a character in a fiction possessed of certain physical and ethical and psychological traits, affecting other characters and the narrator in a certain way" (p. 8). He says that a theological explanation is "essentially nonpoetic"—an appeal to "a scheme which obviates the necessity for thinking of the character as an individual and ultimately, perhaps, of the poem as a poem" (p. 9). Hence the main critical problem concerning Guyon is a matter of old-fashioned character analysis: "If the fiction is to hold us, the cause [of Guyon's faint] must be found in the hero's own unique being, in some conscious or unconscious failure of his moral character, his

248

ethos" (p. 29). Berger's theory of allegory is simply a more rigid and elaborate version of the theory that the poem is a world:

> In the concrete fictional world of the poem the character sees with his eyes the persons and places of the quest; the narrator, telling us of the character's sensory experiences, reveals—through one or another poetic device—their allegorical meanings. . . . The complete world of such an allegorical poem includes both the fictional world through which the hero journeys and the real world in which lies our quest; the two are at every point analogically placed side by side; the poem itself is thus an intelligible world, created by . . . an act of spirit, of the *intellectus spiritualis,* whereby the real and fictional worlds are conjoined (pp. 35, 37).

We begin with two stanzas in which Berger claims that Spenser brings out the difference between the reader's experience and Guyon's. Mammon has just made his first offer to Guyon—a huge display of riches (31)—and has said:

> Loe here the worldes blis, loe here the end,
> To which all men do ayme, rich to be made:
> Such grace now to be happy, is before thee laid.
>
> (32)

The next two stanzas present, first, Guyon's response and then the reaction of the fiend who hovers over him, waiting to tear him to pieces if he touches any of Mammon's goods (see 27):

> Certes (said he) I n'ill thine offred grace,
> Ne to be made so happy do intend:
> Another blis before mine eyes I place,
> Another happinesse, another end.
> To them, that list, these base regardes I lend:
> But I in armes, and in atchieuements braue,
> Do rather choose my flitting houres to spend,
> And to be Lord of those, that riches haue,
> Then them to haue my selfe, and be their seruile sclaue.

> Thereat the feend his gnashing teeth did grate,
> And grieu'd, so long to lacke his greedy pray;
> For well he weened, that so glorious bayte
> Would tempt his guest, to take thereof assay:
> Had he so doen, he had him snatcht away,

More light then Culuer in the Faulcons fist.
Eternall God thee saue from such decay.
But whenas *Mammon* saw his purpose mist,
Him to entrap vnwares another way he wist.

(33–34)

Berger cites the first of these stanzas to illustrate Guyon's "self-suffi-
ciency" and his "awareness and articulation" of his "difference from
Everyman" (pp. 16–17). In the second stanza, "one line [the sev-
enth] . . . is directed straight at the reader, drawing by implication
the central analogy between himself and the hero: 'Guyon is clearly
able to rely on his own powers, but you, Reader, had better invoke
some higher assistance, since it is apparent (experience has shown)
that you and your kind are less able to resist' " (p. 32).

But is the reader really supposed to feel he could not emulate
Guyon's heroic stance or that he would be seriously tempted by Mam-
mon's offer? Mammon puts his offer in terms that are simply an af-
front to a Christian: "Loe here the worldes blis, loe here the end, / To
which all men do ayme, rich to be made." The reader may be fallen,
but surely this strikes him as a challenge, rather than a temptation,
and Guyon's answer is the one he himself would make. (It may be
worth noting that the phrase "my flitting houres" indicates that Guyon
is perfectly aware of his own mortality, and that he is conscious of be-
ing different only from men of "base regardes.") Guyon is explicitly
speaking for Everyman here, because the terms in which he is chal-
lenged and in which he answers—"blis," "happinesse," "end"—are, to
a sixteenth-century reader, crucial concepts in man's definition of
himself in ethics, politics, and theology.[15] By the same token, the sense
of danger and uncertainty in the second stanza must be thought to in-
volve both Guyon and ourselves. The fiend's behavior and the simile
of the culver and the falcon make us feel that Guyon's firm and confi-
dent moral stance, far from being the luxury of "an aristocrat" who
is "immune to the frailties most of us feel" (p. 10), is essential to the
spiritual safety of any moral man. Berger's theory forces him to make
his point about Everyman depend solely on the seventh line of the
stanza. But the change of atmosphere that he rightly notices is a func-
tion of the whole stanza; we no longer see the heroic stance from the
inside—the individual's response to a challenge—but in the context of
Mammon's realm, its dangers and its potential powers. Furthermore,

---

[15] See John M. Steadman, "Felicity and End in Renaissance Epic and Ethics,"
JHI, 23 (1962) 117–132.

the line "Eternall God thee saue from such decay" does not unequivocally turn from the action to the reader. It can equally well be read as a response to Guyon's plight, and Spenser characteristically allows it to include both possibilities without forcing a choice of one or the other. As we would have expected, the reader's and the hero's experience go hand in hand, and the hero, instead of being a different kind of creature from us, expresses and focuses our understanding of ourselves and our moral capacities.

It would be possible to say that Berger is simply being historically ignorant when he fails to understand the force of Guyon's response to Mammon. Consider his paraphrase of Guyon's concluding words: " 'I don't want money,' he replies to Mammon, 'I would rather "be Lord of those, that riches haue, / Then them to haue my selfe, and be their seruile sclaue"—give me some authority over all those rich men, and I'll forego the cash' " (p. 28). Berger's slang is annoying, but Guyon does seem rather arrogant here if we think of him solely as a unique individual and are unaware that he invokes a moral commonplace which, as such, pertains to all men—that a man either masters riches or is mastered by them.[16] Berger's essential failure, however, is not a matter of knowledge, but of sympathetic imagination and historical common sense. Here is his account of the first exchange between Guyon and Mammon: "Having identified himself, Mammon offers the hero money for his service, and this prompts two sententious utterances by Guyon, one on the evil of riches and one, displaying fine Senecan primitivism, on the 'antique world's' Golden Age. These long declarations (7.12–17) should indicate that the hero sees and understands the danger. He should, with this knowledge, want nothing to do with Mammon. Yet when Mammon in effect says, 'Here's my final offer, take it or leave it' (7.18), Guyon's answer is not exactly what we should have expected" (p. 19). Berger assumes that our interest is

[16] "In those mindes where the desire of this metall growes, there cannot remaine so much as a sparke of true honour and vertue: for what thing can be more base, than for a man to disgrade, and to make himselfe a seruant, and a slaue to that, which should be subiect vnto him? *Apud sapientem divitiae sunt in servitute, apud stultum in imperio; Riches serue a wise man, but command a foole.*" Pierre Charron, *Of Wisdome,* tr. Samson Lennard, 1612, p. 84. The quotation is from Seneca, *De Vita Beata* 26.1; see also Horace, *Epistles* 1.10.47. Guyon's stance here probably derives from a story told of Manius Curius Dentatus, who was "famous as a type of ancient Roman virtue and frugality" (*Oxford Companion to Classical Literature*). "When the Samnites had brought him a great mass of gold as he sat before the fire, he declined their gift with scorn; 'for,' said he, 'it seems to me that the glory is not in having the gold, but in ruling those who have it' " ("eis qui haberent aurum imperare"). Cicero, *De Senectute,* 16.56, tr. W. A. Falconer, London: Loeb Classical Library, 1923.

in observing a character in action. But surely we are expected to respond to Guyon's "long declarations" not as the expression of an individual character's perceptions and moral choices, but precisely as speeches. Guyon is giving what we can only call the right answers to a god of money: these are the moral awarenesses and the myths of excellence that all good men can stand by. As an eighteenth-century editor said, the episode "gives occasion to a noble Speech against Riches."[17]

Berger can describe a moral speech only as the expression of a personality: "Guyon has stated his ethical position before entering the Cave. His subsequent reaction, combined with the patently trite nature of his observations, suggests that these are uttered by rote: Guyon is preserved and informed by the proverbial wisdom which one may easily associate with the Palmer. This proverbial wisdom seems connatural, virtually instinctive, evoked as a push-button response to Mammon's self-characterization and statement of aims" (p. 20). Hence Berger looks to the nature of the character and not to the nature of the speech in interpreting Guyon's first words to Mammon:

> What art thou man, (if man at all thou art)
> That here in desert hast thine habitaunce,
> And these rich heapes of wealth doest hide apart
> From the worldes eye, and from her right vsaunce?
>
> (7)

"Curiosity," says Berger, "draws Guyon initially to Mammon" (p. 18). Berger fails to consider that the reader would assent to the notion that there is a "right vsaunce" of riches and that therefore Guyon puts a real question to Mammon. Despite the fact that the initial description of Mammon (especially stanza 5) portrays him as a generalized lord of earthly riches and not simply as an individual miser, Berger assumes that the poetry of this meeting lies in the dramatic interplay of personalities, rather than in posing issues about the human use of wealth.

Berger's argument that Guyon is guilty of curiosity is not at all as eccentric as it can be made to seem. So long as we think of Guyon as a character in a fiction, it is natural and proper to evaluate his personality. Berger simply thought through the implications of one of the

[17] John Hughes, in *The Works of Edmund Spenser: A Variorum Edition*, ed. Edwin Greenlaw, et al., Baltimore, 1932–1957, Book II, p. 248.

commonplaces of Spenser criticism—that Guyon is rather cold and uninteresting—and once he had shown the way, others did not hesitate to make a criticism of Guyon's personality central to their interpretations of the Cave of Mammon and of Book II.[18] In arguing against Berger, then, we should not simply refute his specific interpretations; we must ourselves propose new grounds for understanding the episode. It would be hard to deny that Spenser means us to assent to the speeches in which Guyon attacks riches as the "roote of all disquietnesse" and praises the antique world. But we have not looked at the stanzas that most strongly support the argument that Spenser means us to be critical of Guyon's personality.

The first of these is Guyon's rejection of Mammon's first offer:

> Me ill besits, that in der-doing armes,
> And honours suit my vowed dayes do spend,
> Vnto thy bounteous baytes, and pleasing charmes,
> With which weake men thou witchest, to attend:
> Regard of worldly mucke doth fowly blend,
> And low abase the high heroicke spright,
> That ioyes for crownes and kingdomes to contend;
> Faire shields, gay steedes, bright armes be my delight:
> Those be the riches fit for an aduent'rous knight.
>
> (10)

There is a very evident weakness in the concluding lines: the "riches" Guyon lists are uncomfortably like the literal riches that Mammon would offer him. The question is whether Spenser means this contradiction to indicate some personal weakness in Guyon. Thinking of Despair's debate with the Red Cross Knight, one might expect Mammon to turn the hero's arguments, his presumed moral strengths, against him.[19] By trying to trap Guyon in his metaphor of "riches," he would be saying, "You serve me without knowing it," and the issue would be one that involved the potential weaknesses of the human personality. But instead Mammon reverts to literal money, and the challenging, forensic nature of his speech indicates that the issue here is one of conscious assent to a moral truth:

---

[18] See Maurice Evans, "The Fall of Guyon," ELH, 28 (1961), 215–224; Carl Robinson Sonn, "Sir Guyon in the Cave of Mammon," SEL, 1 (1961), 17–30; Lewis H. Miller, Jr., "Phaedria, Mammon, and Sir Guyon's Education by Error," JEGP, 63 (1964), 33–44; Alastair Fowler, Spenser and the Numbers of Time, London, 1964, p. 113.

[19] On Despair, see below, pp. 350–358.

Vaine glorious Elfe (said he) doest not thou weet,
That money can thy wantes at will supply?
Sheilds, steeds, and armes, and all things for thee meet
It can puruay in twinckling of an eye;
And crownes and kingdomes to thee multiply.
Do not I kings create, and throw the crowne
Sometimes to him, that low in dust doth ly?
And him that raignd, into his rowme thrust downe,
And whom I lust, do heape with glory and renowne?

(11)

This first exchange concerns not individual dramatic behavior, but the nature of the moral dicta and sanctions that human beings subscribe to and invoke. In using the phrase "twinckling of an eye" and speaking of himself as if he were Fortune, Mammon repeats the claim to godhead with which he began his offer to Guyon: "God of the world and worldlings I me call, / Great *Mammon,* greatest god below the skye" (8). When Mammon goes on to say, "Wherefore if me thou deigne to serue and sew, / At thy commaund lo all these mountaines bee" (9), we immediately think, "Ye cannot serve God and Mammon" (Matt. 6:24). But Guyon refuses to serve Mammon not in the name of God, but in the name of knighthood and human moral distinctions (the contrast between "weake men" and "the high heroicke spright"). If we followed Berger and the other commentators on Book II we would interpret this as a personal shortcoming of Guyon's —a sign of his naive overconfidence in human powers. But I think Spenser means us to see a genuine problem here—a difficulty that is inherent in human heroism as it is presented in Book II.

Let us consider some verses from the Sermon on the Mount:

Laye not up for your selves treasure upon earth, where the rust and mothe doth corrupte, and where theves breake through, and steale. But laye up for you, treasures in heven, where nether rust nor mothe doth corrupte, and where theves do not breake thorow nor steale. For where your treasure is, there will youre hert be also. . . .

No man can serve two masters. For ether he shal hate the one and love the other, or els leane to the one, and despyse the other: ye cannot serve God and Mammon. Therfore I saye unto you: be not carefull for your lyfe, what ye shall eate or drincke, nor yet for youre bodye, what rayment ye shall put on. Is not the lyfe more worth then meat: and the body more of value then rayment? Behold, the foules of the ayer: for they sowe not, nether do they reape, nor cary into the barnes: and youre hevenly father fedeth them. Are ye not moch better then they? . . .

And why care ye for rayment? Consydre the lylies of the felde, how they growe. They laboure not, nether do they spynne. . . . Wherfore, yf God so cloth the grasse of the felde (which though it stande to daye, is to morow cast into the fornasse) shall he not moch more do the same for you, O ye of lytle fayth? . . .

Seke ye fyrst the kyngdome of God, and the ryghteousnesse therof, and al these thinges shalbe ministred unto you.

Care not then for the morow, for the morowe daye shall care for it selfe: sufficient unto the daye, is the travayle therof.
(Matt. 6:19–21, 24–26, 28, 30, 33–34)

Seen in its context, "Ye cannot serve God and Mammon" is hardly a sanction of human endeavor, and this is not the first time in Book II that Spenser has drawn our attention to problems raised by the radical unworldliness of the Sermon on the Mount. When Phaedria sings her parody of "Consider the lilies of the field" (2.6.15–17), we know that she is wrong to make Nature the deity of her song, just as we have no difficulty in saying, with Guyon, "*Mammon . . . thy godheades vaunt is vaine*" (9). But the real question is what version of human experience and what moral injunctions we can oppose to Phaedria and Mammon, for it is axiomatic in Book II that we cannot say, "Seke ye fyrst the kyngdome of God, and the ryghteousnesse therof, and al these thinges shalbe ministred unto you." (It is worth recalling that in Book I the presence of such injunctions does not produce a definitive version of Christian heroism that might be invoked against Guyon; rather it creates other problems about human heroism, which are most explicitly stated in the Red Cross Knight's encounter with Contemplation.) To Mammon's appeal to lavish greed, Guyon opposes the delight a man can take in noble deeds and aspirations. The contradiction felt when he speaks of "the riches fit for an aduent'-rous knight" raises questions not about him, but about using purely human terms to reject the evils of this world. This view of Spenser's interest in this passage seems to me to be plausible in itself and to account much better than Berger's interpretation for the nature of Mammon's reply to Guyon and for the fact that Guyon answers him with his speeches on the "disquietnesse" caused by riches and on the primitive contentment of the antique world. These speeches present, respectively, a classic exposé of money as a human evil and the most important secular myth in support of a heroic scorn of riches.

We have still to explain the final exchange, a cornerstone of Berger's interpretation:

> Sonne (said he then) let be thy bitter scorne,
> And leaue the rudenesse of that antique age
> To them, that liu'd therein in state forlorne;
> Thou that doest liue in later times, must wage
> Thy workes for wealth, and life for gold engage.
> If then thee list my offred grace to vse,
> Take what thou please of all this surplusage;
> If thee list not, leaue haue thou to refuse:
> But thing refused, do not afterward accuse.
>
> Me list not (said the Elfin knight) receaue
> Thing offred, till I know it well be got,
> Ne wote I, but thou didst these goods bereaue
> From rightfull owner by vnrighteous lot,
> Or that bloud guiltinesse or guile them blot.
>
> (18–19)

"Guyon's answer," Berger says, "is not exactly what we should have expected," and he interprets it as a symptom of curiosity—"a qualified answer which invites further discussion" (p. 19).

I think most readers would agree with Berger in finding Guyon's answer strange. Mammon has a real point—we do not live in an unfallen world—but he puts it in the most unattractive possible way, and we feel it calls for rejection. But why then should we be surprised that Guyon attempts to make moral distinctions within the context of fallen humanity? Because if this exchange is a debate between contending moralities, Guyon seems rather stupid to respond solely to Mammon's offer of money and not to his broader claims. If our interest is in a version of human experience to oppose to Mammon, any number of things might be said against, "Thou that doest liue in later times, must wage / Thy workes for wealth, and life for gold engage." But Guyon treats the challenge as one that calls for a moral action and not for a debate, and Berger's motive-hunting is simply an attempt to make this fact intelligible. For Berger, however, a moral action is simply a matter of accepting or rejecting, in which the only words that matter are "yes" and "no." But Spenser's interest is in a more complex kind of moral action. When Christ rejects Satan by saying, "It is wrytten, man shall not lyve by bread onlye" and "It is wrytten agayne: Thou shalt not tempte the Lorde thy God" (Matt. 4:4,7), general moral principles become specific acts of rejection; conversely, the act of rejection is not a simple "no" with a supporting reason, but directly takes the form of the invoked moral dictum. (I think the best term for this combination of idea and act is "moral stance," the stating of a general moral principle as an individual dramatic act.) The principles Guyon states in this final exchange hardly exist apart from specific acts of acceptance or rejection. Like the earlier metaphor of riches, the narrowed terms of Guyon's reply here express certain difficulties inherent in rejecting the evils of this world in human terms. These difficulties are now seen to involve not simply the principles one espouses, but also the expression of them in moral action.

The mode of pure debate with which the passage began has now reached an impasse that is registered after Guyon's refusal to handle money stained by robbery or blood:

> Perdy (quoth he) yet neuer eye did vew,
> Ne toung did tell, ne hand these handled not,
> But safe I haue them kept in secret mew,
> From heauens sight, and powre of all which them pursew.

> What secret place (quoth he) can safely hold
> So huge a masse, and hide from heauens eye?
> Or where hast thou thy wonne, that so much gold
> Thou canst preserue from wrong and robbery?
>
> (19–20)

Berger interprets Guyon's questions as sophisticated and culpable, but they seem to me naive in manner ("How can this be in this world of ours?"), and they are based on sound moral considerations. Guyon's first question is part of a sequence, discussed below, in which Spenser brings together the conflicting feelings of closeness and massive size (as in "secret" and "huge") to convey the moral and psychological evil of avarice. These other passages make it clear that Guyon's first question is a real one, which, in the act of turning around Mammon's claim that his riches are safe, introduces the suggestion that the real problem is the possessor's spiritual safety. So far as the development of the episode is concerned, the most important aspect of Guyon's questions here is that they simply repeat and throw back the statement that provokes them. Guyon is asking essentially the same question as he did when he first challenged Mammon (7), but there is now no more to be done, in confronting Mammon, by way of debate. To further understand the realities of Mammon, we must descend to his realm, where, in Milton's words, we can "see and know."

The debate between Guyon and Mammon quite literally produces the rest of the canto. It states all the themes—both phenomena presented and moral attitudes—that will be developed in the exploration of Mammon's kingdom. Mammon's offers to Guyon underground simply repeat those he first made. The heaps of wealth with which we first see him (4–6) reappear in his underground rooms (28–31). Mammon's forge (35–38) is simply a realization—that we might see and know—of his claim to be the source from which riches "do flow into an ample flood" (8) and of Guyon's myth of the beginnings of avarice (17). The ills of worldly ambition catalogued by Guyon (12–14) reappear in the personifications who line the broad highway leading to hell (21–23) and in Philotime's court (47). Mammon's and Guyon's mutual disdain (7, 12, 18) is incarnated in the figure of Disdain (41; compare the references to Guyon's "wilfull mood" and "bold mesprise" in 38 and 39). Repetition, as we have already observed, is an essential poetic technique in this canto.

An especially interesting reprise—and one that gives us a clear view of the changes and complications that occur in the canto—is based on Guyon's speech on the antique world:

> Indeede (quoth he) through fowle intemperaunce,
> Frayle men are oft captiu'd to couetise:
> But would they thinke, with how small allowaunce
> Vntroubled Nature doth her selfe suffise,
> Such superfluities they would despise,
> Which with sad cares empeach our natiue ioyes:
> At the well head the purest streames arise:
> But mucky filth his braunching armes annoyes,
> And with vncomely weedes the gentle waue accloyes.
>
> The antique world, in his first flowring youth,
> Found no defect in his Creatours grace,
> But with glad thankes, and vnreproued truth,
> The gifts of soueraigne bountie did embrace:
> Like Angels life was then mens happy cace;
> But later ages pride, like corn-fed steed,
> Abusd her plenty, and fat swolne encreace

To all licentious lust, and gan exceed
The measure of her meane, and naturall first need.

(15–16)

Both the images and the morals of these stanzas reappear in the portrayal of Tantalus and Pilate (57–62). In presenting Pilate vainly trying to wash away his spiritual stains and Tantalus unable to eat the proffered fruit and cursing heaven, Spenser seems to be "saying the same thing" as in these stanzas. The main difference in meaning between the two passages does not lie in the general principles that can be drawn from them. It lies in our relation to these truths, in the difference between apprehending a moral myth and seeing a "cursed wretch" (60; cf. 57, 59, 61) who embodies the corruptions of human nature of which the myth makes us aware. Tantalus and Pilate are significant in the development of the canto, because of all the creatures we have seen in Mammon's kingdom, they are most like Guyon and ourselves. We have seen a crowd of human beings around Philotime's throne, but Tantalus and Pilate are potential heroes: their evil is a corruption of the goodness that we hope to possess. Whereas the myth of the antique world expresses the good man's sense of the strength that is part of his endowment as a man, Tantalus and Pilate may well provoke us to say, "There but for the grace of God go I." They thus provide the most challenging test of Guyon's stance as a hero.

We have been asking, in effect, what motivates the descent underground and the exploration of Mammon's abode. Berger would say that the motive is Guyon's curiosity, whereas from our point of view the rest of the canto is produced by problems inherent in the initial confrontation with Mammon. If we seek a human center for this motivating force, it is in the poet's and the reader's recognition of these problems. The difference between this position and Berger's is connected with different ways of understanding the canto as a whole. Most commentators follow Berger (cf. p. 18) in asking "Why is Guyon in Mammon's cave?" and they seek the answer in his motives or his character or in some statement that Spenser wants to make about him (everyone recognizes that the canto has no connection with his quest to destroy the Bower of Bliss). But surely the right question is "Why did Spenser devote a canto to the Cave of Mammon?" and the answer is to be found in the subject of Book II. The trials undergone, the evils revealed, the issues raised in the Cave of

259

Mammon—all arise naturally from an interest in understanding temperance.

Temperance as a subject naturally includes heroic personality, but this subject can be directly addressed and considered as a moral subject and need not arise from the dramatic presentation of a hero. Berger's critical assumptions are analogous, in the analysis of narrative, to the dichotomy between concrete and abstract that by now has ceased to bemuse us in dealing with the imagery of Renaissance poems. But in dealing with narrative phenomena it is harder to free ourselves of the notion that the particular has priority over the general. It is difficult for us to feel at ease with the fact that, for a sixteenth-century reader, a topic that we would call general, like temperance, had as much human reality as a fictional hero. Yet to see that this was indeed the case, we need only think of the titles of Bacon's essays, or of the numerous Renaissance books with titles like *Of Wisdom* or *Of Honour*. It is in the context of essays on "The Use of Riches" or "Avarice" that an Elizabethan reader would expect to find statements like:

> All otherwise (said he) I riches read,
> And deeme them roote of all disquietnesse;
> First got with guile, and then preseru'd with dread,
> And after spent with pride and lauishnesse,
> Leauing behind them griefe and heauinesse.
>
> (12)

Or two stanzas later:

> Indeede (quoth he) through fowle intemperaunce,
> Frayle men are oft captiu'd to couetise:
> But would they thinke, with how small allowaunce
> Vntroubled Nature doth her selfe suffise,
> Such superfluities they would despise,
> Which with sad cares empeach our natiue ioyes.
>
> (15)

Neither statement depends, for its truth or relevance, on the presence of a fictional character, but both directly raise questions about human personality. These two speeches show how naturally questions about moral strength and the nature of heroism arise from questions about riches. They equally well show that "heroism" and "moral strength" are themselves general topics, like "the use of riches," that have a direct presence in the poem—in what we ambiguously call the concrete details of its language—that can be quite independent of the dramatic portrayal of a hero.

III

Let us sum up the view we now have of the Cave of Mammon episode. The materials of the canto come from its ostensible subject: at its very simplest it presents the evils of riches and their abuse. But the details of language and the unfolding sequence of stanzas primarily concern moral heroism. In developing his materials, Spenser brings to the surface of the poem topics inherent in a confrontation with riches —problems of man's definition of himself and his sense of his moral strengths. Thus Tantalus' reaching for fruit and water, which traditionally represents the miser's inability to use what he has, is made to render more fundamental problems of human nature:

> Most cursed of all creatures vnder skye,
> Lo *Tantalus,* I here tormented lye:
> Of whom high *Ioue* wont whylome feasted bee,
> Lo here I now for want of food doe dye.
>
> (59)

It has long been recognized that Spenser gives an uncommon version of the story, and that he might have been expected to write, "Who of high Jove wont whilome feasted be."[20] But Spenser is not simply contrasting Tantalus' past and present fortunes, as if to bring out, like a medieval tragedy, the extent of his fall. The line here directly calls up the theme of ambitious self-assertion that we have seen in Disdain and Philotime, and in feasting Jove, Tantalus emulates the lavishness of Mammon himself. The contrast between feasting Jove and dying for want of food is a contrast between exploiting the bounty of Mammon and an inability to satisfy the simplest human needs.

> The antique world, in his first flowring youth,
> Found no defect in his Creatours grace,
> But with glad thankes, and vnreproued truth,
> The gifts of soueraigne bountie did embrace.
>
> (16)

But Tantalus is one of those who "gan exceed / The measure of her meane, and naturall first need" (16), and there is no relief for his

[20] See Sawtelle's note in the *Variorum*, Book II, p. 268. H. G. Lotspeich suggests that Spenser might have learned this version of the story from Comes. *Classical Mythology in the Poetry of Edmund Spenser*, Princeton, 1932, p. 110.

hunger in the kingdom of the god he served. One can say here, as in Horace's passage, "de te fabula narratur." But the moral is addressed not to the miser, but to all heroic men:

> vnto all that liue in high degree,
> Ensample be of mind intemperate,
> To teach them how to vse their present state.
>
> (60)

"Vse their present state," precisely because it shows its origins in the traditional moral of Tantalus' punishment, is an impressive witness to the change Spenser has wrought in his materials.

The best warrant for our view of the canto is Milton's praise of Spenser in *Areopagitica:*

> That vertue therefore which is but a youngling in the contemplation of evill, and knows not the utmost that vice promises to her followers, and rejects it, is but a blank vertue, not a pure; her whitenesse is but an excrementall whitenesse; Which was the reason why our sage and serious Poet *Spencer,* whom I dare be known to think a better teacher then *Scotus* or *Aquinas,* describing true temperance under the person of *Guion,* brings him in with his palmer through the cave of Mammon, and the bowr of earthly blisse that he might see and know, and yet abstain.[21]

Milton is concerned not with a specific sin or virtue, but with the nature of moral strength, and his argument here surely justifies our invoking the phrase "see and know" as the rationale for Spenser's taking us from the opening debate down to the realm of Mammon itself. But Milton says, "see and know, and yet abstain," and there is a problem in the phrase as a whole that will enable us to achieve a true grasp of the nature and development of the canto. There is no question that Spenser makes us "see and know" in the Cave of Mammon. But it is doubtful that anyone feels tempted by what he sees there, and it is therefore not clear in what way abstaining expresses moral strength.

In this episode, unlike the Bower of Bliss, Spenser does not attempt to make us know "the utmost that vice promises to her followers." He seems to be doing something of the sort in Guyon's first test, when a door opens to reveal "of richesse such exceeding store, / As eye of man did neuer see before" (31). But between this wondrous

[21] John Milton, *Complete Prose Works*, Vol. 2, ed. Ernest Sirluck, New Haven, 1959, 515–516.

sight and Mammon's exclamation, "Loe here the worldes blis, loe here the end," the following lines intervene:

> The charge thereof vnto a couetous Spright
> Commaunded was, who thereby did attend,
> And warily awaited day and night,
> From other couetous feends it to defend,
> Who it to rob and ransacke did intend.
>
> (32)

The sense of hostility and suspicion in the covetous soul does more than counteract the impressiveness of the displayed riches. Throughout the canto, Spenser expresses the spiritual deformity of avarice by yoking together a feeling of lavishness with some moral or emotional opposite to it. Thus Mammon calls himself a god who pours out his plenty unto all, but his vast generosity is associated with a sense of laborious striving:

> Riches, renowme, and principality,
> Honour, estate, and all this worldes good,
> For which men swinck and sweat incessantly,
> Fro me do flow into an ample flood.
>
> (8)

In the first description of the cave (28), a feeling of massive richness is succeeded by a description of the spider's "cunning web" and "subtile net." When we first see Mammon with his "heapes of wealth" (7), his first concern is to hide "those pretious hils from straungers enuious sight" (6). The excesses of abundance and closeness are again associated when he tells Guyon that he has hidden all his wealth ("this surplusage," 18) "in secret mew" (19). Passages like these make us feel, when we come to Mammon's first offer, that the presence of a covetous and wary Spirit is inherent in the gathering together of unimaginable riches. We know the false promises of avarice by a direct awareness of their evil and not by feeling their attractiveness in our own souls. Far from being tempted, we see and know the truth of Guyon's first speech against riches:

> All otherwise (said he) I riches read,
> And deeme them roote of all disquietnesse;
> First got with guile, and then preseru'd with dread,
> And after spent with pride and lauishnesse,
> Leauing behind them griefe and heauinesse.
>
> (12)

263

The notion that knowledge of sin comes from feeling its attractions and resisting them is perfectly natural, but quite misleading when we are dealing with this episode. Berger recognizes the dilemma it imposes by saying that if Guyon shares the frailties of Everyman, then his behavior is "resistance to temptation"; if he does not, then it is "fortitude in the face of danger" (p. 10). By "danger" here, Berger seems to mean simply the possibility of physical harm (see pp. 18, 20, 27), because he assumes that no moral or psychological stress can be imposed by a clearly perceived evil. It is certainly true that much moral writing assumes that clarity of vision is an expression of moral immunity and superiority. But when Spenser uses the traditional description of a miser's den, he transforms our relationship to it:

> That houses forme within was rude and strong,
> Like an huge caue, hewne out of rocky clift,
> From whose rough vaut the ragged breaches hong,
> Embost with massy gold of glorious gift,
> And with rich metall loaded euery rift,
> That heauy ruine they did seeme to threat;
> And ouer them *Arachne* high did lift
> Her cunning web, and spred her subtile net,
> Enwrapped in fowle smoke and clouds more blacke then Iet.
>
> (28)

How, precisely, should we characterize our reaction to this stanza? Surely we do not feel attracted or allured, as we do at numerous times in the Bower of Bliss. Yet there is no question that we respond vividly to the moral and emotional qualities conveyed. In a line like "From whose rough vaut the ragged breaches hong," we cannot separate the suggestion of evil qualities, which we reject, from the descriptive felicity, to which we assent. Sometimes, as in "That heauy ruine they did seeme to threat," Spenser invites a very active sympathetic participation on the reader's part. Keats' use of line 5 as a metaphor for the poet's activity is sufficient evidence of our responsiveness to the stanza.[22] It is a real and difficult problem to say how we can take the

[22] Criticizing *The Cenci* in a letter to Shelley (Aug. 16, 1820), Keats said, "A modern work it is said must have a purpose, which may be the God— *an artist* must serve Mammon—he must have 'self concentration' selfishness perhaps. You I am sure will forgive me for sincerely remarking that you might curb your magnanimity and be more of an artist, and 'load every rift' of your subject with ore." *The Letters of John Keats*, ed. Hyder Edward Rollins, Cambridge, Mass., 1958, 2, 322–323.

impression, so to speak, of poetry like this and not be in a state of sin. (This problem—one of Plato's major challenges to poetry—is of great importance for *The Faerie Queene:* consider the notorious seductiveness of Despair and the Bower of Bliss.) In any case, Berger is clearly right to assume that we must in some way be susceptible to these impressions—that an innocent, unfallen man could not respond properly to this stanza. Hence Milton was entirely right to single out this canto as he does, and to say that it is distinguished by the intensity with which we are made to "see and know" the repugnant and terrifying aspects of Mammon. Such an experience, though it is not one of temptation, raises questions about the way in which man can deal with a knowledge of evil, and Spenser confronts these questions by means of Guyon's fortitude, his resistance to Mammon.

Spenser draws attention to this puzzle about man's moral strength as soon as we descend to Mammon's realm. The first thing we see are the personifications that line the highway to Hell, and each of the three stanzas that describes them ends by explicitly mentioning our presence and engaging our feelings:

> And both did gnash their teeth, and both did
> threaten life. (21)

> And Shame his vgly face did hide from liuing eye.
> (22)

> Whiles sad *Celeno,* sitting on a clift,
> A song of bale and bitter sorrow sings,
> That hart of flint a sunder could haue rift.
> (23)

In the next stanza, Guyon is mentioned for the first time since the descent underground; in the characteristic Spenserian way, he serves to intensify our responses:

> All these before the gates of *Pluto* lay,
> By whom they passing, spake vnto them nought.
> But th'Elfin knight with wonder all the way
> Did feed his eyes, and fild his inner thought.
> (24)

These are very odd terms to use in this canto, because avarice is a lust of the eyes. We first see Mammon "feed[ing] his eye" (4), and he fears "straungers enuious sight" (6); he offers his mountains of gold to Guyon's "great mind, or greedy vew" and Guyon in reply rejects "such eye-glutting gaine" (9). Berger interprets Guyon's feeding his eyes as culpable curiosity, but we cannot think that as a dramatic character Guyon is susceptible to lust of the eyes, because two stanzas later Spenser says that he would have been torn to pieces "if euer couetous hand, or lustfull eye, / Or lips he layd on thing, that likt him best" (27). As dramatic behavior, our gazing and Guyon's is a natural activity: we are seeing wondrous evils. But Spenser brings out the problematic nature of our knowing these evils by the metaphor of feeding and by associating our gazing with the sin from which we are presumably immune. The puzzle at the heart of the poetry can be indicated by remembering that the "dread and horrour" (20) that we see are personifications of human passions, and that we are thus engaged in knowing ourselves. This sense of what it means to read the poem is supported by our recognizing that the passage is an imitation of Virgil: we are undergoing again the experience of the arch-hero, Aeneas.

Our awareness of the strains inherent in an encounter with human evil is focused by the fiend who stalks behind Guyon, waiting to tear him to pieces if he even desires, much less touches, anything in Mammon's realm, or even if he yields to the need for sleep (26–27). As we said in an earlier discussion of these stanzas,[23] simply being human is dangerous here. Spenser makes us fully experience our susceptibility to Mammon's terrors, while at the same time he renders human heroism not as a mastery of frailty, but as an immunity from it. After Guyon refuses Mammon's first offer, the fiend is again used to bring out this double perspective on human strength. Guyon's firm and self-conscious espousal of "another happinesse, another end" is followed by a stanza that in no way undercuts the heroic stance as such, yet suddenly makes us see heroism not as a rich human accomplishment, but as the averting of an imminent disaster:

> Thereat the feend his gnashing teeth did grate,
> And grieu'd, so long to lacke his greedy pray;
> For well he weened, that so glorious bayte
> Would tempt his guest, to take thereof assay.

(34)

The first line, which comes with a shock after the nobility of Guyon's speech, has a purely narrative excitement, because it renders only a ghastly action. But Spenser, by using a syntactically parallel verb and the same pattern of alliteration, turns our responsiveness to this line

---

[23] Above, pp. 92–94.

into a sympathetic experience of the fiend's internal feeling in the second. In all Spenser's uses of the phrase, "greedy prey" means "the prey which was greedily desired,"[24] but here, of course, it also means "the prey which was greedy": for a moment we entertain the fiend's notions about Guyon as if they were true. Both meanings enforce our imaginative participation in the fiend's feelings, and we are thus made to register the full force of "glorious bayte" and "tempt": we do not see them simply from the outside, as contrary-to-fact imaginings. Spenser achieves something remarkable with the duplicity of his language here. Although the hero is explicitly not threatened by his character or behavior, but by conditions external to him, we are made to understand these conditions precisely through our knowledge of the human passions that might threaten a heroic stance.

The vision of Mammon's forge repeats the pattern we have seen in the preceding passages. The sight of the "deformed creatures" working at a hundred furnaces (35) is again a direct vision of the evils of avarice—in particular, the association of Mammon with laborious striving. Yet as in the description of the cavelike room, our knowledge is gained by imaginative participation: the verse ensures our full assent when the passage ends, "And euery one did swincke, and euery one did sweat" (36). In the next stanza, Guyon himself feels the strain this experience puts on man's capacities:

> Their staring eyes sparckling with feruent fire,
> And vgly shapes did nigh the man dismay,
> That were it not for shame, he would retire,
> Till that him thus bespake their soueraigne Lord
>   and sire.   (37)

Mammon's offer, which comes in the next stanza, does not follow an experience of attraction to a good, but dismay at an evil.

Even at the end of the canto, when presumably Guyon desires the food and rest offered him, the testing is not rendered as if it were a temptation:

> Infinite moe, tormented in like paine
> He there beheld, too long here to be told:
> Ne *Mammon* would there let him long remaine,
> For terrour of the tortures manifold,
> In which the damned soules he did behold,
> But roughly him bespake. Thou fearefull foole,

[24] See 1.7.20; 4.3.19; 5.4.42, 8.7, 8.31; 6.11.17.

Why takest not of that same fruit of gold,
Ne sittest downe on that same siluer stoole,
To rest thy wearie person, in the shadow coole.

(63)

As this stanza suggests, the passage which it concludes is full of
spiritual struggle and anguish and amazement at them, and it is these
feelings that persuade us that it is difficult to resist Mammon. Mam-
mon himself, far from seeking to allure Guyon, "roughly him be-
spake": he tests him in the mode of the poetry and its effect on us,
not in the manner of a dramatic appeal to the desire for food and
rest. Yet dramatically, as we see in the next stanza, the only chance
to break down Guyon's resolve is to allure his desires:

All which he did, to doe him deadly fall
In frayle intemperance through sinfull bayt;
To which if he inclined had at all,
That dreadfull feend, which did behind him wayt,
Would him haue rent in thousand peeces strayt:
But he was warie wise in all his way,
And well perceiued his deceiptfull sleight,
Ne suffred lust his safetie to betray;
So goodly did beguile the Guyler of the pray.

(64)

Even here, in a direct account of Guyon's behavior, Spenser expects
us to recognize the difference between a character's dealing with his
passions and the general statement that human virtue consists in not
yielding to passion. The line, "To which if he inclined had at all"
must mean that dramatically Guyon was not in the least tempted.
Hence when Spenser says, "Ne suffred lust his safetie to betray," this
"lust" cannot be a desire that Guyon felt; it must directly refer to the
weakness to which a man is potentially liable in this situation. We
ourselves are persuaded of the human susceptibility to this weakness
not by experiencing a desire for Mammon's "sinfull bayt," but
through the terror of "that dreadfull feend"—that is, by a continua-
tion of our experience in reading the preceding stanzas.

The most challenging single question about the canto is to explain
Guyon's fainting at the end of it. We have already said enough to
show that the commonsense explanation is the right one: Guyon is
exhausted from the ordeal of resisting Mammon, and our knowl-
edge of this experience comes from reading stanza after stanza in

which Spenser renders, with exceptional verbal intensity, feelings of gloom, of struggle and labor, of oppressive richness. The canto is perhaps the most extraordinary rendering in world literature of the experience of saying No to an evil. It is extraordinary both for the intimacy and intensity with which the experience is rendered and for the firmness and poise of the double awareness that man has true moral strengths of his own and yet is liable to the weaknesses of his nature. And we have still not given an overall account of the most interesting part of the canto—the successive visions of Philotime, the Garden of Proserpina, and Tantalus and Pilate. In these passages, Spenser turns from the direct rendering of visions of evil and the denial of them to a broader and broader evaluation of the strength that produces the rejection of Mammon.

This movement in the canto begins with Guyon's encounter with Disdain. Guyon rejects Mammon's first offers of unlimited wealth in the name of heroic knighthood, and Spenser renders the scene at Mammon's furnaces as a martial encounter. The fiends see Guyon "glistring in armes and battailous aray" and the motive that prevents him from drawing back is shame (37). Guyon moves directly from this scene to a genuine martial confrontation with Disdain, who is a diabolical parody of all that Guyon is. He personifies an evil version of the scorn Guyon has just shown for Mammon's offers—the "rigour of [Guyon's] bold mesprise" (39) becomes Disdain's "striding stiffe and bold" (40)—and he is compared to "an huge Gyant of the *Titans* race" (41), a traditional symbol of the evil aspects of heroic strength and aspiration. Guyon prepares to battle Disdain

> Till *Mammon* did his hasty hand withhold,
> And counseld him abstaine from perilous fight:
> For nothing might abash the villein bold,
> Ne mortall steele emperce his miscreated mould.
>
> (42)

These lines are perhaps the most puzzling in the canto. If Mammon has a dramatic motive here—say, a recognition that Guyon can be defeated only by a temptation—Spenser admirably conceals it. He makes Mammon seem rather like the Palmer, and the next stanza begins, "So hauing him with reason pacifide" (43). Moreover, there is no obvious rationale for an impasse here, as there is in Guyon's other encounters with personifications—his battle with Furor (2.4.10) and his confrontation with Shamefastness in the House of Alma

269

(2.9.43). But even though these problems exist, one point seems clear. For all Guyon's confidence in "armes, and in atchieuements braue" (33), his victory over Mammon cannot be expressed by heroic battle.

The encounter with Disdain indicates that martial prowess inadequately expresses moral strength. The vision of Philotime contains a more far-reaching criticism of heroic strength. So far as dramatic action goes, we are as sure of ourselves as ever. We directly perceive the evils of worldly ambition in Philotime and her court, and we are no more tempted by Mammon's offer of her hand than we were by his previous offers of gold. But as we have already observed, our testing in this episode is not by way of temptation, but in respect to our evaluation of our moral strengths. When Spenser gives the golden chain to Philotime, he transfers to Mammon's realm a myth that we might well expect a hero to invoke. The same switch occurs when Mammon says that Philotime will "thee aduance for workes and merites iust" (49). It was relatively easy to reject Mammon when he displayed heaps of gold and said: "Loe here the worldes blis, loe here the end, / To which all men do ayme, rich to be made" (32). He now appropriates words that might formerly have been used against him:

> Honour and dignitie from her alone,
> Deriued are, and all this worldes blis
> For which ye men do striue: few get, but many mis.
>
> (48)

The truth of the last line is hard to deny in this episode, and when Guyon refuses Philotime's hand, we are not surprised that he no longer takes a heroic stance:

> Gramercy *Mammon* (said the gentle knight)
> For so great grace and offred high estate;
> But I, that am fraile flesh and earthly wight,
> Vnworthy match for such immortall mate
> My selfe well wote, and mine vnequall fate.
>
> (50)

Spenser seems to be moving us to a point where our awareness of the problematic nature of heroism will move us to recognize a truer model for human goodness. But as Guyon's rejection of Philotime continues, we see that this is not at all what Spenser has in mind:

270

And were I not [an unworthy match], yet is my
    trouth yplight,
And loue auowd to other Lady late,
That to remoue the same I haue no might:
To chaunge loue causelesse is reproch to warlike knight.

                                                (50)

These lines are wonderfully characteristic of Spenser's poetry—not least, of course, because we cannot tell whether this "other Lady" is the Fairy Queen (cf. 2.9.4) or a fiancée invented on the spot. But it is less important to decide whether someone, either Guyon or Spenser, is improvising here, than to pay attention to the moral terms that this nonce-bethrothal provides. To use a fine phrase of Empson's, Spenser has been screwing a moral case up tight in this episode: we are made to ask, what are true honor and dignity? But we would be quite wrong to look for a definite answer to this question—to think that when Guyon speaks of his lady, a knightly ethic of martial achievement has been superseded by an ethic of chivalric love. Spenser is not so much proceeding by dialectical stages as he is keeping alive the moral problem that has concerned him from the beginning of the canto: what secular sanctions can be invoked against Mammon? Guyon's final maxim, like his speaking of "the riches fit for an aduent'rous knight," expresses a confidence that there are such sanctions. The significance of his rejection of Philotime lies not so much in its specific ethical content as in its developing the stance of a "warlike knight" from a consciousness of being "fraile flesh and earthly wight."

We can now see how important the Garden of Proserpina is in the development of the canto. Four stanzas after Guyon's rejection of Philotime, Spenser has restored us to the world of mythological heroism. Even in the lines that are meant to remind us how imperfect human heroism is, he does not deny feelings of glamor and nobility: "And had of her, faire *Helen* for his meed, / That many noble *Greekes* and *Troians* made to bleed" (55). Moreover, three of the four myths connected with the golden apples are stories of love, and it is in the name of love that Guyon rejected Philotime. The transition from the Philotime episode to the description of the golden apples shows the poise and openness of Spenser's mind, the refusal to act as if issues were definitively settled. When Mammon takes Guyon into the Garden of Proserpina, the first thing we are told is that its "hearbs and fruits" are "direfull deadly blacke" (51):

There mournfull *Cypresse* grew in greatest store,
And trees of bitter *Gall,* and *Heben* sad,
Dead sleeping *Poppy,* and blacke *Hellebore,*
Cold *Coloquintida,* and *Tetra* mad,
Mortall *Samnitis,* and *Cicuta* bad,
With which th'vniust *Atheniens* made to dy
Wise *Socrates,* who thereof quaffing glad
Pourd out his life, and last Philosophy
To the faire *Critias* his dearest Belamy.

(52)

With characteristic insouciance, Spenser tells us that the deadly plants "whose kinds mote not be red" in the preceding stanza are in fact familiar poisons and funereal trees. There is an important sense in which what naturally grows in Mammon's realm is "not such, as earth out of her fruitfull womb / Throwes forth to men, sweet and well sauoured" (51), but in this stanza we turn to the other half of that truth to acknowledge that such plants can be thought of as natural on earth. One is not surprised, then, to see the second half of the stanza turn to a notoriously wicked human use of these poisons. What might seem surprising—though to me it is characteristic of Spenser's breadth of mind and his aliveness to the interest of moral issues—is the fact that the stanza concludes by reminding us not of the Athenians' injustice, but of the nobility of Socrates.[25]

We can now see the full importance of the descriptions of Tantalus and Pilate. In the first place, they are the last of the evils we see: they present to us, more directly than anything else in the canto, the human suffering entailed in serving Mammon. They embody the corruptions of human nature projected by the myth of the antique world, and their activity in hell is the "labour vaine and idle industry" (61) that is one of the main motifs of the canto. But Tantalus and Pilate are a fitting climax to the canto because they combine the intense experience of knowing an evil with a severe testing of our valuation of heroism. This can most readily be seen by considering their relation to the myth of the antique world. That myth is a version of pastoral: it shadows forth what are now heroic strengths by a vision of humble simplicity. Up to this point we have been sure of ourselves in taking the myth as a myth; there is an important sense in which we

[25] For an explanation of Spenser's mistaken reference to Critias here—probably due to his conflating or confusing the death of Socrates with that of the philosopher Theramenes—see the *Variorum* notes to the stanza.

believe in it, but we accept Mammon's home truth that men are no longer like that. But Tantalus and Pilate show us the human disasters that occur when a man is not like the men of the antique world—when he does not know, in Milton's phrase, "the good before him" (*PL* 4.203), and when he does not have clean hands and a pure heart. And the model of such a man is not a humble or innocent figure, but the hero, the man with responsibilities in this world:

> Nay, nay, thou greedie *Tantalus* (quoth he)
> Abide the fortune of thy present fate,
> And vnto all that liue in high degree,
> Ensample be of mind intemperate,
> To teach them how to vse their present state.
>
> (60)

The breadth and generosity of Spenser's mind are nowhere more apparent than in the fact that he does not present Guyon's words to Tantalus as a final moral stance, but ends the stanza by acknowledging the human pain caused by this moral severity:

> Then gan the cursed wretch aloud to cry,
> Accusing highest *Ioue* and gods ingrate,
> And eke blaspheming heauen bitterly,
> As authour of vniustice, there to let him dye.
>
> (60)

The clash between the hero's judgment and the torment of the "cursed wretch" suggests how far we are from the pastoral antique world. In that world, man "found no defect in his Creatours grace, / But with glad thankes, and vnreproued truth, / The gifts of soueraigne bountie did embrace" (16). In this world, in which Mammon parodies God's grace and bounty (8, 18, 32, 33, 50), it is Tantalus who cries, "Of grace I pray thee, giue to eat and drinke to mee" (59), and Guyon's refusal of this grace is an act of justice. The pathos of Tantalus' plea to him and the anguish with which he curses the heavens in no way qualify our moral judgment of his merits, but we are made vividly aware of the human toll that justice takes. And yet when we go on to Pilate, Spenser restores the just man to us as a model of human worth and integrity:

> I *Pilate* am the falsest Iudge, alas,
> And most vniust, that by vnrighteous
> And wicked doome, to Iewes despiteous

273

Deliuered vp the Lord of life to die,
And did acquite a murdrer felonous.

(62)

The naming of Christ as "the Lord of life" brings to mind the fact
that the myth of the antique world and, by negation, the various en-
counters with Mammon's world base human goodness on nature. But
it is not simply a pastoral feeling that produces our sense that there is
an obvious, a sadly obvious, wrongness in what Pilate did. That feel-
ing comes primarily from the firmness with which Spenser appeals to
our own sense of justice. The line, "And did acquite a murdrer felon-
ous," though it seems so much less resonant than the preceding line,
does an essential job of placing Pilate's sin in the context of real hu-
man judgments. Similarly, Spenser's condemning the Jews as "despit-
eous" immediately after Guyon's failure to pity Tantalus shows his
confidence that we know the difference between the two cases.

And yet the canto turns around once again. Guyon's faint is the
culminating expression of our awareness that there *are* limits to hu-
man strength. To the explanation we have already given of the faint
—that it is the result of the inherent strains of knowing an evil—we
must add an account of its relation to the way in which Spenser has
been evaluating human heroism. It is in this respect that Guyon's faint
has caused a great deal of interpretive difficulty. Most critics regard
the faint as a moral judgment against Guyon. But surely Spenser re-
gards it as natural in both senses of the word. It is due to man's na-
ture, and it is the inevitable result of the trial Guyon has endured:

> And now he has so long remained there,
> That vitall powres gan wexe both weake and wan,
> For want of food, and sleepe, which two vpbeare,
> Like mightie pillours, this fraile life of man,
> That none without the same enduren can.

(65)

The last two lines make it evident that no man is exempt from the
weakness that besets Guyon. Moreover, Spenser gives a real grandeur
to the inevitability of Guyon's exhaustion. It could indeed be an irony
against heroic pretensions to faint from want of food and sleep. But
when they are called "mightie pillours," to do without them, to find
a substitute for their strength, *is* noble. When it comes to behavior in
which we can morally distinguish one man from another, Guyon is
praised for resisting "frayle intemperance" (64). When Spenser goes

on to make his hero the victim of "this fraile life of man," he is not confusedly trying to pass a moral judgment, but indicating something problematic or paradoxical about human moral strength: to exercise it, to resist human frailty, takes a psychological toll because of human frailty.

The compatibility of the heroic and the humble—a promise held out by the myth of the antique world and shown as a human reality in Guyon's rejection of Philotime and in the stance we take in confronting Tantalus and Pilate—turns out to be subject to the conditions of a mortal world. The two poles are at the end incompatible. The inability to take the proffered fruit, which metaphorically expresses Tantalus' state of sin, is a dramatic expression of Guyon's virtue. Guyon as a character is not humiliated by his faint. But the pointed paradox in the closing lines—that when he "gan sucke this vitall aire into his brest, . . . the life did flit away out of her nest" (66)—prepares us for the statement, in the opening stanzas of the next canto, of the context in which the paradox of strength through humility is literally true:

> And is there care in heauen? and is there loue
> In heauenly spirits to these creatures bace,
> That may compassion of their euils moue?
>
> (2.8.1)

And yet it is not enough to say that Guyon's faint moves us, as if by dialectic, to the expression of man's dependence on God. What most impresses us at the end of the Cave of Mammon is the full and poised awareness that has been evident throughout. We never lose sight of Guyon's heroism. The model for his three days in Mammon's realm is Christ's Harrowing of Hell, and the stanza which tells us that his "vitall powres gan wexe both weake and wan" concludes by referring to his "hardie enterprize" (65). The reiterated references to life in the final stanza—"liuing wight," "liuing light," "vitall aire"—are not simply there as ironic preparation for Guyon's faint. They are a witness to the goodness in nature and human life that has been a main source of our strength while we were in Mammon's realm. The angel's succoring of Guyon, after all, is not the same as the rescue of the Red Cross Knight from Orgoglio's dungeon. It expresses a recognition of human frailty, but it is based on the conclusion of the Temptation in the Wilderness: "Then the devyl leaveth him, and behold, the angels came, and ministred unto him" (Matt. 4:11).

275

PART III

Chapter Nine

The Nature of Spenser's Allegory

I

When we ask what makes a given work allegorical, we can be thinking either of what it is in itself—the nature of its subject matter, its formal elements, and the like—or of its interest for and effect on us as readers. Both these problems will concern us as we consider, in a more general way than in other chapters, the kind of interest and value *The Faerie Queene* has. The main problem we have to deal with is the relation of Spenser's poetry to action. Yeats' famous statement neatly summarizes the modern objection to allegory in general and *The Faerie Queene* in particular: "He wrote of knights and ladies, wild creatures imagined by the aristocratic poets of the twelfth century . . . ; but he fastened them with allegorical nails to a big barn-door of common sense, of merely practical virtue."[1] Yeats criticizes, as if they were the same thing, didactic purpose and the rational structuring of realities within the poem. The two objections belong together. The double hostility to disembodied intellect and to action in the world comes from a basic assumption of modern aesthetic—that a poem has its own special reality and that it is produced by and appeals to a special mode of vision.[2] Hence John Crowe Ransom says—in what might itself be regarded as a didactic vein—"Over every poem which looks like a poem is a sign which reads: This road does not go through to action; fictitious."[3] The rationale of this motto is Ransom's attack on what he calls Platonic Poetry:

> Platonic Poetry is allegory, a discourse in things, but on the understanding that they are translatable at every point into ideas. (The usual ideas are those which constitute the popular causes, patriotic, religious, moral, or social.) . . . Platonism, in the sense I mean, is the name of an impulse that is native to us all. . . . We are led to believe that nature is rational and that by the force of reasoning we shall possess it. . . . We love to view the world under universal or scientific ideas to which we give the name truth; and

[1] William Butler Yeats, *Essays and Introductions*, New York, 1961, p. 367.
[2] See Frank Kermode, *Romantic Image*, London, 1957.
[3] "Poetry: a Note in Ontology," in *The World's Body*, New York, 1938, p. 131.

this is because the ideas seem to make not for righteousness but for mastery. . . . Now the fine Platonic world of ideas fails to coincide with the original world of perception, which is the world populated by the stubborn and contingent objects, and to which as artists we fly in shame.[4]

In some ways, the best answer to this is the one Rosemond Tuve gives in the final chapter of *Elizabethan and Metaphysical Imagery*. She points out that Ransom's metaphysical and psychological assumptions not only are entirely different from Spenser's—and thus impede entering into the aesthetic experience he offers—but also make for a much cruder notion of didacticism. Miss Tuve remarks, "What these modern theories all share is an antipathy toward that moving of the will toward good or evil which is an integral part of the didactic theory as the Renaissance understood it."[5] One well understands this antipathy when the notion of the will is represented by Yeats' dictum, with which Allen Tate begins an attack on "Platonic Poetry,"[6] that rhetoric is the will trying to do the work of the imagination. Didactic poetry, on this view, is inherently false, because it satisfies callow and self-ignorant needs. But the proper text to start with is Sidney's statement, in the midst of his most exalted praise of poetry, that "our erected wit maketh vs know what perfection is, and yet our infected will keepeth vs from reaching vnto it."[7] As Miss Tuve says, "A theory which sees poetry as speaking to the will . . . suited with the picture these men had of how the human mind works, so that poetry's moral aspect is simply a natural part of its rational functioning. In the total process of perceiving, understanding, and taking an attitude toward reality, the final linkage in the normal chain of intellectual-distinguishing-of-true-from-false-and-moral-choosing-of-good-rather-than-bad was broken only by an 'infected will.' . . . To be *moved* to do that which we know—there is the rub."[8]

However, to clear away modern misconceptions does not solve the problem that interests us. Miss Tuve's main concern was to enable us to see the Elizabethans clearly, and particularly to persuade us that rational and sensitive men could hold the views of poetry that Spenser

[4] *Ibid.*, pp. 122–123.

[5] *Elizabethan and Metaphysical Imagery*, Chicago, 1947, p. 400.

[6] "Three Types of Poetry," in *Reactionary Essays on Poetry and Ideas*, New York, 1936, p. 87.

[7] Sir Philip Sidney, *An Apologie for Poetrie*, in *Elizabethan Critical Essays*, ed. G. Gregory Smith, Oxford, 1904, 2 vols., 1, 157. Page references to the *Apologie* that appear in the text are to this volume.

[8] *Op. cit.*, pp. 400–401.

and Sidney did. She was rightly impatient with the kind of complacent ignorance enshrined in Tate's remark that *The Faerie Queene* is the first proletarian poem.[9] On the other hand, Elizabethan scholars sometimes fall into a false historicism that simply inverts the views of critics like Ransom and Tate and praises *The Faerie Queene* for being rational and didactic in more or less the way they mean those words. It is not enough to say that the Elizabethans believed that poetry should move a man to virtuous action, and that Spenser said that his purpose was "to fashion a gentleman or noble person in vertuous and gentle discipline." The problem of the moral effect of *The Faerie Queene* is a real one, and it was felt by Spenser himself:

> The rugged forhead that with graue foresight
> Welds kingdomes causes, and affaires of state,
> My looser rimes (I wote) doth sharply wite,
> For praising loue, as I haue done of late,
> And magnifying louers deare debate;
> By which fraile youth is oft to follie led,
> Through false allurement of that pleasing baite,
> That better were in vertues discipled,
> Then with vaine poemes weeds to haue their fancies fed.
>
> (4.Proem.1)

Spenser gives two answers to this attack. He begins by saying, "Such ones ill iudge of loue, that cannot loue, / Ne in their frosen hearts feele kindly flame" (4.Proem.2), and the argument applies as well to the judging of poetry. But Spenser then goes on to claim that true love "of honor and all vertue is / The roote, and brings forth glorious flowres of fame"—in other words, that his poem, rightly construed, will have exactly the moral effect that Burleigh thinks it ought to have. A man like Burleigh looks to results, and one feels the constraint when Spenser equates "moral effect" with "actions produced":

> Which who so list looke backe to former ages,
> And call to count the things that then were donne,
> Shall find, that all the workes of those wise sages,
> And braue exploits which great Heroes wonne,
> In loue were either ended or begunne.
>
> (4.Proem.3)

Spenser surely would not have the worth of his poem depend on the

[9] "A Note on Elizabethan Satire," in *Reactionary Essays*, p. 82.

literal truth of this statement, and he would not say that love and love poetry are justified solely because they produce brave exploits and wise works. Yet in trying to answer Burleigh on his own terms, his only room for maneuver lies in a play on words—the allusion to the presumed derivation of "hero" from "eros" and to the etymological meaning of "philosophy" (the word is used in the next line), "love of wisdom."[10] The real answer to Burleigh is that he does not know what it is like to love or to read a poem. Spenser therefore turns from "these Stoicke censours"—"To such therefore I do not sing at all"—and concludes the proem by addressing his queen.

Spenser was not alone in feeling how difficult it is to close the gap between the morally valuable experience of reading poetry and its results in moral action. The problem weighs heavily on Daniel's Musophilus, when he defends learning against Philocosmus, and it is rather concealed than resolved in Sidney's *Apologie*. The heart of Sidney's defense of poetry lies in the passages in which he describes, sometimes in ravishing prose, the psychological effect of poetry—in particular, the way it makes us see and love virtue and virtuous acts. Yet when it comes to showing that poetry *produces* virtuous acts, his main examples (p. 174) are Menenius Agrippa's tale of the belly and the parable of Nathan the Wise—humble fictions that are expressly framed to provoke an action. At another point, when he is showing that "a fayned example hath as much force to teach as a true example," the temporary equation of moral lesson with action produced leads Sidney into a trivial argument, couched in a tasteless jest:

> *Herodotus* and *Iustine* do both testifie that *Zopirus,* King *Darius* faithfull seruaunt, seeing his Maister long resisted by the rebellious *Babilonians,* fayned himselfe in extreame disgrace of his King: for verifying of which, he caused his own nose and eares to be cut off: and so flying to the *Babilonians,* was receiued, and for his knowne valour so far credited, that hee did finde meanes to deliuer them ouer to *Darius.* Much like matter doth *Liuie* record of *Tarquinius* and his sonne. *Xenophon* excellently faineth such another strata-geme, performed by *Abradates* in *Cyrus* behalfe. Now would I fayne know, if occasion bee presented vnto you to serue your Prince by such an honest dissimulation, why you doe not as well learne it of *Xenophons* fiction as of the others verity: and truely so much the

---

[10] See Martha Alden Craig, "Language and Concept in the *Faerie Queene*," Ph.D. dissertation, Yale, 1959, pp. 68–69.

better, as you shall saue your nose by the bargaine; for *Abradates* did not counterfet so far (p. 169).

Yet when, in the next sentence, Sidney returns to the psychological experience of poetry, he produces one of the most vigorous and memorable statements in the *Apologie:* "So then the best of the Historian is subiect to the Poet; for whatsoeuer action, or faction, whatsoeuer counsell, pollicy, or warre stratagem the Historian is bound to recite, that may the Poet (if he list) with his imitation make his own; beautifying it both for further teaching, and more delighting, as it pleaseth him: hauing all, from *Dante* his heauen to hys hell, vnder the authoritie of his penne."

Although it is a false reduction to test moral poetry by the actions it produces, it is worth inquiring whether moral action is a model for what occurs within the reader of a didactic poem. Sidney himself raises this question when he speaks of "the highest end of the mistres Knowledge, by the Greekes called *Arkitecktonike*, which stands, (as I thinke) in the knowledge of a mans selfe, in the Ethicke and politick consideration, with the end of well dooing and not of well knowing onely" (p. 161). "The end of well dooing" consistently controls the idea of self-knowledge in the *Apologie*. Sidney's psychology is very different from I. A. Richards', but he would agree with Richards' formulation of the relation between the experience of reading and real moral action: "*In a fully developed man a state of readiness for action will take the place of action when the full appropriate situation for action is not present.* The essential peculiarity of poetry as of all the arts is that the full appropriate situation is *not* present. It is an *actor* we are seeing upon the stage, not Hamlet. So readiness for action takes the place of actual behaviour."[11]

Richards' distinction is the one we would invoke to explain what Sidney means when he says that heroic poetry stirs us to emulate noble actions: "For as the image of each action styrreth and instructeth the mind, so the loftie image of such Worthies most inflameth the mind with desire to be worthy, and informes with counsel how to be worthy. *Only let Aeneas be worne in the tablet of your memory;* how he gouerneth himselfe in the ruine of his Country; in the preseruing his old Father, etc." (p. 179, my italics). Even when Sidney seems to speak of poetry as knowledge, virtuous action is his model for knowing. His characterization of poetry as a speaking picture implies a

---

[11] *Science and Poetry*, New York, 1926, p. 29. The italics are Richards'.

mind poised for action: "No doubt the Philosopher . . . replenisheth the memory with many infallible grounds of wisdom, which, notwithstanding, *lye darke before the imaginatiue and iudging powre,* if they bee not illuminated or figured foorth by the speaking picture of Poesie" (p. 165, my italics). When Sidney goes on to describe the way poetry shows us "all vertues, vices, and passions so in their own naturall seates layd to the viewe" (p. 166), "their natural seats" refers to various actions (the madness of Ajax, the valor of Achilles, "the soone repenting pride of *Agamemnon*") which he imagines not that the reader will emulate or avoid on the spot, but that he will carry, in their full liveliness, in "the tablet of his memory." There is nothing unusual about Sidney's assumptions about the relation of mental processes to action. As Miss Tuve suggests, they are what we would expect from an Elizabethan writer interested in "what poetry achieves in a reader's mind."[12]

With this as background, let us ask what kind of moral understanding or knowledge of ourselves *The Faerie Queene* gives us. Many readers, whether they start with modern or Elizabethan assumptions, expect to find in Spenser the kind of moral analysis and decision that is called casuistry. Hence most interpreters of *The Faerie Queene* feel that their job is to determine the rights and wrongs of particular cases and to assign praise or blame for particular actions. Yet Spenser's kind of moral understanding is almost the direct opposite of this. The most important opportunity he has for genuine casuistical reasoning is when he pauses to evaluate Calidore's remaining among the shepherds:

> Who now does follow the foule *Blatant Beast,*
> Whilest *Calidore* does follow that faire Mayd,
> Vnmyndfull of his vow and high beheast,
> Which by the Faery Queene was on him layd,
> That he should neuer leaue, nor be delayd
> From chacing him, till he had it attchieued?
> But now entrapt of loue, which him betrayd,
> He mindeth more, how he may be relieued
> With grace from her, whose loue his heart hath sore
>   engrieued.
>
> That from henceforth he meanes no more to sew
> His former quest, so full of toile and paine;
> Another quest, another game in vew

[12] *Elizabethan and Metaphysical Imagery*, p. 399.

He hath, the guerdon of his loue to gaine:
With whom he myndes for euer to remaine,
And set his rest amongst the rusticke sort,
Rather then hunt still after shadowes vaine
Of courtly fauour, fed with light report
Of euery blaste, and sayling alwaies on the port.

Ne certes mote he greatly blamed be,
From so high step to stoupe vnto so low.
For who had tasted once (as oft did he)
The happy peace, which there doth ouerflow,
And prou'd the perfect pleasures, which doe grow
Amongst poore hyndes, in hils, in woods, in dales,
Would neuer more delight in painted show
Of such false blisse, as there is set for stales,
T'entrap vnwary fooles in their eternall bales.

(6.10.1–3)

No wonder critics have been unable to agree whether Calidore is right or wrong to remain in the country. These stanzas are designed *not* to permit a decision on this question, but rather to make us see the sanctions and motives on both sides. The two points of view are unequivocally stated, and there is no attempt or desire to qualify one by the other. It is no mystery that the mind can hold these different evaluations and regard each as in some way true. What is unusual is that Spenser is content to treat the elements of a complex moral case as distinct and self-contained moral perspectives, and feels no need to combine them into a single structure of judgment. We feel the presence of a clear and decisive moral intelligence in these stanzas, and yet by ordinary standards they seem unclear (what *does* the speaker think of the court?) and indecisive. The quality of mind these stanzas reveal has been best appreciated by William Empson:

The size, the possible variety, and the fixity of this unit [the Spenserian stanza] give something of the blankness that comes from fixing your eyes on a bright spot; you have to yield yourself to it very completely to take in the variety of its movement, and, at the same time, there is no need to concentrate the elements of the situation into a judgment as if for action. As a result of this, when there are ambiguities of idea, it is whole civilisations rather than details of the moment which are their elements; he can pour into the even dreamwork of his fairyland Christian, classical, and

285

chivalrous materials with an air, not of ignoring their differences, but of holding all their systems of values floating as if at a distance, so as not to interfere with one another, in the prolonged and diffused energies of his mind.[13]

It is rather difficult to relate the noncasuistical quality of Spenser's mind to didactic theories of poetry. In the stanzas just quoted, Spenser is not being didactic in the vulgar modern sense: he is not imposing his will on his materials in order to make the reader think or do a certain thing. (The modern objection to these stanzas would be either to the unreality of a moral case conceived in such general and conventional terms, or to Spenser's refusal to make up his mind about Calidore.) But it is not clear whether or how such poetry as this speaks to the will in Sidney's sense. The stanzas about Calidore surely do not appeal to the reader in the way that is suggested when Sidney says: "Truely, I haue knowen men, that euen with reading *Amadis de Gaule* (which God knoweth wanteth much of a perfect Poesie) haue found their harts mooued to the exercise of courtesie, liberalitie, and especially courage. Who readeth *Aeneas* carrying olde *Anchises* on his back, that wisheth not it were his fortune to perfourme so excellent an acte?" (p. 173). Spenser's stanzas assume that the reader is a good person—that in real life he desires to do acts of courtesy, liberality, and courage. Their moral interest and value has to do with the understanding of one's situation that comes from seeing it in more than one perspective.

Sidney's discussion of the reader's mind assumes, as Aristotle did, that "the virtues are modes of choice or involve choice" and that "choice is either desiderative reason or ratiocinative desire."[14] Spenser might agree with these statements insofar as real action is concerned, but he does not see the reader of a poem as constantly making choices analogous to those involved in real action. Since his poetry does not attempt to depict dramatic action, it could hardly arouse the feelings of emulation or rejection that Sidney envisages in the reader of a heroic poem. But there is a kind of moral action that we do assume the reader of *The Faerie Queene* (and of most works of literature) to be engaged in—the judging of issues and actions presented. Judging, which is an action and of which choice is the essence, is precisely

---

[13] *Seven Types of Ambiguity*, 3rd edn., London, 1953, p. 34.

[14] *Nicomachean Ethics*, 2.5, 6.2, tr. W. D. Ross, in *The Basic Works of Aristotle*, ed. Richard McKeon, New York, 1941. See also *Nic. Eth.* 3.2. Note that Sidney cites Aristotle's dictum that "it is not *Gnosis* but *Praxis* must be the fruit" (p. 171; *Nic. Eth.* 1.3).

what Spenser does not expect of us. In most cases, as in the Cave of Mammon, he assumes that the hero's behavior is good, and devotes his poetry to making us see and understand general themes, issues, and problems of man's life. In the rare case that is genuinely doubtful, like Calidore's, he makes us see both sides of the question. In the most important instance of wrong behavior on the part of a hero, he deliberately, and for reasons that are at the heart of the subject of Book I, prevents us from passing judgment on the Red Cross Knight or making any single determination about the nature of his plight. Even when judging is part of the action of the poem—in Mercilla's trial of Duessa—Spenser's interest is more in the elements of the judgment than in the act of decision itself. The stanzas recounting the personifications who appear as witnesses (5.9.44–45)—which are not, of course, to be read as action, but as a listing of motives and sanctions —are genuinely impressive, because they make us entertain the reasons on both sides of the case. Even when more reasons are brought against Duessa, and Arthur, who had pitied her, "gan repent" "his former fancies ruth" (5.9.49), the conflict between justice and mercy is unresolved:

> But she [Mercilla], whose Princely breast was
>   touched nere
> With piteous ruth of her so wretched plight,
> Though plaine she saw by all, that she did heare,
> That she of death was guiltie found by right,
> Yet would not let iust vengeance on her light;
> But rather let in stead thereof to fall
> Few perling drops from her faire lampes of light;
> The which she couering with her purple pall
> Would haue the passion hid, and vp arose withall.
>
>   (5.9.50)

This stanza ends the canto. The condemnation of Duessa, which we would expect to resolve the issues of the trial, is deferred until the next canto, where its context is not the single process of judgment, but a general account of mercy and praise of Mercilla for possessing this virtue (5.10.1–4).

If moral understanding in *The Faerie Queene* does not take the form of an action, perhaps we should regard it as a form of knowledge. We can imagine, and some critics espouse, a Platonic model of *The Faerie Queene*. C. S. Lewis says: "It is Spenser's method to have in each book an allegorical core, surrounded by a margin of what is called 'romance of types,' and relieved by episodes of pure fantasy. Like a true Platonist he shows us the Form of the virtue he is studying not only in its transcendental unity (which comes at the allegorical core of the book) but also 'becoming Many in the world of phenomena.' "[15] According to this description of the poem, our moral understanding would consist of the perception of the Forms or Ideas of various virtues. This theory would require the allegorical cores of *The Faerie Queene* to be much more truly visionary than they are. Instead, these cantos are characterized by the same kind of activity—the provisional adopting of attitudes and evaluations—that is Spenser's way of rendering the moral truth of Calidore's stay among the shepherds. The Cave of Mammon shows us that the poetic intensity of Spenser's allegorical cores is to a great extent an intensification of this kind of activity, and it is nowhere better exemplified than in the major visionary experience in *The Faerie Queene*—when the Red Cross Knight sees the New Jerusalem (1.10.53–67). Spenser devotes most of this passage, the climax of the allegorical core of Book I, not to the vision that shows man his ultimate goal, but to the dialogue between the knight and the hermit Contemplation, the purpose of which is to evaluate earthly action and human moral imperatives in the light of that vision. Similarly, Calidore's vision of the Graces (6.10.10–17) gives way to Colin Clout's disquisition on their significance for human life (6.10.21–28).

With the Red Cross Knight's changes of mind and the hermit's inconsistencies about the value of earthly glory, their colloquy wonderfully shows that Spenser's moral intelligence lies in his ability to see all around a complex issue, and not in his making moral decisions. What we want particularly to observe here is that each aspect of the issue is presented in the form of a moral action—an attitude taken or choice made:

> But deeds of armes must I at last be faine,
> And Ladies loue to leaue so dearely bought?
> What need of armes, where peace doth ay remaine,
> (Said he) and battailes none are to be fought?
> As for loose loues are vaine, and vanish into nought.

> (1.10.62)

In isolation, these lines seem to exemplify Sidney's ideas of the moral knowledge a poem gives us. What is peculiarly Spenserian is the no-

---

[15] *The Allegory of Love*, Oxford, 1936, p. 334.

tion that the moral reality illuminated by this stanza will be further illuminated by taking the opposite stance in the next:

> O let me not (quoth he) then turne againe
> Backe to the world, whose ioyes so fruitlesse are;
> But let me here for aye in peace remaine,
> Or streight way on that last long voyage fare,
> That nothing may my present hope empare.
> That may not be (said he) ne maist thou yit
> Forgo that royall maides bequeathed care,
> Who did her cause into thy hand commit,
> Till from her cursed foe thou haue her freely quit.

(1.10.63)

(Note that although this injunction *could* be made consistent with the preceding stanza—"you must fulfill your earthly obligations before turning to heaven"—Spenser makes us feel the elements of conflict and incompatibility by his radically different namings of "Ladies loue.") Spenser's mind, as much as Sidney's, is directed to this world —to moral choices, attitudes, and conflicts, and to the realities of human psychology. He differs from Sidney in that he does not conceive reading his poem to entail the judging and choosing that are inseparable from real moral action. What Spenser expects of and creates in his reader is best called simply moral understanding. I think that term suggests our active interest in the moral realities we are shown, while at the same time it indicates that these realities are phenomena we contemplate—permanent conditions of human nature and human life—and that we know more about them than we can express by particular choices and decisions.

We can see the strengths of understanding as opposed to judging if we compare the pastoral episode in Book VI of *The Faerie Queene* with the pastoralism of Book I of Sidney's *Arcadia*. In a passage that is often cited to show the seriousness with which the Elizabethans took the idea of didactic poetry, Fulke Greville tells us the moral lessons to be learned from the *Arcadia*:

> May not the most refined spirits, in the scope of these dead images (even as they are now) finde, that when Sovaraign Princes, to play with their own visions, will put off publique action, which is the splendor of Majestie, and unactively charge the managing of their greatest affaires upon the second-hand faith, and diligence of Deputies, may they not (I say) understand, that even then they

bury themselves, and their Estates in a cloud of contempt, and under it both encourage, and shaddow the conspiracies of ambitious subalternes to their false endes, I mean the ruine of States and Princes? . . . Lastly, where humor takes away this pomp, and *apparatus* from King, Crown, and Scepter, to make fear a Counsellor, and obscurity a wisdom; be that King at home what the current, or credit of his former Government, for a while, may keep him: yet he is sure among forrain Princes to be justly censured as a Princely Shepherd, or Shepherdish King: which creatures of scorn seldome fail to become fit sacrifices for home-born discontentments, or ambitious forrain spirits to undertake, and offer up.[16]

These statements are a just interpretation of the initiating action of the *Arcadia*—Basilius' retreat to the country because of his superstitious belief of an oracle. Our interest is in the way this kind of decisive moral consciousness restricts the interest and value of pastoral experience in the *Arcadia*. As Greville's scornful reference to a "shepherdish king" might suggest, there is no figure in Arcadia like Spenser's Melibee. The wise spokesman in Sidney is the responsible aristocrat Kalander, while the representative rustic is Dametas, the boor whom Basilius has elevated to a position of trust and whom Sidney rather tiresomely mocks whenever he appears. We hear of other, more admirable shepherds, but Dametas is much the most prominent, because we are seeing Arcadia under the aspect of the moral judgment on Basilius' retreat.

A similar judgment—that love undermines heroism—controls the heroes' experience of pastoral realities. When Musidorus gently rebukes Pyrocles for giving himself up to solitariness, "the slye enimie, that doth most separate a man from well doing,"[17] Pyrocles replies:

Doth not the pleasauntnes of this place carry in it selfe sufficient reward for any time lost in it? Do you not see how all things conspire together to make this country a heavenly dwelling? . . . Doth not the aire breath health, which the Birds (delightfull both to eare and eye) do dayly solemnize with the sweet consent of their voyces? Is not every *eccho* therof a perfect Musicke? and these fresh and delightful brookes how slowly they slide away, as loth to leave the

[16] *Life of Sir Philip Sidney*, ed. Nowell Smith, Oxford, 1907, pp. 11–13.
[17] *The Countesse of Pembrokes Arcadia*, in Sir Philip Sidney, *Works*, ed. Albert Feuillerat, Cambridge, 1912, 1, 55. All page references in the text are to this volume.

company of so many things united in perfection? and with how sweete a murmure they lament their forced departure? Certainelie, certainely, cosin, it must needes be that some Goddesse enhabiteth this Region, who is the soule of this soile: for neither is any, lesse then a Goddesse, worthie to be shrined in such a heap of pleasures: nor any lesse then a Goddesse, could have made it so perfect a plotte of the celestiall dwellings (p. 57).

The Tempest shows that these *topoi* can render valuable experiences:

> Where should this music be? I' th'air, or th'earth?
> It sounds no more; and sure it waits upon
> Some god o' th'island. Sitting on a bank,
> Weeping again the King my father's wrack,
> This music crept by me upon the waters,
> Allaying both their fury and my passion
> With its sweet air.   (1.2.387–393)

When Ariel's songs lead Ferdinand to Miranda, he says, "Most sure, the goddess / On whom these airs attend!" (1.2.421–422). These poetic extravagances are in the fullest sense true to human nature. Their truth to Ferdinand's feelings has a corresponding truth to the nature of Prospero's island and of Miranda: when Ferdinand addresses her, "O you wonder!" he is simply naming her. But Pyrocles' fine words merely mask—they can hardly be said to rationalize—what he himself feels to be a shameful desire. Musidorus considers the speech "an affected praising of the place," and he forces Pyrocles' secret from him with words that have a different force here than they do in the *Apology for Poetry:* "I think you will make me see, that the vigor of your witte can shew it selfe in any subject: or els you feede sometimes your solitarines with the conceites of the Poets, whose liberall pennes can as easilie travaile over mountaines, as molehils: and so like wel disposed men, set up every thing to the highest note; especially, when they put such words in the mouths of one of these fantasticall mind-infected people, that children and Musitians cal Lovers" (p. 58). The word "lover" strikes Pyrocles to the quick, and he appears "armed with the verie countenance of the poore prisoner at the barr, whose aunswere is nothing but guiltie" (p. 59). Sidney's metaphor shows that our witty awareness of the springs of Pyrocles' rhetoric is indeed a mode of judgment.

In the pastoral episode in Book VI, Spenser uses a point about

Calidore similar to Sidney's point about Pyrocles. When Melibee finishes praising "this lowly quiet life, which I inherite here" (6.9.25), Spenser says that Calidore is

> rapt with double rauishment,
> Both of his speach that wrought him great content,
> And also of the obiect of his vew [i.e. Pastorella],
> On which his hungry eye was alwayes bent.
>
> (6.9.26)

When Calidore himself goes on to praise the country life, Spenser says that he does so "to occasion meanes, to worke his mind, / And to insinuate his harts desire" (6.9.27). In the *Arcadia* this awareness is a judgment that undermines the validity of Pyrocles' speech, because the speech is reduced to its dramatic motivation. Spenser uses the dramatic point not to make a decision, but to complicate an issue that he presents in general terms. We assent to a great deal in Calidore's speech—his characterization of "this worlds gay showes" and "fortunes wrackfull yre, / Which tosseth states" (6.9.27). But by suggesting a selfish motive, Spenser brings out a problem in the knight's wish that

> th'heauens so much had graced mee,
> As graunt me liue in like condition;
> Or that my fortunes might transposed bee
> From pitch of higher place, vnto this low degree.
>
> (6.9.28)

Melibee rebukes the way men "the heauens of their fortunes fault accuse" (6.9.29), and says that each man must accept what is allotted him, because "it is the mynd, that maketh good or ill" (6.9.30). Calidore's selfishness has been silently changed from an individual dramatic motive to a mode of self-regard inherent in pastoralism—a sentimental longing for relief and simplicity. (Note too that in order to make this point, Spenser allows Melibee to directly contradict his representation, in 6.9.20–25, of country life as in itself better than the court.) As in the Cave of Mammon, the hero's stance is a function of general themes and issues, not of a continuous dramatic narration.

Hence the passage concludes not with a dramatic resolution, but with a metaphor that beautifully indicates the courtier's complex relation to the country:

> Since then in each mans self (said *Calidore*)
> It is, to fashion his owne lyfes estate,

Giue leaue awhyle, good father, in this shore
To rest my barcke, which hath bene beaten late
With stormes of fortune and tempestuous fate,
In seas of troubles and of toylesome paine,
That whether quite from them for to retrate
I shall resolue, or backe to turne againe,
I may here with your selfe some small repose obtaine.

(6.9.31)

In Melibee's speech, the truth that each man fashions his life takes the form of apothegms, which are not only dramatically appropriate to a rustic character, but which can also be regarded as the verbal equivalent to the dramatic assumption of rustic pastoral—that all men have the same simple needs. Calidore, on the other hand, uses a metaphor that expresses the nature of the courtier's life. Where before he simply repeated Melibee's speeches, he now shows that he has learned a deeper lesson of pastoral: knowledge of self is inseparable from knowing and accepting one's circumstances; a man's ability to "*fashion* his owne lyfes estate" comes precisely from recognizing what his life's estate is. The image of the ship in port suggests genuine rest, but does not deny that the courtier spends his life on the high seas. The conflict between active knighthood and pastoral retirement is thus presented in a way that shows the attractiveness of pastoral ease without therefore abandoning the problem of choosing between it and heroic action. But Spenser's interest is in the elements of the choice, not the choice itself. Whatever the hero's decision, the value of pastoral experience here lies in the understanding conveyed in the "small repose" of this stanza.

In these two passages, Spenser and Sidney are equally self-conscious and intelligent about the human implications of pastoral conventions. But Sidney fails to render the claims and interest of pastoral experience, because he identifies intelligence with judging. Judging is not simply moral judgment, but, to give it a broader sense, thinking that takes the form of a choice between clearly rendered alternatives. Sidney's treatment of his heroes' pastoralism is the result not of moral severity, pure and simple, but of a decisive analytic intelligence that is his greatest strength as a writer. Consider the song Musidorus sings when he disguises himself as a shepherd in order to woo Pamela:

Come shepheard's weedes, become your master's minde:
Yeld outward shew, what inward change he tryes:

293

Nor be abasht, since such a guest you finde,
Whose strongest hope in your weake comfort lyes.

Come shepheard's weedes, attend my woefull cryes:
Disuse your selves from sweete Menalcas' voice:
For other be those tunes which sorrow tyes,
From those cleere notes which freely may rejoyce.
      Then power out plaint, and in one word say this:
      Helples his plaint, who spoyles himselfe of blisse.[18]

As David Kalstone has said, "The pressure of judgment touches even the slightest lyrics"; he points out that Musidorus' self-reproach makes this lament very different from the ordinary shepherd's "innocent surprise at the pains of love."[19] And judging in the broad, as well as the narrow, sense accounts for the impoverishment of pastoral experience in this lyric and elsewhere in the *Arcadia*.

The distinction Musidorus makes between his singing and Menalcas' is based on the general distinction between courtier and shepherd that we saw in Spenser. But the analytic clarity and decisiveness of Sidney's mind turns it into a rigid compartmentalization of pastoral experiences. When Pyrocles is telling Musidorus about his taking on the disguise of an Amazon, he says: "For after I had runne over the whole petigree of my thoughts, I gave my selfe to sing a little, which as you know I ever delighted in, so now especially, whether it be the nature of this clime to stir up Poeticall fancies, or rather as I thinke, of love; whose scope being pleasure, will not so much as utter his griefes, but in some forme of pleasure" (p. 86). The end of the sentence suggests the intimate relation between love and "Poeticall fancies" that normally gives one kind of pastoral experience its peculiar potentiality for human enrichment. But it is the analytic mode of the first half of the sentence that prevails in the *Arcadia*. On the one hand, Sidney scarcely mentions the role of love when he tells us that the Arcadians are natural poets.[20] On the other hand, poetry is provoked in Pyrocles and Musidorus by the pricks of desire alone, and

---

[18] *Ibid.*, p. 113. The text of this poem is taken from *The Poems of Sir Philip Sidney*, ed. William A. Ringler, Jr., Oxford, 1962, p. 13.

[19] *Sidney's Poetry*, Cambridge, Mass., 1965, pp. 52–53. See pp. 53–59 for a comparison of Sidney and Spenser that parallels the comparisons made here.

[20] Kalander says, "Ordinary it is among the meanest sorte, to make Songes and Dialogues in meeter, either love whetting their braine, or long peace having begun it" (p. 28), but the alternatives here are not held in even balance. The rest of this passage and the earlier description of Arcadia (pp. 13–14) make it clear, as the next sentence says, that "ease [is] the Nurse of Poetrie."

not at all by "the nature of this clime." Real pastoral song and the experience of love are brought together only in the eclogues that are set off from the narrative, and even there, Kalstone points out, there is a "sharp distinction between courtiers and shepherds."[21] The only characters who are genuinely enriched by a pastoral experience of love, Strephon and Claius, are meticulously kept distinct from everyone else in the book. The special character of their fate and history is indicated by the mythic terms in which their love for Urania is narrated (pp. 5–6); so far are they from being typical shepherds that they scorn mere rustics (p. 6), and their love has caused them to *leave* Arcadia and its "sweete life" (p. 14). Kalander's aristocratic condescension to their claim that love, not desire for knowledge, has improved their minds (p. 27) indicates that their experience is not held out as a serious possibility for Musidorus and Pyrocles.

With the humiliating transformations of Sidney's heroes into an Amazon and a shepherd, compare the transformation of Calidore when Pastorella scorns his courtly manners:

> Which *Calidore* perceiuing, thought it best
> To chaunge the manner of his loftie looke;
> And doffing his bright armes, himselfe addrest
> In shepheards weed, and in his hand he tooke,
> In stead of steelehead speare, a shepheards hooke,
> That who had seene him then, would haue bethought
> On *Phrygian Paris* by *Plexippus* brooke,
> When he the loue of fayre *Oenone* sought,
> What time the golden apple was vnto him brought.
>
> (6.9.36)

In its use of pastoral values and the myth of Paris, Spenser's stanzas reveal the same kind of self-conscious and witty understanding of poetic materials that we find in Sidney. It is not simply that Spenser brings out the context of Calidore's behavior by comparing him to Paris just before he made the decision that brought on the Trojan War and with it a world of heroic action. There is wit too in the fact that Calidore's act of "doffing his bright armes" produces not a contrasting appearance of rustic humility—hinted by "shepheards weed" —but a glamorous form of pastoralism that concludes with an appeal, in the physical attractiveness of the golden apple and the heroic context it evokes, to the kinds of feeling aroused by the "bright armes" that have been cast off. But Spenser is quite unlike Sidney in

[21] *Sidney's Poetry*, p. 65.

that he is not moved to make any one of the perspectives that wit provides here decisive against the others. The Paris simile is full of irony, but it does not provide us with a definite structure of judgment. The image of Paris in his state of innocence has a genuine value for us and holds our imaginations. The sign of this in the simile itself is the straightforward freshness with which the pastoral action is described. But the major indication that we are to have our pastoralism both ways here, yielding to its claims and powers and yet acknowledging its limitations, is the pivotal line of the stanza, "In stead of steele-head speare, a shepheards hooke." Spenser sees the general phenomenon of the warrior turned shepherd for love under the aspect of the most august pastoral *topos* in our literature: "They shall breake theyr swerdes also into mattockes, and theyr speares to make sythes. And one people shall not lyft vp weapen against another, neyther shal they learne to fyght from thens forth" (Isaiah 2:4). Spenser is not concerned to make us judge favorably the dramatic motive indicated at the beginning of the stanza: it is precisely this mode of thinking that forces Sidney into his continual discriminations and distinctions. The dramatic action is simply a taking off point for Spenser to show us all the human truths implied in the transformation of the hero by pastoral experience.

If we turn our attention from the mind and temperament implied here to the means by which they are conveyed, we see that what enables Spenser to have his cake and eat it is the additive progression of his verse that is the result of his ways with syntax and his formulaic sense of language. Each line in this stanza—most importantly the fifth and ninth—brings to light values, truths, and cultural memories, without requiring, or even allowing, one to predominate over or structure the others. It is impossible to read the verse that way; we simply take in each line as it comes. As with the lines, so with the stanzas: we are next shown Calidore's transformation under the aspect of genuine rusticity (6.9.37). In the *Arcadia,* on the other hand, where the prose is grounded on logical and rhetorical oppositions and discriminations, the versions of pastoral that Spenser's inclusive mind and methods bring together so richly remain separated and mutually exclusive.

II

While we have been examining the mind of the poet (and hence of the reader) and the relation of its behavior to action, we have found ourselves observing again that dramatic action is not depicted within

The Faerie Queene. It is not surprising that Spenser does not think of his characters' moral situations as dramatic, when his own moral understanding has so little analogy to the operation of the mind in action. We have seen numerous instances in which potentially dramatic narration is transmuted by Spenser's verse into the statement and examination of a general theme or issue. This phenomenon is part of what we mean when we call *The Faerie Queene* allegorical. But although we are well acquainted with the fact itself, it will be worth our while to inquire into the relation between dramatic action within the poem and the moral insights the poem conveys. We have already seen enough to recognize that lack of dramatic narration is a source of poetic strength for Spenser. One of the reasons Sidney compartmentalizes pastoral experiences is that his imagination is thoroughly dramatic: he assumes that different men, with different stations in society and roles to play, and with different temperaments, histories, and relations with other people, cannot have "the same" experience. By contrast, Spenser is able to bring together the realms of Pyrocles and Musidorus, on the one hand, and Strephon and Claius, on the other, because he does not assume that the human reality and value of Calidore's vision of the Graces is determined by Calidore's dramatic relation to it. Although Calidore causes the Graces to disperse, the vision itself is in the world of Colin Clout. Spenser's verse enables us to conflate the hero's and the poet's pastoral experience, although, as the rest of the episode makes clear, the two men dramatically belong to different realms.

Now let us turn the question around and ask what is the effect on Spenser's poetry when he attempts to write dramatically. The pastoral passages we have already discussed are followed by an account of the jealousy of Coridon, Pastorella's rustic suitor, and Calidore's magnanimous treatment of him (6.9.38–46). Where Spenser's moral interest in the passages about Melibee and Pastorella lies in revealing what is challenging and rich in pastoral experience, his purpose here is to present Calidore as a model of courteous behavior, and he can show us little more than his hero's patronizing condescension to a rustic lout. The passage is genuinely shallow, in ways that are most apparent when the shepherds hold wrestling games and Coridon challenges Calidore in hopes that he will "worke his foe great shame" (6.9.43):

> But *Calidore* he greatly did mistake;
> For he was strong and mightily stiffe pight,

That with one fall his necke he almost brake,
And had he not vpon him fallen light,
His dearest ioynt he sure had broken quight.
Then was the oaken crowne by *Pastorell*
Giuen to *Calidore,* as his due right;
But he, that did in courtesie excell,
Gaue it to *Coridon,* and said he wonne it well.

(6.9.44)

One can agree that a courteous man acknowledges the worth of a defeated opponent, and still object to the direct conflict between Calidore's resounding victory and his saying that Coridon won the garland well. A passage in *The Courtier* shows that we are right to feel that this stanza strikes a false note. Federico Fregoso, the most narrow-minded and legalistic member of the company gathered at the court of Urbino, is discussing the courtier's public appearances:

> After this, he ought to have a great consideration in presence of whome hee sheweth him selfe, and who be his matches. For it were not meet that a gentleman should be present in person and a doer in such a matter in the countrey, where the lookers on and the doers were of a base sorte.
>
> Then said the Lorde Gasper Pallavicin. In our countrey of Lumbardy these matters are not passed upon, for you shall see the yong gentleman upon the holy dayes come daunce all the day long in the sunne with them of the countrey, and passe the time with them in casting the barre, in wrastling, running and leaping. And I believe it is not ill done. For no comparison is there made of noblenesse of birth, but of force and sleight, in which thinges many times the men of the countrey are not a whit inferiour to gentlemen, and it seemeth this familiar conversation conteyneth in it a certaine lovely freenesse.
>
> This dauncing in the sunne, answered Sir Fredericke, can I in no case away with all: and I can not see what a man shall gaine by it.
>
> But who so will wrastle, runne and leape with men of the countrey, ought (in my judgement) to doe it after a sorte: to prove himselfe and (as they are wont to say) for courtisie, not to try maistry with them: and a man ought (in a manner) to be assured to get the upper hand, else let him not meddle withall, for it is too ill a sight and too foule a matter and without estimation, to see a gentleman overcome by a carter, and especially in wrastling.

Therefore I believe it is well done to abstaine from it, at the least wise in presence of many, because if hee overcome his gaine is small, and his losse in being overcome very great.[22]

Spenser wants to have it both ways. There is not the slightest doubt that Calidore will win, but Spenser still would like us to believe that his behavior exemplifies the "certaine lovely freenesse" that depends precisely on the willingness to risk defeat. When it comes to real action, one cannot have one's cake and eat it. The peculiar Spenserian relationship to the complexity and truth of the great commonplaces about man's existence makes for mere simplemindedness in relation to dramatic action.

Spenser has a radical inability to render dramatic action and to express the importance and interest of moral issues by its means. (This is not to say that he would not have been alive to the moral interest and importance of actions in real life and in other works. He was an excellent reader of *Orlando Furioso* and, one presumes, of the *Arcadia,* but he could have written neither.) The fact that dramatic action is inherent in the subjects of the last three books of *The Faerie Queene* is the fundamental reason that they are more uneven than the first three. It is commonly recognized that the weaknesses of Book V are due to its subject, but the reasons are ones essential to the whole poem. Consider Artegall's encounter with the egalitarian giant (5.2.29–54), which modern readers often find distasteful. Spenserians usually defend this episode on the grounds that Spenser's notions of justice and political equity were different from ours. But the modern reader is perfectly capable of appreciating these ideas, as he does when he reads Shakespeare's histories, even if he disagrees with them. Any reader who sees what is valuable elsewhere in *The Faerie Queene* will feel the gravity and justness of Artegall's reply to the giant:

> Likewise the earth is not augmented more,
> By all that dying into it doe fade.
> For of the earth they formed were of yore,
> How euer gay their blossome or their blade
> Doe flourish now, they into dust shall vade.
> What wrong then is it, if that when they die,
> They turne to that, whereof they first were made?

---

[22] Baldassare Castiglione, *The Book of the Courtier,* tr. Sir Thomas Hoby, London: Everyman's Library, 1928, pp. 97–98.

All in the powre of their great Maker lie:
All creatures must obey the voice of the most hie.

They liue, they die, like as he doth ordaine,
Ne euer any asketh reason why.
The hils doe not the lowly dales disdaine;
The dales doe not the lofty hils enuy.
He maketh Kings to sit in souerainty;
He maketh subiects to their powre obay;
He pulleth downe, he setteth vp on hy;
He giues to this, from that he takes away.
For all we haue is his: what he list doe, he may.

(5.2.40–41)

Artegall's argument is directed not to the value of social hierarchy (as is Ulysses' in *Troilus and Cressida*), but to accepting one's lot, on the grounds that man is mortal and cannot presume to control his destiny. No doubt these sentiments could have been used, as they are to this very day, simply to justify the possession of wealth and power by those who have them. But these stanzas cannot be accused of such shallowness or dishonesty, because Spenser in no way suggests that princes and noblemen are exempt from the common lot: "How euer gay their blossome or their blade / Doe flourish now, they into dust shall vade." The point is unequivocally put in political and social terms when "He maketh Kings to sit in souerainty," which everyone expects to find here, is balanced by "He pulleth downe, he setteth vp on hy." The gravity, scope, and poise of these stanzas entirely justify Spenser's having Artegall continue his challenge to the giant with an argument modeled on God's challenge to Job (5.2.42–43; cf. Job 38 and 2 Esdras 4).

The problem in this episode is not the basic political assumptions, but their poetic manifestations. What the modern reader rightly objects to is the conclusion of the episode, in which Talus sends the giant crashing down the cliff and disperses the mob with his flail (5.2.49–54). The verse here is disturbing, because Spenser seems to expect us to relish the violence and fearfulness of Talus' power. The limitations of the poetry here, the loss of the complexity and poise of understanding found in Artegall's speech, come from the fact that political attitudes are now being expressed as action. Not only is the purely physical action of Talus presented as the resolution of the moral situation. We also see Artegall discriminating and choosing paths of ac-

300

tion, in a manner that is frequent in the *Arcadia,* but rare in *The Faerie Queene:*

> Which lawlesse multitude him comming too
> In warlike wise, when *Artegall* did vew,
> He much was troubled, ne wist what to doo.
> For loth he was his noble hands t'embrew
> In the base blood of such a rascall crew;
> And otherwise, if that he should retire,
> He fear'd least they with shame would him pursew.
> Therefore he *Talus* to them sent, t'inquire
> The cause of their array, and truce for to desire.
>
> (5.2.52)

We can agree that here, as elsewhere in Book V, there are personal reasons for the failure of Spenser's poetry. Lewis says, not without justice, "Spenser was the instrument of a detestable policy in Ireland, and in his fifth book the wickedness he had shared begins to corrupt his imagination."[23] We may prefer to think that Spenser had good cause to fear and resent the mob or that real public action, the fact or the idea, released untamed aggressions in him, as in many men; nevertheless, we should agree with Lewis that "to explain by causes is not to justify by reasons."[24] But we find failures similar to those in the episode with the giant, even when the subject of justice does not bring out Spenser's personal relation to political reality. When Britomart rescues Artegall, two stanzas render wonderfully the dismay caused by "that lothly vncouth sight, / Of men disguiz'd in womanishe attire" (5.7.37):

> Not so great wonder and astonishment,
> Did the most chast *Penelope* possesse,
> To see her Lord, that was reported drent,
> And dead long since in dolorous distresse,
> Come home to her in piteous wretchednesse,
> After long trauell of full twenty yeares,
> That she knew not his fauours likelynesse,
> For many scarres and many hoary heares,
> But stood long staring on him, mongst vncertaine
>   feares.
>
> Ah my deare Lord, what sight is this (quoth she)

---

[23] *The Allegory of Love,* p. 349.
[24] *Ibid.,* p. 321.

What May-game hath misfortune made of you?
Where is that dreadfull manly looke? where be
Those mighty palmes, the which ye wont t'embrew
In bloud of Kings, and great hoastes to subdew?
Could ought on earth so wondrous change haue wrought,
As to haue robde you of that manly hew?
Could so great courage stouped haue to ought?
Then farewell fleshly force; I see thy pride is nought.

(5.7.39–40)

These stanzas are distinguished first by their grandeur—their just representation of heroic toil and accomplishment and hence their grasp of the transformation wrought in the hero—and second by their holding in poise the conflicting evaluations that Spenser has suggested to us throughout the episode—that Artegall's predicament is either an abandoning or a product of his nobility (cf. 5.5.17, 20, 23, 26, 56; 6.1, 2). (The balance is struck so well here, because the Ulysses simile, which suggests that the whole process has been a heroic endeavor, represents the hero as humiliated, while Britomart's speech, which verges on reproach, continually reminds us of Artegall's prowess.) But the stanzas are also notable for their indication of Britomart's situation and behavior, and the reader may well ask why we do not call them dramatic.

Clearly the stanzas use the dramatic situation, but they do not bear or reward inspection as a rendering of dramatic action. Part of the brilliance of the comparison of Britomart to Penelope is that it counteracts what is suggested by the narrative action—Britomart's angry and impatient campaign to free her lover from another woman—and presents Britomart's faithfulness under the aspect of domesticity and patience. Spenser splendidly renders Britomart's tone of voice in the first two lines of her speech; but the mimetic interest decreases as the stanza progresses, and the last line expresses a sentiment that is quite out of character. These stanzas are concerned with the significance of the basic situation of these cantos—Artegall's surrendering himself, like Hercules (cf. 5.1.2, 5.5.24), to a woman. In their relation to the *immediate* situation, the dramatic action at this point, the stanzas are simply an interruption. In the preceding stanza, we are told that Britomart

then too well beleeu'd, that which tofore
Iealous suspect as true vntruely drad,

302

Which vaine conceipt now nourishing no more,
She sought with ruth to salue his sad misfortunes sore.

(5.7.38)

(Note how difficult it is to tell exactly what goes through Britomart's mind here.) Britomart's subsequent speech is full of love, but it expresses itself as dismay, and in no way can be regarded as an attempt "to salue his sad misfortunes sore." We do not find her acting on this purpose—that is, the action proper does not resume—until the stanza following her speech:

> Thenceforth she streight into a bowre him brought,
> And causd him those vncomely weedes vndight;
> And in their steede for other rayment sought,
> Whereof there was great store, and armors bright,
> Which had bene reft from many a noble Knight;
> Whom that proud Amazon subdewed had,
> Whilest Fortune fauourd her successe in fight,
> In which when as she him anew had clad,
> She was reuiu'd, and ioyd much in his semblance glad.

(5.7.41)

No reader of *The Faerie Queene* will object to the flat story-telling of the first half of the stanza. The faults here lie in what the dramatic mode does to the moral interest of the second half. Compare the use of Fortune as a moral tag here—the false goddess invoked to explain why the wicked are temporarily successful—with the truth and intelligence of "What May-game hath misfortune made of you?"—a line which by its metaphor suggests how a man is mocked by life, and by its tone how sad the spectacle is. And are we really to believe that Britomart, after all her jealousy, anger, and shame, is "reuiu'd" simply by Artegall's change of costume? Or that, as is implied, Artegall's "semblance glad" shows no sign that he has felt himself humiliated by Radigund or that he is ashamed in the sight of Britomart? The two preceding stanzas show that Spenser understood perfectly well what would go on between the two lovers in this situation, but he was incapable of rendering his insights as dramatic action. From the restoration of the right relation between the sexes, Spenser moves to the restoration of social and political order. But this rich and noble theme (consider *The Winter's Tale*) lies inert when he renders it as dramatic action:

303

So there a while they afterwards remained,
Him to refresh, and her late wounds to heale:
During which space she there as Princess rained,
And changing all that forme of common weale,
The liberty of women did repeale,
Which they had long vsurpt; and them restoring
To mens subiection, did true Iustice deale:
That all they as a Goddesse her adoring,
Her wisedome did admire, and hearkned to her loring.

(5.7.42)

The contradictions here—the princess who restores women to men's subiection and then is adored as a goddess—are annoying because they are presented in a dramatic mode: no one can fill, in so simply reported an action, the many roles given Britomart here. But in the Penelope simile and in Britomart's dream in Isis Church (5.7.15–16), such conflicting perspectives are used in ways that illuminate human character and relationships.

Spenser's inability to render moral awareness as dramatic action puts Guyon's much-debated destruction of the Bower of Bliss in its true light. The abundant critical discussion of this canto has been much hampered by the notion that we are simply to decide, *tout court*, whether the Bower of Bliss is good or bad. The main burden of Lewis' celebrated discussion is to point out "danger signals"[25] and to attach hostile moral labels—as when he vulgarly renames the bathing girls Cissie and Flossie, and dismisses the reader's fascination with the metal ivy on the fountain as showing a lamentable taste for "metal vegetation as a garden ornament."[26] But in seeking to justify Spenser on such grounds, Lewis was unjust both to Spenser and to his own best insights. When we read about the Bower of Bliss, our interest is not in rendering a moral judgment, but in the depth and quality of our moral understanding. Consider the climax of the passage in which Acrasia is revealed to us, the description of Verdant sleeping on her lap:

The young man sleeping by her, seemd to bee
Some goodly swayne of honorable place,
That certes it great pittie was to see
Him his nobilitie so foule deface;
A sweet regard, and amiable grace,

25 *Ibid.*, p. 332.
26 *Ibid.*, p. 325. See above, pp. 45–46.

Mixed with manly sternnesse did appeare
Yet sleeping, in his well proportiond face,
And on his tender lips the downy heare
Did now but freshly spring, and silken blossomes beare.

His warlike armes, the idle instruments
Of sleeping praise, were hong vpon a tree,
And his braue shield, full of old moniments,
Was fowly ra'st, that none the signes might see;
Ne for them, ne for honour cared hee,
Ne ought, that did to his aduauncement tend,
But in lewd loues, and wastfull luxuree,
His dayes, his goods, his bodie he did spend:
O horrible enchantment, that him so did blend.

(2.12.79–80)

These stanzas are the fullest explicit expression of Spenser's moral intelligence in the canto. Because they are concerned with displaying and understanding what Verdant has done to himself—and not simply with deciding whether it was good or bad—all the moral terms retain meanings that point to the human realities that both cause and make regrettable this waste of budding youth. "Idle instruments" and "sleeping praise" are only the simplest and most obvious of these phrases. What is truly remarkable is the way these stanzas, in their nondramatic mode, keep in touch with dramatic realities. The second half of the first stanza gives literal truth to "Him his nobilitie so foule deface." When we heed the social realities and obligations indicated by "honorable place," "honour," and "aduauncement," we recognize that the full meanings of "lewd," "wastfull," and "spend" express the same concrete sense of human loss in moral abandonment that is expressed by the similar double meanings in Shakespeare's line, "The expence of spirit in a waste of shame." The understanding registered in the final exclamation is firm and unambiguous in point of moral judgment, yet it in no way denies the hold the Bower of Bliss has had on us as readers or could have on us as men.

Now compare Guyon's destruction of the Bower:

But all those pleasant bowres and Pallace braue,
Guyon broke downe, with rigour pittilesse;
Ne ought their goodly workmanship might saue
Them from the tempest of his wrathfulnesse,
But that their blisse he turn'd to balefulnesse:
Their groues he feld, their gardins did deface,

Their arbers spoyle, their Cabinets suppresse,
Their banket houses burne, their buildings race,
And of the fairest late, now made the fowlest place.

(2.12.83)

Instead of the complex and poised intelligence that we find three stanzas earlier, we have the simple destructiveness of Guyon's "rigour pittilesse" (compare the use of "deface" in this stanza). We cannot argue that Spenser means to characterize Guyon in a way that will allow us to "place" him as a moral intelligence: two stanzas later he says that the men transformed to beasts show, in a fine phrase, the "mournefull meed of ioyes delicious," and the sadness of the spectacle prompts him to ask that they "returned be vnto their former state" (2.12.85). It is only in this stanza, when moral awareness manifests itself as action, that we find something disturbing in Spenser's evaluation of the Bower of Bliss. This is not to say that the narrative necessity for rendering an action explains away what is disturbing here—the vindictive hostility that has prompted many critics to speak of this stanza as a moralistic revulsion against the Bower of Bliss. It is surely not surprising that a man who has written a canto like this has a complex and indeed ambivalent relation to the phenomena he has brought to life. But through the whole magnificent canto, it is only when he renders action that Spenser's moral intelligence loses its clarity and poise, and that we feel, to return to the problem of which Sidney reminded us, that he is wanting in self-knowledge.

Of all the parts of *The Faerie Queene,* Book VI is most radically affected by Spenser's inability to render dramatic action. There is, as Lewis points out,[27] a great deal of plain story-telling in this book, and the reason is to be found in the subject. Spenser by no means identifies courtesy with external forms of behavior, and he pays much attention to the inner conditions that produce right behavior. But courtesy is not wholly an inner condition: unlike (for example) temperance, it does not exist apart from specific external acts and ways of behaving. The necessity of depicting actions for their own sake impoverishes Spenser's poetry in almost every canto of Book VI and makes it distinctly inferior to each of the first three books of *The Faerie Queene.* Justifying this judgment would require a much fuller examination of Book VI than we have space for here, and my interest is in establishing what makes for the poetic strengths of *The Faerie Queene* wherever they occur. But I think that the passages discussed

[27] *The Allegory of Love,* p. 353.

in the following pages are representative of Book VI, and that our memories of Calidore's stay among the shepherds and the vision of the Graces on Mount Acidale should not blind us to the weaknesses that appear throughout the other cantos of the book.

In one of the best known episodes in Book VI, a savage man rescues Serena and Calepine from the villainous Sir Turpine and tends their wounds in his den in the woods. Readers remember the episode because it is a truly affecting story, but the story gains very little from being turned into Spenserian verse. When Sir Turpine runs away, Serena fears she is in as great danger from the savage:

> But the wyld man, contrarie to her feare,
> Came to her creeping like a fawning hound,
> And by rude tokens made to her appeare
> His deepe compassion of her dolefull stound,
> Kissing his hands, and crouching to the ground;
> For other language had he none nor speach,
> But a soft murmure, and confused sound
> Of senselesse words, which nature did him teach,
> T'expresse his passions, which his reason did empeach.
>
> (6.4.11)[28]

This stanza unquestionably presents one of the "sweet images of humility" that Lewis considered to be a hallmark of Book VI.[29] But its interest is purely narrative: in the context in which it appears, we are concerned to know only whether the savage will harm Serena or feel pity for her. Hence the account of his soft murmuring is, by Spenserian standards, rather facile and sentimental. Our tender feelings for a less than human creature are fully evoked, but the savage's subhumanity in no way complicates the validity or pertinence of his compassion, in the way the satyrs' simplicity, which makes their worship of Una so right and attractive, limits its validity and pertinence as a rendering of our love of Una.

If the only point of interest belongs to pure story, it is not surprising that Spenser's verse is unable to generate the unfolding complications that characterize the passages written in his natural, rhetorical mode. There is no doubt that the issue here is simply whether the

[28] "Fawning" (line 2) means "to show delight or fondness" when used of an animal (*OED* 1) and suggests servility and the like only when used of human beings. Spenser uses it in a favorable sense of subhuman creatures like the savage, Una's lion (1.3.6), and the satyrs (1.6.12, where there is a contrast with Sansloy's "fawning wordes," 1.6.4).

[29] *The Allegory of Love*, p. 352.

savage, the "natural" man, will react like a good man or a bad man. The first two stanzas of the canto are full of the moral labeling that Spenser is often, but wrongly, thought to be engaged in whenever he uses moral or abstract terms. Turpine is called "that faytour bold" and "this most discourteous crauen"; Calepine is "this most courteous knight" and "the gentle *Calepine*"; Serena is said to be "in pitifull affright" and she emits a "loud and piteous shright." When the savage arrives in the next stanza, all the moral terms are fixed:

> The saluage man, that neuer till this houre
> Did taste of pittie, neither gentlesse knew,
> Seeing his sharpe assault and cruell stoure
> Was much emmoued at his perils vew,
> That euen his ruder hart began to rew,
> And feele compassion of his euill plight.
>
> (6.4.3)

The point is simple: even the savage feels compassion, and that is all that is needed to resolve this moral situation (it is all that was needed to make Turpine behave rightly to Calepine and Serena in the first place; see 6.3.31–34, 41, 43). Hence it is not surprising that the heart of the stanza in which the savage creeps to Serena simply repeats the last lines quoted here: "And by rude tokens made to her appeare / His deepe compassion of her dolefull stound" (6.4.11).

Compare the rendering of a similar moment in Book I, when the lion "forgat his furious forse" (1.3.5) at the sight of Una:

> In stead thereof he kist her wearie feet,
> And lickt her lilly hands with fawning tong,
> As he her wronged innocence did weet.
> O how can beautie maister the most strong,
> And simple truth subdue auenging wrong?
> Whose yeelded pride and proud submission,
> Still dreading death, when she had marked long,
> Her hart gan melt in great compassion,
> And drizling teares did shed for pure affection.
>
> (1.3.6)

Although the story by itself makes a similar point—the beast reacts more truly to Una than the man who has deserted her—this stanza engages us more fully and complexly than its analogue in Book VI. The speaker's wonder in lines 4 and 5 encompasses both the directness and spontaneity with which one naturally responds to Una and dismay at the fact that beauty and simple truth have been of no avail to her. The rhetorical question points not to a simple division of good and bad, but to the paradox that provokes Spenser's lament for Una in the first three stanzas of the canto: we feel Una's power over us, and yet she is now "Forsaken, wofull, solitarie mayd / Farre from all peoples prease, as in exile" (1.3.3). The stanza beautifully renders the puzzles about human nature that underlie (and are in turn, through Spenser's verse, expressed by) this narrative situation. Even the "as" in line 3 makes its force felt. Unlike the lion, we do know Una's "wronged innocence": the epithets in "wearie feet" and "lilly hands" have just evoked the main elements in the pathos of her situation—her unflagging devotion and her beauty.

The next lines give direct expression to our desire to love Una simply and directly. Yet their force is due to the presence of other elements in our nature that are acknowledged in the phrase "maister the most strong." The paradox latent here emerges in line 6. "Yeelded pride" can be regarded as direct narration and is consonant with the simple tenderness of the first three lines. But "proud submission" is an explicit paradox, and one which indicates a dignity and strength in man's nature. A proud submission is a knowing one: the "as" in line 3 rebukes us, but it also makes clear that the lion's pastoral simplicity, like that of the satyrs later, has its full value only when it becomes a human reality. The disparity between the real lion and what his strength can stand for in man's nature is the basis of Una's lament in the next stanza:

> The Lyon Lord of euery beast in field,
> Quoth she, his princely puissance doth abate,
> And mightie proud to humble weake does yield,
> Forgetfull of the hungry rage, which late
> Him prickt, in pittie of my sad estate:
> But he my Lyon, and my noble Lord,
> How does he find in cruell hart to hate
> Her that him lou'd, and euer most adord,
> As the God of my life? why hath he me abhord?
>
> (1.3.7)

The issues here are not limited to narrative action. The terms in which Una speaks of the lion and of the knight bring to full life issues broached in the preceding stanza—the relations between humility and strength, service and lordship.

These passages from Books I and VI indicate some important general distinctions. In the episode from Book VI, moral issues are limited to those that can be expressed by narrative action. (Observe that this fact in no way contradicts the fact that the episode makes a general point—that man naturally feels pity at the distress of others.) By contrast, the episode in Book I is concerned with realities of feeling and attitude rather than of behavior—with the way a man responds to beauty and purity and the relation of his response to the whole of his moral and emotional nature. Spenser is of course concerned with the savage's response to Serena, but only insofar as it is a right reaction and leads to right behavior. He does not exploit the truths or problems about nature, reason, and passion that seem to come to the surface of the poem in the lines about the savage's attempts at speech. Instead, the next stanza (6.4.12) tells us that having seen Calepine's wound and making "great mone after his saluage mood," the savage runs off to the woods to pick an herb that he knows has healing powers.

In the episode in Book I, our response to Una is put in the context not of right action, but of man's response to beauty. When Una takes off her veil,

> her angels face
> As the great eye of heauen shyned bright,
> And made a sunshine in the shadie place;
> Did neuer mortall eye behold such heauenly grace.
>
> (1.3.4)

Taken literally, these lines register the inaccessibility to mortal man of the vision of heavenly truth: Una wears her veil in mourning for her parents' captivity in Eden, and when she takes it off here she is "in secret shadow, farre from all mens sight" (1.3.4). Yet in another sense, these lines are a praise of female beauty, and Spenser would regard this too as a literal meaning—both because of Neoplatonic accounts of earthly beauty and because of the authority of witness and usage that lies behind these conventional formulas. From this point of view, Una's beauty is accessible to our love, and the first stanza of the canto shows that Spenser means us to see this sense of the words:

> I, whether lately through her [beauty's]
> brightnesse blind,
> Or through alleageance and fast fealtie,
> Which I do owe vnto all woman kind,

310

Feele my heart perst with so great agonie,
When such I see, that all for pittie I could die.

(1.3.1)

The formulas that describe Una's beauty have the characteristic Spenserian lucidity and poise: we cannot separate the meanings and give them a structured relation to each other. In encompassing both meanings, we bring to life the psychological realities that underlie our interest in the pastoral figure of the lion: we both can and cannot take on this simplicity. Our relation to Una is not identical with the lover's relation to a woman's beauty, but that is the aspect under which, in this episode, we see Una and the Red Cross Knight's abandonment of her. In other words, we see the moral situation as a version of a permanent psychological or spiritual condition and not, as in Book VI, as a dramatic situation that calls for one or another kind of reaction and action. Even the psychological phenomena that can lead to action—such as the humble obedience to the mistress—are here presented as internal experiences and paradoxes.

Spenser's poetry has its characteristic excellences when it is rendering the realities of human psychology. By "psychology" I mean simply "what happens in the soul, in man's mind and feelings," and I wish to distinguish these realities from those of cosmology, eschatology, politics, society—all that belongs to an external world. We should observe that moral attitudes—evaluations of oneself and the world—are psychological phenomena, and that they are quite independent of specific external action when their terms are as general as they are in the Cave of Mammon or the Red Cross Knight's encounter with Contemplation. We can recognize that Spenser's concern is preponderatingly with psychological truths if we simply recall some of the most impressive and characteristic episodes of *The Faerie Queene*: first, episodes that are explicitly psychological—the battle with Error, the Cave of Despair, the story of Phedon, the transformation of Malbecco —and second, the great allegorical cores with their complex and exhaustive renderings of feelings and attitudes. Even the Garden of Adonis and the Mutability cantos are not cosmologies in the strict sense, though of course they use cosmological materials. The first is a myth about the naturalness of love, and the second is explicitly devoted not to describing change in the universe, but to understanding and coming to terms with it. (Hence the "antimasque" of Faunus and Molanna, in which the story of Actaeon and Diana is given a

311

benign, comic form, is as much a part of the affirmation in these cantos as Nature's cryptic assertion at the end.) In *The Faerie Queene,* the vision of things as they are is always subsumed by the rendering and exploration of the reader's feelings and attitudes. The episodes in which our interests are not ultimately psychological, like those based on historical materials, are the least interesting in the poem.

We can see Spenser's notion of psychological realities and our relation to them if we consider another point of contrast between the two episodes we have been comparing. A major shortcoming of the episode in Book VI is that it displays what Harry Berger, Jr. calls "the soap-opera morality of the poem conceived as a narrative of external actions."[30] Spenser, whose renderings of evil are among the triumphant successes of Books I and II, can find no interest in Sir Turpine beyond labeling him "a rude churle" (6.3.33), "vnknightly Knight" (6.3.35), and "this most discourteous crauen" (6.4.2), and his actions "fowle discourtesie, vnfit for Knight" (6.3.33), "vngentle" and "currish" (6.3.42, 43), and "vncomely for a knight" (6.4.8). In Book I, the verse occasioned by Turpine's analogue, Sansloy, is intelligent and interesting even in its ordinary moments. At the end of canto 3, Una is left at the mercy of Sansloy, who snatches her from the ass on which she rides:

> But her fierce seruant full of kingly awe
> And high disdaine, whenas his soueraine Dame
> So rudely handled by her foe he sawe,
> With gaping iawes full greedy at him came,
> And ramping on his shield, did weene the same
> Haue reft away with his sharpe rending clawes:
> But he was stout, and lust did now inflame
> His corage more, that from his griping pawes
> He hath his shield redeem'd, and foorth his swerd
>   he drawes.   (1.3.41)

This stanza repeats the formulas used to render the lion's initial rush towards Una (1.3.5) and his subsequent yielding to her; it is no mistake that Sansloy has grabbed her, "her visage to behold" (1.3.40). However, the interest of this stanza lies in transferring these formulas to the context of human heroism. The first two lines, which render the paradoxes and values of true chivalric heroism, give way to a view of heroism as martial strength, for which evil as well as noble feelings

---

[30] *The Allegorical Temper*, New Haven, 1957, p. 13.

can be a source of energy. We are not asked to judge the combatants or their actions (for the lion is as fierce as Sansloy), but to perceive the relation Spenser's formulas have to our knowledge of human nature and moral values, particularly as we know them in epic poetry.

In the next stanza, Spenser complicates the issues by rendering Sansloy's prowess in the dignified language that we associate with good warriors:

> O then too weake and feeble was the forse
> Of saluage beast, his puissance to withstand:
> For he was strong, and of so mightie corse,
> As euer wielded speare in warlike hand,
> And feates of armes did wisely vnderstand.
> Eftsoones he perced through his chaufed chest
> With thrilling point of deadly yron brand,
> And launcht his Lordly hart: with death opprest
> He roar'd aloud, whiles life forsooke his stubborne
>   brest.   (1.3.42)

This is genuine heroic combat, not the pitting of good against evil. Spenser is showing us the other side of the coin of Una's lament for "my Lyon, and my noble Lord." We desire to make the metaphor a human reality and take on the kingly beast's relation to Una. But there is something in human nature that makes becoming like a lion fearsome, not noble. In the next stanza, words that were used of the lion now render Sansloy's evil: not only do we hear of his desire for "raging spoile," but Una is his "yeelded pray" and he is now "Lord of the field" (1.3.43).

In responding to the language of heroic poetry in these stanzas, we acknowledge that Sansloy's evil is a potentiality of human nature. Neither the reader nor the characters are conceived dramatically here, so that we are not put in the position, as we are in Book VI, of saying, "I am or am not, ought or ought not to be, like that person." Our sense of and assumptions about ourselves here are like those found in another characteristically Elizabethan poem:

> I know my Bodi's of so fraile a kinde,
> As force without, feauers within can kill;
> I know the heauenly nature of my minde,
> But tis corrupted both in wit and will:
>
> I know my *Soule* hath power to know all things,
> Yet is she blind and ignorant in all;

313

I know I am one of *Natures* litle kings,
Yet to the least and vilest things am thrall.

I know my life's a paine, and but a span,
I know my *Sense* is mockt with euery thing;
And to conclude, I know myselfe a *Man,*
Which is a *proud* and yet a *wretched* thing.[31]

A man who thinks of himself this way would reject with horror the thought of behaving like Sansloy, yet he would agree that Sansloy expresses a reality of human nature, which the virtuous man therefore acknowledges to exist within himself. The acknowledgment of general truths as personal truths—which has a restricted and accessible form in Sir John Davies' sententious dignity—underlies the intelligence, poise, and humanity of *The Faerie Queene.* The passage we are examining—a perfectly ordinary stretch of verse and a valuable example for just that reason (also because it makes the comparison with Book VI relevant and fair)—has its life and interest precisely because in it "heroism" and "human nature" are general concepts. Spenser concludes the canto by depicting Una's ass following her and Sansloy in order "to be partaker of her wandering woe," just as we were at the beginning of the canto. Because Spenser assumes that the reader will find all the truths of man's nature within himself, he can encourage our tentative identification with the "seruile beast" without assuming, as he would in Book VI, that we are immune from the epigrammatic rebuke that concludes the canto—the statement that the ass is "more mild in beastly kind, then that her beastly foe" (1.3.44).

The treatment of evil characters is the most direct index we have of a poet's negative capability—the fullness with which he renders and understands the human reality of the situation or action he presents to us. It is difficult to define our relation to villain-heroes like Faustus, Macbeth, and Satan, but we would agree that their greatness as poetic creations involves our feeling some degree of identification with them, and that their creators achieve this by vitality of dramatic depiction.[32] This is not at all Spenser's way. Of course it is hard to imagine a poet wanting to bring Sir Turpine to dramatic life, but then there seems no reason to tell us over and over that he is a wretch: later in

---

[31] Sir John Davies, *Nosce Teipsum,* 1599.

[32] Some students of the English Renaissance, I suppose, would not agree with this. The best answer to them is Helen Gardner, "Milton's 'Satan' and the Theme of Damnation in Elizabethan Tragedy," *Essays and Studies,* 1 (1948), 46–66; reprinted in *Elizabethan Drama: Modern Essays in Criticism,* ed. R. J. Kaufmann, New York, 1961, pp. 320–341.

Book VI, Arthur goes on for three dreadful stanzas in this vein (6.6.33–35). As we would expect, Spenser establishes our kinship with an evil by directly appealing to us—by engaging some feeling or attitude that we acknowledge as ours. Everyone who does not have a critical case to argue agrees that we feel attracted to dangerous *loci amoeni* like the Red Cross Knight's fountain, Phaedria's island, and of course the Bower of Bliss. But the Bower of Bliss, though a representative example of Spenser's rendering of evil, can mislead us if we think that we experience its pleasures and temptations as dramatic realities. Throughout *The Faerie Queene,* our relation to evils is established in the way represented by the verses on Sansloy or the transformation of Malbecco—by language evoking feelings and attitudes that we acknowledge to be true of ourselves.

The frankest form this takes is the use of an aphoristic statement, one that covers all cases, to prevent us from judging the Red Cross Knight at the fountain or Artegall when he spares Radigund:

> At sight thereof his cruell minded hart
> Empierced was with pittifull regard,
> That his sharpe sword he threw from him apart,
> Cursing his hand that had that visage mard:
> No hand so cruell, nor no hart so hard,
> But ruth of beautie will it mollifie.
>
> (5.5.13)

Similarly the first stanza of Book I, canto 3 puts a new perspective on the Red Cross Knight's pitying Duessa and being blinded by her beauty in the preceding canto:

> Nought is there vnder heau'ns wide hollownesse,
> That moues more deare compassion of mind,
> Then beautie brought t'vnworthy wretchednesse
> Through enuies snares or fortunes freakes vnkind:
> I, whether lately through her brightnesse blind, [etc.]
>
> (1.3.1)

Very often the narrative situation gives rise, sometimes with no dramatic justification, to language that states or suggests values that we honor. The stanzas describing Sansloy are an example of this, and there is a particularly fine instance when the bathing girls in the Bower of Bliss, whom Lewis wants us to believe suggest sterility, are compared to Venus rising from "th' Oceans fruitfull froth" (2.12.65). At other times, frail or corrupt feelings and attitudes are attributed to

315

man in general, and for one reason or another we assent to their truthfulness. Thus we are told that the wandering islands that Guyon passes on his way to the Bower of Bliss "seemd so sweet and pleasant to the eye, / That it would tempt a man to touchen there" (2.12.14). The nature of our interest in the loveliest part of the description of the bathing girls—"their snowy limbes, as through a vele, / So through the Christall waues appeared plaine"—emerges in the next two lines: "Then suddeinly both would themselues vnhele, / And th'amarous sweet spoiles to greedy eyes reuele" (2.12.64).

Perhaps the most extraordinary use of these tactics is when Phaedria stops the battle between Guyon and Cymochles. Her appeal begins in her usual vein of self-indulgent charm, but it comes to resemble Spenser's argument in the proem to Book IV, and the image of Mars disarmed by love is one that Spenser himself uses in his invocation to Cupid at the beginning of the poem (1.Proem.3):

> Debatefull strife, and cruell enmitie
> The famous name of knighthood fowly shend;
> But louely peace, and gentle amitie,
> And in Amours the passing houres to spend,
> The mightie martiall hands doe most commend;
> Of loue they euer greater glory bore,
> Then of their armes: *Mars* is *Cupidoes* frend,
> And is for *Venus* loues renowmed more,
> Then all his wars and spoiles, the which he did of yore.
>
> (2.6.35)

The next stanza confirms the claim these words have on us:

> Therewith she sweetly smyld. They though full bent,
> To proue extremities of bloudie fight,
> Yet at her speach their rages gan relent,
> And calme the sea of their tempestuous spight,
> Such powre haue pleasing words: such is the might
> Of courteous clemencie in gentle hart.
>
> (2.6.36)

These stanzas are extraordinary both because of Spenser's willingness to ignore Phaedria's dramatic character and for the sureness with which he uses the verse that results. The lines last quoted register the full attractiveness of Phaedria and her realm; line 4 confirms the maxim that underlies the interest of the Idle Lake as an allegorical

316

image: "So easie is, t'appease the stormie wind / Of malice in the calme of pleasant womankind" (2.6.8).

These stanzas bring to life a distinction that perhaps struck us as mechanical and preacherly in its earlier dramatic form. When Phaedria flirts with Guyon in her boat,

> The knight was courteous, and did not forbeare
> Her honest merth and pleasaunce to partake;
> But when he saw her toy, and gibe, and geare,
> And passe the bonds of modest merimake,
> Her dalliance he despisd, and follies did forsake.
>
> (2.6.21)

Our responsiveness to the later stanzas not only acknowledges that there is something valuable and attractive which Phaedria's realm parodies, but also brings to life our own resources of "honest merth and pleasaunce," because of which we (like Guyon) do not feel genuinely tempted there. These resources come into full play in the comic conclusion of the episode. Guyon replies to Phaedria's courtesy with his own—"the Faery knight / Besought that Damzell suffer him depart" (2.6.36)—and we last see Phaedria experiencing pettish relief at his departure:

> She no lesse glad, then he desirous was
> Of his departure thence; for of her ioy
> And vaine delight she saw he light did pas,
> A foe of folly and immodest toy,
> Still solemne sad, or still disdainfull coy,
> Delighting all in armes and cruell warre,
> That her sweet peace and pleasures did annoy,
> Troubled with terrour and vnquiet iarre,
> That she well pleased was thence to amoue him farre.
>
> (2.6.37)

Our moral understanding is expressed by comedy here: the point that Guyon simply does not belong with Phaedria is made by showing what a nuisance he is to her. Spenser keeps in touch with Phaedria's point of view by repeating "she" and "her" and by making each line a separate accusation against Guyon. But the wit of the stanza also lies in its deployment of verbal formulas. Most of the lines mean one thing to Phaedria and another to Guyon and us, and there are fine shifts of perspective in the middle of the stanza, where the noblest representation of Guyon, one that grounds his heroism in delight, is preceded by Phaedria's most telling criticism of him.

The last example reminds us, as did the Red Cross Knight's encounter with Contemplation, that Spenser's poetry has many moments that are at least quasi-dramatic and that, more importantly, the moral understanding we find in *The Faerie Queene* involves dramatic awareness—a sympathetic and intelligent knowledge of the way men and women act. But Spenser is incapable of making dramatic action the mode of his poetry. When he has to represent dramatic action, as he does in Book VI, he cannot make it express the moral understanding he has of it. Consider the episode in which Calidore and Priscilla bring the wounded Aladine home to his father Aldus. After an entire stanza in which the old man laments, "Such is the weakenesse of all mortall hope; / So tickle is the state of earthly things" (6.3.5), we are told:

> So well and wisely did that good old Knight
> Temper his griefe, and turned it to cheare,
> To cheare his guests, whom he had stayd that night,
> And make their welcome to them well appeare:
> That to Sir *Calidore* was easie geare.
>
> (6.3.6)

Spenser makes it impossible to discriminate between the cheer (if it is that) that comes from wisely accepting grief and the cheer with which one greets one's guests. Where his normal practice in repeating words is to open up their different meanings, here he is constrained to ignore them and insist on their identity. He can only render by a pun the courteous behavior that gets its just dramatic presentation in the *Arcadia*. While Musidorus (calling himself Palladius) is a guest of Kalander, his host receives word that his son Clitophon has been captured by the rebelling helots. Kalander tells his servants "diligentlie to waite and attend upon *Palladius,* and to excuse his absence with some necessarie busines he had presentlie to dispatch" (p. 29). But Musidorus observes that something is wrong; upon his urging, Kalander's steward tells him of his master's passionate lamenting and concludes:

> Now sir (said he) this is my maisters nature, though his grief be such, as to live is a griefe unto him, and that even his reason is darkened with sorrow; yet the lawes of hospitality (long and holily observed by him) give still such a sway to his proceeding, that he

will no waie suffer the straunger lodged under his roofe, to receyve (as it were) any infection of his anguish, especially you, toward whom I know not whether his love, or admiration bee greater. But *Palladius* could scarce heare out his tale with patience: so was his hart torne in peeces with compassion of the case, liking of *Kalanders* noble behaviour, kindnesse for his respect to himwarde, and desire to finde some remedie (p. 30).

We find Kalander's behavior noble and worthy of emulation because it acknowledges the conflicting dramatic pressures of the situation in which he finds himself. By contrast, it is unrealistic and, on the face of it, insensitive, for Spenser to report approvingly that Aldus simply turned his grief—called, in the preceding stanza, "bale and bitter sorrowings"—into hospitality. And matters get worse as the stanza continues:

> But that faire Lady [Priscilla] would be cheard
>   for nought,
> But sigh'd and sorrow'd for her louer deare,
> And inly did afflict her pensiue thought,
> With thinking to what case her name should now be
>   brought.   (6.3.6)

Spenser is not being ironic about Priscilla's fears for her reputation: he praises Calidore for protecting it the next day (6.3.15–19). But he seems not to consider that the reader of this stanza will compare the sorrows of Aldus and Priscilla and wonder how we can take seriously the lady's inability to be cheered when the old man can "so well and wisely . . . temper his griefe." Conversely we might wonder how we can believe in the old man's cheerfulness, if potential loss of reputation is an affliction of the spirit. In any case, it is clear that when Spenser's poetry attempts or is constrained to be dramatic, it exhibits the "want of imaginative common sense" of which G. Wilson Knight accused it.[33]

I think we must attribute the failure of passages like this to Spenser's inability to render dramatic action, because the points, attitudes, and perceptions that he fails to convey persuasively in Book VI come to poetic life elsewhere in *The Faerie Queene,* when he is directly concerned with permanent realities of feeling and attitude. Spenser seems rather unthinking when he tells us, after explaining why Priscilla fears her loss of reputation,

[33] "The Spenserian Fluidity," in *The Burning Oracle,* London, 1939, p. 16.

> But *Calidore* with all good courtesie
> Fain'd her to frolicke, and to put away
> The pensiue fit of her melancholie;
> And that old Knight by all meanes did assay,
> To make them both as merry as he may.
>
> (6.3.9)

Might it not, we ask, be the mark of true courtesy to leave Priscilla alone with her melancholy?—the more so as the source of her concern is acknowledged by both her lover and Calidore to be genuine. And Aldus' pitching in to make everyone merry seems grotesque when we recall his lament four stanzas earlier. In failing to allow for the dramatic realities of the situation, Spenser makes himself appear didactic in the worst sense. He enjoins us to be cheerful to others, but shows no sense of the value of this rule—its place in relation to the claims of other human values, acts, feelings.

Yet in another context, it is clear that he does know how to value the courteous knight's attempt to cheer someone in grief. When Arthur meets Una,

> With louely court he gan her entertaine;
> But when he heard her answeres loth, he knew
> Some secret sorrow did her heart distraine:
> Which to allay, and calme her storming paine,
> Faire feeling words he wisely gan display,
> And for her humour fitting purpose faine,
> To tempt the cause it selfe for to bewray.
>
> (1.7.38)

In itself this is dramatic action, and the verse is undistinguished. But this stanza does not arouse the objections that we bring against analogous moments in Book VI, because our attention is not focused on a dramatic situation and the way to behave in it. The context of Arthur's courtesy is a contrast between two attitudes towards the value of earthly existence. As we have already noted,[34] the description of Arthur restores to the canto a sense of the worth and nobility of human achievement; it counteracts the sense of earthly vanity that gets its fullest statements in the portrayal of Orgoglio (1.7.8–18) and the drastic *contemptus mundi* of Una's lament for the Red Cross Knight (1.7.22–23). Arthur's tenderness to Una and his solicitude for her grief bear witness to the value of human life, but they are not ends

[34] Above, pp. 151–152.

in themselves. They support and enrich the examination of general attitudes with which Spenser is concerned:

> O but (quoth she) great griefe will not be tould,
> And can more easily be thought, then said.
> Right so; (quoth he) but he, that neuer would,
> Could neuer: will to might giues greatest aid.
> But griefe (quoth she) does greater grow displaid,
> If then it find not helpe, and breedes despaire.
> Despaire breedes not (quoth he) where faith is staid.
> No faith so fast (quoth she) but flesh does paire.
> Flesh may empaire (quoth he) but reason can repaire.
>
> (1.7.41)

In the aphoristic stichomythy of this stanza, Spenser is able to exploit Arthur's courteous manner and its significance, and we are persuaded, as we seldom are in Book VI, that

> His goodly reason, and well guided speach
> So deepe did settle in her gratious thought,
> That her perswaded to disclose the breach,
> Which loue and fortune in her heart had wrought.
>
> (1.7.42)

The exception in Book VI that proves the rule for *The Faerie Queene* is the episode in which the cannibals attempt to sacrifice Serena and Calepine rescues her. Here Spenser writes in the mode of the first three books, and the result is his most beautiful statement of the value of courteous behavior. The basis of the grim comedy with which the episode begins is that the cannibals' decision to sacrifice Serena to their god and to eat her "dainty flesh" (6.8.38) is a literalization of the lover's praise of his mistress:

> Some with their eyes the daintest morsels chose;
> Some praise her paps, some praise her lips and nose;
> Some whet their kniues, and strip their elboes bare.
>
> (6.8.39)

But the catalogue description of Serena turns the parody of lover's religion into the thing itself:

> Her yuorie necke, her alablaster brest,
> Her paps, which like white silken pillowes were,
> For loue in soft delight thereon to rest;

> Her tender sides, her bellie white and clere,
> Which like an Altar did it selfe vprere,
> To offer sacrifice diuine thereon;
> Her goodly thighes, whose glorie did appeare
> Like a triumphall Arch, and thereupon
> The spoiles of Princes hang'd, which were in battel won.
>
> (6.8.42)

Spenser makes his point explicit when he produces, from the sensu-ousness of the first four lines, an image of praise that exactly corre-sponds to what the cannibals mean to do. What, then, has happened to the distinctions that seem so firm in the preceding stanza?

> Now being naked, to their sordid eyes
> The goodly threasures of nature appeare:
> Which as they view with lustfull fantasyes,
> Each wisheth to him selfe, and to the rest enuyes.
>
> (6.8.41)

On the one hand, the description of Serena has made us engage in something akin to "lustfull fantasyes." And yet such verse is the proper way to celebrate "the goodly threasures of nature": it is as beautiful and compelling as anything in the Song of Songs. When we return to the narrative action, our relation to it has been transformed:

> Those daintie parts, the dearlings of delight,
> Which mote not be prophan'd of common eyes,
> Those villeins vew'd with loose lasciuious sight,
> And closely tempted with their craftie spyes;
> And some of them gan mongst themselues deuize,
> Thereof by force to take their beastly pleasure.
> But them the Priest rebuking, did aduize
> To dare not to pollute so sacred threasure,
> Vow'd to the gods: religion held euen theeues
>   in measure.   (6.8.43)

But our eyes too are "common": the image of the triumphal arch hung with spoils was a glamorous naming of Serena's "daintie parts." Hence though we reject the frank lustfulness of the villains in the middle of the stanza, we take on, for the moment, the role of the priest who guards "so sacred threasure."

The description of Serena is a perfect example of Spenser's verse. A set piece that could be dropped from the poem without disturbing the narrative action, it brings to life an august convention of western poetry, our assent to which ensures our participation in all the human realities that the narrative can potentially express: for just as the image of the altar is a version of what the cannibals are doing, so the arch hung with trophies gives a sanction and dignity to Calepine's "restlesse paines" and "endlesse toyles" (6.8.33, 47). It is in this context, when the poetry engages everything relevant that we know of ourselves, that Spenser best renders the moral values that we find throughout the Book of Courtesy. First he exploits the sheer narrative excitement of the sacrifice:

> To whom the Priest with naked armes full net
> Approching nigh, and murdrous knife well whet,
> Gan mutter close a certaine secret charme,
> With other diuelish ceremonies met:
> Which doen he gan aloft t'aduance his arme,
> Whereat they shouted all, and made a loud alarme.

> Then gan the bagpypes and the hornes to shrill,
> And shrieke aloud, that with the peoples voyce
> Confused, did the ayre with terror fill,
> And made the wood to tremble at the noyce:
> The whyles she wayld, the more they did reioyce.
>   (6.8.45–46)

The mixture of fascination, awe, dismay, and alarm make us imaginatively grasp the terrible joy of the last line, and we come to understand, better than we do in a dozen episodes with Turpine, the impulse that underlies his villainy. From this catharsis of sadism, Spenser suddenly shifts to the toiling and weary Sir Calepine, who, awakened by the cannibals' shouts, comes and disperses them. He then turns to succor his terrified beloved, whom he cannot see and recognize:

> From them returning to that Ladie backe,
> Whom by the Altar he doth sitting find,
> Yet fearing death, and next to death the lacke
> Of clothes to couer, what they ought by kind,
> He first her hands beginneth to vnbind;
> And then to question of her present woe;
> And afterwards to cheare with speaches kind.
> But she for nought that he could say or doe,
> One word durst speake, or answere him a whit thereto.
>   (6.8.50)

This stanza is so beautiful because all that has preceded makes us understand the value of Calepine's gentleness. Precisely because we have participated in "lustfull fantasyes," we recognize that his kindness is the right translation into action of the dignity conferred on the beloved by poetry like the description of Serena. The knight's obligation to fair ladies, so boringly insisted on as a rule of behavior throughout Book VI, here shows its human truth.

When the mode of his poetry is rhetorical, Spenser is able to do justice to a dramatic moment. This is most fully evident in the stanza that concludes the episode:

> So inward shame of her vncomely case
> She did conceiue, through care of womanhood,
> That though the night did couer her disgrace,
> Yet she in so vnwomanly a mood,
> Would not bewray the state in which she stood.
> So all that night to him vnknowen she past.
> But day, that doth discouer bad and good,
> Ensewing, made her knowen to him at last:
> The end whereof Ile keepe vntill another cast.

(6.8.51)

In the book of the poem that most puzzles over nature and fortune and that purports to depict, on the small scale of daily living and the large scale of a life's history, the ordinary realities of human life, it is a grand affirmation to have the simple rising of the sun reveal the lovers to each other. What is most moving is the character of the affirmation in the formula, "day, that doth discouer bad and good." There is no poetizing here—no attempt to render a dawn that would answer to the catalogue description of Serena's "goodly threasures of nature." This is the sun of the Sermon on the Mount: "That ye maye be the children of your father which is in heaven: for he maketh his sonne to aryse on the evell, and on the good, and sendeth rayne on the just and on the unjust" (Matt. 5:45). In concluding with it, Spenser not only reminds us of the context of actual human life in which courtesy is an important virtue; he enacts the moral by his solicitude for Serena. Serena's shame, like its medium, the night, is dispelled by the sunrise, but Spenser's formula does not dispel, as an epic, mythological dawn would have, her reasons for feeling it. In this loving and true conclusion, Calepine's courtesy becomes Spenser's and our own.

III

The moral understanding that *The Faerie Queene* gives us is, in a profound sense, self-knowledge. But if the reader's mind does not organize and impose itself as if it were in action, the question arises whether the mode of Spenser's poetry does not contradict the very nature of self as we understand it. The poet's selflessness in *The Faerie Queene* has been rightly emphasized by the romantic tradition of Spenserian criticism, and it is perhaps the main cause of the modern reader's hostility to or uneasiness with Spenser's verse. Lewis' tribute to Spenser is a sublime rendering of this characteristic:

> It . . . gives us, while we read him, . . . a feeling that we have before us not so much an image as a sublime instance of the universal process—that this is not so much a poet writing about the fundamental forms of life as those forms themselves spontaneously displaying their activities to us through the imagination of a poet. The invocation of the Muse hardly seems to be a convention in Spenser. We feel that his poetry has really tapped sources not easily accessible to discursive thought. . . . Milton has well selected wisdom as his peculiar excellence—wisdom of that kind which rarely penetrates into literature because it exists most often in inarticulate people. It is this that has kept children and poets true to him for three centuries, while the intellectuals (on whom the office of criticism naturally devolves) have been baffled even to irritation by a spell which they could not explain.[35]

Recent Spenser criticism has been nothing if not intellectual; from the desiccating discussion of the "ideas" of *The Faerie Queene,* one turns gladly to the critics in the romantic tradition, with their emphasis on the immediate, experienced realities of Spenser's verse. And yet Lewis' statement about the wisdom of inarticulate people is simply ridiculous. It can be understood only as an attempt to remain true to the character of Spenser's verse without calling him, as have critics from Hazlitt to G. Wilson Knight, a voluptuary. Our readings of specific passages continually show that Spenser's strengths are those of sane and generous moral understanding, and not the specialized strengths of voluptuous imagination or inarticulate wisdom. The modern scholar, then, is essentially right to reject the romantic version of Spenser's poetical character and to appeal to Milton's reference to "our sage and serious poet." Our problem is to explain how this

[35] *The Allegory of Love,* pp. 358–359.

characterization of Spenser is compatible with his selflessness as a poet.

The notion of the poet's selflessness is based on a dramatic conception of his relation to his work. But to understand Spenser's selflessness, we must recognize that there is no dramatic analogy to the way his mind worked. Coleridge said that *The Faerie Queene* reminded him of some lines of his own:

> Oh! would to Alla!
> The raven or the sea-mew were appointed
> To bring me food!—or rather that my soul
> Might draw in life from the universal air!
> It were a lot divine in some small skiff
> Along some ocean's boundless solitude
> To float for ever with a careless course,
> And think myself the only being alive![36]

The image conveys essential characteristics of Spenser's mind—its passivity, its abeyance of will, its endless receptivity. Coleridge then says, "Indeed Spenser himself, in the conduct of his great poem, may be represented under the same image," and he quotes:

> As Pilot well expert in perilous waue,
> That to a stedfast starre his course hath bent,
> When foggy mistes, or cloudy tempests haue
> The faithfull light of that faire lampe yblent,
> And couer'd heauen with hideous dreriment,
> Vpon his card and compas firmes his eye,
> The maisters of his long experiment,
> And to them does the steddy helme apply,
> Bidding his winged vessell fairely forward fly.
>
> (2.7.1)

The setting is similar, but the human center is directly opposite to what it is in Coleridge's lines—confident, purposeful, outgoing, energetic. And this image conveys an equal truth about Spenser's mind: it is not for nothing that in the proem to Book II he invokes the Elizabethan discoveries to justify his creation of Fairyland.

Any attempts to dramatize the active and passive aspects of Spenser's mind, as in the images just quoted, must represent them as con-

---

[36] *Coleridge's Miscellaneous Criticism*, ed. T. M. Raysor, Cambridge, Mass., 1936, p. 36. The lines are from *Remorse*, act 4, sc. 3, lines 13–20.

flicting. Yet when we read *The Faerie Queene,* they strike us as compatible, and I think it is because of the wholehearted and untroubled way in which Spenser treats truths as having an existence external to him. This explanation of the puzzle about Spenser's mind appears most distinctly in the cantos in which he is most conscious of his creative role as a poet—the Garden of Adonis and the Mutability cantos. The Garden of Adonis canto begins with the myth of Chrysogone's impregnation by the sun. After telling the story, which is his own invention, Spenser says:

> Miraculous may seeme to him, that reades
> So straunge ensample of conception;
> But reason teacheth that the fruitfull seades
> Of all things liuing, through impression
> Of the sunbeames in moyst complexion,
> Doe life conceiue and quickned are by kynd:
> So after *Nilus* invndation,
> Infinite shapes of creatures men do fynd,
> Informed in the mud, on which the Sunne hath shynd.
>
> (3.6.8)

The gesture in the opening lines is so potent, because the preceding stanza, with its account of the sunbeams playing on and penetrating Chrysogone's naked body, *has* been miraculous to read. Yet when Spenser invokes reason and the nature of things to make his poetic myth valid, we have a sense not of a new category of experience, but of a continuation of the old. His scientific account exploits the ravishing language of the preceding stanza, and his example is as wondrous as his story (and yet it is one of the most familiar illustrations of nature's "miracles"), and makes even broader claims for the naturalness of human fertility. Throughout the description of the Garden of Adonis, Spenser moves between the myth he has created and the natural truths that it expresses, and it is the complete ease of these movements that underlies the poised gravity with which he speaks to us. Spenser's poetry, recognizing no division between the seer and the seen, dissolves the ambiguities of the word "vision."

But it was not the truths of nature so much as the truths of poetry itself that possessed Spenser's imagination. At the end of his description of the Garden of Adonis, Spenser lists the flowers that grow in the grove of myrtle trees. All are metamorphosed youths who suffered unhappy fates in love, and at the end of the stanza, Spenser points di-

rectly to the transforming force of poetry in making love's victims
flowers in her garden:

> Sad *Amaranthus,* in whose purple gore
> Me seemes I see *Amintas* wretched fate,
> To whom sweet Poets verse hath giuen endlesse date.
>
> (3.6.45)

When Spenser then moves to his description of Adonis as Venus' lover
and as "eterne in mutabilitie," we expect him to be consciously and
fully in possession of his visionary powers. Yet a formula suggesting
the exact opposite occurs in each of the three stanzas:

> There yet, some say, in secret he does ly.
>
> (3.6.46)

> And sooth it seemes they say: for he may not
> For euer die, and euer buried bee.
> For him the Father of all formes they call.
>
> (3.6.47)

> In a strong rocky Caue, which is they say,
> Hewen vnderneath that Mount, that none him losen may.
>
> (3.6.48)

Spenser's authority for the most august moment of the canto—the
climax of an account that began, "Well I wote by tryall, that this same
/ All other pleasant places doth excell" (3.6.29)—is not his own vi-
sion but the myth itself. The pronouns "some" and "they" (compare
the plural "sweet Poets" of 3.6.45) remind us that the myth is a cre-
ation of many men and has taken on a life of its own, independent of,
but still obviously capable of nourishing, an individual poet.

The attitude towards poetic truth represented by these stanzas in-
forms the Mutability cantos. Consider what Spenser says about Muta-
bility at the beginning of the cantos:

> Ne shee the lawes of Nature onely brake,
> But eke of Iustice, and of Policie;
> And wrong of right, and bad of good did make,
> And death for life exchanged foolishlie:
> Since which, all liuing wights haue learn'd to die,
> And all this world is woxen daily worse.
> O pittious worke of *MVTABILITIE!*
> By which, we all are subiect to that curse,

And death in stead of life haue sucked from our Nurse.

(7.6.6)

If we take this as a stanza about a real mythological figure—and Spenser has just told about the Titaness' birth and compared her to Hecate and Bellona (7.6.3)—it is very bold indeed: the myth Spenser has invented is an account of the Fall of Man. And yet if we take "O pittious worke of *MVTABILITIE!*" to be simply about an abstraction, the stanza is almost commonplace, in the manner of the first stanza:

> What man that sees the euer-whirling wheele
> Of *Change,* the which all mortall things doth sway,
> But that therby doth find, and plainly feele,
> How *MVTABILITY* in them doth play
> Her cruell sports, to many mens decay?

(7.6.1)

With this as a starting point, one is not surprised to find Spenser characterizing himself as simply a recorder of truths:

> I will rehearse that whylome I heard say.

(7.6.1)

> But first, here falleth fittest to vnfold
> Her antique race and linage ancient,
> As I haue found it registred of old,
> In *Faery* Land mongst records permanent.

(7.6.2)

The poetics of these cantos combines self-effacing acceptance and bold inventiveness in yet another way. On the one hand, we can regard Spenser's mythologizing as deriving its authority from Ovid: the influence and example of his most august passages—the account of Creation (*Metamorphoses* 1.1ff.) and the vision of Pythagoras (*Metamorphoses* 15.60ff.)—are evident throughout the Mutability cantos.[37] Or we can regard Spenser as rivaling Ovid—presenting a new version of Actaeon and Diana in the myth of Faunus and Molanna and a grander and truer procession of the months than is to be found in the *Metamorphoses*.[38] Clearly Spenser would have re-

[37] See William P. Cumming, "The Influence of Ovid's Metamorphoses on Spenser's Mutabilitie Cantos," SP, 28 (1931), 241–256.

[38] A. J. Smith discusses the relation between imitation and emulation in "Theory and Practice in Renaissance Poetry: Two Kinds of Imitation," *Bulletin of the John Rylands Library*, 47 (1964), 216, 218. He quotes Giraldi Cinthio's remark that "imitation always wants to be accompanied by emulation, which is nothing but a firm desire to surpass the man whom one imitates" (p. 216).

garded both relations to Ovid as true. By the same token, it is impossible to separate imitation and emulation in his use of another model, Chaucer's *Parliament of Foules* (see 7.7.1–9). Elsewhere Spenser makes his double relation to his masters explicit when he begins the story of Cambel and Triamond by asking Chaucer to infuse his spirit in him as "I follow here the footing of thy feete" (4.2.34)—for Spenser purports to complete the unfinished "Squire's Tale"—and ends by saying of the Nepenthe that Cambina brings:

> Much more of price and of more gratious powre
> Is this, then that same water of Ardenne,
> The which *Rinaldo* drunck in happie howre,
> Described by that famous Tuscane penne.

> (4.3.45)

In saying this, Spenser in effect claims that he has "emulated and overgone" Ariosto.[39]

Allegory, Rosemond Tuve has splendidly said, makes us think about things we already know.[40] Spenser's great achievement was to unfold before us and make us participate in man's traditional wisdom about himself and the truths inherent in the traditions and conventions of poetry. The next two chapters attempt to show both aspects of this achievement as they are seen in whole books of the poem. But we quite misapprehend Spenser's value for us if we ourselves become too "sage and serious" about his acceptance of traditional truths at face value. Our attitude towards Spenser's habit of mind inevitably reflects our living at a time when it is impossible. Lewis' cozy accounts of Spenser's mind, his eagerness to see in him "the brave appeal of a cause nearly lost,"[41] show this as much as the severer moral and intellectual structures that characterize the American tradition of Renaissance studies. But Spenser's clear and generous intelligence took the form it did because the vigor and seriousness with which he perceived all that he knew to be true of man were not incompatible with a sense of ease and freedom among these truths.

Perhaps we see Spenser's sense of poetic truth most clearly if we think of *The Faerie Queene* as a series of performances. The admiration for the poem when it appeared unquestionably involved a recog-

---

[39] The words are Gabriel Harvey's, who attributes them to Spenser. Spenser-Harvey Letters 5, in *The Works of Edmund Spenser: A Variorum Edition*, ed. Edwin Greenlaw, et al., Baltimore, 1932–1957, *Prose Works*, p. 471.

[40] In the Christian Gauss Seminar, Princeton University, May 1959. Quoted by Thomas P. Roche, Jr., *The Kindly Flame*, Princeton, 1964, p. 30.

[41] *The Allegory of Love*, p. 360.

nition that on both the large and small scales, Spenser had brilliantly "done" an immense number of kinds of poetry. The first canto of the first book indicates the spirit in which we read. It is full of passages that declare that Spenser can do the kinds of things that we expect great poets to do—catalogues of trees, heroic similes, the descent to the House of Sleep that is a rivaling imitation of Ovid and of Ovid's imitators, who include Chaucer and Ariosto.[42] And yet, as even this summary account indicates, Spenser does not have a personal and dramatic relation to his performances. They are determined by what is to be performed, and we can imagine Spenser becoming a different kind of poet for each passage of the poem. In reading *The Faerie Queene,* our delight is expressed by "How fine a catalogue of trees!" "How moving a love lament!" "How lifelike a description of a tapestry!" "How challenging or attractive a version of pastoral!" When we say "How Spenserian!" we tend to perceive only what the nineteenth century saw in Spenser.[43] Spenser's performances show the same double attitude towards poetry that we saw in the Garden of Adonis and the Mutability cantos. They bear witness to highly individual powers and pleasures, and yet we can think of their life as coming entirely from outside the individual poet. Hence in the performance of our own reading, our passivity and selflessness are not incompatible with outgoing energies and free play of the mind.

The nondramatic mode that is the essence of Spenser's poetry and the source of its greatness is at the same time its limitation. As G. Wilson Knight has said, "something is wanting" in *The Faerie Queene:*

> That something is to be related to (i) the New Testament and great tragedy generally; (ii) individual human personality as an indissoluble and realized unit. . . . There is not that impact of terrific importance and native direction in the human adventure found in the New Testament drama and in Shakespeare: which indeed generally forces a dramatic, often tragic, expression. Conversely dramatic form helps to force creative profundity. Drama, with its close plot-texture and disciplinary limits, its centralized and realistic human concern, was the condition of full Elizabethan expres-

---

[42] *Metamorphoses* 11.592ff.; *The Book of the Duchess,* 153ff.; *OF* 14.92–94.
[43] Compare the force of our saying, "How Dickensian!" My thinking about Spenser's performances was much clarified by Robert Garis' *The Dickens Theatre,* Oxford, 1965. "The Dickens problem" makes an interesting comparison with our difficulties in reading *The Faerie Queene,* and Dickens' quirky, exuberant, intensely personal theatricality suggests how different are the civilizations that nurtured his and Spenser's nondramatic narratives.

sion. The Elizabethan mind was too flooded with diversity of ideas and images: Shakespeare knew no more than Spenser, but gained by being forced to say less. Steep banks make a stream deep, swift, and forceful which without them is slothful, leisurely, and expansively shallow. And yet the greatest dramatic expression depends also on a sense of human personality which I feel Spenser, to a final judgement, lacks. He is rarely inside his fictions, enduring their joys and terrors. Shakespeare writes from a hard core of trust in human personality—his own or others'—which Spenser's fluid impressionism does not reach, so getting underneath his dramatic figure or action, creating from within and forcing others to share from within; and finally, the structure of his art-form has, with little explicit doctrine, the tough-corded sanity of an unswerving experienced realism.[44]

As we saw in comparing Spenser and Sidney, the vagueness of the poet's self-definition is a positive strength of *The Faerie Queene*. Spenser's ability to enter into and entertain truth after truth, perspective after perspective, gives the poem its generosity and richness as it unfolds line by line, stanza by stanza. But Spenser's selflessness is what makes him a lesser poet than the greatest masters—Shakespeare, Dante, Milton. The most serious limitation of *The Faerie Queene* when we compare it to the *Divine Comedy* or *Paradise Lost* is the absence of the deep organizing structures that arise from and in turn give life to individual parts. This lack is a sign of Spenser's failure to maintain a dramatic identity in relation to his poem. The condition of his poetry is the abeyance of will, and as a result linear sequence takes the place of structure in the sentences that make up stanzas, in the stanzas that make up cantos, in the cantos that make up books. And Spenser's selflessness accounts, as Knight says, for his not having a tragic sense. Eliot said of Pound that his hells are for other people. Spenser's limitation—not nearly so telling, but still, finally, a limitation—is that his hells are for Everyman. He seems not to have imaginatively grasped that the potentialities of human nature could actually transform individuals, could show themselves in dramatic actions whose consequences, in both the personality and the external world, could not be undone. The story of Phedon is a model of Spenser's poetry in this respect. It renders the psychological experience of rage with awesome force and clarity, and thus, in one way, shows "a sense of human personality" to which Knight does not do sufficient jus-

[44] *The Burning Oracle*, pp. 16–17.

tice. And yet Knight is, in another sense, entirely right. Phedon is totally unmarked by his dreadful experience and by what he has done. And just as he is not conceived as a dramatic personality, so the two murders he commits are not conceived as dramatic acts. Even murder, in Spenser's verse, is transformed into the rendering of a psychological state and thus can be purged by the Palmer's grave speech.

Spenser's inability to conceive tragedy can be seen by comparing the Despair episode in Book I with *Doctor Faustus*. Spenser's episode shows despair as a potential development of any man's religious experience. Its genesis is in the Red Cross Knight's confidence in his own powers in their most honorable form, knightly obligations; in his personal sense of world-weariness and sinfulness, which must be part of any Christian's self-knowledge; most of all, in his vivid belief in the God of Justice. The episode magnificently brings to life the truism that only a believer can feel despair. But Spenser cannot show us despair as a tragic state, in which a single man, because of what he is, what his past acts and choices have made him, is torn by his inability to act in the one way that would relieve him from being himself. Spenser's great genius is to make us participate in attitudes and states of feeling, but this participation does not involve the pressure of feeling them as dramatic potentialities at the moment of reading. At any moment of reading *The Faerie Queene,* we are ready to go on to the next line, the next stanza. The poetry is a mode of understanding, not of experience. Spenser, as Knight says, knew a great deal of what Shakespeare knew, but he could never have written *King Lear.*

Chapter Ten

Heroism and Human
Strength in Book I

I

Book I is one of the most admired books of *The Faerie Queene,* but, to judge from published criticism, we have not as yet made clear to ourselves what its value and interest is. One does not look forward with either pleasure or confidence to treating it as genuine theological exposition. But that approach to it seems the inevitable consequence of our traditional notions of allegory, and of assumptions like A. S. P. Woodhouse's that "whatever be true of some other poets, the aesthetic patterning of Spenser and Milton is based upon ideas, upon conceptual thinking."[1] But the truth and human use of Christian belief take many forms, and our interest in Book I need not consist of creating structures of theological ideas, or of trying to decide, as earlier generations of scholars did, to which Protestant doctor or Anglican divine Spenser owed allegiance.[2] In this book, as in every other, it is with a poet's means that Spenser makes us "think about things we already know."

It would be impossible, in a single essay, to treat Book I comprehensively and at the same time keep our attention where the life of the poem is—in the detailed workings of stanzas, passages, and episodes. In order to do justice to both the whole and its parts, I would like to show one theme at work throughout the book. The problem of human heroism and human strength is a main point of interest for Spenser in Book I, as it is in one of his most memorable statements:

> What man is he, that boasts of fleshly might,
> And vaine assurance of mortality,
> Which all so soone, as it doth come to fight,
> Against spirituall foes, yeelds by and by,
> Or from the field most cowardly doth fly?
> Ne let the man ascribe it to his skill,
> That thorough grace hath gained victory.

[1] "Nature and Grace in *The Faerie Queene,*" ELH, 16 (1949), 197.
[2] On this subject, see Virgil K. Whitaker, *The Religious Basis of Spenser's Thought,* Stanford, 1950, and Robert Ellrodt, *Neoplatonism in the Poetry of Spenser,* Geneva, 1960, pp. 195–209.

If any strength we haue, it is to ill,
But all the good is Gods, both power and eke will.

(10.1)

Here are both terms of our subject—human strength, a topic that constantly appears in the religious writings of Spenser's contemporaries, and human heroism, which is both a moral topic for Spenser and his main poetic material. This stanza gives a drastic account of human frailty: more than any other in Book I it invites the term "Calvinist." But Spenser can give us an entirely different sense of human nature. Una is rescued from her exile among the satyrs by Satyrane, who recognizes her true worth and "her wisedome heauenly rare" (1.6.31), and undertakes the role of servant and protector that the Red Cross Knight had forsaken. Spenser pointedly makes Satyrane a creature who is "of the earth, earthy": he is the son of a human mother and of a satyr who raped her as she wandered in the woods searching for her husband Therion (Greek for "beast"), "a loose vnruly swayne" (6.21). Satyrane is also fully human in the best sense: he is "a noble warlike knight" of "well deserued name":

> He had in armes abroad wonne muchell fame,
> And fild far landes with glorie of his might,
> Plaine, faithfull, true, and enimy of shame,
> And euer lou'd to fight for Ladies right,
> But in vaine glorious frayes he litle did delight.

(6.20)

Clearly Spenser regards the subject of human strength and heroism as problematic—not so much because it imposes conflicting feelings or alternatives of action, as because the truth about it is a profound puzzle about human nature. The puzzle is presented to us in the first episode of Book I:

> His Lady sad to see his sore constraint,
> Cride out, Now now Sir knight, shew what ye bee,
> Add faith vnto your force, and be not faint:
> Strangle her, else she sure will strangle thee.
> That when he heard, in great perplexitie,
> His gall did grate for griefe and high disdaine,
> And knitting all his force got one hand free,
> Wherewith he grypt her gorge with so great paine,
> That soone to loose her wicked bands did her constraine.

(1.19)

Critics usually quote "Add faith vnto your force" in isolation and as if it made Spenser's whole intent plain. But Spenser uses the context of heroic action to draw our attention to problems that concern any religious thinker: what are man's natural strengths and to what extent are the strengths God's grace gives him "his own"? In the Epistle to the Ephesians, Saint Paul says, "For by grace are ye made safe thorow fayth, and that not of youre selves. It is the gyfte of God, and commeth not of workes, lest eny man shulde boast him selfe" (2:8–9); yet the epistle concludes with a heroic image of the strength that comes through faith—the description of the "whole armoure of God" (6:11–17) to which Spenser refers in the Letter to Raleigh. Spenser's interest is not in asserting that a paradox, strength comes from humility, is true, or in determining the particular meaning of the paradox (think how variously theologians might interpret "Add faith vnto your force" if it were a biblical text). The knight's heroic effort, particularly the phrase "knitting all his force," is designed to make us aware of a' puzzle, and not to render a structured judgment about it. The Red Cross Knight's adventures in Book I end with the same puzzle: "Then God she praysd, and thankt her faithfull knight, / That had atchieu'd so great a conquest by his might" (11.55). The uncertain reference of "his" makes this quite ambiguous as theology. But it would be more accurate to say that the grammatical ambiguity enables Spenser to render the full truth about human strength and its dependence on God.

The episode that begins Book I, the Red Cross Knight's encounter with Error, shows us the nature of Spenser's interest in human heroism. It is first of all a means of rendering psychological motivation—both the driving energies of man's spirit and the moral sanctions he consciously invokes. The stanza in which the knight adds faith unto his force is directly concerned with spiritual energies, while at the beginning of the episode, motivation takes the form of a self-conscious moral stance:

> Ah Ladie (said he) shame were to reuoke
> The forward footing for an hidden shade:
> Vertue giues her selfe light, through darkenesse
>   for to wade.   (1.12)

While Spenser enforces our sympathetic participation in these states of mind and feeling, his verse also allows us to see them from the outside, to evaluate what they tell us about spiritual experience and strength. When we are told that the knight leapt at Error "As Lyon

fierce vpon the flying pray" (1.17), the simile renders the energies
that impel "the valiant Elfe" to action. At the same time, the simile
makes us see a likeness between the knight and the dragon, who is de-
scribed as "turning fierce" and "threatning her angry sting." The bat-
tle thus becomes a genuine psychomachia, an expression of conflicting
potentialities within a single mind: because of the simile, we see that
the same fund of energy can manifest itself as either rage or bold
prowess. We should note that Spenser's interest in the hero's fierce-
ness, greedy eagerness, or rage, here and throughout the book, is not
in these particular emotions as they are dramatically experienced and
distinct from others. It is rather that these emotions appropriately reg-
ister the general point that man's spiritual resources inevitably partake
of his earthly, sinful nature.

Spenser maintains the double perspective on man's strengths
throughout this opening episode:

> But full of fire and greedy hardiment,
> The youthfull knight could not for ought be staide,
> But forth vnto the darksome hole he went,
> And looked in: his glistring armor made
> A litle glooming light, much like a shade,
> By which he saw the vgly monster plaine,
> Halfe like a serpent horribly displaide,
> But th'other halfe did woman's shape retaine,
> Most lothsom, filthie, foule, and full of vile disdaine.
>
> (1.14)

Lines 4 and 5 are a celebrated bit of Spenserian description, but the
stanza's real interest—the claim it has on us as serious and complex
poetry—is in the way it develops the Red Cross Knight's confident
assertion that "Vertue giues her selfe light, through darkenesse for to
wade." We are aware that the knight may be, in Una's words, "too
rash." Nevertheless, the tradition that heroic prowess is a sign of
moral worth prepares us to see his bold claim as natural and right,
worthy of a man's honor and assent. The stanza in which the knight
enters the dragon's cave plays out the ways in which we can evaluate
this heroic claim. The first two lines continue the suggestion that his
boldness is impetuous, but more important is the pointedly ambiguous
nature of the light that the virtuous hero's "glistring armor" gives off.
It is "glooming," "much like a shade," and yet at the same time it en-
ables the knight to see "the vgly monster plaine." As in the Cave of
Mammon, Spenser is concerned with a puzzle inherent in the percep-

tion of an evil: seeing it for what it is suggests our immunity from it, and yet the fact that we are men, not angels, makes us in a sense partakers of it. Hence each of the next two stanzas begins with a repulsive and threatening portrayal of Error; **yet** each ends with the daunting effect of light on her. The second of these stanzas in particular shows that the obvious ironies about "Vertue giues her selfe light" are not the only truth about the knight's heroism:

> She lookt about, and seeing one in mayle
> Armed to point, sought backe to turne againe;
> For light she hated as the deadly bale,
> Ay wont in desert darknesse to remaine,
> Where plaine none might her see, nor she see any plaine.
>
> (1.16)

Even where the language most encourages us to see the earthly frailty inherent in human heroism, our understanding of it is not limited to that perspective on it:

> Thus ill bestedd, and fearefull more of shame,
> Then of the certaine perill he stood in,
> Halfe furious vnto his foe he came,
> Resolv'd in minde all suddenly to win,
> Or soone to lose, before he once would lin;
> And strooke at her with more then manly force,
> That from her body full of filthie sin
> He raft her hatefull head without remorse;
> A streame of cole black bloud forth gushed from her
>   corse.
>
> (1.24)

We begin with the purely human sanction of shame and the motivating energy of anger, yet the syntax of lines 5 and 6 makes it plain that what is "more then manly" in the knight's force cannot be separated from these earthbound sources of strength. One is not surprised, then, that the episode ends not only with the statement that the knight goes on his way "with God to frend" (1.28), but also with Una's praise of him as a hero:

> Faire knight, borne vnder happy starre,
> Who see your vanquisht foes before you lye:
> Well worthy be you of that Armorie,
> Wherein ye haue great glory wonne this day,
> And proou'd your strength on a strong enimie.
>
> (1.27)

Spenser does not attempt to redefine heroism as Milton does when he rejects "the wrath Of stern *Achilles*" and the "rage Of *Turnus* for *Lavinia* disespous'd" for "the better fortitude Of Patience and Heroic Martyrdom."[3] In itself, human heroism in Book I is consistently represented as it is in the opening episode. When Arthur joins battle with Orgoglio,

> his mightie shild
> Vpon his manly arme he soone addrest,
> And at him fiercely flew, with courage fild,
> And eger greedinesse through euery member thrild.
>
> (8.6)

In his final battle with the dragon, the Red Cross Knight is impelled by the same motives—wrath, shame, and the like—as in the battle with Error. The interest and complexity of Spenser's treatment of heroism lie not in the way it is represented in itself, but in Spenser's willingness to examine it from every perspective—to ask as fully as possible what it tells us about human nature. In almost every canto of Book I, there is a criticism of human strength as it is expressed by heroism; yet in each of these cantos, the claims and values of heroism are in some way re-established. The value of Spenser's moral intelligence lies in the breadth and variety with which these movements of attitude are registered in canto after canto of the book.

Cantos 3 and 6 contain the simplest and most direct manifestations of the movement from a criticism of heroism to a reassertion of it. In both cantos, human heroism is rebuked by pastoral simplicity: the lion and the satyrs worship and protect Una, while the Red Cross Knight has abandoned and Archimago and Sansloy attempt to abuse her. It is not enough to say that Archimago and Sansloy are false and wicked knights. Knighthood itself is called into question by Archimago's entirely plausible imitation of the Red Cross Knight (3.28–29), which deceives Una, and by the heroic terms in which we are made to see Sansloy's battle with the lion (3.41–42). But the pastoral figures in themselves offer no alternative to heroic knighthood. The lion's lordly service and the satyrs' humble worship have their full value only when they become human realities through the reader's response to and comprehension of them. In the very moment of rebuking human sinfulness, the pastoralism of these cantos figures forth our human strengths, and in both cantos these strengths are expressed by rein-

[3] John Milton, *Paradise Lost*, 9.14–17, 32–33, ed. Merritt Y. Hughes, New York, 1962.

stating the values of heroic knighthood. The presentation of Sansloy challenges us to be lionlike in a different way—to be noble, not beastly —and the implicit appeal to heroic values is made explicit in the opening stanza of the next canto (4.1). In canto 6, Satyrane arrives to give Una proper protection and return her to the world of men, where alone she can be truly worshipped. Similarly, the noble and glamorous figure of Arthur appears in canto 7 after what seem almost unqualified renderings of the weakness and sinfulness of man's nature and the vanity of life on earth.

Of the middle cantos of Book I, the fifth contains the most far-reaching criticism of heroism and human strength. The canto begins by speaking of "The noble hart, that harbours vertuous thought, / And is with child of glorious great intent" (5.1). The next stanza gives us a glamorous sense of the hero by showing him clad (as Arthur is later, 7.29) in "sun-bright armes" after a ravishing description of the dawn that is based on Psalms 19:4–5: "the sunne, which commeth forth as a brydgrome out of hys chambre, and reioyseth as a giaunt to runne his course." Yet this noble heroism is under the patronage of Lucifera, who supplies the bards and chroniclers to record the deeds of heroes (5.3), the wine "to kindle heat of corage priuily" (5.4), and the proper setting for the knights' combat (5.5). When the battle begins, Spenser describes both the good and the bad knight in the same terms: both have "shining shieldes" and "burning blades" ("the instruments of wrath and heauinesse"), and "with greedy force each other doth assayle" (5.6). And yet to indicate that any heroism is bound up with human sinfulness does not eliminate the distinction between what the argument to the canto calls "the faithfull knight" and "his faithlesse foe":

> The Sarazin was stout, and wondrous strong,
> And heaped blowes like yron hammers great:
> For after bloud and vengeance he did long.
> The knight was fiers, and full of youthly heat,
> And doubled strokes, like dreaded thunders threat:
> For all for prayse and honour he did fight.
>
> (5.7)

The knights are distinguished here in terms of purely human motives, and the Red Cross Knight's "youthly heat" does not impugn his worth —any more than the terms in which Spenser describes the noble heart's yearning to produce "th'eternall brood of glorie excellent" are invalidated by the dramatic manifestation of that desire: "Such restlesse passion did all night torment / The flaming corage of that Faery knight" (5.1).

As the battle with Sansjoy develops, Spenser changes our relation to it in order to complicate the double perspective on heroism that the opening stanzas give us. The stanza that follows the contrast between the two knights begins, "So th'one for wrong, the other striues for right." But the simile that occupies the rest of the stanza recognizes no moral discriminations:

> As when a Gryfon seized of his pray,
> A Dragon fiers encountreth in his flight,
> Through widest ayre making his ydle way,
> That would his rightfull rauine rend away:
> With hideous horrour both together smight,
> And souce so sore, that they the heauens affray:
> The wise Southsayer seeing so sad sight,
> Th'amazed vulgar tels of warres and mortall fight.
>
> (5.8)

The phrase "rightfull rauine" beautifully summarizes the central puzzle about heroism. But the distinctive development here is that the puzzlement we feel as observers has changed from clear moral understanding into fearful amazement. In the next stanza, this development is recapitulated in terms of the battle itself. Once again the stanza begins, "So th'one for wrong, the other striues for right." But our desire simply to cheer on the good against the bad is made impossible by the realities of warfare—the blood covering "the armes, that earst so bright did show." The stanza ends:

> Great ruth in all the gazers harts did grow,
> Seeing the gored woundes to gape so wyde,
> That victory they dare not wish to either side.
>
> (5.9)

The awed fascination that Spenser creates in these stanzas is exploited, two stanzas later, in one of the most brilliant bits of poetic duplicity in *The Faerie Queene*. Sansjoy makes a final effort to finish off the Knight:

> Therewith vpon his crest he stroke him so,
> That twise he reeled, readie twise to fall;
> End of the doubtfull battell deemed tho

341

The lookers on, and lowd to him gan call
The false *Duessa,* Thine the shield, and I, and all.

(5.11)

It is not just the battle that is doubtful here. The reference of "him" is entirely ambiguous, and Duessa's cry so fully continues our excitement at the battle that we do not use what she says to determine to which knight she is calling. Our involvement causes us to be confused in just the way the knight is in the next stanza:

Soone as the Faerie heard his Ladie speake,
Out of his swowning dreame he gan awake,
And quickning faith, that earst was woxen weake,
The creeping deadly cold away did shake:
Tho mou'd with wrath, and shame, and Ladies sake,
Of all attonce he cast auengd to bee,
And with so'exceeding furie at him strake,
That forced him to stoupe vpon his knee;
Had he not stouped so, he should haue clouen bee.

(5.12)

The fact that we have made the same mistake about Duessa's call means, first of all, that we do not sit in judgment on the knight: we share his fallibility, which therefore is seen as innately human. Hence we feel the full weight of the problematic rendering of heroism in this stanza. We cannot, on the one hand, dismiss the fact that, Duessa or no, the knight experiences "quickning faith," just as he did when Una called to him. But the confusion out of which he (along with us) emerges and the recognition that it is "the false *Duessa*" who is "his Ladie" enforce the suggestion that "swowning dreame" and "creeping deadly cold" define his spiritual condition. In this context, the pivotal line of the stanza—"Tho mou'd with wrath, and shame, and Ladies sake"—manages to hold in solution, in simply recording the realities of heroic motivation, essential puzzles about man's energies and resources.

We must now ask how our moral strength can be reasserted after a criticism of heroism that so fully engages our own capacities. As the Red Cross Knight is about to kill Sansjoy, a dark cloud falls upon the body and it vanishes from sight. While the knight stands poised for action but confused, Duessa runs to greet him as a hero ("O prowest knight"), urges him to "abate the terror of your might" and leave

Sansjoy for dead, and concludes, echoing her initial cry, "The conquest yours, I yours, the shield, and glory yours" (5.14):

> Not all so satisfide, with greedie eye
> He sought all round about, his thirstie blade
> To bath in bloud of faithlesse enemy;
> Who all that while lay hid in secret shade:
> He standes amazed, how he thence should fade.
>
> (5.15)

In these lines we begin to stand outside the knight's experience. From his standpoint, line 4 expresses puzzlement, whereas for us it is simple narrative fact. (Similarly in the preceding stanza, we see the duplicity —and hence can deal with Duessa—in "lo th'infernall powres / Couering your foe with cloud of deadly night, / Haue borne him hence to *Plutoes* balefull bowres" (5.14)—which is a literal truth, but does not, as the knight is to think, report Sansjoy's death.) Unlike the Red Cross Knight, we are not "amazed, how he thence should fade." Hence in the next stanza, the home truth that human heroism is bound up with man's sinfulness—which earlier was the grounds for making us share the Red Cross Knight's plight—now appears in iconic form as a clear moral perception: the knight bows to Lucifera ("that soueraine Queene") and offers his service, while she is shown "greatly aduauncing his gay cheualree" (5.16). We are not led to condemn the knight as wicked, because in both this stanza and the preceding one, he is swept along by the celebrations of his victory and the honor paid him: his aggrandizement is a continuation of his confusion in the battle and not the result of a direct act of the will. But we ourselves are not swept along now, and in two more stanzas, we find ourselves completely outside the knight's experience. The heroic simile of the crocodile whose false tears arouse a traveler's foolish pity renders the dramatic fact that Duessa is fooling the Red Cross Knight, but it in no way fools us. Unlike the "wearie traueller," we are not "vnweeting of the perillous wandring wayes" (5.18).

Our moral strength at this point lies in recognizing that human heroism inherently serves Lucifera—that the House of Pride is its natural home. In the next episode Spenser develops almost the same point, but in such a way that the strength we derive from the recognition is much more uncertain. The episode begins when Duessa journeys to Night and urges her to show "that dreaded *Night* in brightest day hath place, / And can the children of faire light deface" (5.24). But Night replies:

> Who can turne the streame of destinee,
> Or breake the chayne of strong necessitee,
> Which fast is tyde to *Ioues* eternall seat?
> The sonnes of Day he fauoureth, I see.
>
> (5.25)

We have a confident relation to these stanzas: "Ye are all the chyldren of lyght, and the chyldren of the daye. We are not of the nyght nether of darknes" (1 Thessalonians 5:5). Elsewhere in the passage, our moral assurance is rendered by the wit of the narrative situation—the play on Duessa's "true" and "false" appearances, particularly in the recognition scene between her and Night (5.26–27)—and by the wit of local details, such as the fact that Duessa's "sunny bright" appearance, which dismays Night, is artificial (5.21), or locutions like "the false resemblance of Deceipt" (5.27), or "the fowle welfauourd witch" (5.28). But our relation to the powers of darkness begins to change when Night comes to take Sansjoy's body into her chariot:

> And all the while she stood vpon the ground,
> The wakefull dogs did neuer cease to bay,
> As giuing warning of th'vnwonted sound,
> With which her yron wheeles did them affray,
> And her darke griesly looke them much dismay;
> The messenger of death, the ghastly Owle
> With drearie shriekes did also her bewray;
> And hungry Wolues continually did howle,
> At her abhorred face, so filthy and so fowle.
>
> (5.30)

What begins as an extraordinary mythological event concerning a creature called Night becomes a rendering of what any night is like on earth. The stanza makes us aware that there is an ordinary, but important sense in which "dreaded *Night* in brightest day hath place." We are thus not in a position to consider ourselves solely "chyldren of the daye" when we descend into Hell with Night and Duessa:

> There creature neuer past,
> That backe returned without heauenly grace;
> But dreadfull *Furies,* which their chaines haue brast,
> And damned sprights sent forth to make ill men aghast.
>
> (5.31)

344

We "ill men" are saved from such powers not by what we are in ourselves—"chyldren of lyght"—but by the external force of "heauenly grace."

To be sure, what we are and what grace makes us are the same, but the theological controversies of the sixteenth century are sufficient evidence that there is an essential puzzle here. To recognize that human heroism belongs to Lucifera's realm is, in a sense, to recognize our dependence on grace. But the recognition can be regarded as "our own" source of strength. The stanzas last quoted break down this assumption, and it is tested with exceptional breadth and stringency in the long passage that concerns the visit to Aesculapius. Aesculapius is condemned to hell because he restored Hippolytus to life after he was torn to pieces when the monsters called up by Theseus' curse terrified the horses drawing his chariot. Spenser spends three stanzas telling the story before we reach Aesculapius, and the passage, which seems pure digression, serves to build into this underworld the whole range of human values and possibilities:

> *Hippolytus* a iolly huntsman was,
> That wont in charet chace the foming Bore;
> He all his Peeres in beautie did surpas,
> But Ladies loue as losse of time forbore.
>
> (5.37)

Hippolytus resembles the young Arthur (9.9–12), and throughout the passage it is never forgotten that the evil passions of Phaedra and Theseus destroyed something lovely and valuable. Hence it seems a piece of human dignity when Theseus repents and

> gathering vp the relicks of his smart
> By *Dianes* meanes, who was *Hippolyts* frend,
> Them brought to *Æsculape,* that by his art
> Did heale them all againe, and ioyned euery part.
>
> (5.39)

And yet "Such wondrous science in mans wit to raine / When *Ioue* auizd," he thrust him into Hell (5.40). The condemnation of all purely human achievement is so forceful because we have been made to recognize how much we value Aesculapius' art. This is the context of the grave and searching exchange when Night asks Aesculapius to heal Sansjoy:

345

Ah Dame (quoth he) thou temptest me in vaine,
To dare the thing, which daily yet I rew,
And the old cause of my continued paine
With like attempt to like end to renew.
Is not enough, that thrust from heauen dew
Here endlesse penance for one fault I pay,
But that redoubled crime with vengeance new
Thou biddest me to eeke? Can Night defray
The wrath of thundring *Ioue,* that rules both night
    and day?

Not so (quoth she) but sith that heauens king
From hope of heauen hath thee excluded quight,
Why fearest thou, that canst not hope for thing,
And fearest not, that more thee hurten might,
Now in the powre of euerlasting Night?
Goe to then, O thou farre renowmed sonne
Of great *Apollo,* shew thy famous might
In medicine, that else hath to thee wonne
Great paines, and greater praise, both neuer to be
    donne. (5.42–43)

This is, as it were, a noble and dignified version of despair. All that has preceded makes us ask whether not simply our sins, but all that we value of ourselves is not "in the powre of euerlasting Night." Night's magnificent appeal to Aesculapius as a hero of knowledge ends by explicitly turning her terrors into a claim on us. If "great paines" ended the sentence, it would unequivocally mean torment in hell. But when the line continues with the answering phrase, "greater praise," it turns into a formula for noble endeavor.

At this point we can well believe that no mortal has "backe returned without heauenly grace." Our rescue comes in the next stanza, when after "the learned leach" begins to exercise "his cunning hand" and "his art," Night, "the mother of dread darknesse,"

backe returning tooke her wonted way,
To runne her timely race, whilst *Phoebus* pure
In westerne waues his wearie wagon did recure.

(5.44)

We leave Hell because of the natural cycle of the day and night. There is indeed a sense in which we are the protected children of "thundring *Ioue,* that rules both night and day." But our sense of strength is

346

equivocal here. The reassertion of an order that can cherish as well as condemn us is in terms of a recovery from weariness and illness (because of the suggestions of "recure" in the context of this episode).[4] In the next stanza we return with Duessa to the House of Pride, where she finds that the Red Cross Knight has departed in a condition that we recognize is similar to ours: "his woundes wide / Not throughly heald, vnreadie were to ride" (5.45). Yet he has left because of human moral capacities. "His wary Dwarfe" has seen Lucifera's dungeon (5.45), and he has recognized the House of Pride for what it is. The dungeon is filled with the great figures of the pagan world—not simply the monstrously wicked, blasphemous kings and lustful queens, but also great conquerors and noble Romans. The passage in one sense simply repeats the point made in the battle with Sansjoy, that heroic achievement belongs to Lucifera. Similarly the sense of earthly sinfulness and vanity has, in some sense, been our moral strength throughout this canto and the preceding one, in which we saw the Seven Deadly Sins. But the vehemence of the *contemptus mundi* in this passage implies what is explicit in the narrative action, that our escape from this hell is a narrow one. The Red Cross Knight leaves by his own resources, but the heroic stance he took against the procession of the Seven Deadly Sins (4.37) is now associated with the "great," "mighty," "stout," and "high minded" inhabitants of Lucifera's dungeon.

I I

Canto 5 does not entirely deny that man has moral and spiritual strengths, but it certainly seems to rule out heroic knighthood as an expression of them. Yet in the very next canto the satyrs' adoration of Una produces the figure of Satyrane, and Arthur first appears in the canto after that. Spenser is quite unwilling to decide against heroism in its usual forms and propose an alternative to it. This attitude is most apparent in canto 10, where it is the only explanation for Contemplation's praise of heroic action and his insisting on the Red Cross Knight's obligation to it. Canto 10 begins by saying, "If any strength we haue, it is to ill," and it is full of manifestations of *contemptus mundi*. But the attitude expressed towards the world is by no means a simple one—the Red Cross Knight is twice recalled from too drastic

[4] The first meaning of "recure" here is "to bring back to a normal state or condition; to restore after loss, damage, exhaustion" (*OED* 1b), as in *FQ* 1.9.2, 2.1.54. Note that *OED* treats this as a subdivision of the meaning, "to cure (one) *of* or *from* a disease."

a loathing of human life (10.21–23, 63)—and for our purposes the most important aspect of the canto is the form that human strengths and values take in it. Throughout there are lovely and affecting portrayals of the bonds that exist between men—the "comely courteous glee" with which Zeal greets Una and the knight (10.6), Caelia's joyous welcome of Una (10.9), the habitually loving behavior of Fidelia, Speranza, and Charissa, and most important the "holy Hospitall" in which we see the corporal works of mercy (10.36–43). Spenser's management of this passage shows how little he wishes our knowledge of man's sinfulness and frailty to produce a rejection of humanity. He deviates from the traditional seven corporal works of mercy, as codified by St. Thomas (*S.T.* 2.2.32.2), by combining two works, feeding the hungry and giving drink to the thirsty, into one (10.38), and adding, as the seventh work, the care of widows and orphans (10.43). His authority for this is Lactantius,[5] but he surely means us to remember Lactantius' authority: "And se that ye be doars of the worde and not hearers onely, deceaving your awne selves. For yf eny man heare the worde and declareth not the same by his workes, he is lyke unto a man beholding his bodely face in a glasse. . . . Pure devocyon and undefyled before God the father, is this: to visyt the fatherlesse and widdowes in theyr adversyte, and to kepe him selfe unspotted of the worlde" (James 1: 22–23, 27). By this allusion (to which Spenser adds the duty of defending the "rightfull causes" of widows and orphans against "the powre of mighty men"), Spenser makes explicit the solicitude for human life that continually appears in the portraits and actions already noted, in the description of the third corporal work of mercy (10.39), and in language like "She cast to bring him, where he chearen might" (10.2), "Now when their wearie limbes with kindly rest, / And bodies were refresht with due repast" (10.18), "Him dearely kist, and fairely eke besought / Himselfe to chearish" (10.29).

It is essential to recognize that everything humanly valuable we see in the first two-thirds of canto 10 derives its sanction from the realm of grace, not of nature. The virtues Spenser, like St. James, celebrates are those that belong—to use the title of a short discourse by Tasso—to *carità* and not to *virtù eroica*. The context of the whole canto, no less than the nature of the dramatic occasion, makes it surprising that the hermit Contemplation qualifies the knight's statement that the heavenly city is fairer than Cleopolis, the city of glory:

[5] See Charles E. Mounts, "Spenser's Seven Bead-men and the Corporal Works of Mercy," PMLA, 54 (1939), 974–980.

Most trew, then said the holy aged man;
Yet is *Cleopolis* for earthly frame,
The fairest peece, that eye beholden can:
And well beseemes all knights of noble name,
That couet in th'immortall booke of fame
To be eternized, that same to haunt,
And doen their seruice to that soueraigne Dame,
That glorie does to them for guerdon graunt:
For she is heauenly borne, and heauen may iustly vaunt.

(10.59)

There is no way of reconciling, in a single structure of judgment, this stanza with what has preceded it. The last line keeps "immortall" and "eternized" from being positively irreligious, but the perspective and sanctions of this stanza are those of earthly heroism.[6] Heroism seems very different when viewed, as it is in the next stanza, *sub specie aeternitatis:*

But when thou famous victorie hast wonne,
And high emongst all knights hast hong thy shield,
Thenceforth the suit of earthly conquest shonne,
And wash thy hands from guilt of bloudy field:
For bloud can nought but sin, and wars but sorrowes
   yield.   (10.60)

Canto 10 does not produce the praise of earthly glory in the way canto 6 produces the figure of Satyrane or canto 7 the figure of Arthur. Contemplation's praise of Cleopolis is occasioned by Spenser's concern in this particular passage—to do justice to the claims on man of both the Earthly and the Heavenly Cities and to register the inherently problematic nature of our relationship to them. In admiring Spenser for producing this stanza at this moment of the poem, we admire a habit of mind, not a fresh complication or realization in a continuous poetic development. But in the cantos that precede and follow this one, the criticism of heroism and the sense of its validity are inwoven with each other, and heroism is a main means of rendering, as it is not in canto 10, the complex nature of human strength.

The episode in the Cave of Despair is a radical criticism of human heroism. If we ask, as we did in the Cave of Mammon, what is the

---

[6] Rosemond Tuve cites and illuminates this line in discussing why a Christian knight owes duty to his king and why it is the king who rewards him. *Allegorical Imagery*, Princeton, 1966, p. 349.

simplest understanding we have of the episode, we must say, "If any strength we haue, it is to ill, / But all the good is Gods, both power and eke will" (10.1). The Red Cross Knight encounters Despair not as the inevitable result of his weakened condition, but because he seeks him out to test his strength and to avenge what Despair has done to Sir Terwin. Despair's main sophistry, his speaking only of God's justice and never of His mercy, simply turns against the knight the terms in which he originally challenged him:

> And to the villein said, Thou damned wight,
> The author of this fact, we here behold,
> What iustice can but iudge against thee right,
> With thine owne bloud to price his bloud, here shed
>   in sight.
>
> What franticke fit (quoth he) hath thus distraught
> Thee, foolish man, so rash a doome to giue?
> What iustice euer other iudgement taught,
> But he should die, who merites not to liue?
>
> (9.37–38)

Five stanzas later, Despair returns to the *lex talionis* invoked by the knight:

> The lenger life, I wote the greater sin,
> The greater sin, the greater punishment:
> All those great battels, which thou boasts to win,
> Through strife, and bloud-shed, and auengement,
> Now praysd, hereafter deare thou shalt repent:
> For life must life, and bloud must bloud repay.
>
> (9.43)

But although our awareness that human strength is frailty is unequivocal in this episode, it is by no means single-minded. Our evaluation of the Red Cross Knight's heroism is immensely enriched and complicated by the episode that begins the canto—Arthur's account of his upbringing and his falling in love with the Fairy Queen. Critics invariably neglect this episode when they discuss the encounter with Despair, but its relevance is a striking indication of the fact that Spenser thinks of a canto as a poetic unit. Arthur's story—which also concerns the humbling of a naively overconfident hero—dignifies the Red Cross Knight's motives in two ways. In the first place, it makes it impossible to consider human feelings as in themselves unworthy and dangerous. Arthur is brought up "in gentle thewes and martiall might" (9.3); his tutor Timon, whose name means honor and who was once "in warlike feates th'expertest man aliue" (9.4), is a pagan version of the knight turned hermit; Arthur's heroism is confirmed by his being humbled by the God of Love, "that proud auenging boy" (9.12). In almost every stanza of Arthur's narration, there is a formula for human feeling and experience that reminds us of the imperfections of the flesh.[7] And yet when Una sees "his visage wexed pale, / And chaunge of hew great passion did bewray," she says:

> O happy Queene of Faeries, that hast found
> Mongst many, one that with his prowesse may
> Defend thine honour, and thy foes confound:
> True Loues are often sown, but seldom grow on ground.
>
> (9.16)

In addition to complicating our sense of human motives in general, Arthur's story makes the Red Cross Knight's reaction to Sir Trevisan seem natural and right. The Red Cross Knight's comment—"For neuer knight I saw in such misseeming plight" (9.23)—justly confirms the description in the preceding stanza: "About his neck an hempen rope he weares, / That with his glistring armes does ill agree" (9.22). The difference between Arthur's story and that of Trevisan's friend, Sir Terwin—the lady who caused Terwin's despair is unworthy of a knight's devotion (9.27)—suggests that differences between good and bad, worthy and unworthy, can be defined in purely human terms, and that the Red Cross Knight's confidence in human powers is therefore not inherently foolish. Similarly, Arthur's relation to the Red Cross Knight makes the Red Cross Knight's relation to Sir Trevisan —his attempt to bring him out of his fears and restore his knightly boldness, and his willingness to champion his cause—seem entirely honorable. The canto begins:

> O Goodly golden chaine, wherewith yfere
> The vertues linked are in louely wize:
> And noble minds of yore allyed were,
> In braue poursuit of cheualrous emprize,

---

[7] Arthur speaks of his rankling wound of love (9.7), the "feruent fury" and the "rage" of the flames of love (9.8, 9), the general uncertainty of "fleshly might" (9.11), the "iollitie / Of looser life, and heat of hardiment" that motivated him before love struck him down (9.12), the ravishing delight of his dream of the Fairy Queen (9.14), the sorrow and care he experiences when she has left and the "labour, and long tyne" with which he now seeks her (9.15).

That none did others safety despize,
Nor aid enuy to him, in need that stands,
But friendly each did others prayse deuize,
How to aduaunce with fauourable hands,
As this good Prince redeemd the *Redcrosse* knight
    from bands. (9.1)

In the light of this, we are not surprised to find that the description of
the Red Cross Knight's indignation when he sees the "piteous spec-
tacle" of the dead Sir Terwin—"with firie zeale he burnt in courage
bold" (9.37)—uses the same terms as were used of Arthur when he
releases the Red Cross Knight from Orgoglio's dungeon, "with con-
stant zeale, and courage bold" (8.40).

Because of Arthur's presence in the canto, we see the inevitability
of the Red Cross Knight's encounter with Despair less as the dra-
matic result of his enfeebled condition than as a fatal necessity of
man's sense of his own dignity and strength. Consider the force given
by earlier episodes to what seems the most apparent sophistry:

Who trauels by the wearie wandring way,
To come vnto his wished home in haste,
And meetes a flood, that doth his passage stay,
Is not great grace to helpe him ouer past,
Or free his feet, that in the myre sticke fast?

    (9.39)

These lines are based on a psalm that appeals to God's mercy: "Saue
me, O God, for the waters are come in euen vnto my soule. I sticke
fast in the depe myre, where no ground is: I am come into depe wa-
ters, so that the floudes renne ouer me" (Psalm 69:1–2). This allu-
sion and the play on "grace" tell us what is wrong with Despair's
example: it invites us (as the Red Cross Knight suggests two stanzas
later) to act as God. But the lines are also plausible and persuasive,
because they render a worthy sense of human endeavor and obliga-
tion. The first two lines state the plight of Una and (with less exact-
ness) Arthur in the mortal world. Even more important is the fact
that "grace" is not simply a tag to indicate Despair's fallaciousness.
The word recalls its use, several stanzas earlier, to render the ties of
friendship that bind knights:

Certes (said he) hence shall I neuer rest,
Till I that treachours art haue heard and tride;
And you Sir knight, whose name mote I request,

> Of grace do me vnto his cabin guide.
> I that hight *Treuisan* (quoth he) will ride
> Against my liking backe, to doe you grace.

(9.32)

(Note that the last phrase would be more simply ironic if it were not for the Red Cross Knight's conversational "of grace.") To men who speak this way, Despair's argument suggests that assisting a miserable man out of the world is a moral obligation. This is not, of course, to deny that Despair's argument is fallacious and meant to deceive, and that there is a terrible irony in his use of the word "grace." It is to say that he turns to our disadvantage not a weakness but a strength—here the quality of humane feeling that is suggested by the epithet "gentle" (cf. stanzas 3, 16, 17, 24, 37), as in the preceding stanza he turned against us our sense of justice and righteous indignation.

In the encounter with Despair, the stakes are high for all men, not just for the Red Cross Knight. The experience of despair in the strict sense—the individual soul's conviction that its sinfulness is beyond salvation—does not begin until the second half of the episode. Despair's first effort of persuasion is not personal accusation of the Red Cross Knight (which does not occur until stanza 45), but an appeal to truths about the human condition that give man the dignity of self-understanding and that are often associated with heroic motivation and choice. Kathrine Koller has pointed out that Despair's enticement to death is a pastiche of pagan sentiments that became part of the Christian literature on "the art of dying well":

"You have sleep, death's counterfeit, and this you daily put on like a garment" (Cicero, *Tusc. Disp.* 1.38); "How foolish is it to fear it [death], since men simply await that which is sure, but fear only that which is uncertain!" (Seneca, *Ep. Mor.* 30.10–11); "No great pain lasts long" (*ibid.* 30.14); "For our part, if it so fall out that it seems a sentence delivered by God, that we depart from life, let us obey joyfully and thankfully and consider that we are being set free from prison and loosed from our chains, in order that we may pass on our way to the eternal home which is clearly ours, or else be free of all sensation and trouble" (*Tusc. Disp.* 1.49); "The nearer I approach death the more I feel like one who is in sight of land at last and is about to anchor in his home port after a long voyage" (Cicero, *De Senectute* 19).[8]

---

[8] This list is based on Koller's "Art, Rhetoric, and Holy Dying in the *Faerie Queene* with Special Reference to the Despair Canto," SP, 61 (1964), 131.

Everyone feels the seductiveness of Despair's invitation to "Sleepe after toyle, port after stormie seas" (9.40), but only when we recognize his use of these classical dicta do we see the justness of the knight's response: "The knight much wondred at his suddeine wit" (9.41). The knight tries to answer him in kind:

> The knight much wondred at his suddeine wit,
> And said, The terme of life is limited,
> Ne may a man prolong, nor shorten it;
> The souldier may not moue from watchfull sted,
> Nor leaue his stand, vntill his Captaine bed.
> Who life did limit by almightie doome,
> (Quoth he) knowes best the termes established;
> And he, that points the Centonell his roome,
> Doth license him depart at sound of morning droome.
>
> (9.41)

This stanza makes it explicit that Despair is engaged in turning man's strengths against himself. The Red Cross Knight invokes a venerable metaphor that suggests not simply the necessity of enduring the burdens of the flesh and the world, but also the dignity of accepting that necessity.[9] Despair's response is simply to continue the metaphor. "Quoth he" officially indicates a change of speaker, but since the pronoun is ambiguous it is possible to read the stanza as if the Red Cross Knight spoke the last four lines.[10]

Nor would this mistaken reading be corrected by the next stanza:

However, I give the translations in the respective volumes of the Loeb Classical Library: *Tusculan Disputations*, tr. J. E. King, London, 1927; *Epistulae Morales*, tr. Richard M. Gummere, vol. 1, London, 1917; *De Senectute*, etc., tr. W. A. Falconer, London, 1923.

[9] Cf. *De Senectute* 20, tr. Falconer: "Pythagoras bids us stand like faithful sentries and not quit our post until God, our Captain, gives the word." This passage is cited by Helen Gardner in her discussion of the metaphor, *The Business of Criticism*, Oxford, 1959, p. 49. In Sidney's *Arcadia*, Philoclea uses the metaphor to dissuade Pyrocles from suicide. *Works*, ed. Albert Feuillerat, Cambridge, 1912, 2, 108.

[10] At least one sixteenth-century reader made this mistake. Despair's words appear as an argument *against* suicide in *The Return from Parnassus*, Part 2, lines 1397–1398:

> Oh no, the sentinell his watch must keepe,
> Vntill his Lord do lycence him to sleepe.

The Three Parnassus Plays, ed. J. B. Leishman, London, 1949. That the author is remembering Spenser here is confirmed by the fact that twenty lines later he closely imitates 1.9.33—the description of Despair's abode.

Is not his deed, what euer thing is donne,
In heauen and earth? did not he all create
To die againe? all ends that was begonne.
Their times in his eternall booke of fate
Are written sure, and haue their certaine date.
Who then can striue with strong necessitie,
That holds the world in his still chaunging state,
Or shunne the death ordaynd by destinie?
When houre of death is come, let none aske whence,
     nor why.   (9.42)

With the exception of "to die againe" all of this could be put in the mouth of the Red Cross Knight. To appeal to God's inscrutability and power (as Arthur does, 9.6) may lead to, but is by no means identical with, the fatal mistake of remembering only His justice and wrath. Quite the contrary, the final lines of this stanza—reminiscent of heroes from Achilles to Hamlet—bespeak the moral fortitude that comes from accepting necessity, and they make a stronger argument for the Red Cross Knight's position than for Despair's. The awesome power that all readers have felt in Despair's arguments is due to the fact that they are directly generated by our own heroic energies and values. Even when Despair turns to accusing the Red Cross Knight and arguing him into death, he begins by invoking truths that are part of the self-knowledge of any Christian (9.43, quoted above). Many a sixteenth-century minister knew, from the spiritual distresses of his congregation,[11] how perilously close Despair's words are to Contemplation's "For bloud can nought but sin, and wars but sorrowes yield" (10.60). Similarly we cannot deny the truth of Despair's *contemptus mundi* in the next stanza:

For what hath life, that may it loued make,
And giues not rather cause it to forsake?
Feare, sicknesse, age, losse, labour, sorrow, strife,
Paine, hunger, cold, that makes the hart to quake;
And euer fickle fortune rageth rife,
All which, and thousands mo do make a loathsome life.
                                        (9.44)

    Up to this point in the episode, the narrative action is primarily the occasion for verse that directly engages the reader's energies and atti-

---

[11] See H. C. Porter, *Reformation and Reaction in Tudor Cambridge*, Cambridge, 1958, pp. 217, 285–286, 310, 320–321, 333, 340–342.

tudes. But at stanza 45 our relation to the verse changes. As Ernest Sirluck has observed, "We may safely take it . . . that here, if not earlier, the contemporary reader recognized the nature of Despair's fraud, and was able to observe both it and its effect upon Redcross from a point of vantage."[12] Sirluck specifically refers to Despair's attempt to dismiss Arthur's rescue of the knight from Orgoglio as "good lucke." Equally decisive, I think, is the opening line of the stanza: "Thou wretched man, of death hast greatest need." Despair's challenging manner provokes our dissent, and we are confirmed in it by recognizing that the statement, to be true, should substitute the word "grace" for "death." It is natural for our "point of vantage" to be established in this stanza, because for the first time the knight appears as a separate individual with a history of his own. But even though Despair's persuasiveness is now displayed in a drama external to us, the verse remains fully allegorical. Thus when we are told that "all his manly powres it did disperse, / As he were charmed with inchaunted rimes" (9.48), we know from our own experience the power of language to dissipate heroic strength. To the knight's earlier question—"How may a man . . . with idle speach / Be wonne, to spoyle the Castle of his health?"—we can say, with Trevisan, "I wote . . . whom triall late did teach" (9.31). In the next stanza, "hellish anguish did his soule assaile" produces its literal enactment in the lines that follow:

> He shew'd him painted in a table plaine,
> The damned ghosts, that doe in torments waile,
> And thousand feends that doe them endlesse paine
> With fire and brimstone, which for euer shall remaine.
>
> (9.49)

The act of reading, our taking in the full significance of "hellish anguish," makes us see these visions—which were a familiar symptom of despair[13]—not simply as diseased hallucinations, but as a potentiality of spiritual grief.

The most striking example of the way Spenser's verse generates allegorical realities is the rescue of the Red Cross Knight by Una. After Despair shows the torments of Hell, Spenser says:

> The sight whereof so thoroughly him dismaid,
> That nought but death before his eyes he saw,

[12] "A Note on the Rhetoric of Spenser's 'Despair,'" MP 47 (1949), 10.
[13] See Robert Burton, *Anatomy of Melancholy*, 3.4.2.6, ed. A. R. Shilleto, London, 1896, 3, 485.

And euer burning wrath before him laid,
By righteous sentence of th'Almighties law.

(9.50)

Our recognizing the disaster of only seeing death before your eyes directly depends on our knowing what it is that the Red Cross Knight does not see: that, in Una's words, "where iustice growes, there grows eke greater grace." It is our understanding—which includes our dismay here—that generates Una's intervention. Spenser makes it explicit that Una is not a *dea ex machina,* but that her rescue and the knight's spiritual distress are actions of a single mind. When Despair gives the knight a dagger,

> his hand did quake,
> And tremble like a leafe of Aspin greene,
> And troubled bloud through his pale face was seene
> To come, and goe with tydings from the hart,
> As it a running messenger had beene.
> At last resolu'd to worke his finall smart,
> He lifted vp his hand, that backe againe did start.

(9.51)

The last half-line is extremely important. It means that the Red Cross Knight feels a natural revulsion from self-murder,[14] and Una's intervention is generated by her experiencing this revulsion:

> Which when as *Vna* saw, through euery vaine
> The crudled cold ran to her well of life,
> As in a swowne: but soone reliu'd againe,
> Out of his hand she snatcht the cursed knife,
> And threw it to the ground, enraged rife.

(9.52)

Her feelings exactly parallel the knight's. This may be an act of grace —as a matter of theology, Spenser would certainly say that it was— but it is here represented as an action of the human soul. And what is most important for us is that the saving knowledge or remembrance

[14] A similar episode is discussed in M. S. and G. H. Blayney, "*The Faerie Queene* and an English Version of Chartier's *Traité de l'Espérance,*" SP, 55 (1958), 154–163. The narrator of Chartier's work (probably written between 1428 and 1433) is moved to suicide by Despair, whereupon "Nature, fearful of death, trembles and quakes so greatly that she awakens Understanding, who lies asleep" (p. 158). But the man remains oppressed by melancholy until Understanding calls forth Faith, Hope, and Charity.

takes the form of heroic self-reproach. Una matches Despair rhetorical question for rhetorical question:

> And to him said, Fie, fie, faint harted knight,
> What meanest thou by this reprochfull strife?
> Is this the battell, which thou vauntst to fight
> With that fire-mouthed Dragon, horrible and bright?
>
> Come, come away, fraile, feeble, fleshly wight,
> Ne let vaine words bewitch thy manly hart,
> Ne diuelish thoughts dismay thy constant spright.
> In heauenly mercies hast thou not a part?
> Why shouldst thou then despeire, that chosen art?
>
> (9.52–53)

The point of the whole episode has seemed to be the spiritual disasters inherent in human heroism, and yet the rescue from despair is rendered as an act of heroic self-consciousness. The question is how we are to interpret this fact. If we look into the literature of despair, we find that, in Burton's words, "Faith, hope, repentance, are the sovereign cures and remedies, the sole comforts in this case."[15] Repentance is the most important: Burton earlier calls it "the sole means to be relieved."[16] A desperate person, then, is rescued from himself by what we find in canto 10, in the House of Holiness. The character of Una's rescue of the Red Cross Knight is, to my knowledge, unexampled in literary treatments of despair.[17] When martial heroism appears as a spiritual metaphor, it characteristically renders protection against despair and not a rescue from it.[18] This fact confirms what would seem to be the significance of Spenser's rendering the rescue as a natural revulsion that produces heroic self-consciousness. If the spiritual energies that produce despair imply the resources to rescue us from it, then we can never truly be in Faustus' condition. But on the other hand, the very continuity of spiritual resources, the fact that

[15] *Anatomy*, ed. Shilleto, 3, 488.

[16] *Ibid.*, p. 473.

[17] In following up the various works mentioned in the *Variorum*, I found only one example of heroic self-consciousness producing an escape from despair—Tasso's *Rinaldo*, 11.54ff. But the episode does not involve despair of the soul's salvation; it is a story, like Sir Terwin's, of love despair.

[18] See Thomas Becon, *The Christian Knight*, in *The Catechism*, etc., ed. John Ayre, Cambridge: Parker Society, 1844, p. 624; George Wither, "Of Despaire," *Abuses Stript and Whipt*, 1.11. I learned of Becon's work from William Nelson, *The Poetry of Edmund Spenser*, New York, 1963, p. 152.

the rescue is not effected by a new spiritual experience, confirms what was so broadly and richly developed earlier in the canto—the inevitability of man's undergoing spiritual distress. (Hence we assent when Spenser begins the next canto by saying, "If any strength we haue, it is to ill.")

Even at this most "dramatic" of moments, the poem unfolds its truths, as William Nelson remarks, by way of analysis rather than history.[19] The rescue here does not render a new stage in a drama of conversion and regeneration. It is used to put us in full possession of the kind of truth stated by Hooker when he expounds "the certainty and perpetuity of faith in the elect," even in the most grievous spiritual distress: "The 'seed of God' abideth in them, and doth shield them from receiving any irremediable wound. Their faith, when it is at the strongest, is but weak; yet even then when it is at the weakest, so strong, that utterly it never faileth, it never perisheth altogether, no not in them who think it extinguished in themselves."[20]

The affirmation made at the end of the Despair canto is extremely problematic. Consider the confident way in which the puzzle about man's strength is maintained by Thomas Becon's Christian knight, as he resists Satan's temptation to despair: "Here hast thou mine armours, darts, and sword. [He has just asserted his dependence on God's grace and his trust in God's promises.] I am not able to resist thee with mine own strength and wisdom. But I can do all things through Christ Jesus, which hath overcome thee, and delivered me from thee. Even he teacheth, ruleth, governeth, confirmeth, strengtheneth, and defendeth me by his holy Spirit. Therefore seeing that God himself is on my side, who shall damn me?"[21] The knight's manner here is that of a man who, in the words of the various titles to the work "comforteth himself with the sweet promises of the holy scripture" and "liue[s] before God with a quiet and mery conscience."[22] Una's words, by comparison, are harrowing. Their vehemence is informed by the fearful revulsion from suicide, and we do not forget that she is "enraged rife." She invokes the firmest stays of our belief, and yet her heroic rhetoric shakes our souls, because it lays hold of and reverses the spiritual energies that were engaged by Despair's appeal.

[19] *Ibid.*, p. 173. Nelson's terms, of course, come from the Letter to Raleigh.
[20] The sermon is reprinted in *Of the Laws of Ecclesiastical Polity*, London: Everyman's Library, 1907, 1, 5.
[21] *The Christian Knight*, p. 633.
[22] *Ibid.*, pp. 626, 620.

In respect to the relation between the attitudes taken and the feeling with which they are charged, the rescue of the Red Cross Knight intensifies a puzzle developed earlier in the canto about Trevisan's escape from Despair. Trevisan is possessed by a violent and demeaning fear (9.21–23), which has motivated his flight (9.30). On the other hand, he attributes his escape to "greater grace" (9.26), says parenthetically of Despair, "God from him me blesse" (9.28), and says to the Red Cross Knight, "God you neuer let his charmed speeches heare" (9.30). Moreover, there is a sense in which Trevisan's fear is a proper means of his escape. He is described as standing astonished, "as one that had aspide / Infernall furies, with their chaines vntide" (9.24), and in fact he has been in the presence of "a man of hell" (9.28). Trevisan's calling himself "more fearefull, or more luckie wight" (9.30) is explicitly problematic, and when Una turns her fear into reproach, Spenser manages to turn all the elements of the puzzle into a single action of the mind without coming to a moral or theological determination about the cause of the knight's rescue. Moreover, it is not simply the status of the knight's fear that makes his rescue problematic. Although it is generated by and continues to express the knight's spiritual distress, Una's heroic reproach expresses a real strength. "Arise, Sir knight arise, and leaue this cursed place" (9.53), she says, and the canto concludes:

> So vp he rose, and thence amounted streight.
> Which when the carle beheld, and saw his guest
> Would safe depart, for all his subtill sleight,
> He chose an halter from among the rest,
> And with it hung himselfe, vnbid vnblest.
> But death he could not worke himselfe thereby;
> For thousand times he so himselfe had drest,
> Yet nathelesse it could not doe him die,
> Till he should die his last, that is eternally.
>
> (9.54)

The next canto immediately shows what our knowledge of Christian doctrine would in any case tell us—that the experience of despair has by no means been brought to a conclusion. Yet this stanza does give, for the moment, a sense of completion—not simply because we are told that the knight departs safely, but also because of the portrayal of Despair. Although he is acknowledged to be a permanent reality in human affairs, he is represented as self-defeating, and the stanza

360

encourages in us the confident relation to him that Becon's Christian Knight has to Satan.

I I I

The nature of our spiritual strength seems inherently problematic. Man's natural strengths by themselves seem insufficient and potentially disastrous, and yet they also seem to be essential sources of spiritual energy and moral value. On the other hand, though our strengths come from God, they in some sense become our own. Una's rescue of the Red Cross Knight from Despair contains both aspects of the puzzle: she speaks in man's heroic accents, and she is an agent of Heaven who becomes part of our minds. But we must now take notice of the fact that the two major statements about human strength in Book I do not represent it as problematic—the first stanza of canto 10 (quoted above) and the first stanza of canto 8:

> Ay me, how many perils doe enfold
> The righteous man, to make him daily fall?
> Were not, that heauenly grace doth him vphold,
> And stedfast truth acquite him out of all.
> Her loue is firme, her care continuall,
> So oft as he through his owne foolish pride,
> Or weaknesse is to sinfull bands made thrall.

How do we reconcile these statements with the affirmation, implicit in treating human strength as a puzzle, that man in some sense has strengths of his own?

Woodhouse recognized this problem when he spoke of "Spenser's partial adherence to two different traditions," which are represented by Hooker and Calvin: "In the one tradition grace could build on the sure foundation of nature. In the other it seemed, rather, to demand a new start. Spenser tries to do justice to the facts of human experience which support these two rival views."[23] It is unclear whether Woodhouse thought the poem suffered from this double allegiance. He seems to have felt there was a problem of theological consistency, for he says that Spenser's "task was rendered more difficult" and he speaks of one tradition being "crossed and partly cancelled" by the other. But the advantage and importance of poetry in general, and of Spenser's kind of poetry in particular, is that it can coherently express attitudes that prove contradictory when worked out philosophically.

---

[23] "Nature and Grace," p. 225.

As Empson has observed, "Literary uses of the problem of free-will and necessity, for example, may be noticed to give curiously bad arguments and I should think get their strength from keeping you in doubt between the two methods."[24] Furthermore, it is important to recognize that Spenser's drastic statements would be acceptable to almost any Christian, short of a heretic like Arminius. For example, Lancelot Andrewes, whose views on nature and grace resemble Hooker's, says: "It is dangerous to ascribe too little to the grace of God for then we rob him of his glory, but if we ascribe too little to ourselves there is no danger; for whatsoever we take from ourselves, it cannot hinder us from being true Christians; but if we ascribe that to the strength of our own nature which is the proper work of grace, then do we blemish God's glory."[25]

Nevertheless, we cannot deny that there is a contradiction—of the sort that generated some of the profoundest theological controversies of the sixteenth century—between the first stanza of canto 10 and the praise of Cleopolis at the end, or the stanza in which Contemplation says to the knight whom he has called "thou man of earth" (10.52):

> [A ploughman] brought thee vp in ploughmans state
>   to byde,
> Whereof *Georgos* he thee gaue to name;
> Till prickt with courage, and thy forces pryde,
> To Faery court thou cam'st to seeke for fame,
> And proue thy puissaunt armes, as seemes thee best
>   became.   (10.66)

We have praised Spenser for the habit of mind that allows him to include a stanza like this in canto 10. But when we say that Spenser's poetry gives coherent expression to potentially conflicting attitudes, do we mean any more than that he allows them to exist side by side? It could be argued that the traditions of Hooker and Calvin are kept segregated in Book I—the former dominating cantos 3 and 6, for example, and the latter cantos 5, 8, 9, and 10. Whatever recognition of human strengths we find in these four cantos, they do not hold the two traditions of which Woodhouse speaks in an even balance, and it is coherent expression of conflicting attitudes in this sense that we expect to find somewhere in Book I. We do find it, appropriately, at the end of the book, in the battle with the dragon in canto 11.

---

[24] William Empson, *Some Versions of Pastoral*, London, 1935, p. 115.
[25] *Sermons*, London, 1875–1882, 5, 316; quoted by H. C. Porter, *Reformation and Reaction in Tudor Cambridge*, p. 393.

Simply by looking at the narrative action, we can see that canto 11 is a criticism of human heroism of the sort with which we are now familiar in Book I. The Red Cross Knight and the dragon are both described as motivated by wrath, outrage, and the like (11.16, 17, 22, 24–27, 37, 39, 40, 42, 44). At the end of each day's fighting, the knight is in extreme danger, from which he is saved only by accidentally falling first into the Well of Life and then under the Tree of Life —restoring agents that are clearly sacred in character.[26] Much of the verse is devoted to the ills inherent in human heroism. In a series of similes that Milton must have remembered, the dragon, the principle of evil, is described in terms of honorable human endeavor. His scales are like "an Armour bright" (11.9), and his wings are like the sails of a ship (11.10). The most interesting of these stanzas is:

> His blazing eyes, like two bright shining shields,
> Did burne with wrath, and sparkled liuing fyre;
> As two broad Beacons, set in open fields,
> Send forth their flames farre off to euery shyre,
> And warning giue, that enemies conspyre,
> With fire and sword the region to inuade;
> So flam'd his eyne with rage and rancorous yre:
> But farre within, as in a hollow glade,
> Those glaring lampes were set, that made a dreadfull
>   shade. (11.14)

Our sense of the human reality of this evil is immensely complicated when the dragon's eyes are compared to friendly fires, as if he were on our side and the enemy were somewhere else. The stanza, which begins with a simple comparison of the dragon to something heroic, ends with ambivalent pastoralism.

Spenser's fullest and most searching examination of human heroism comes, fittingly, at the climax of the first day's battle, when the dragon breathes fire on the knight and makes him burn in his own armor:

> Not that great Champion of the antique world,
> Whom famous Poetes verse so much doth vaunt,

---

[26] They have usually been identified with the Anglican sacraments of baptism and the eucharist. But there has never been any positive evidence for the latter identification, and Rosemond Tuve has now shown that they figure forth something that is more fundamental spiritually and less specific historically—the operation of grace in the human heart, with the basic image being the heart as a garden. *Allegorical Imagery*, pp. 110–112.

And hath for twelue huge labours high extold,
So many furies and sharpe fits did haunt.

(11.27)

The formulas with which Hercules is described indicate how high the stakes are here. Heroism at its noblest turns out to be self-destructive: "That erst him goodly arm'd, now most of all him harm'd" (11.27). The knight who was just before filled with mighty wrath is now reduced to an extremity that resembles his distress in the Cave of Despair (11.28). The dragon then strikes him down, and he is saved only because he falls into the Well of Life.

What we have so far seen is decisive taken by itself, but it is not all that canto 11 shows us of human heroism. The canto begins with a glamorous presentation of the Red Cross Knight. Una says to him:

The sparke of noble courage now awake,
And striue your excellent selfe to excell;
That shall ye euermore renowmed make,
Aboue all knights on earth, that batteill vndertake.

(11.2)

He wears "glistring armes, that heauen with light did fill" (11.4). The poet asks for the muse's inspiration, "That I this man of God his godly armes may blaze" (11.7). Though the knight's motivating energies are pointedly like the dragon's, his powers are genuine:

For neuer felt his [the dragon's] imperceable brest
So wondrous force, from hand of liuing wight;
Yet had he prou'd the powre of many a puissant knight.

(11.17)

Spenser emphasizes the Red Cross Knight's prowess even to the point of allowing what would seem a crucial contradiction in the narrative action. After emerging from the Well of Life, the knight wounds the dragon in the head. Spenser says:

I wote not, whether the reuenging steele
Were hardned with that holy water dew,
Wherein he fell, or sharper edge did feele,
Or his baptized hands now greater grew;
Or other secret vertue did ensew;
Else neuer could the force of fleshly arme,
Ne molten mettall in his bloud embrew:

364

For till that stownd could neuer wight him harme,
By subtilty, nor slight, nor might, nor mighty charme.

(11.36)

According to this stanza, there seems to be no question about whose strength quells the dragon. Yet despite the last lines, the dragon has already been wounded in the first day's fighting, when the knight, putting "three mens strength vnto the stroke," "wrought a wound full wyde" with his spear (11.20).

In narrative action, the two perspectives on human strength produce inconsistencies. They are made coherent and harmonious by the workings of the verse—most complexly and impressively in the two passages that take us from the end of each day's fighting to the beginning of the next. When the Red Cross Knight falls into the Well of Life, we are told that

> vnto life the dead it could restore,
> And guilt of sinfull crimes cleane wash away,
> Those that with sicknesse were infected sore,
> It could recure, and aged long decay
> Renew, as one were borne that very day.

(11.30)

Four stanzas later, he emerges from the well

> As Eagle fresh out of the Ocean waue,
> Where he hath left his plumes all hoary gray,
> And deckt himselfe with feathers youthly gay,
> Like Eyas hauke vp mounts vnto the skies,
> His newly budded pineons to assay,
> And marueiles at himselfe, still as he flies:
> So new this new-borne knight to battell new did rise.

(11.34)

The simile is based on a famous metaphor in Psalm 103 (verse 5), but the nature of the knight's "new-borne" strength is not as unequivocal as the two quoted stanzas suggest. As we go from one to the other, our attention is on nature, not grace. First there is a description of the sunset:

> Now gan the golden *Phoebus* for to steepe
> His fierie face in billowes of the west,
> And his faint steedes watred in Ocean deepe,
> Whiles from their iournall labours they did rest.

(11.31)

365

In the next stanza, Una, mistakenly "weening that the sad end of the warre," spends the night watching and praying. The stanza that follows combines the elements of these two as the mythical rendering of nature harmonizes with human expectations and desires:

> The morrow next gan early to appeare,
> That *Titan* rose to runne his daily race;
> But early ere the morrow next gan reare
> Out of the sea faire *Titans* deawy face,
> Vp rose the gentle virgin from her place,
> And looked all about, if she might spy
> Her loued knight to moue his manly pace.

(11.33)

When the knight begins "to moue his manly pace" in the next stanza, we are encouraged to see his revival as the result not simply of grace, but also of the orderly processes of nature. Even his fall, in light of the description of the sunset, can be regarded as a natural weariness from which he can recover. These stanzas bring directly into the poem the fact that the dragon, which we have associated with the realities of a fallen world, is in an important sense unnatural (see especially stanzas 4, 21, 37, 44, 54, in which he is compared to various upheavals in the elements). The comparison of the new-risen knight to an eagle serves not simply to invoke the realm of grace, but to confirm our newly awakened sense of nature, for it looks back to and qualifies an earlier comparison of the dragon to "an Eagle, seeing pray appeare" (11.9). The point is made again three lines later, when the comparison of the knight to an "eyas [young, untrained] hauke" counterbalances the earlier comparison of the dragon to a "hagard [wild, adult] hauke" (11.19).

The balance between the orders of nature and grace that begins to develop in this passage is fully achieved in its analogue at the end of the second day's battle. Even the narrative framework contributes to the even poising of the two perspectives on human strength. The knight falls not because he is helpless, but because he strategically retreats "a little backward for his best defence" (11.45). But then:

> It chaunst (eternall God that chaunce did guide)
> As he recoyled backward, in the mire
> His nigh forwearied feeble feet did slide,
> And downe he fell, with dread of shame sore terrifide.

(11.45)

Where before he longed for death, here he reacts heroically, "with dread of shame." This moment recalls two earlier ones. The first occurs after the knight is thrown from his horse:

> [he] can quickly ryse
> From off the earth, with durty bloud distaynd,
> For that reprochfull fall right fowly he disdaynd.
>
> (11.23)

The second is when the dragon knocks him to the ground with his tail and drives his sting into his shoulder:

> But yet more mindfull of his honour deare,
> Then of the grieuous smart, which him did wring,
> From loathed soile he can him lightly reare.
>
> (11.39)

In the context of these earlier occurrences, we expect the knight to rise again, and he does so by means of the long passage which in effect concludes the battle with the dragon.

The passage begins with three stanzas that describe the Tree of Life:

> In all the world like was not to be found,
> Saue in that soile, where all good things did grow,
> And freely sprong out of the fruitfull ground,
> As incorrupted Nature did them sow,
> Till that dread Dragon all did ouerthrow.
>
> (11.47)

It is precisely in the state of "incorrupted Nature" that the puzzles about man's nature cease to be problematic. And Spenser proceeds to put us in as full possession of that Eden as we can have. The stanza continues by recognizing, in Milton's words, that "next to Life / Our Death the Tree of Knowledge grew fast by" (*PL* 4.220–221). But the fact that "one mans fault hath doen vs all to dy" (11.47) is only the beginning of the drama of man's destiny, and Spenser therefore returns us to the Tree of Life. He describes the healing balm that flows from it, and says

> Life and long health that gratious ointment gaue,
> And deadly woundes could heale, and reare again
> The senselesse corse appointed for the graue.
> Into that same he fell: which did from death him saue.
>
> (11.48)

The next stanza makes our security from the dragon, our possession of life, explicit:

> For nigh thereto the euer damned beast
> Durst not approch, for he was deadly made,
> And all that life preserued, did detest.
>
> (11.49)

From this point, Spenser returns us, with perfect poise, to the nature of the world in which we live:

> By this the drouping day-light gan to fade,
> And yeeld his roome to sad succeeding night,
> Who with her sable mantle gan to shade
> The face of earth, and wayes of liuing wight,
> And high her burning torch set vp in heauen bright.
>
> (11.49)

We are aware that night can be the element of evil and the enemy of life, and yet it arrives as part of an orderly process, and the last line describes, truthfully, how beautiful it can be. Then, just as in the earlier passage, we turn to Una:

> When gentle *Vna* saw the second fall
> Of her deare knight, who wearie of long fight,
> And faint through losse of bloud, mou'd not at all,
> But lay as in a dreame of deepe delight,
> Besmeard with pretious Balme, whose vertuous might
> Did heale his wounds, and scorching heat alay,
> Againe she stricken was with sore affright,
> And for his safetie gan deuoutly pray;
> And watch the noyous night, and wait for ioyous day.
>
> (11.50)

The stanza that described Una after the first day's battle was wholly from her point of view. Now Spenser juxtaposes her notion of what has happened and her consequent fearfulness with our knowledge of the knight's condition. The double perspective could produce a dichotomy between nature and grace. But when Spenser returns us to Una's "sore affright" after describing the action of the "pretious Balme," he makes it explicit that her distress is as important as our secure knowledge in motivating the prayer and expectation with which the stanza ends.

When the "ioyous day" arrives—as before, in the form of a myth-ological sunrise, of the sort we associate with epic poetry—there is no single realm to which it can be assigned:

> The ioyous day gan early to appeare,
> And faire *Aurora* from the deawy bed
> Of aged *Tithone* gan her selfe to reare,
> With rosie cheekes, for shame as blushing red;
> Her golden lockes for haste were loosely shed
> About her eares, when *Vna* her did marke
> Clymbe to her charet, all with flowers spred,
> From heauen high to chase the chearelesse darke;
> With merry note her loud salutes the mounting larke.
>
> (11.51)

On the one hand, this is a glamorous rendering of ordinary nature, not a description of "incorrupted Nature." On the other hand, the lit-eralness with which the dawn is personified draws Una into an action of the gods. And now the hero who had fallen "with dread of shame sore terrifide," arises:

> Then freshly vp arose the doughtie knight,
> All healed of his hurts and woundes wide,
> And did himselfe to battell readie dight.
>
> (11.52)

It takes only one stanza to dispatch the dragon (11.53), and he falls to earth in a stanza in which some formulas render his terrifying ef-fects on nature and others his evanescence and unreality (11.54). To the very end the canto is concerned with the double perspective it has so fully developed. Even when the dragon falls, Una fears to approach:

> But yet at last, when as the direfull feend
> She saw not stirre, off-shaking vaine affright,
> She nigher drew, and saw that ioyous end.
>
> (11:55)

And the canto concludes with the puzzle about man's strengths in a form in which it most inspires trust and confidence:

> Then God she praysd, and thankt her faithfull knight,
> That had atchieu'd so great a conquest by his might.
>
> (11.55)

369

Chapter Eleven

Heroic and Pastoral
in Book III

I

In the proem to Book IV, Spenser answers the "Stoicke censours" who have reproved him for "magnifying louers deare debate." Love, Spenser says, is a fit subject of poetry, because true love inspires man to noble deeds:

> For it of honor and all vertue is
> The roote, and brings forth glorious flowres of fame.
>
> All the workes of those wise sages,
> And braue exploits which great Heroes wonne,
> In loue were either ended or begunne.
>
> (4.Proem.2, 3)

The same claim about love is made in Book III (see 3.1–2, 5.1), which is clearly the object of the attacks that are dealt with in this proem. It would be absurd for us to take these statements literally and say that they define the moral point of Book III or adequately represent its moral complexity. On the other hand, we should not simply ignore them, and we certainly cannot ignore the fact that in Book III true love is consistently represented by the heroic actions and attitudes of Britomart and Arthur. Similarly, false love is often associated with a defection from or the destruction of knightly heroism. Heroic action, while neither the literal aim nor the moral justification of true love, is a pervasive metaphor for its nature and qualities, and it is used to express Spenser's central attitude towards human love.

But given that *The Faerie Queene* is a heroic poem and that Spenser's materials are those of chivalric romance, in what way do his materials express the themes of Book III? Heroism is a complex phenomenon in Books I and II, but at the same time the heroic action in these books makes sense in the simplest kind of reading. If we are presented with a scenario of either book, we see the relevance of heroic quest and battle as ways of rendering the moral and psychological phenomena with which Spenser is concerned. But the scenario of Book III does not make this kind of sense. Unlike the battles in which the Red

Cross Knight and Guyon engage, Britomart's battles have no discernible relation to the struggles of the mind. Nor is there any other kind of simple, obvious relation between narrative action and moral idea when, for example, Britomart defeats Marinell. Rather, Britomart's heroic action acquires its significance by being placed in a specific poetic context—the traditional opposition of heroic and pastoral. The first questions we must ask concern the version of pastoral we find in Book III and the way in which the heroic is opposed to it.

In Book III Spenser is hardly ever concerned with the depiction of rustic life, idealized or not, as a foil to the life of civilization. The characteristic pastoral setting is the woods—with some excursions to the sea—and the characteristic inhabitants of the pastoral world are not shepherds, but mythological figures. This type of pastoral is frankly based on literary images, and it deals with a harmonious and benign nature—the vision that informs Virgil's fourth eclogue and Milton's Eden. Its human use lies not in depicting or praising a real way of life, but in making nature a projection of human nature—in particular, a projection of human erotic desires. Our concern is the way this type of pastoral operates in a heroic poem, and we can take as a point of departure the first chorus of Tasso's *Aminta:*

> O bella età de l'oro,
> non già perché di latte
> se 'n corse il fiume e stillò mèle il bosco;
> non perché i frutti loro
> diêr da l'aratro intatte
> le terre, e gli angui errâr senz'ira o tòsco;
> non perché nuvol fosco
> non spiegò allor suo velo,
> ma in primavera eterna,
> ch'ora s'accende e verna,
> rise di luce e di sereno il cielo;
> né portò peregrino
> o merce o guerra a gli altrui lidi il pino.[1]

O lovely golden age, not because the river ran with milk and the wood dripped honey; not because the lands gave their fruits untouched by the plow, and snakes wound their way without anger or venom; not because dark cloud did not then spread its veil, but in eternal spring, which now grows hot and cold, the sky

[1] Torquato Tasso, *Aminta*, ed. Bruno Maier, Milan, 1952, act 1, lines 570–582.

smiled clear and light; nor did the wandering ship carry trade or
war to others' shores.

Borrowing extensively from Virgil's fourth eclogue, Tasso describes
the golden world by listing several features of the idealized nature of
idyllic pastoral. The two major images—spontaneous growth and per-
petual spring—are ones we shall meet again in the Garden of Adonis.
In the next stanza, Tasso takes rhetorical advantage of his initial ne-
gations to assert that the golden world was golden because honor, "the
tyrant of our nature,"

> non mischiava il suo affanno
> fra le liete dolcezze
> de l'amoroso gregge.

$$(1.589–591)$$

did not mingle its troubling effects among the sweet joys of the
amorous flock.

All the natural wonders of the golden world are a setting for unin-
hibited erotic delight:

> Allor tra fiori e linfe
> traean dolci carole
> gli Amoretti senz'archi e senza faci;
> sedean pastori e ninfe,
> meschiando a le parole
> vezzi e susurri, ed a i susurri i baci
> strettamente tenaci;
> la verginella ignude
> scopria le fresche rose,
> ch'or tien ne 'l velo ascose,
> e le poma de 'l seno acerbe e crude;
> e spesso in fiume o in lago
> scherzar si vide con l'amata il vago.

$$(1.596–608)$$

Then among flowers and streams, Cupids without bows and
torches led sweet dances; nymphs and shepherds sat about, mix-
ing caresses and whispers with their words, and with the whispers
kisses tightly clinging; the virgin bared the fresh roses, which she
now keeps hidden in a veil, and the young, unripened apples of
her bosom; and often in river or lake, the desirous lover was seen
sporting with his beloved.

The honor that has destroyed this golden world has the usual double definition, which is developed in the last two stanzas of the chorus. It is woman's honor, which makes her deny the favors of love, and it is the warrior's honor, which makes him seek high achievement rather than pastoral ease.

When the erotic pastoral vision occurs in a Renaissance heroic poem, we expect that the values expressed in Tasso's chorus will simply be inverted, as Tasso himself inverted them in *Gerusalemme Liberata*.[2] The "joyous, golden law" ("legge aurea e felice") of the golden world—"If it pleases, it is allowed" ("S'ei piace, ei lice")—is categorically rejected. In a fallen world, the impulses that cause man to create images of ideal gardens are seen as inherently sinful. The heroic then is not simply "the best way of life," but expresses something essential to any good life: noble impulses must either overcome or succumb to sinful ones. Hence the heroic and the pastoral are often radically opposed, and if this is not Spenser's only view of their relation, it is certainly the one that underlies Guyon's mission to destroy the Bower of Bliss.

The pastoral in Book III is very different from what it is in Book II: the erotic paradise, the Garden of Adonis, now expresses a moral norm for human love, rather than a mortal threat to human temperance. The Garden of Adonis is in the tradition exemplified by Tasso's vision of the golden age; what is curious is that it cannot be understood in the moral terms provided by Tasso's chorus and by its inversion in *Gerusalemme Liberata* and Book II of *The Faerie Queene*. The relation between heroic and pastoral in Book III is not a matter of moral choice—whether the choice is between good and bad or between two forms of the good, such as the active and contemplative lives. The pastoral image of love in the Garden of Adonis confers value on the heroic human lover: the heroic and the pastoral are thus seen as mutually dependent, not mutually exclusive. To complicate matters further, Spenser reconciles the heroic and the pastoral by developing the opposition between them. At the same time as the pastoral expresses a valuable and true vision of human love, it also represents modes of human feeling that are inferior to and incompatible with Britomart's heroic love. Even so, Britomart, unlike Guyon and Tasso's Rinaldo, is not threatened or endangered by pastoral settings and the characters identified with them. In neither its "good" nor its

---

[2] Armida's garden, like the Bower of Bliss, is a false paradise. On the other hand, the rustic pastoral (Erminia's stay among the shepherds, 7.1–22) provides an image of virtuous life and security from warfare.

"bad" aspects does the pastoralism of Book III satisfy our ordinary expectations of its relation to the heroic. (Sidney's *Arcadia,* to take still another example, does satisfy our expectations: it is axiomatic that kings cannot retire to the countryside and that heroism and love, the pastoral occupation, will conflict with each other.) We must take Book III on its own terms, and these are not the terms of any other Renaissance heroic poem—not even Book II of *The Faerie Queene.* Spenser announces the theme of heroic and pastoral in the first canto of Book III, and in doing so he indicates, both in details of expression and in the character of his narration, the particular responses and awarenesses that are appropriate to this book of his poem.

I I

Just after Britomart and the Red Cross Knight enter Malecasta's castle, they encounter the tapestries that portray the love of Venus and Adonis (1.34–38). Everyone recognizes that the tapestries are a characteristic piece of Spenserian pastoral, but our understanding of them has been considerably clouded by C. S. Lewis' discussion:

> Let us compare the pictured Venus and Adonis in the house of Malecasta with the real Venus and Adonis in the Garden. We find at once that the latter (the good and real) are a picture of actual fruition. Venus, in defiance of the forces of death, the Stygian gods,
>
> > Possesseth him, and of his sweetnesse takes her fill.
>
> Nothing could be franker; a dainty reader might even object that the phrase "takes her fill" brings us too close to other and more prosaic appetites. But daintiness will be rebuked (as Spenser is always ready to rebuke it) if any one tries to prefer the pictured Venus on Malecasta's wall. For she is not in the arms of Adonis: she is merely looking at him,
>
> > And whilst he bath'd, with her two crafty spyes,
> > She secretly would search each daintie lim.
>
> The words "crafty," "spies," and "secretly" warn us sufficiently well where we have arrived. The good Venus is a picture of fruition: the bad Venus is a picture not of "lust in action" but of lust suspended—lust turning into what would now be called *skeptophilia.*[3]

[3] *The Allegory of Love,* Oxford, 1936, pp. 331–332. The fact is that in the stanza after the one Lewis quotes, Spenser says that the bad Venus "ioyd his loue in secret vnespyde" (1.37).

Let us look at the stanzas from which Lewis takes his quotations:

> And whilst he slept, she ouer him would spred
> Her mantle, colour'd like the starry skyes,
> And her soft arme lay vnderneath his hed,
> And with ambrosiall kisses bathe his eyes;
> And whilest he bath'd, with her two crafty spyes,
> She secretly would search each daintie lim,
> And throw into the well sweet Rosemaryes,
> And fragrant violets, and Pances trim,
> And euer with sweet Nectar she did sprinkle him.
>
> (1.36)

> There wont faire *Venus* often to enioy
> Her deare *Adonis* ioyous company,
> And reape sweet pleasure of the wanton boy;
> There yet, some say, in secret he does ly,
> Lapped in flowres and pretious spycery,
> By her hid from the world, and from the skill
> Of *Stygian* Gods, which doe her loue enuy;
> But she her selfe, when euer that she will,
> Possesseth him, and of his sweetnesse takes her fill.
>
> (6.46)

From the character of the description, one would certainly not say that the good Venus is defying the Stygian gods. Her love, as much as that of her wicked counterpart, depends on pastoral seclusion. If we look at the whole stanza in canto 1, we find that the two lines quoted by Lewis are imbedded in a lovely and attractive context, and that it is precisely the poetic mode of this context that Spenser draws on in such lines as "reape sweet pleasure of the wanton boy" and "Lapped in flowres and pretious spycery." Similarly, the "bad" Venus' transformation of the dead Adonis into a flower (1.38) is directly echoed by the grove in which the "good" Venus enjoys her love: "all about grew euery sort of flowre, / To which sad louers were transformd of yore" (6.45). Spenser is not attempting to depict two modes of real existence that are polar opposites. The primary reality in these two passages is verbal—the pastoral mode that gives us two versions of sweet erotic pleasure. In these terms we can explain a line that Lewis cannot: "There yet, some say, in secret he does ly." For Lewis, "secretly" is a danger signal to warn us against the bad Venus, so that he can hardly allow "secret" to be used of the good. But Spenser uses not only "secret," but "wanton" in this stanza. He deliberately repeats words that have previously suggested corrupt feeling, as he does throughout this passage.[4] Evidently he thinks that in certain contexts the pastoral expression of sweet erotic pleasure is valid, in others it is not. As we shall see, Spenser treats the pastoral as a valid expression of human love when we understand it as visionary or mythological. However, as a metaphor for the feelings of an individual human being, it expresses limitations of personality, and is thus an appropriate introduction to the self-indulgence found in Malecasta's castle.

Lewis oversimplifies when he speaks of a bad and a good Venus, and he is incorrect when he makes the issue a matter of preferring one or the other. In the description of the tapestry Spenser does not try to elicit from us a categorical moral judgment, and he does not try to create the sense of evil that makes such judgments appropriate. When he wants such a response from us, he gives a drastic and terrifying portrayal of skeptophilia:

> He, like an Adder, lurking in the weeds,
> His wandring thought in deepe desire does steepe,
> And his fraile eye with spoyle of beautie feedes;
> Sometimes he falsely faines himselfe to sleepe,
> Whiles through their lids his wanton eies do peepe,
> To steale a snatch of amorous conceipt,
> Whereby close fire into his heart does creepe:
> So, he them deceiues, deceiu'd in his deceipt,
> Made drunke with drugs of deare voluptuous receipt.
>
> (2.5.34)

Every detail of imagery and diction is devoted to expressing a radical corruption of desire. When we compare the stanza from Book III, it is impossible to equate Venus and Cymochles, as Lewis does.[5] Spenser's diction in describing Venus' eyes is notably less severe than in the description of Cymochles, and the alliteration produces a softer effect: compare "secretly would search" with "steale a snatch." Even more decisive is the fact that Spenser does not continue the vein of "She secretly would search each daintie lim" to the end of the stanza. Instead he introduces a second main verb, "throw," and the sentence turns into a brief catalogue of flowers. The stanza ends unequivocally

---

[4] Cf. his use of "wanton" in 6.42, 44, 49, and of "paramour" in 6.41, 45.

[5] *The Allegory of Love*, p. 332. "Armed," as he says, by his analysis of the two Venuses, Lewis returns to the Bower of Bliss and discusses the description of Cymochles.

with the sweetness that is its most prominent characteristic and that is conveyed by the consistently pretty and decorative language.

Surely this stanza does not express anything that can properly be called diseased. The two lines dealing with Venus' "crafty spyes" modify our sense of erotic sweetness, but they do not control and determine our responses. They suggest a quality of erotic self-indulgence that is entirely appropriate to the stanza and to the whole description of Venus and Adonis. Spenser's criticism of Venus' love is that it is self-regarding, cloistered, and fragile. It depends on her keeping Adonis from going out "to hunt the saluage beast in forrest wyde" (1.37), and when he is killed, she can only behave as she did when he was her lover: "euermore / With her soft garment wipes away the gore, / Which staines his snowy skin with hatefull hew" (1.38). The pastoral prettiness that dominates these stanzas indicates emotional inadequacy, rather than corruption. Hence the tapestries conclude:

> But when she saw no helpe might him restore,
> Him to a daintie flowre she did transmew,
> Which in that cloth was wrought, as if it liuely grew.

> (1.38)

In the Bower of Bliss, the "liveliness" of artifacts endangers the viewer; here it simply enforces our awareness that this resolution of erotic tragedy is merely picturesque and hence valid only in a world of mythological pastoral. The sufferings of human love—we soon see them in Britomart as well as in Malecasta—are deeper and more violent than Venus'. The image of their resolution must acknowledge the turbulence of human feeling and express more vigor than the dainty flower does.

Such an image is provided by heroic action. When the revellers have gone to bed, Malecasta, "panting soft, and trembling euerie ioynt," creeps to Britomart's chamber:

> And to her bed approching, first she prooued,
> Whether she slept or wakt, with her soft hand
> She softly felt, if any member mooued,
> And lent her wary eare to vnderstand,
> If any puffe of breath, or signe of sence she fond.

> Which whenas none she fond, with easie shift,
> For feare least her vnwares she should abrayd,
> The'embroderd quilt she lightly vp did lift,
> And by her side her selfe she softly layd,

377

Of euery finest fingers touch affrayd;
Ne any noise she made, ne word she spake,
But inly sigh'd.   (1.60–61)

All Malecasta's movements and gestures are rendered by the delicate, sensuous vocabulary with which Spenser characterizes Venus' behavior to Adonis. In the next stanza, Spenser executes a characteristic shift of diction:

Where feeling one close couched by her side,
She lightly lept out of her filed bed,
And to her weapon ran, in minde to gride
The loathed leachour. But the Dame halfe ded
Through suddein feare and ghastly drerihed,
Did shrieke alowd, that through the house it rong,
And the whole family therewith adred,
Rashly out of their rouzed couches sprong,
And to the troubled chamber all in armes did throng.

(1.62)

"The loathed leachour" renders Britomart's instinctive and indignant reaction at finding what she thinks is a man in her bed. Malecasta's sensual softness produces not a moral judgment, but a farcical action. Spenser then makes us see this action in terms of the opposition of heroic and pastoral. When Malecasta's courtiers are afraid to attack Britomart, the knight Gardante shoots an arrow at her:

The mortall steele stayd not, till it was seene
To gore her side, yet was the wound not deepe,
But lightly rased her soft silken skin,
That drops of purple bloud thereout did weepe,
Which did her lilly smock with staines of vermeil steepe.

(1.65)

This is unmistakably—indeed, almost too emphatically—in the mode of the Venus and Adonis tapestries. Britomart reacts as if she were on the field of battle:

Wherewith enrag'd she fiercely at them flew,
And with her flaming sword about her layd,
That none of them foule mischiefe could eschew,
But with her dreadfull strokes were all dismayd:
Here, there, and euery where about her swayd
Her wrathfull steele, that none mote it abide.

(1.66)

In order to understand just what the opposition of heroic and pastoral expresses here, we must consider the character of the episode in Malecasta's castle. The concluding scene has a farcical aspect because the whole episode has a comic basis—the confusion about Britomart's sex. Like the disguised heroine of any comedy, Britomart is immune to sexual assault simply because she is a woman. On this basis, Spenser portrays her as immune to corrupted feeling. The finest example is the passage in which Britomart sympathizes with Malecasta's "strong extremitie" because she too knows "what paines do louing harts perplexe"; since she will not despise love, she behaves courteously to Malecasta and thus encourages her attempted seduction (1. 53–55). The scene is wonderfully comic, but if we read it dramatically it is absurd, and Britomart seems rather a fool. She sympathizes with Malecasta because she is a woman, but unlike Shakespeare's Viola, she is entirely unaware of the sexual grotesqueness of the situation. If we are not bothered by this, it is because Britomart's relation to Malecasta is never really dramatic. Our first sight of her inside the castle is as the moon breaking through the clouds to cheer the lost traveler (1.43), and we continue to see her under the aspect of a natural fact (cf. 1.46, 49, 54, 58), rather than as a real person reacting to and dealing with her hostess. Hence, we do not anticipate that unnaturalness will be resolved dramatically—by events that reveal Britomart's true identity. We anticipate no resolution (whereas we know that there is a male twin of Viola for Olivia to marry), and naturalness is not something worked out; it is always present in Britomart's behavior and the images that are associated with her.

The importance of all this is the way it affects our moral criticism of Malecasta—our sense of the way Britomart foils her. Malecasta herself is sufficiently awesome and menacing; her chaotic feelings play out the sexual grotesqueness of the situation. But because Spenser does not treat the situation as dramatic, he is able to present Britomart with all the liveliness and ease of a comic exposé of the unnatural. Our moral criticism is rendered by Britomart's innocence, spontaneity, and unsophisticated generosity. The comic handling of Britomart exactly expresses Spenser's point—that she is not at all in danger, any more than she is threatened by a loathsome lecher when Malecasta is softly sighing in the bed beside her. Britomart is passionate and impetuous, but unlike Guyon and the Red Cross Knight, she is never in trouble because she is moved by human impulse: she is triumphantly innocent.

Now let us return to Britomart's martial victory in her bedchamber. Britomart's laying about her with her sword is obviously not heroic in the normal sense. Her "triumph" involves none of the arduousness, daring, and endurance that make the Homeric hero noble and that are still present, at however great a remove, in the moral heroism of Guyon and the Red Cross Knight. Where the traditional hero magnificently responds to a challenge, Britomart simply flies off the handle. It is not that Spenser makes her absurd; rather, her warfare here concludes a comic rather than a heroic pattern. It expresses the spontaneity, the instinctive vigor and directness, with which she thwarts Malecasta.

Spenser concludes canto 1 by opposing Britomart's heroism to the pastoralism that is associated with Malecasta and her household. But the point and interest of the episode lie in Spenser's development of the social comedy—Malecasta's flirtation with Britomart, the raging of her desires, the decorations of her castle and her forms of entertainment, and Britomart's unflagging innocence and vigor. The concluding opposition of heroic and pastoral confirms our sense of what has happened, but it does not reveal anything that is new to us. Though we recognize that Britomart's martial violence is entirely appropriate to her, we by no means know the full significance of heroism here, nor do we understand why it should be introduced to support an essentially comic concept. Moreover, we do not fully understand why pastoralism is associated with Malecasta: her violent feelings and abandoned behavior seem more opposed to than equated with Venus' tender self-indulgence. These questions point us ahead to the rest of the book, in which we encounter real heroic action and, even more important, real pastoral settings. As we shall see, it is in his treatment of the pastoral that Spenser brings out the central moral emphasis that is expressed by the heroic.

III

In Britomart's second adventure, the conflict of heroic and pastoral is explicit and prominent, and the point of the conflict is the point of the episode. The major action is Britomart's wounding of Marinell, the meaning of which is revealed in an account of Marinell's genealogy and education (4.19–28). Proteus, the prophet of sea gods, has warned Cymoent, Marinell's mother, that "of a woman he should haue much ill, / A virgin strange and stout him should dismay, or kill" (4.25):

For thy she gaue him warning euery day,
The loue of women not to entertaine;
A lesson too too hard for liuing clay,
From loue in course of nature to refraine:
Yet he his mothers lore did well retaine,
And euer from faire Ladies loue did fly;
Yet many Ladies faire did oft complaine,
That they for loue of him would algates dy:
Dy, who so list for him, he was loues enimy.

(4.26)

Marinell's pride in his prowess and fame as a warrior (4.20–21) is matched by his arrogance in claiming immunity from love, and his battle with Britomart initiates him into the realities of love as well as of warfare. It is true that Cymoent "vainely did expound" Proteus' prophecy to mean "hart-wounding loue" (4.28): the "deadly wound" turns out to be real, for the enemy virgin is a warrior, not a lover. But as Spenser says, "the termes of mortall state" are "full of subtile sophismes, which do play / With double senses" (4.28). This is an allegory, and the real sophism is that Britomart is the champion of love and that Marinell's cure will be his learning to love Florimell. Marinell's wound jolts him into the "course of nature" both as a warrior and as a man.

Marinell is not "loues enimy" in the sense that Pyrocles—the implacable foe representing a constant psychological force—is the enemy of temperance. Marinell is not a personification, but a human type, an overprotected adolescent. The most important thing about him is his immature arrogance, which Spenser conveys by associating it with the pastoral. Marinell's mother is a sea nymph, and "Her Sea-god syre she dearely did perswade, / T'endow her sonne with threasure and rich store" (4.21):

The God did graunt his daughters deare demaund,
To doen his Nephew in all riches flow;
Eftsoones his heaped waues he did commaund,
Out of their hollow bosome forth to throw
All the huge threasure, which the sea below
Had in his greedie gulfe deuoured deepe,
And him enriched through the ouerthrow
And wreckes of many wretches, which did weepe,
And often waile their wealth, which he from them did
    keepe.

381

Shortly vpon that shore there heaped was,
Exceeding riches and all pretious things,
The spoyle of all the world, that it did pas
The wealth of th'East, and pompe of *Persian* kings;
Gold, amber, yuorie, perles, owches, rings,
And all that else was pretious and deare,
The sea vnto him voluntary brings,
That shortly he a great Lord did appeare,
As was in all the lond of Faery, or elsewheare.

(4.22–23)

Spenser makes "great Lord" suggest not the vigor of real magnificence but Marinell's callow self-sufficiency. The effect is due to the way in which the fine pomp of "The sea vnto him voluntary brings" is modified by all that precedes it, and especially by the wonderful gaudiness and crowding of "Gold, amber, yuorie, perles, owches, rings." This line and expressions like "heaped," "exceeding riches," and "the spoyle of all the world" (a phrase that picks up all of stanza 22) make us feel that Marinell's grandeur is mere collecting—naive, vulgar, and childish—instead of the full and harmonious strength of a hero. Spenser brilliantly adapts the rationale of the idyllic pastoral—that nature responds to and is in a sense created by man's desires. The criticism of Marinell is precisely that he expects to live in a pastoral world: he is so childish a great lord because he assumes that the sea, with all its vast force and indifference to man, is his major-domo. The description of the jeweled shore adapts the decorative side of the pastoral mode (cf. 4.18), and the whole conception is related to the action of the canto by the fact that the sea's generosity helps the nymph keep her son secluded and in a state of innocence.

Britomart is opposed to Marinell not because she stands for a moral or psychological category, but because of her emotional vigor, of which her superior physical strength is an expression. Canto 4 begins with Britomart's complaint as she watches the waves,

That gainst the craggy clifts did loudly rore,
And in their raging surquedry disdaynd,
That the fast earth affronted them so sore,
And their deuouring couetize restraynd.

(4.7)

This is a very different sea from the one in which Cymoent lives (4.31–34) and which pours riches at her son's feet. Britomart makes it a metaphor for the turbulence of her passion:

Huge sea of sorrow, and tempestuous griefe,
Wherein my feeble barke is tossed long,
Far from the hoped hauen of reliefe,
Why do thy cruell billowes beat so strong,
And thy moyst mountaines each on others throng,
Threatning to swallow vp my fearefull life?
O do thy cruell wrath and spightfull wrong
At length allay, and stint thy stormy strife,
Which in these troubled bowels raignes, and rageth rife.

(4.8)

Although the real sea apparently rages as a matter of course, Britomart shifts the metaphor to that of a stormy sea. Hence her complaint ends with a prayer to the "God of winds" to "at last blow vp some gentle gale of ease" (4.10). Ease, however, comes not from Glauce's comforting words (4.11), but from Britomart's own martial reaction when she sees Marinell galloping towards her:

Her dolour soone she ceast, and on her dight
Her Helmet, to her Courser mounting light:
Her former sorrow into suddein wrath,
Both coosen passions of distroubled spright,
Conuerting, forth she beates the dustie path;
Loue and despight attonce her courage kindled hath.

(4.12)

The turbulent feelings of love turn into martial wrath; Britomart does not master passion, but rather finds a way to express it. The intimate connection between love and despight (the angry disdain that spurs the warrior into battle) is made clear in the heroic simile of the next stanza:

As when a foggy mist hath ouercast
The face of heauen, and the cleare aire engrost,
The world in darkenesse dwels, till that at last
The watry Southwinde from the seabord cost
Vpblowing, doth disperse the vapour lo'st,
And poures it selfe forth in a stormy showre;
So the faire *Britomart* hauing disclo'st
Her clowdy care into a wrathfull stowre,
The mist of griefe dissolu'd, did into vengeance powre.

(4.13)

The metaphor is very pointedly the same as that of Britomart's complaint, even down to an analogous gale of ease. Britomart's martial prowess is identified with the quality of her feelings even more explicitly than in canto 1.

We can now see the basic contrast between the heroic and the pastoral as expressions of human love. The heroic deals with, and indeed finds its source in, all the pain and turbulence of erotic desire that the pastoral ignores. But so stated, the contrast only serves to distinguish two types of individual, and its meaning is sufficiently expressed by the battle: emotional and physical strength are equated and the stronger knight wins. The battle, however, is not simply a decision procedure, the outcome of which tells us to prefer Britomart to Marinell, the heroic to the pastoral. The battle concerns Marinell's emotional experience, and its meaning, the significance of his wound, is rendered by a magnificent heroic simile:

> The wicked steele through his left side did glaunce;
> Him so transfixed she before her bore
> Beyond his croupe, the length of all her launce,
> Till sadly soucing on the sandie shore,
> He tombled on an heape, and wallowd in his gore.

> Like as the sacred Oxe, that carelesse stands,
> With gilden hornes, and flowry girlonds crownd,
> Proud of his dying honor and deare bands,
> Whiles th'altars fume with frankincense arownd,
> All suddenly with mortall stroke astownd,
> Doth groueling fall, and with his streaming gore
> Distaines the pillours, and the holy grownd,
> And the faire flowres, that decked him afore;
> So fell proud *Marinell* vpon the pretious shore.

$$(4.16–17)$$

From the description of the battle, in which language suggests physical violence, Spenser shifts to the decorative vocabulary and full rhythms of the simile. We now see the battle as a ceremony, which Marinell, the innocent dumb ox, cannot understand. Where the battle itself renders Marinell's view of his wound as a harsh and humiliating blow, the simile places it in the context of an orderly and benign process: thus Spenser is genial, rather than ironic, when he says that the ox is "proud of his dying honor and deare bands." The shift in perspective comes about through Spenser's use of the decorative and sensuous pastoral mode. It so controls the stanza that although Spenser has not previously mentioned Marinell's "pretious shore," we feel it is a perfectly natural fictional detail just because of the language with which the simile begins and ends.[6]

The pastoral mode does not simply identify particular agents and settings in the action of this canto. As in the simile of the sacred ox, it also renders our perspective on all the action. Nowhere is this more striking than when Spenser endorses Britomart's martial wrath as an image of value for human love. Clearly Britomart is not an exemplary knight in the sense that her behavior sets a pattern for the man or woman in love. In terms of the way she acts, Britomart is a public menace; more soberly, we can say that Spenser by no means recommends "suddein wrath" as a way of calming the "distroubled spright." Britomart is "good" in her conquest of Marinell, because the heroic simile of the storm makes us feel that the dissipation of turbulent passion by heroic wrath is a natural process. The incessant and chaotic storm of Britomart's complaint is now seen as the dispersal of mists that cloud the face of heaven. As the canto proceeds, the images of the dispelled storm and the calm sea become directly associated with pastoral nature.

The point of Marinell's wound is that it is "a lesson too too hard for liuing clay, / From loue in course of nature to refraine." One use of the pastoral in this episode is to suggest that the lessons of love are necessarily painful. But the painfulness of human experience is itself seen, under the aspect of the pastoral, as part of the "course of nature." This double perspective is fully developed in the passage in which Cymoent hears of Marinell's wound, crosses the sea to where he lies, laments over his body, and when she discovers signs of life, brings him to her bower under the waves and tries to cure him (4.29–44). The poetic strategy of the whole passage is extremely simple. The pastoral mode in all its decorative loveliness is used to characterize Cymoent's two sea-voyages (4.31–34, 42), the secluded spot where she first hears of Marinell's wound (4.29), and even the delicacy of the dolphins that draw her chariot (4.34). This mode is consistently opposed by violent language that expresses grief and, less often, the physical actuality of Marinell's wound. The oppositions occur within stanzas (4.29, 34) and between groups of stanzas: the

[6] The effect is largely due to the pause after "holy grownd" and the consequent isolation of the next to last line; despite the syntax, we do not feel that the flowers are stained by blood. Spenser is thus able, in the last line, to produce the precious shore from the pastoral mode.

lovely voyage, in which Cymoent's dolphins skim over a sea calmed in sympathy with her grief, is followed by her long and vehement lament (4.36–39). These passages recapitulate what happens to Marinell when Britomart wounds him and his pride. Where Britomart's love sorrows are natural in the world she inhabits, grief disrupts Cymoent's world. To some extent, then, the pastoral expresses the limited possibilities of feeling and experience in the world of women in which Marinell's mother, like Achilles' (also a sea-nymph), has secluded him to keep him from the normal risks and disasters of man's world.

At the same time, Spenser treats pastoral nature as in itself attractive and even grand:

> Great *Neptune* stood amazed at their sight,
> Whiles on his broad round backe they softly slid
> And eke himselfe mournd at their mournfull plight,
> Yet wist not what their wailing ment, yet did
> For great compassion of their sorrow, bid
> His mightie waters to them buxome bee:
> Eftsoones the roaring billowes still abid,
> And all the griesly Monsters of the See
> Stood gaping at their gate, and wondred them to see.
>
> A teme of Dolphins raunged in aray,
> Drew the smooth charet of sad *Cymoent;*
> They were all taught by *Triton,* to obay
> To the long raynes, at her commaundement:
> As swift as swallowes, on the waues they went,
> That their broad flaggie finnes no fome did reare,
> Ne bubbling roundell they behind them sent;
> The rest of other fishes drawen weare,
> Which with their finny oars the swelling sea did sheare.
>
> (4.32–33)

There is a remarkable poise in these stanzas: while they suggest all the limitations of the nymphs' delicate feelings, they also create a sense of genuine wonder at the calming of the seas and the progress of the chariot. Supported by stanzas like these, Spenser can use the pastoral mode to render the care with which the nymphs bind Marinell's wounds and take him home (4.40–43). The pastoral assures us that for all the vehemence of Cymoent's grief, Marinell will be cured, just as it shows Marinell "tombled on an heape" to be participating in a ceremony. The passage ends with the nymphs lamenting and cursing Britomart (4.44), but their mourning takes place in an underwater bower that fully assimilates Britomart's storms to pastoral nature:

> Deepe in the bottome of the sea, her bowre
> Is built of hollow billowes heaped hye,
> Like to thicke cloudes, that threat a stormy showre,
> And vauted all within, like to the sky,
> In which the Gods do dwell eternally.
>
> (4.43)

Spenser is very much at his ease in this episode. His brilliant variations on the pastoral mode serve not so much to explore and develop poetic meanings as to put us in full possession of the double meaning of the pastoral. While the canto by no means expresses the full significance of the contrast between heroic and pastoral, it does establish the basic terms of the contrast. When the pastoral is a metaphor for personal feelings, it expresses an excessive tenderness and lack of vigor that is criticized by the robust passion of the heroic; but as an image of nature, the pastoral expresses a benign harmony that gives a sanction to human love and its heroic image. It is this second use of the pastoral that we must now examine. For it is precisely by developing the pastoral as an image of value that Spenser makes us see why the heroic must be the metaphor for individual experience.

I V

The most important pastoral passages in Book III are those in which Spenser uses the vision of harmonious nature to represent human love as it ought to be. Our first encounter with this type of pastoral is the description of Belphoebe's glade (5.39–40, quoted above, p. 190). In describing this *locus amoenus,* Spenser adds suggestions of grandeur and stateliness to the predominating source of order—the sweetness and friendliness of the stream and the birds. In this way he establishes a pastoral mode that he will use later to develop the portrait of Belphoebe as the exemplar of heroic virginity. Virginity is not equivalent to chastity in Book III, but it is an important aspect, or phenomenon, of chaste love. Spenser uses the pastoral to present its most complete and admirable form—the form in which it really defines an individual's being and is not the result of psychological fear or social fastidiousness, as it is in almost all the chaste damsels who refuse the Squire of Dames' advances (7.57–60; the only exception was a country lass).

387

With Belphoebe, Spenser uses the simplifying separateness of a pastoral world to isolate an important single phenomenon of human love. There is another, and extraordinarily brilliant, use of this strategy in the description of the satyrs, where the pastoral becomes the setting for sexual vigor and jollity. This version of pastoral is slightly different from Belphoebe's, for Spenser gives it some rustic elements. The satyrs keep a herd of goats, and their chief daytime activity is dancing around Hellenore, their queen of the May (10.44). Nevertheless, the passage returns to and ends with the artificial, decorative mode. When the sun sets, with a standard circumlocution—"Till drouping *Phoebus* gan to hide his golden hed" (10.45)—

> Tho vp they gan their merry pypes to trusse,
> And all their goodly heards did gather round,
> But euery *Satyre* first did giue a busse
> To *Hellenore*: so busses did abound.
> Now gan the humid vapour shed the ground
> With perly deaw, and th'Earthes gloomy shade
> Did dim the brightnesse of the welkin round,
> That euery bird and beast awarned made,
> To shrowd themselues, whiles sleepe their senses
>   did inuade.   (10.46)

The going in from the fields and the bussing of Hellenore are seen under the aspect of a glamorized nature and the feelings of loveliness and friendliness it inspires. The pastoral, conveying the peacefulness with which the birds and the beasts go to sleep, provides the context in which the satyrs go to bed. Their "ioyous play" (10.48)—"When one so oft a night did ring his matins bell"—is not ironically contrasted to the pastoral setting, but is given a sanction by it. The pastoral beautifully eliminates both the ethical question of lust and the problematic emotional aspects of passion; it makes us recognize that these jolly satyrs exemplify an admirable directness and gaiety of sexual appetite. The satyrs' goats are symbols of lust for man, and they butt Malbecco; but to the satyrs, who are half goat themselves, they are simply goats. The satyrs completely lack the elements that can make man's sexual passion destructive. They do not have the fastidious self-consciousness and obsession with sexual appetite that drive Malbecco mad.

Spenser's most important use of pastoral nature to define what is normative for human love is, of course, the Garden of Adonis. The

Garden of Adonis has all the marks of the innocent golden world—perpetual spring, spontaneously ordered growth, and the like. But Spenser, unlike Tasso, does not depict a separate world that is innocent in a way man and nature as we know them can never be. In the Garden of Adonis, the ideal world and the real are not opposed. Spenser makes a point of saying that the Garden of Adonis is Venus' earthly residence (6.29), and the episode that leads up to the description of the garden concerns a nontranscendental, earthly virgin birth—the impregnation of a human woman by the beams of the sun (6.5–9). Spenser sets up a very active and intimate relationship between the ideal world of the Garden of Adonis and the real world of change and turbulent desires. He uses aspects of an ideal garden as visionary resolutions of fundamental problems and imperfections of nature as we know it. Thus the flowers are seen as welling up from chaos (6.36), the "continuall spring, and haruest" (6.42) is a resolution of the ravages of earthly time (6.39), and the little grove on top of the mountain (6.45) makes lovers' tragedies participate in natural cycles. The Garden of Adonis keeps changing in appearance because it is not a circumscribed world that in its innocence and perfection mocks human desire. It is really a series of pastoral images that are responsive to and complete human desires and that give them the sanction of nature.

If all this is so, then in what sense is the heroic opposed to the pastoral in Book III? Let us look at the exemplary figures who emerge from the three pastoral worlds we have just discussed. The issues Spenser is concerned with are defined by Malbecco's madness at seeing the abundant delight of Hellenore and her satyrs. His transformation into Jealousy simply acts out his psychological reaction as a man. The feelings of the *vieux jaloux* who is at the mercy of his obsessions are consistently rendered in terms that are equally appropriate to the figure of Jealousy: "[he] did his hart with bitter thoughts engore," and "all his hart with gealosie did swell."[7] Malbecco's transformation represents not a change in him, but a terrible remaining what he is. Spenser's central concern in this passage, as we have seen in chapter 7, is to present the deformed emotion of jealousy as a reality of human feeling and a potentiality of any human love. Even the ultimate expression of Malbecco's monstrosity is that he has "forgot he was a man." And this is a possibility only for human beings.

What Spenser opposes to Malbecco is not the human being without

[7] 10.45, 48. See also 10.14, 15, 17, 18, 22.

passion, but precisely the person who is passionate in a different way
—the hero, who instead of turning passion against himself, converts
it into energy, turns it outward into action. In what she represents of
erotic psychology, the heroic Britomart is the human version of the
satyrs. Her passionate vigor is unself-conscious and is always ex-
pended in action; to use Spenser's image, the cloud that gathers al-
ways pours itself forth in a shower. This is not to say that Spenser
holds up Britomart's tempestuous militancy as a model of human be-
havior. It rather expresses a categorical moral statement—that human
love must be in some way passionate. The quality of Malbecco's pas-
sion destroys him, but the persistence and intensity of his passion—
which make his ultimate monstrosity an image of human tragedy—
express something that is true of all human feeling.

Spenser's insistence on passion as human, not wicked, explains
why Belphoebe, the heroic figure produced by the pastoral environ-
ment, is an unsatisfactory image of human erotic desire. Just to say
this indicates the reason: Belphoebe has no erotic desires. At just
the point where virginity becomes truly heroic—that is, when the ideal
defines the personality—erotic desire is eliminated. Spenser specif-
ically connects this limitation in Belphoebe with the pastoral envi-
ronment that produces her:

> That dainty Rose, the daughter of her Morne,
> More deare then life she tendered, whose flowre
> The girlond of her honour did adorne:
> Ne suffred she the Middayes scorching powre,
> Ne the sharp Northerne wind thereon to showre,
> But lapped vp her silken leaues most chaire,
> When so the froward skye began to lowre:
> But soone as calmed was the Christall aire,
> She did it faire dispred, and let to florish faire.
>
> (5.51)

Belphoebe may tender her chastity more dear than life, but it is still
a dainty flower. Where the hero expresses his scorn for mere living
by rushing into the face of death, Belphoebe withdraws from anything
that is not benign. She is simply ignorant of Timias' erotic suffering
and tries to treat his metaphoric wound of love with pastoral pharma-
copoeia. Belphoebe can only be herself, and Spenser does not criti-
cize her in the way Shakespeare criticizes Isabella. Rather he limits
her as an exemplary image of the human individual, and the limitation

is expressed by the fact that her heroism is dependent on the perpetual spring of the pastoral world.

The issue Spenser develops here is the human relevance of the pastoral vision. In the Garden of Adonis, the same details that limit Belphoebe as an image of the human individual render, without any implied criticism, the ideal landscape that provides the sanction of nature for human love. For example, the little grove of trees with intertwining branches is fashioned so that "nether *Phoebus* beams could through them throng, / Nor *Aeolus* sharp blast could worke them any wrong" (6.44). Spenser can repeat this detail (as he repeats details from Malecasta's tapestries) because he uses the separateness of a pastoral world to "place" the Garden of Adonis. Rather than making the pastoral vision identical with idealized human feeling, he sets it into a certain relation to actual human feeling.

This placing of the pastoral vision is done through the two most important human (or quasi-human) figures in the Garden of Adonis canto, Chrysogone and Amoret. We have seen that Spenser brings the Garden of Adonis into close contact with human life by making Chrysogone's virgin conception occur by the same processes that cause fertilization and growth in nature as we know it. This sets, as it were, an upper limit to the significance of the mythological miracle. But a lower limit is set too. Venus and Diana discover Chrysogone just after she has borne her twins "in slombry traunce" (6.26):

> Vnwares she them conceiu'd, vnwares she bore:
> She bore withouten paine, that she conceiued
> Withouten pleasure.   (6.27)

These marvellously plain lines contain one of Spenser's most humane perceptions. Mythical experiences are not real experiences, and only we, who undergo pleasure and pain in love, can understand the true wonder of the miraculous birth. Venus and Diana, for all their amazement at finding babes in the woods, simply divide the twins and go home. In these lines, Spenser places Chrysogone perfectly. She stands for the category of what is specifically human, but not for the human individual; she is a model of human fertility and thus of the naturalness of human love, but she is not a model of human experience.

Again, Spenser is emphasizing the visionary aspect of a pastoral world: it can image attitudes and awarenesses that contribute to and determine the way we are. But our experiences themselves cannot be represented under the aspect of the pastoral world. They specifically belong to the world of turmoil, change, and pain—the world of man and nature as we know them. Spenser makes this distinction very clear when Venus sends Amoret from the Garden of Adonis down to earth (the "which" of the first line refers to "all the lore of loue, and goodly womanhead" in 6.51):

> In which when she to perfect ripenesse grew,
> Of grace and beautie noble Paragone,
> She brought her forth into the worldes vew,
> To be th'ensample of true loue alone,
> And Lodestarre of all chaste affectione,
> To all faire Ladies, that doe liue on ground.
> To Faery court she came, where many one
> Admyrd her goodly haueour, and found
> His feeble hart wide launched with loues cruell wound.
>
> (6.52)

To say that Amoret is the lodestar of all chaste affection does, in a sense, tell us what she is. Her beauty and purity are things of permanent value in what we understand of man. This is the Neoplatonic doctrine that all beautiful things, and especially beautiful women, body forth and participate in the divine essence of Beauty itself. But Spenser is really turning this doctrine around and saying that understanding Beauty itself is impossible without human feeling: love of Beauty must involve love for a beautiful woman. And human love, which springs from erotic desire, necessarily introduces a whole area of feeling and experience that would destroy the pastoral world and that is indicated here by the image of the "hart wide launched with loues cruell wound."

The central moral imperative of Book III is that love must be a human experience. Its exemplary image must be developed from the world of action and turbulence, and it is therefore associated with the traditional world of heroism in warfare. The benign pastoral world can present the reader's awareness of "what love is" and can stand as an image of value for heroism.[8] But our interest is always directed towards individual human experience. We start with Venus and Adonis in a tapestry, but we end with Malecasta; the fabliau of Malbecco ends not with the satyrs' comic celebration, but with the

---

[8] Spenser defines the relation between pastoral poetry and the human reader in the stanzas (5.52–54) that follow the description of Belphoebe's "dainty Rose." He turns from Belphoebe's dramatic sense of her chastity and addresses the female reader, who understands that the rose does not define a personality, but symbolizes a virtue. Once the flower becomes explicitly metaphoric, it acquires new scope and energy as an image of value.

old man's terrible transformation. Our interest is not in the personalities and specific experiences of separate individuals, but in the general aspect of our experiences—the fact that they belong to human life and involve human feelings. Hence the characteristic setting of Book III is not a specific society, but the reverse of the pastoral *locus amoenus*—the vague and mysterious woods in which all the knights wander.[9] Britomart's behavior—what she specifically does—is unimportant in itself; but the nature of her behavior consistently reveals that she, unlike Belphoebe, is heroic under the conditions of human life. It is precisely because she is heroic that Spenser in his similes can appeal to the grand and benign appearances of the moon and sun that are associated with her throughout the book.

V

The point about Britomart's heroism—that human love must involve human experience—is not primarily established by the actions of Britomart herself. It comes out in the complexities of the pastoral worlds; in sexual grotesques like Malecasta, Malbecco, and the twin giants Argante and Ollyphant; and in the unheroic characters who act out various inadequate versions of erotic feeling. Marinell, the Squire of Dames, and Paridell are, respectively, the callow adolescent, the cynically submissive servant of ladies, and the egotistic philanderer. These characters are supported by the figures of Proteus and the lecherous old fisherman, the witch and her loutish son (a rustic pair who are moved by love to create a dazzlingly artificial false Florimell), and Braggadocchio and Trompart. In the midst of all this, Britomart herself is essentially a comic figure. The comic role we have already seen her play in Malecasta's castle continues, in cantos 2 and 3, in her adolescent love pangs and Glauce's attempts to cure them, and in her naive pleasure in the lies that make the Red Cross Knight praise Artegall. Spenser's treatment of Britomart throughout most of Book III is characterized by a passage that occurs when she and Glauce visit Merlin to seek a love cure. Glauce lies elaborately until Merlin interrupts her:

> The wisard could no lenger beare her bord,
> But brusting forth in laughter, to her sayd;
> *Glauce,* what needs this colourable word,

[9] See especially 1.14 and 11.6. The setting of the woods introduces us to the first adventures in the book (most notably the pursuit of Florimell) and to Britomart's discovery of Scudamour and her final adventure against Busyrane.

To cloke the cause, that hath it selfe bewrayd?
Ne ye faire *Britomartis,* thus arayd,
More hidden are, then Sunne in cloudy vele.

(3.19)

Merlin's metaphor is true; Britomart really is like the sun:

The doubtfull Mayd, seeing her selfe descryde,
Was all abasht, and her pure yuory
Into a cleare Carnation suddeine dyde;
As faire *Aurora* rising hastily,
Doth by her blushing tell, that she did lye
All night in old *Tithonus* frosen bed.

(3.20)

The image of Aurora is both grand and charming, and the ease with which Spenser confirms Merlin's metaphor makes Britomart wonderfully comic without making her at all ridiculous. She is at the mercy of her incipient erotic desires, and the gaiety of Spenser's treatment makes his point about her love for Artegall. When Britomart gazes in the mirror that gives an image of the looker's desire, she is engaged in a real-life version of the myth of Chrysogone. For all her pain and turmoil, her feelings are perfectly natural; we do not need Merlin's British history to assure us that her vision will take flesh and that she will finally meet her lover.

The significance of Britomart's comic role is developed by episodes that we have hardly noticed so far and that occur when Britomart is off stage. In these episodes, Spenser provides a context for understanding Britomart through a cluster of conventional events—the sight of a beautiful face, the pursuit of the maiden, and the quest for the beloved. These events occur separately and in combination with each other. The simplest versions of them are Scudamour's knightly quest to rescue Amoret; the parody quest when Malbecco, aided by the mock-heroic Braggadocchio, goes in search of Hellenore; Argante's lustful pursuit of the Squire of Dames; and the provocative effects of Florimell's beauty, which stirs the old fisherman to attack, the witch's son to wooing, and Proteus to a combination of persuasion and force. These motifs are interwoven in Timias' adventures. Like Arthur, he sets out in pursuit of Florimell when her dazzling beauty flashes through the woods. But he soon finds himself in pursuit of her pursuer, the "foul foster"; this knightly mission leads to his real wound, which in turn leads to the wound of love received when he opens his eyes to see his physician, the divinely beautiful Belphoebe. It will be observed that Spenser makes the narrative action produce some of the crucial conceits of Renaissance love poetry.

Spenser's major use of this cluster of events is to make paradoxical relations among them express the major concerns of Book III. Thus, for Arthur the quest for the beloved object and the pursuit of any desirable object are identical. Arthur chases Florimell because her beauty makes him think she might be Gloriana, whom he has never seen. In presenting erotic impulse under the aspect of heroic enterprise, Spenser expresses both the worth and the paradox of searching for Beauty itself in a beautiful woman. The climax of the pursuit is Arthur's complaint against Night (4.55–60): he protests not only against a malicious darkness, but against the very alternation of day and night that characterizes nature as we know it.

Florimell's role is the reverse of Arthur's. Simply because she is beautiful, her search for Marinell is a constant flight from pursuers. This paradoxical quest by flight expresses the sexual fearfulness that is the ambiguous source of her fidelity. This is not to say that Spenser questions an individual personality in Shakespeare's manner. Florimell's fearfulness is developed by a rather light-hearted treatment of her as the maiden in distress. By presenting her in a comic role, Spenser makes her need for protection express a positive need for union with her lover, rather than a psychological inadequacy. But her role as the unprotected woman suggests something of the emotional complexities that arise when the woman is a lover as well as the beloved. When we come to the pain and terror that Amoret undergoes in the name of fidelity, we can see what Florimell contributes to Book III. Spenser makes us aware that fidelity must be the product of erotic desire: precisely because it has its source in problematic human impulses, it has dignity as a moral virtue.

The whole complex of events we have been discussing, and particularly its development in Arthur and Florimell, converges on Britomart. Like Arthur, she has seen her lover only in a vision; her quest, like his, has no definable goal, but gets its purpose solely from her confidence in her own feelings and desires. On the other hand, she shares Florimell's role of the desirable maiden; whenever she takes off her helmet, she arouses the desires of those who see her. These links with the roles and actions of Arthur and Florimell act out Britomart's paradoxical status as a female warrior. But where Arthur's quest by pursuit and Florimell's quest by flight suggest problematic aspects of human love, there is nothing at all problematic about Britomart. Although she is entirely passionate, she never feels sexual attraction for anyone until she meets Artegall. Although she arouses desire, she disarms it simply by being herself: she is as unself-conscious and spontaneous in awing Paridell (9.20–25) as in foiling Malecasta. Britomart is defined by paradoxes, but she embodies their resolutions; she is comic insofar as we feel confident that these resolutions are adequately expressed by her naive and spontaneous vigor. As a comic figure, Britomart completes a pattern by which we see that what is paradoxical in love is not ultimately problematic.

The complex of episodes we have just discussed occurs under the auspices of what we may call the cosmic pastoral—images of the heavens as ordered and beneficent. Britomart is constantly associated with the moon and the sun,[10] and the night that hides Florimell from Arthur participates in human feeling at the same time that it is majestic:

> Yet he her followd still with courage keene,
> So long that now the golden *Hesperus*
> Was mounted high in top of heauen sheene,
> And warnd his other brethren ioyeous,
> To light their blessed lamps in *Ioues* eternall hous.

(4.51)

Here again, however, the pastoral does not characterize the "world" of Book III, but renders the reader's perspective on the action. When night encloses Arthur, Spenser's visual trickery interlaces two responses to the event:

> All suddenly dim woxe the dampish ayre,
> And griesly shadowes couered heauen bright,
> That now with thousand starres was decked fayre;
> Which when the Prince beheld, a lothfull sight, etc.

(4.52)

To Arthur, darkness is "griesly shadowes" because he can no longer see his way or the maiden he pursues; to the reader, the heavens remain bright as the stars come out. Similarly, Arthur uses light as an image of value in his complaint against night. But his actual request of nature (as opposed to his metaphoric statement of faith) is almost Quixotic:

[10] 1.43, 3.19–20, 9.20. See also Artegall's appearance in the mirror "as *Phoebus* face out of the east, / Betwixt two shadie mountaines doth arize" (2.24); the Neoplatonic image in 3.1; Chrysogone's fertilization by the sun (6.6–9), and the descriptions of night and sunrise in 1.57 and 10.1.

O *Titan,* haste to reare thy ioyous waine:
Speed thee to spred abroad thy beames bright,
And chase away this too long lingring night,
Chase her away, from whence she came, to hell.
She, she it is, that hath me done despight:
There let her with the damned spirits dwell,
And yeeld her roome to day, that can it gouerne well.

(4.60)

Coming as it does after a contrast of Day and Night as cosmic prin-
ciples of good and evil (4.59), this stanza expresses much more than
a longing for sunrise. Arthur wants the sun to stay in the sky forever,
the earth to become the Garden of Adonis. In his heroic appeal to
the sun, seen as the rebel Titan, he is asking the impossible. Hence
when the sun does rise in its ordinary fashion, Arthur goes forth
"with heauie looke and lumpish pace" (4.61). But the reader is not
only aware of the dramatic event that produces this not very remark-
able irony; he also sees Arthur's plight as part of a benign process. At
the very moment when Arthur trudges off, we see the common sun
under the aspect of the cosmic pastoral: "And earely, ere the morrow
did vpreare / His deawy head out of the *Ocean* maine" (4.61). The
pastoral poetry of the universe is true for our sense of the action, but
false for the action itself.

V I

We can see that the sanctions given human love in Book III could
lead to a series of marriages in which pastoral images would become
the world of the poem. Something like this happens in the last two
cantos of Book IV, when the marriage of the Thames and the Med-
way becomes the setting for the betrothal of Florimell and Marinell.
But even there, pastoral images remain metaphors expressing value;
they do not become metaphors for human experience.[11] It is not sur-
prising, therefore, that Book III ends with a genuinely heroic episode
in which Britomart no longer plays a comic role. Where her previous
battles were accidental and supererogatory, her rescue of Amoret is
a real quest and an arduous endeavor. Britomart is no longer char-
acterized simply by her spontaneous vigor; like the heroes of Homer,
Virgil, and Tasso, she is now self-conscious and articulate about her
role as a knight (11.14, 19). Under the aspect of Britomart's heroism,
Spenser presents the final and most comprehensive vision of human

[11] See above, pp. 121–123.

love in Book III. In the House of Busyrane, as in the rest of the book, Spenser treats love as a general phenomenon; he is still concerned with "what love is," rather than with the dramatic experience of it by individual lovers. But he now renders his statements on love by directly involving the reader in a psychological experience that is characterized (in both the adventure itself and the two long set pieces) by terror, violence, humiliation, fear, and pain. These feelings belong to the realm of actual experience, in which, as we have seen, heroism must be the metaphor for human love. Our final sense of love as harmonious comes from a felt response to Britomart's rescue of Amoret, and not from images that allow us to see love as a phenomenon sanctioned by pastoral nature.

We have already seen that Amoret's torture does not render a moral judgment against her, but presents, in the form of a "speaking picture," the main issues of Book III. We must now ask what is the meaning of Amoret's release. Clearly, to say that her wound is closed "as it had not bene bor'd" (12.38) is to affirm, with the rest of Book III, that love, though apparently problematic and paradoxical, is ultimately harmonious and benign: it leaves no scars, exacts no consequences. On the other hand, harmony and benignity are precisely what we do not feel in this episode. The pastoral endorsement of love is entirely absent, and the comic energy of earlier cantos has been replaced by terror and uncertainty. The healing of Amoret's heart repeats, in its broad terms, the affirmation made throughout Book III. But the character of this affirmation, the particular significance it has in this episode, is quite new. To understand it, we must consider Britomart and her heroic role.

Spenser develops Britomart's role when she and Scudamour come to Busyrane's castle and find the entrance choked by a wall of flame:

> Greatly thereat was *Britomart* dismayd,
> Ne in that stownd wist, how her selfe to beare;
> For daunger vaine it were, to haue assayd
> That cruell element, which all things feare,
> Ne none can suffer to approchen neare:
> And turning backe to *Scudamour,* thus sayd;
> What monstrous enmity prouoke we heare,
> Foolhardy as th'Earthes children, the which made
> Battell against the Gods? so we a God inuade.

>   (11.22)

At this point, Britomart, Scudamour, and the reader are united in a single response to the fire. But when Britomart discovers that this unassailable wall of flame is the only entrance to the castle, she takes her stand for "noble cheuisaunce" (11.24). Foolhardiness becomes heroic daring:

> Therewith resolu'd to proue her vtmost might,
> Her ample shield she threw before her face,
> And her swords point directing forward right,
> Assayld the flame, the which eftsoones gaue place,
> And did it selfe diuide with equall space,
> That through she passed; as a thunder bolt
> Perceth the yielding ayre, and doth displace
> The soring clouds into sad showres ymolt;
> So to her yold the flames, and did their force reuolt.

> (11.25)

The image that in 4.13 appeared in the explicit relation of simile to action, now comes as the climax of action. While before the simile described a natural event, it is now entirely paradoxical: flesh and blood penetrates fire as fire penetrates air, so that the yielding flames are metaphorically transformed (in fact, melted) into sad showers. And yet our attention is hardly drawn to these paradoxes. The directness and lucidity of Spenser's diction and rhythms give a sense of ease and naturalness, and suggest once again Britomart's naive vigor. In earlier cantos, Britomart's magical immunity was a metaphor for her innocence and energy, which in turn were seen under the aspect of a harmonious nature. Here, in this astonishing combination of paradox and simplicity, Britomart's symbolic importance is totally identified with her role as the magical heroine who can penetrate Busyrane's flames.

When she is a comic figure, Britomart's paradoxical nature is a triumphant expression of normal humanity. In this canto she is explicitly magical, as the next stanza makes clear:

> Whom whenas *Scudamour* saw past the fire,
> Safe and vntoucht, he likewise gan assay,
> With greedy will, and enuious desire,
> And bad the stubborne flames to yield him way:
> But cruell *Mulciber* would not obay
> His threatfull pride, but did the more augment
> His mighty rage, and with imperious sway

Him forst (maulgre) his fiercenesse to relent,
And backe retire, all scorcht and pitifully brent.

(11.26)

The usual interpretation of this stanza—that it indicates a moral fault in Scudamour—is surely ungenerous. The phrases "greedy will," "enuious desire," and "threatfull pride" are the kind of term that Spenser uses of any knight, including Arthur,[12] who is engaged in combat. Their importance in this stanza is not to register moral criticism, but to indicate that Scudamour's martial wrath is that of a human hero; similarly Spenser emphasizes the raging might of the flames in order to render the dust and heat of battle. Scudamour retreats "all scorcht and pitifully brent" because he is merely human. The fire, "cruell *Mulciber,*" is in fact, for ordinary mortals, the god against which Britomart exclaimed. We do not morally reject Scudamour—leave him grovelling in the grass—and identify ourselves with the triumphant Britomart. Our feeling that Britomart is magical makes us all the more ready to participate in the ordinary knight's struggle and pain, and to identify ourselves with his common humanity. Hence in the next stanza (11.27), Spenser juxtaposes Scudamour's "burning torment" and violent grief with a half-incantatory narration of Britomart's entrance into the castle. Our understanding of Busyrane's wall of flame involves feelings of both magical immunity from and intense susceptibility to the potent and raging fire.

When Britomart returns to the scene of action after the description of the tapestries, she alone carries this double response of the reader's. On the one hand, her experience merges with and intensifies ours: her frail senses are dazzled (11.49) and she is awed by the loneliness of the palace (11.53). At the same time, she is immune to Busyrane's power in a way the reader is not. She gazes with impunity at the darts the reader must fear to behold (11.48–49). She cannot understand Busyrane's menacing command "Be bold" (11.50, 54), yet she safely obeys it and the final mocking warning "Be not too bold." The walls of living gold and Cupid's trophies (11.51–52) fascinate us and suggest the real terror of the palace; but Britomart, though she gazes with "greedy eyes" can only wonder "that none was to possesse / So rich purueyance, ne them keepe with carefulnesse" (11.53). This is the innocence with which we are familiar: these lines resemble her wondering who pays for Malecasta's costly tapestries

[12] Cf. 1.8.6, 29; 2.8.31, 40, 42; 2.11.32–34.

(1.35). But in the setting of Busyrane's palace, the immunity of innocence is magical. We have no way of understanding why Britomart is unharmed by the palace, and we simply accept the fact that she is not. On the basis of this magical immunity, Spenser develops Britomart as a hero. She obeys Busyrane's command "Be bold" by going "forward with bold steps into the next roome" (11.50). She is "the warlike Mayde" (11.53) when she gazes at the "warlike spoiles . . . / Of mighty Conquerours and Captaines strong" (11.52). At the end of the canto, she awaits her enemy with heroic scorn of fear and weariness:

> Thus she there waited vntill euentyde,
> Yet liuing creature none she saw appeare:
> And now sad shadowes gan the world to hyde,
> From mortall vew, and wrap in darkenesse dreare;
> Yet nould she d'off her weary armes, for feare
> Of secret daunger, ne let sleepe oppresse
> Her heauy eyes with natures burdein deare,
> But drew her selfe aside in sickernesse,
> And her welpointed weapons did about her dresse.
>
> (11.55)

The sweet sleep that in Malecasta's castle suggested Britomart's naturalness and simplicity (1.58) is now associated with the human reader, from whom the hero stands apart.

Britomart's magical heroism brings out something implicit in the fact that our intimate experience of Spenser's poetry does not make us identical with Busyrane's victims. We feel the sadness and terror of Busyrane's palace, but we still recognize not only that love's wound is unavoidable, but also, through the mythological grandeur and variety of the tapestries, that it is the source of full and rich experience. But how much is there really to choose between the pastoral endorsement of love and the kind of affirmation Spenser seems to be making here? We hardly seem exposed to love's power if our ability to deal with it is reposed in a virgin warrior who is magically immune to it. It is not enough to say that Britomart is an element in the reader's complex awareness: this element may very well be nothing more than the general pastoral confidence in the benignity of love to which Busyrane's spectacles apparently give the lie. Such doubts as these hardly arise as we read canto 11, for we do not fully identify ourselves with Britomart's magical heroism. They would, however, become very pressing indeed if Spenser concluded the episode by having Britomart score another of her automatic victories.

We are brought back to the meaning of Amoret's release. Spenser asks, "Ah who can loue the worker of her smart?" as if it were impossible to be a human lover. But the rest of the episode shows that the answer to this question is not "no one," but "anyone." When this affirmation is embodied in a magical heroine, "anyone" remains a visionary abstraction, analogous to the vision of nature in the Garden of Adonis. But in the stanza in which Spenser asks his question, he indicates another way in which the affirmation can be made:

> And her before the vile Enchaunter sate,
> Figuring straunge characters of his art,
> With liuing blood he those characters wrate,
> Dreadfully dropping from her dying hart,
> Seeming transfixed with a cruell dart,
> And all perforce to make her him to loue.
> Ah who can loue the worker of her smart?
> A thousand charmes he formerly did proue;
> Yet thousand charmes could not her stedfast heart remoue.
>
> (12.31)

The core of the episode is the contrast between "Dreadfully dropping from her dying hart" and "Yet thousand charmes could not her stedfast heart remoue." The two lines suggest the poles of ordinary and heroic experience in these cantos, and heroism, so far as we can tell, is magical. But there is nothing magical about Amoret here. Her heart is steadfast because though it is dying, it is not dead. The last line means "a thousand charms could not shift her affections from Scudamour," but Spenser draws all our attention to the literal meaning of the metaphorical action, and he supports this emphasis by drawing on the rationale of the speaking picture: the voice and rhythm of the firm last line assure us of the reality of the emblem and the feelings associated with it. Spenser thus insists on the simple truth that there is no suffering without a sufferer, and the assurance of Amoret's life is precisely the intensity of her suffering. In making his affirmation, Spenser now appeals to the integrity and actuality of individual experience.

Because Amoret's release is seen under the aspect of individual experience, Britomart is not permitted to rescue her in the conventional manner—that is, by destroying her captor. When Britomart lays hold of Busyrane, he turns his weapon to her, and

Vnwares it strooke into her snowie chest,
That little drops empurpled her faire brest.
Exceeding wroth therewith the virgin grew,
Albe the wound were nothing deepe imprest,
And fiercely forth her mortall blade she drew,
To giue him the reward for such vile outrage dew.

(12.33)

As in Malecasta's house, the pastoral wound provokes the heroic response. But wrath is no longer an appropriate expression of normal vigor; it can be so only when we also see the wound of love as a pastoral scratch. These paradoxes were formerly enjoyed as paradoxes, because Spenser's comic ease expressed a generous confidence in love's benignity. But the paradoxes are now dissolved as Spenser appeals to what is axiomatic in the painfulness of love. Britomart is about to kill Busyrane when Amoret

Dernely vnto her called to abstaine,
From doing him to dy. For else her paine
Should be remedilesse, sith none but hee,
Which wrought it, could the same recure againe.

(12.34)

Once again Spenser describes Busyrane with a formula that ordinarily describes the object of desire. Busyrane's torment is now seen not only as characterizing human love, but as essential to the experience of it. Hence Britomart assures the integrity of the experience not by exercising her magical prowess but by being assimilated to Amoret's suffering. As Busyrane reverses his charms, the immune virgin feels their force:

Horror gan the virgins hart to perse,
And her faire locks vp stared stiffe on end,
Hearing him those same bloudy lines reherse;
And all the while he red, she did extend
Her sword high ouer him, if ought he did offend.

(12.36)

Britomart's vigilance is no longer preparation for the enemy, as it nominally was at the end of canto 11. It is now literally a type of endurance, the heroic version of Amoret's steadfastness of heart.

What Spenser has done with Britomart's heroism is even more apparent in the next stanza:

403

> Anon she gan perceiue the house to quake,
> And all the dores to rattel round about;
> Yet all that did not her dismaied make,
> Nor slacke her threatfull hand for daungers dout,
> But still with stedfast eye and courage stout
> Abode, to weet what end would come of all.
> At last that mightie chaine, which round about
> Her tender waste was wound, adowne gan fall,
> And that great brasen pillour broke in peeces small.

> (12.37)

Taken by themselves, the quaking and rattling of the first two lines seem to belong to the realm of the Gothic thriller. In fact they are a brilliant development of two earlier passages in the canto. In the very first stanzas, a whirlwind shakes the palace, and Britomart, undaunted, awaits her foe (12.1–2). But instead of producing an embodiment of its force (like Orgoglio, who has similar imagery associated with him), the whirlwind brings forth the richly clad figure of Ease, whose function is that of prologue to the masque. At the end of the masque, Cupid, "riding on a Lion rauenous" and more satanic than cherubic, unbinds his eyes in a grandly malicious gesture to behold Amoret, his victim:

> With that the darts which his right hand did straine,
> Full dreadfully he shooke that all did quake,
> And clapt on hie his coulourd winges twaine,
> That all his many it affraide did make.

> (12.23)

In the first passage, the hero who stands firmly against the quaking of the castle finds that from the warrior's point of view the enemy is insubstantial, for there is no one to fight. (The same thing happens in 12.29–30, when Britomart enters the inner chamber and finds that the masque has vanished.) In the second passage, the reader is associated with Cupid's troop and with the helpless Amoret in feeling the terror of Love's power. When Busyrane reverses his charm, Britomart stands up against the shaking of the house not as if it were a hypothetical foe, but as an experience of terror. This is endurance in the sense suggested by the preceding stanza, and it produces not heroic victory, but the wondrous dissolving of the mighty chain and the brazen pillar. With Britomart assimilated to the reader's experience of the palace, the sense of wonder is evoked not by her magical embodiment of paradox, but by the healing of Amoret's heart, an event that occurs as if it were a natural process. Britomart's endurance is transmuted into the erotic feeling of "The cruell steele, which thrild her dying hart, / Fell softly forth, as of his owne accord" (12.38). Spenser's affirmation that human love is essentially a harmony is registered not through our wonder at the hero who embodies an assertion, but through wonder as the product of a felt experience.

These last two cantos of Book III emphasize love's painfulness, which is finally presented under the aspect of individual experience. But Spenser demands no trial by fire: he is not saying that fullness of love depends on the lover's undergoing genuine torment. In other words, he does not project love's necessary pain as individual dramatic experience, either in his characters or in his reader. "Individual experience" is both the mode of the reader's understanding and, like "painfulness," something of which he is aware in Spenser's definition of love. But Spenser does not present—and indeed, in his poetry, could not present—individual experience that actually involves such drastic suffering as Amoret's emblematic torment. In Britomart's heroism and Amoret's torture (not to mention the considerable attention given to jealousy), the episode in the House of Busyrane contains the components of *Othello*. But the greatness of the episode is precisely that it can end with a sense of naturalness, wonder, and shared humanity. The range and intensity of feeling and expression and the humanity of insight we find in it deepen and extend the comic sense of love that characterizes all of Book III. If we feel that this episode is the valid, the necessary conclusion to Book III, we are simply acknowledging that this book of *The Faerie Queene* is one of the great comic poems in English, and that to find its equal we must go to Chaucer and Shakespeare.

Index to *The Faerie Queene*

Index

CHARACTERS AND PLACES

Index

409

General Index

Abrams, M. H., 19n
Addison, Joseph, 3
Aeneas, 20, 190, 266, 283, 286
Agnelli, Giuseppe, 163n
Alciati, Andrea, 200n, 202n, 206, 209n, 213, 214n, 219n, 230, 246
alexandrine line, *see* stanza
allegory, 3-4, 18-19, 38, 50, 53, 66, 86, 90, 134, 140, 145n, 152-53, 160-61, 164, 171, 173-74, 201-204, 208, 212-14, 217, 220, 232-38, 240n, 249, 279, 287-88, 297, 311, 330, 334
alliteration, 37, 39, 48, 65, 97-99, 102, 215-17, 266, 376
Allot, Robert, 158-59
Andrewes, Lancelot, 362
Aquinas, St. Thomas, 262, 348
Ariosto, Lodovico, 105, 203; *Cinque Canti,* 221n; *Orlando Furioso,* 24-25, 28-29, 33, 55-60, 62-63, 67-68, 108, 139-40, 144-47, 160-99, 201-202, 212, 218, 220, 226, 299, 330-31
Ariosto, allegorizers of, 140-41, 145-46, 160-72, 174-75, 179, 181, 187n, 188, 194, 200. *See also* Bononome, Dolce, Fornari, Guidicciolo, Harington, Horologgio, Pigna, Porcacchi, Ruscelli, Toscanella, Valvassori
Aristotle, 104n, 113, 207, 223, 286
Augustine, St., 6n, 240

Babb, Lawrence, 222
Bacon, Francis, 260
Bamborough, J. B., 222n, 224n
Batman uppon Bartholome, 209n, 222n
Becon, Thomas, 358n, 359, 361
Berger, Harry, Jr., 26n, 235, 248-56, 259-60, 265, 312
Bible, 27, 127, 240, 254-55, 257, 275, 296, 300, 322, 324, 336, 340, 344, 352, 365
Blayney, M. S. and G. H., 357n
Bligh, E. W., 106n
Boccaccio, Giovanni, 217, 218n, 221, 223
Bocchi, Achilles, 210n
Boiardo, Matteo, 164
Bononome, Gioseffo, 165, 187
Botticelli, Sandro, 236

Bronzino, 212
Bruno, Giordano, 226
Burleigh, William Cecil, Lord, 281-82
Burton, Robert, 222, 223n, 224, 225n, 226, 356n, 358

Calvin, John, 361
Camden, William, 224n
canto, as basic unit, 107, 125, 131, 350
Capaccio, G. C., 206n
Cartari, Vincenzo, 200, 206
Castiglione, Baldassare, 298-99
Chapman, George, 103, 105
Charron, Pierre, 225, 251n
Chartier, Alain, 357n
Chaucer, Geoffrey, 71, 126n, 160, 330-31, 405
Chew, Samuel C., 220n, 222n
Cicero, 220-21, 251, 353, 354n
Cinthio, Geraldi, 329n
Ciris, 182n
Coleridge, Samuel T., 11, 71, 77, 326
Comes, Natalis, 200, 221n, 237-38, 241-42, 245-46, 261n
Craig, Martha, 98-101, 106n, 282n
Crawford, Charles, 158n
Cumming, William P., 329n

Dallett, Joseph B., 9n, 133n
Daniel, Samuel, 12n, 226, 282
Dante, 10n, 22, 105, 107, 124, 198, 232, 283, 332
Davies, Sir John, 313-14
Della Casa, Giovanni, 219n, 225-27
Dickens, Charles, 331n
diction, 7, 45-46, 376-78, 384-85, 399
Digby, Sir Kenelm, 106, 201
Discord, 212n
Dixon, John, 152-54
Dodge, R. E. Neil, 185n
Dolce, Lodovico, 163n, 164
Donne, John, 72-73, 78
Drayton, Michael, 78-81, 226
Drummond, William, 214n
Dryden, John, 198
Du Bellay, Joachim, 104n
Durling, Robert M., 134n, 177n, 195n

Ebreo, Leone, 165n
Eliot, T. S., 198, 332
Ellrodt, Robert, 5n, 165n, 200, 334n
emblems, 9, 16-18, 153n, 200, 202,

411

Index

Williams, Arnold, 247n
Wind, Edgar, 200n, 203n, 210n, 212n
Wither, George, 358n
Woodhouse, A. S. P., 132n, 334, 361-62
Wordsworth, William, 13, 198

world, poem as, 19-22, 26-27, 29, 32-34, 36, 112, 134, 228, 249

Yeats, William Butler, 71-72, 75-76, 279-80
Yunck, John A., 247n

415